COST-BENEFIT ANALYSIS

AN INFORMAL INTRODUCTION

BY

E. J. MISHAN

THIRD EDITION

London
GEORGE ALLEN & UNWIN
Boston   Sydney

George Allen & Unwin (Publishers) Ltd,
40 Museum Street, London WC1A 1LU, UK

George Allen & Unwin (Publishers) Ltd,
Park Lane, Hemel Hempstead, Herts HP2 4TE, UK

Allen & Unwin Inc.,
9 Winchester Terrace, Winchester, Mass 01890, USA

George Allen & Unwin Australia Pty Ltd,
8 Napier Street, North Sydney, NSW 2060, Australia

First published in 1971
Second Edition 1975
Third Impression 1978
Fourth Impression 1979
Third Edition 1982

British Library Cataloguing in Publication Data

Mishan, E. J.
　　Cost benefit analysis.—3rd ed.
1. Cost effectiveness
I. Title
339.4″1　　　HD47

ISBN 0-04-338099-9

Library of Congress Cataloging in Publication Data

Mishan, E. J. (Edward J.), 1917–
　　Cost benefit analysis.

Bibliography: p.
1. Welfare economics.　2. Cost effectiveness.
3. Expenditures, Public.　I. Title.
HB846.2.M55　1982　　658.1′554　　82-3933
ISBN 0-04-338099-9　　　　AACR2

Printed in Great Britain by Billing and Sons Ltd Guildford,
London and Worcester

COST-BENEFIT ANALYSIS

by the same author

THE ECONOMIC GROWTH DEBATE: AN ASSESSMENT

ELEMENTS OF COST-BENEFIT ANALYSIS

ECONOMIC EFFICIENCY AND SOCIAL WELFARE

TO
DAVID AND FREDA

Contents

Preface to the Third Edition

Since the second edition of this work, which appeared in 1975, several textbooks on the subject have been published. All of them, however, are better compared with my *Elements of Cost-Benefit Analysis* than with the present volume, being, like the former, more limited in scope and treatment and directed more to the attention of the beginner than to the more mature student. Only in response to one aspect of the treatment in these new textbooks, that of the foundations of cost-benefit analysis, has there been an important revision to this book. It consists of a new Part IV, 'The Choice of a Cost-Benefit Criterion', which includes matter that appeared in Note *A* of the second edition along with two new chapters, 25 and 26, that (so far as I can tell) make explicit, for the first time, the analytic and ethical implications of the alternative valuation criteria proposed by different economists. The student of the earlier editions will note, in passing, that I conclude my review of these criteria with a predilection in favour of using compensating variation alone, as in my first edition.

This new Part IV is inserted between Parts III and IV of the second edition, the old Part IV, 'Investment Criteria', appearing in this new edition as Part V. Needless to say, both these parts have been revised; Part III, 'External Effects', has undergone cosmetic surgery only, but the latter half of the new Part V is radically different from that in the second edition and somewhat shorter. The old chapters, on the social opportunity cost of investment and three on the normalization procedure, along with the final chapter on calculating parameters, have been replaced by a crisper and more lucid treatment of the essentials in Chapters 36 and 37, which constitute also a general critique of all DPV methods, one that has regard to the more recent contributions to this controversial literature. The new Chapter 40 tackles the inter-generation problem, one that has been neglected, if not evaded, in the literature on investment criteria, but looks as if it will become increasingly important as economists seek to appraise projects with environmental repercussions that will fall on future generations.

Part II in the second edition, 'Economic Concepts of Costs and Benefits', has also been revised, with particular attention to Chapter 9 on consumer surplus and Chapter 12 on transfer payments and double counting.

Part V in the second edition, 'Particular Problems in Project Evaluation', has sustained a number of mainly expository revisions in becoming Part VI of the present edition. In view of the proliferation of journal articles on the subject, I took the occasion of carefully reconsidering the chapters on life and limb—though without, as it transpired, having to alter the general conclusions reached in my second edition.

Although the literature on uncertainty continues to grow, the greater part is singularly impractical for the sort of uncertainty encountered in evaluating public projects. In actual studies the methods for dealing with the increasing uncertainty of future magnitudes turn out to be crude—often consisting of no more than the use of a cut-off period and/or some simple sensitivity analysis applied to one or two of the more important prices or schedules. For this reason I have, for the time being, forborne from revision of the earlier treatment.

A final word on 'risk-benefit analysis'. The reader will look in vain for reference to this notion in the present volume, for the simple reason that it is no more than fashionable nomenclature used (though not often by economists) when the cost of a mooted project contains a preponderant element of risk. No change of principle, however, is involved in economic calculation appropriate to risk, which is discussed in detail in Chapters 45 and 46.

Preface to the Second Edition

Only Part I of this new edition, containing some simplified examples of cost-benefit studies, remains (apart from a small correction in Chapter 4) virtually the same as it was in the first edition. All other parts of the book have been revised and additional material incorporated in many places.

Part II, 'Concepts of Costs and Benefits' has been extensively revised with additional chapters which I hope improve both the exposition and the logical development of these aspects of the subject. Further, a number of ambiguities have been removed, minor errors corrected, and some additional analysis added in various parts.

Part III, 'External Effects' has been the subject of largely stylistic changes, and the chapters on the Loss of Life and Limb (somewhat amplified) have been transferred to a new Part V, 'Particular Problems in Project Evaluation', which also includes some new chapters on the valuation of time, unemployment, pollution damage, and recreation.

The chapters in what is now Part VI, 'Uncertainty', have come in for moderate revision, with a little new material added to the chapters on Game Theory and a lot more in the last two chapters.

The last three chapters in Note *A* of Part VII are far more developed than their two counterpart chapters in the first edition. My reconsideration of the conceptual basis of a cost-benefit criterion in Chapter 58 was stimulated by the valuable criticism of my first edition by Professor James Meade in *The Economic Journal* for March 1972, while the enlargement of the arguments in the following two chapters arose in response to recent publications on cost-benefit analysis and to further reflection on the methodology of the subject.

Part IV, 'Investment Criteria', came in for the most thorough revision of all. Apart from the first four chapters, this part of the book has been rearranged, rewritten, amplified, and supplemented by additional chapters. In the first edition I had not done justice to Stephen Marglin's 1963 proposals for calculating the 'social opportunity cost' of public investments, nor, indeed, to my own normalization procedure of 1967. In these respects, at least, I believe the reader will find the treatment of investment criteria much superior in this new edition.

References and bibliographies for each part of the book have been brought up to date.

Preface to the First Edition

There is very little in this volume beyond the grasp of any person who has absorbed the contents of a good introductory economics textbook. Other than the occasional resort to some elementary algebra, no mathematics are used in the text, and the diagrams are of the kind familiar to all economics students. I am aware that in certain sections of the book, especially those to be found in Parts IV and VI, recourse to mathematical formulation would have appeared more elegant and saved many pages. But the student's time is a lot scarcer than printed paper, and the chief concern of an introductory textbook ought to be the digestibility of its contents. With this in mind I have sought to avoid abstraction and develop the essential concepts by use of simple examples. My guiding aim, in writing each Part, has been to convey to the interested reader with a smattering of economics some of the crucial notions and procedures that lie behind the techniques used in cost-benefit studies. There should be enough in this volume to make him become more critical of the proposals of government officials and the reports of committees of 'experts'—enough, at any rate, to enable him to ask sensible questions of an official body, and possibly embarrassing ones also.

There is some additional warrant for this pedagogic device of illustrating concepts by simple examples in a treatment of cost-benefit analysis. First, the advantages of elegance, generality, and compactness of statement lie with those branches of the subject that have already passed through a phase of controversy and development and appear to be settling down to a more pedestrian existence. Such is not the state of cost-benefit analysis which is—as readers will soon recognize—an application of welfare economics. Like the parent subject, cost-benefit can be made to look deceptively simple, whereas there are everywhere pitfalls for the unwary. If, therefore, a writer on this subject is vain enough to believe that he has useful advice to offer, he has every incentive to make his meaning clear.

Second, there is not at present, so far as I am aware, any introductory textbook wholly devoted to cost-benefit analysis. There are some well-known works on public investment, such as that by R. N. McKean, *Efficiency in Government through Systems Analysis* (1958), or that by Krutilla and Eckstein on *Multiple Purpose River Development* (1958), which cover an important part of the subject matter. Also there are several weighty volumes of case studies with valuable introductions such as the *Measurement of Benefits of Government Investments*, edited by Robert Dorfman (1965), or the studies put out by the Brookings Institute, *Problems in Public Expenditure*, edited by S. Chase, Jr. (1968) or those by Arthur Maass and others, entitled *Design of Water Resource Systems* (1962). Finally, there are any number of excellent treatises on decision theory with particular reference to problems of uncertainty, to say nothing of the number of works on mathematical programming, operations research, game theory, and the like, that have something to offer in the way of ideas or techniques to cost-benefit analysis. On the subject proper, however, there are, apart from the individual case studies throughout the more technical literature, only some short surveys, the best known being that of Prest and Turvey in the *Economic Journal* for 1965, and an excellent introduction by G. H. Peters put out as a sixty-page Eaton Paper by the Institute of Economic Affairs in 1968.

Without reliable antecedents in the form of a *Principles* of the subject, one is obviously more exposed. All the more is the temptation to retreat into abstract generality about which there is always some penumbra of ambiguity and some latitude of interpretation. But the growing popularity of cost-benefit studies in an age imbued with the notion of efficiency is a sobering thought. The influence on our daily lives of vast investment projects need hardly be stressed. Nor, consequently, need the required appreciation of its scope and limitations by those trained to apply its techniques. If, then, there are critical errors of omission and commission, it is important that the exposition be such that they stand out starkly enough to attract the strictures of competent critics. Any success I have in making the arguments explicit and unequivocal will increase the relevance and the particularity of the criticisms of professional colleagues, as a result of which I, and others, may become the better equipped to produce more suitable cost-benefit treatises.

Notwithstanding these expressions of brave intent, I have had recourse to some form of self-insurance by placing two of the more controversial aspects in Part VII, which carries the noncommittal title of 'Further Notes Relating to Cost-Benefit Analysis'. Logically, Note *A*, 'The Welfare Basis of Cost-Benefit Analysis', should have appeared at the beginning of the book. Pedagogic reasons could be always found, however, for placing it at the end: for one can pick up a lot about the applications of a subject while remaining untroubled about its 'foundations'. But, as suggested above, my own view concerning the basis of cost-benefit analysis is very particular. It is as well, then, to keep it apart from the text which, though it has occasional pretensions to novelty, ought to go over well enough—apart from possible errors— with the profession. Like considerations impelled me to place Note *C*, on 'Allocation, Distribution, and Equity', in the same place of refuge. Note *B*, 'More Accurate Measures of Economic Surplus', however, was relegated to Part VI for the very simple reason that it was, perhaps, too exacting for the ordinary reader. And though it will, I hope, be of interest to some, it is obviously more of a refinement than a requisite.

The sophisticated practitioner may observe that the analytic structure erected in this volume is somewhat monolithic. I state explicitly that cost-benefit analysis is an application of welfare economics and, more particularly, that the rationale of cost-benefit analysis is based on that of a potential Pareto improvement. This thesis runs through the book, and what is valid and what is relevant is consistently determined by reference to it.

There can be two possible objections to this procedure. First, it can be said that it ignores considerations of distribution and equity; second, that it ignores indices of merit other than Pareto-based ones.

The first objection is not a strong one. In the first place, there is an overt concern with distribution and equity in Part III on External Effects, and also in Note *C*, on 'Allocation, Distribution, and Equity'. In addition, it is pointed out in several places, and especially in Note *A*, on 'The Welfare Basis of Cost-Benefit Analysis', that although the outcome, or magnitude, of a cost-benefit evaluation is independent of its potential distribution effects, a project which meets an adopted cost-benefit test can properly be rejected on grounds of distribution or equity. Moreover, the economist has a duty to point up all relevant effects that do not enter the cost-benefit computation.

But having said all this, the cost-benefit calculation remains a thing apart. Notwithstanding attempts made from time to time in the literature to integrate the distributional effects with the 'efficiency' effects—usually by weighting with, say, utility indices the dollar value of net benefits enjoyed by the various income groups—the tradition of separating the cost-benefit calculation from the distributional effects continues in practice, and is unlikely to change in the foreseeable future. I might add in passing that even if a system of distributional weights could be agreed upon, a concern with distributional justice would continue to require reference to the expected effects on distribution. For allowing that a dollar of net benefit to the 'poor' is more heavily weighted than a dollar of net benefit to the 'rich', a project which (using the system of agreed weights) qualifies for admission on some adopted criterion may still be one that makes the rich richer and the poor poorer.

As for the second objection, I again defer to tradition and current practice, though not without recognizing the scope for innovation in the choice of other social merit indicators which—though not having quite the same sanction as a Pareto-based indicator—may yet become acknowledged as revealing and pertinent for particular sorts of projects. But until such social merit indicators have become more widely established, an introductory text may be justified in disregarding them.

Current applications of cost-benefit analysis do not, as it happens, require fastidious equipment in the way of statistical methods or simulation techniques, though obviously familiarity with them will extend the reach and the versatility of the practitioner. There is, however, no advantage in including sections on curve-fitting and identification, and so on, not only because there are already quite a number of competent textbooks devoted to the problems they give rise to, but also because such techniques have a wide range of applications that are not peculiar to cost-benefit methods. The present volume has concentrated wholly on the concepts underlying the applications: on the interpretation to be given to the magnitudes. In short, the volume can be regarded as an essay on what is and what is not agenda; on what is to count and what is not to count in a cost-benefit evaluation. And if the reader ever becomes master of this difficult craft, he need not worry too much if his knowledge of statistics remains somewhat skimpy. There is no lack of good statisticians among economists. But there is, at present, an acute shortage of economists skilled in the design of cost-benefit studies.

Like yesterday's lovers, today's textbook writers act in haste and repent at leisure. Before the War, the practice among academic authors was to mull over a script for several years before offering one's work, with some diffidence if not trepidation, to a more limited community of scholars. The profession was then both more learned and more fastidious. Style and proportion were qualities valued and cultivated. Yet, the fact is that they could afford to move at a more leisurely pace. The numbers in any academic discipline were a small fraction of those today. And the sheer output and pace of development were not there to goad them into indecent haste. These things will be in the mind of the charitable critic as he detects occasional parochialisms and superficialities.

The task of revising a first draft was made easier by the generous response of a couple of my colleagues, and friends, at the London School of Economics. Mr Kurt Klappholz scrutinized Part III, on External Effects, and brought to light a number of errors and ambiguities. Mr Lucien Foldes undertook to vet Parts IV and VI—on Investment Criteria and Uncertainty, respectively—in the course of which he made many valuable suggestions. While making the conventional disclaimer on behalf of both, I wish to record my gratitude to them.

I wish to acknowledge the kindness of the Editors of *The American Economic Review, The Canadian Journal of Economics, The Economic Journal, The Journal of Political Economy* and *Oxford Economic Papers*, for permission to make use of the ideas and exposition in a number of my papers that appeared in these journals between 1960 and 1970.

E.J.M.

Foreword

1 The general question that a cost-benefit analysis sets out to answer is whether a number of investment projects, A, B, C, etc., should be undertaken and, if investible funds are limited, which one, two, or more, among these specific projects that would otherwise qualify for admission, should be selected. Another question to which cost-benefit analysis sometimes addresses itself is that of determining the level at which a plant should operate or the combination of outputs it should produce. In this introductory volume, however, we follow custom in confining our attention chiefly to the former question, about the choice of investment projects.

But why bother with cost-benefit analysis at all? What is wrong with deciding whether or not to undertake any specific investment, or to choose among a number of specific investment opportunities, guided simply by proper accounting practices and, therefore, guided ultimately by reference to profitability. The answer is provided by the familiar thesis that what counts as a benefit or a loss to one part of the economy—to one or more persons or groups—does not necessarily count as a benefit or loss to the economy as a whole. And in cost-benefit analysis we are concerned with the economy as a whole, with the welfare of a defined society, and not any smaller part of it.

A private enterprise, or even a public enterprise, comprises only a segment of the economy, often a very small segment. More important, whatever the means it employs in pursuing its objectives—whether rules of thumb or more formalized techniques such as mathematical programming or operations research—the private enterprise, at least, is guided by ordinary commercial criteria that require revenues to exceed costs. The fact that its activities are guided by the profit motive, however, is not to deny that it confers benefits on a large number of people other than its shareholders. It also confers benefits on its employees, on consumers, and—through the taxes it pays—on the general public. Yet the benefits enjoyed by these four groups continue to exist only for as long as they coincide with the yielding of profits to the enterprise. If it makes losses the enterprise cannot survive unless it receives a public subsidy. If it is to survive unaided as a private concern and, moreover, to expand the scale of its operations it must, over a period of time, produce profits large enough either to attract investors or to finance its own expansion.

There is, of course, the metaphor of the 'invisible hand', the *deus ex machina* discovered by Adam Smith that so directs the self-seeking proclivities of the business world that it confers benefits on society as a whole. And one can, indeed, lay down simple and sufficient conditions under which the uncompromising pursuit of profits acts always to serve the public interest. These conditions can be boiled down to two: that all effects relevant to the welfare of all individuals be properly priced on the market, and that perfect competition prevail in all economic activities.

Once we depart from this ideal economic setting, however, the set of outputs and prices to which the economy tends may not serve the public so well as some other set of outputs and prices. In addition to this possible misallocation of resources among the goods being produced, it is also possible that certain goods which can be economically justified are not produced at all, while others that cannot be economically justified continue to be produced. If, for example, technical conditions and the size of the market are such that a number of goods can be produced only under conditions of increasing returns to scale (falling average cost), it is possible that, although some of these goods will be produced by monopolies charging prices above marginal cost, other such goods will not be produced since there is no single price at which the monopolist can make any profit. But the production of these latter goods is not necessarily uneconomic. It may simply be the case that the monopolist who sells each good at a single price cannot transfer enough of the benefits from his potential customers to make the venture worthwhile.

Again, certain goods having beneficial, though unpriced, spillover effects also qualify for production on economic grounds; but they cannot be produced at a profit so long as the beneficial spillovers remain unpriced. The reverse is also true and more significant: profitable commercial activities sometimes produce noxious spillover effects to such an extent that, on a more comprehensive pricing criterion, they would be regarded as uneconomic.

2   The economist engaged in the cost-benefit appraisal of a project is not, in essence then, asking a different sort of question from that being asked by the accountant of a private firm. Rather, the same sort of question is being asked about a wider group of people—who comprise society—and is being asked more searchingly. Instead of asking whether the owners of the enterprise will become better off by the firm's engaging in one activity rather than another, the economist asks whether society as a whole will become better off by undertaking this project rather than not undertaking it, or by undertaking instead any of a number of alternative projects.

Broadly speaking, for the more precise concept of revenue to the private firm, the economist substitutes the less precise yet meaningful concept of *social benefit*. For the costs of the private firm, the economist substitutes the concept of *opportunity cost*—the social value foregone when the resources in question are moved away from alternative economic activities into the specific project. For the profit of the firm, the economist substitutes the concept of *excess social benefit over cost*, or some related concept used in an investment criterion.

3   It transpires that the realization of practically all proposed cost-benefit criteria—often cast as investment criteria in order to take account of costs and benefits through time—implies a concept of social betterment that amounts to a *potential* Pareto improvement (sometimes referred to in the older literature as a 'test of hypothetical overcompensation'). The project in question, to be considered as economically feasible, must, that is, be capable of producing an excess of benefits such that everyone in society could, by a costless redistribution of the gains, be made better off.

The essential idea is straightforward enough. But once the net is thrown wider, and the repercussions over the economy at large are brought into the calculus, a number of problems arise which require extended treatment. Chief among them are the concepts and measurements of consumers' surplus and rents, the distinction between benefits and transfer payments, the concept of shadow pricing, external economies and diseconomies, the choice of investment criteria, and the problems of uncertainty. They are dealt with in that order in the following chapters.

4   Finally, the reader should bear in mind that the techniques employed in cost-benefit analysis can be put to related uses. One use arises in considering the desirability of transfers in kind since political decisions to help the less fortunate members of society need not always entail direct cash transfers. The available cash, for instance, can be used to promote economic opportunity among such groups. Financing education or medical services, recreational facilities, the building of dams or irrigation works, the provision of tools, technical equipment and advice, and the establishing of industries or information centres, are different ways in which the state can help others to help themselves.

Of course, none of these ways might meet a strict cost-benefit criterion. Yet some or all of them might be regarded by society as superior to direct cash transfers. The economist can then contribute to such decisions to the extent of selecting—within the limits of a number of seemingly equally appropriate ways of helping these less privileged groups—those opportunities which yield the maximum social benefit per dollar transferred in such ways to these groups. Clearly, the discounted present value of the maximum benefit per dollar invested in these socially approved ways may turn out to be *less* than a dollar. But such projects do have the merit of encouraging people to help themselves—an intangible benefit, no less important just because it cannot easily be quantified.

Similar calculations arise when transfers in kind are not the immediate goal, the beneficiaries being a mixed income group or the greater part of the community. The economist in such cases is required to restrict his estimates to the 'cost effectiveness' of a number of alternative projects, any one of which is thought to be politically desirable. Should the government wish to discover the resource costs involved—though *not* the benefits—of maintaining alternative standards of water purity along different stretches of the Delaware Estuary, the economist would be able to provide cost estimates leaving it to the community to decide, through the political process, just which standards to adopt. Another example of cost-effectiveness would be the comparison of the social costs of alternative airport sites, on the assumption—possibly unwarranted—that the airport site confers benefits that more than cover all the social costs.

PART I. SOME SIMPLIFIED EXAMPLES OF COST-BENEFIT STUDIES

Chapter 1

INTRODUCTORY

1 Each of the following five chapters contains brief notes on a hypothetical example of a cost-benefit analysis, albeit one that is based on one or more actual studies. Their main purpose is to bring to the reader's attention some of the ideas that shape the form these benefits and costs take in particular instances. These ideas themselves derive from propositions familiar in that branch of the subject known as welfare economics, although no more than an elementary knowledge of economic principles is needed for their appreciation.

If the reader does not, at a first reading, fully understand the significance of some of the ways of calculating the costs and benefits that are described briefly in the following chapters, he is urged not to worry about it at this stage, but to read on. It is enough if these crude and sometimes partial constructions convey a rough picture of what a cost-benefit study is about and, in doing so, perhaps whet his appetite for the more detailed exposition of the principles that follow. Indeed, these hypothetical examples are placed at the beginning of the book with no purpose in mind other than to engage the reader's mind and to stimulate his imagination. They are not, properly speaking, a part of the instruction and could in fact be omitted on a first reading. Once he has worked through the book, the reader can always return to these chapters, which will then, I feel sure, appear to him straightforward enough.

1

2 Occasionally I have drawn a distinction between, on the one hand, the methods of calculation that are often proposed or that have already been proposed and, on the other, the methods that I hold to be correct in that they are consistent with the basic concepts that emerge from the discussion of criteria in Part IV. These differences in methods of calculating benefits or costs are far from being in the nature of a refinement. The use of some popular but erroneous method of estimating benefits or costs can make an enormous difference to the resulting figures, and possibly a critical one, so that a project appears economically acceptable when in fact it ought to be rejected unhesitatingly or *vice versa*.

I choose to touch on these differences in methods of calculation in this first part of the book so that even though the reader may not be wholly convinced by my brief arguments at this stage, his mind will become more receptive to the exposition of the crucial concepts and *caveats* in later parts of the book.

Chapter 2

AN UNDERGROUND
RAILWAY

1 A city with public surface transport is to consider building an underground railway of a given design. There is no difficulty in estimating the initial capital outlays which will be spread over five years and against which have to be set the stream of future net benefits (gross benefits less operating costs) spread over fifty years.

These net benefits are not likely to accord with the net financial receipts expected from the enterprise, if only because a lower fare structure could produce greater net benefits while reducing net receipts. The largest net benefit accrues when services are such that the fare is equal to the marginal operating cost at all times, on all lines. If this marginal operating cost were zero everywhere, maximum net benefit would correspond to zero revenues.

Marginal operating case is not likely to be zero all the time, however, unless the capacity of the underground railway is much larger than is economical. We should expect it to be positive at peak hours, if only because of congestion costs. But it is troublesome to charge fares equal to the marginal operating costs prevailing at different times during the day. It is also likely to be politically inexpedient, inasmuch as peak hours tend to coincide with the times at which the working population is travelling. In the event, it is not uncommon to hold the fare constant at about average operating cost, or somewhat above average, with possible concessions for early-morning travel.

2 If we suppose the fare is set at 50 cents for any one journey at any time, we may properly infer that the journey undertaken at that fare is worth at least 50 cents to the traveller. A part of the annual gross benefit of the underground railway is therefore equal to the total receipts expected in each of the fifty years, and the net benefit corresponding to this part of the annual gross benefit is calculated simply by subtracting from such gross benefit the annual operating cost.

It is obviously necessary to make some calculation of the remaining gross benefits from having the underground railway service—which, since operation costs have already been subtracted, will also be net benefits. In a very general way, we may say that the appropriate notion to apply is the most that people will be prepared to pay for having the new service when the fare is set at 50 cents a journey. And it should be clear that the higher the cost of the existing alternative forms of road transport, private as well as public, the more are people willing to pay for the new service.

3 When it comes to an actual calculation of these remaining benefits based on willingness to pay, the economist may have recourse to a variety of devices. For some portion of the expected users, for example, the benefits would be calculated as a cost saving as compared with their existing form of travel. For those who currently use private means of travel there may be no saving in operation cost but possibly some saving of time. For those who, instead, currently use public surface transport the saving will be of time, possibly augmented by some estimate of the value of the greater comfort if travelling by underground rail.

In addition to the benefits by the users of the underground railway, other groups will benefit. In so far as road congestion is reduced as a result of the underground railway, those who continue to travel on the roads benefit. Such benefits can be broken down into a saving of time, an increase in safety and an increase in comfort. Again, following the concept of what is known as option demand, even those who never expect to use the underground railway derive a benefit from its construction in the form of an alternative that is always open to them should their customary means of travel fail—a partial form of insurance, in effect. Finally, there is a group that might not travel at all if there were no provision for underground railway services.

Any rise in land values resulting from the new underground service is not, however, to be counted among the benefits. To do this would be to count a given benefit twice, once as a flow and once as a stock. For a rise in the value of land in a particular location, arising from the faster communication from that location to the town centre and

4

other locations, reflects only the capitalized value of the expected future benefits of faster communication. Further discussion of this point will be found in Chapter 12.

4 Since the cost of construction is spread over five years and the expected operation of the underground railway is fifty years, it would be conventional practice to compound forward the five years' outlays at the appropriate rate of interest to 'year zero'. This capitalized value of the outlays is then compared with that of the benefits, the latter being the sum of the values of each of the annual expected benefits over following fifty years when discounted to 'year zero' at the same interest rate.

If the capitalized value of the outlays were equal to $100 million in 'year zero', and there were no other use for this $100 million at that time but to leave it in its existing use, there is an economic case for building the underground if the sum of the discounted future benefits exceeded the $100 million of capital cost. At least, this is the popular view.

Later (in Chapters 36 and 37), however, the reader will discover arguments to the effect that, in general, the use of a single discount rate is erroneous.

Chapter 3

DISEASE CONTROL

1 In what is known as a cost-effective analysis, the economist seeks to estimate the costs only of employing alternative methods of implementing a politically desirable programme using concepts and methods familiar in cost-benefit analysis. It is also possible, though less common, for the economist to seek to estimate the benefits only of a given project or programme. An example would be an estimate of the benefits of controlling or eliminating a particular disease or addiction, a mission undertaken in the hope, perhaps, of impressing the public with the desirability of government action in this connection.

We might, for example, want to have an idea of the benefits to society of reducing the incidence of cancer by a given per cent or—since no difference in principle arises—of eliminating it altogether in any or all of its forms.

2 One method of calculating the benefits of reducing or eliminating a disease that has been used and is still popular is that of estimating the current costs that will be averted if the incidence of the disease is reduced or if it is eliminated altogether.

These benefits or averted costs can be split into three broad categories: (1) expenditures on medical care, (2) losses of current production and (3) the pain and discomforts associated with the disease, all of which are eliminated along with the disease.

(1) The expenditures on medical care include the costs of the services of physicians and other medical personnel, also the costs of drugs, hospital facilities and equipment. (2) The losses of current production—at the stage where complications set in—are reckoned (a) as the loss of gross earnings (earnings of housewives, incidentally, being calculated by reference to the earnings of domestic servants) for time taken up with diagnosis and treatment and (b) any reduc-

6

tion in gross earnings in consequence of the person's being less employable or less productive as a result of having suffered from cancer and its treatment. (3) The pain and discomforts associated with cancer are not easy to evaluate, and whatever procedure is adopted is somewhat arbitrary.

An estimate of these three categories of averted costs can be made for each of two groups, those whose cancers are benign and those whose cancers are malignant. In order to calculate an average figure for each group of the three cost items, it would be convenient to divide the annual number in each group into, say, three income classes and three age groups.

3 Suppose that the combined figure for the community of costs averted from cancer elimination comes to $15 billion for an average year based on the past five years, the capitalized value of all future benefits so calculated would be equal to the sum of each of such annual benefits over an infinite span of time, when each is discounted to the present at an appropriate rate of interest. If the appropriate rate of interest is 4 per cent, the capitalized value of the benefits is 25 times $15 billion, or $375 billion.

It is possible, however, for the population to be expected to grow at 2 per cent per annum for an indefinite number of years and/or for the disease to be expected to grow at 1 per cent per annum on average, if it is not eliminated. In such cases, the annual benefit would grow at some average rate over the indefinite future.

The benefit calculation would, of course, be in real terms: that is to say, all future benefits are to be valued at prices existing in the initial year. The rate of discount used would also be a real figure— for instance, the 4 per cent chosen being unaffected by changes in nominal interest rates (or money interest rates) which tend to vary with the rate of inflation.

4 The above method of calculating the benefits of eliminating a disease cannot strictly be justified by reference to economic principle. A reduction in cost can be directly translated into a benefit for society only when—as in an increment of consumer surplus from a fall in price—we are operating on the demand curve for a specific good. If, for example, the good in question were a standardized health unit which could be purchased on the market, and the unit cost fell by an amount that resulted in a saving of $5 billion a year for the same number of health units bought, then the benefit would indeed be equal to the cost saving of $5 billion a year.

But in the above example of cancer elimination we are not reducing the cost of providing an existing and specific good that is already enjoyed by the public. We are effectively contemplating creating a new good—or, rather, eradicating an existing bad. (If, instead, the disease were already eradicated but measures to ensure that it did not reappear required an expenditure of $2 billion each year, a reduction of this cost—of maintaining the existing good—to $1.5 billion entails a cost saving of $0.5 billion a year, which can, of course, be counted as a net benefit.)

5 Doubt about the correctness of the method illustrated above occurs if one considers an extreme case, that in which cancer strikes only people over 70 and is immediately lethal, so that medical treatment is regarded as futile. There are no medical costs to be averted by eliminating the disease; neither are there productivity losses to be averted. On this method, therefore, there is no benefit from eliminating this hypothetical form of cancer. Nonetheless, there can be no room for doubt that the over-seventies, at least, would regard the elimination of this cancer as a benefit.

By reference to accepted economic principle, the benefit conferred by a new good, or by the elimination of an existing bad, is properly to be calculated as the largest sum that the community is willing to pay for it. Only a moment's reflection is needed to perceive that the sum a community is ready to pay for eradicating a particular disease has no necessary relation to the costs incidental to its current treatment (which costs, as indicated above, could conceivably be zero).

True, the simplicity of the economic conception of the benefit does not ensure that it will be a simple matter to capture the relevant data in such instances. But, as argued in Chapter 46, there is a presumption in favour of guiding one's search for data by reference to a correct conception of the specific benefit or cost, even where the data are apt to be elusive or incomplete.

Chapter 4

RESERVOIR CONSTRUCTION

1   One of the most popular applications of cost-benefit techniques is that of water control, involving the construction of a reservoir or a dam, and the machinery for electricity generation, flood control, or irrigation. There is already some very specialized literature on the methods of estimating costs and benefits for such projects, possibly because the range of practicable schemes for any one or multiple-purpose project is much larger than it is for other common applications of cost-benefit techniques, such as tunnels, highways, bridges, and airports.

2   The following highly simplified example provides the reader with an idea of a possible cost-benefit approach to reservoir construction. A reservoir is to be built on each, or on either, of two tributaries to a river in order to reduce flood damage beyond the point of confluence.

From the data collected over, say, fifty years, it is possible to construct a frequency, or probability, curve of the flood damage to be expected. If, for instance, flood damage valued at $75,000 occurred in four out of the fifty years, we may be able to judge whether climatic and other conditions are likely to change little enough to warrant our using a frequency of 4/50 or 8 per cent for this amount of damage over the future. If we decide that we can accept the events over the past fifty years as a fair sample, then the expected benefit of any construction designed to prevent damage above a certain figure is the value of the damage it can prevent times the probability of its occurrence.

The distribution shown in Figure I.1 is to be interpreted as showing that the minimum damage of $10,000, which can certainly be prevented by the construction of either a single reservoir or two reservoirs, has an 8 per cent probability of occurring in any year. An estimate of the benefit B_1 of such a construction can therefore be reckoned as equal

9

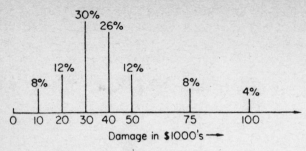

Figure I.1

to the minimum saving times the probability of its occurrence. Thus B_1 is equal to $10,000 times 8 per cent, or $800.

There will, however, be some larger construction which will prevent the occurrence of a larger damage, say $20,000. Since damage of this magnitude is expected to occur with a frequency of 12 per cent, this larger construction offers a benefit B_2 equal to $20,000 times 12 per cent *plus* the B_1 benefit of $800—since this larger construction will also prevent the smaller damage of $10,000 from ever happening.

A larger construction yet would prevent with certainty the occurrence of a greater damage, say of $30,000, occurring and, therefore, prevent the smaller damage possibilities of $20,000 and $10,000 also. If the probability of flood damage equal to $30,000 is 30 per cent, the total benefit B_3 of the larger project is equal to ($30,000 × 30%) + ($20,000 × 12%) + ($10,000 × 8%), or $12,200.

And so we continue until the seventh alternative construction, that which is most costly and which will prevent all damage up to $100,000 from occurring.

It should be clear that the expected value of the damage caused, and therefore the value of the expected benefit from eliminating the damage, depends upon the prices expected for the crops which can be destroyed by flood. The probability distribution depicted in Figure I.1 may be accurate enough with respect to the physical damage over the area, but the expected value of such damage must depend also on the expected price of the crops and the extent and intensity of the farming in the region. If the output of the crops is expected to increase year by year, and/or if the prices of the crops are expected to rise relative to the prices of other goods over time, then the value of potential damage has to be increased in successive years. In that case, the B_3 expected benefit, for instance, would not be a stream of benefits of $12,200 per annum over the future, but a stream of benefits beginning with $12,200 and increasing over time. Whatever the ultimate shape of the expected B_3 benefit stream, we can discount it to a present value using a chosen rate of discount.

3 Having got a present discounted value for each of the expected streams of benefits $B_1, B_2, \ldots, B_7$ (each of such streams corresponding, successively, to a more expensive reservoir construction), the cost of these reservoirs has to be estimated.

Now, in general, the elimination of flood damage which corresponds to some given benefit stream, say B_1, can be effected by a variety of reservoir systems. In our simple instance of a maximum of two reservoirs, we have the choice of building a single reservoir on one tributary to the river, or a single reservoir on the other tributary, or a reservoir across the river itself, or some combination of these. The costs over the future of constructing each of these alternative reservoir systems are compared, and the alternative having the lowest discounted present value, say C_1, is selected as the appropriate one for preventing the expected damage associated with B_1. Exactly the same procedure is gone through for each of the other expected benefit

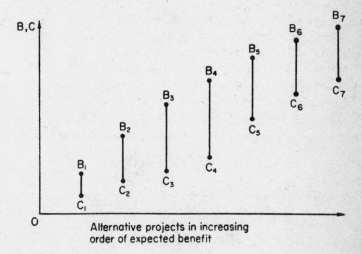

Figure I.2

11

streams, $B_2, B_3, \ldots, B_7$, in order to produce them at the lowest cost constructions, $C_2, C_3, \ldots, C_7$, respectively.

These alternative cost-benefit magnitudes are plotted vertically in Figure I.2 for each of $B_1, B_2, \ldots, B_7$ in that order. The reservoir system chosen is that giving the largest excess benefit over cost, here B_4-C_4, provided that there are no constraints on the funds available.

If the variations in benefit and cost were conceived as continuous, and a continuous B-curve and C-curve were drawn, the reader would perceive the analogy between Figure I.2 and the total cost and total revenue curves of the firm, measured against output along the horizontal axis. Given the conventional shape of the total cost and total revenue curves, maximum net revenue (revenue less cost) is at the output for which the tangents to the two curves are parallel.

Chapter 5
AN UNDER-RIVER TUNNEL

1 The River K is currently crossed by boats and ferries, and the proposal being mooted is the construction of a tunnel as a faster means of travel for vehicles. For simplicity we may assume that there is only one technically feasible tunnel for the River K, the only question being whether the construction of such a tunnel is also economically feasible whether, that is, the capitalized value of its benefits exceeds that of the outlays.

2 For the purpose of estimating the future benefits, the total traffic anticipated can be broken into three types: passengers, vehicles (including private automobiles) and freight. A division of this traffic may also be made between (1) traffic that is *diverted* from the existing means of travel and (2) additional traffic that would be *generated* only in consequence of the new tunnel. An impression of the relevance of this distinction is afforded by comparing areas D and G in Figure I.3, along the horizontal axis of which is measured number of journeys per annum, and along the vertical axis of which is measured the unit cost per journey.

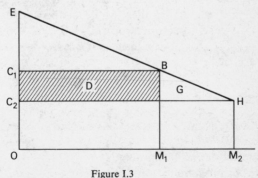

Figure I.3

Assuming that the tunnel is large enough to avoid congestion, the fare may be set to cover (constant) unit cost of operation, OC_2, whereas the existing unit cost of the boat journey across the river is, let us say, OC_1. Constructing a demand curve for the cross-river journeys in this way assumes that people are quite indifferent about the alternative means of crossing the river and will always choose that offering the lowest fare. This is unlikely to be true, but it will serve for illustrative purposes.

Since the cost of the journey falls from OC_1 to OC_2, the people who would, prior to the construction of the tunnel, have made OM_1 journeys will be better off by the saving in cost equal to the shaded rectangular area D. If as a result of this lower cost, however, an additional $M_1 M_2$ journeys are made, the additional gain from this generated traffic is equal to the triangular area G.

3 As indicated above, this way of looking at the problem is useful only for a first impression in which—since the tunnel crossing and the boat crossing are regarded as perfect substitutes—the diverted traffic OM_1 must be equal to all the traffic that was ferried across the river prior to the construction of the tunnel. More generally, the tunnel crossing will be an imperfect substitute for all the other means of crossing the river, so that even the if cost of the tunnel crossing is lower and the travel time less, many will continue to cross the river by boat or ferry.

In this more likely case, the demand schedule for tunnel crossings, passing through EH in Figure I.3, is determined (among other things) by the current costs of the alternative means of travel. If the operating cost per journey were constant at OC_1, the same as the cost of other means of travel, there would still be a net benefit above operating costs equal to the area of triangle $EC_1 B$. Should the cost be lower, equal to OC_2, the net benefit would be equal to the area of the larger triangle $EC_2 H$.

It is against this annual measure of the tunnel benefits that the capital outlays have to be set and a decision reached.

4 It may be thought that against such benefits of the tunnel we should have to set losses from having to scrap a lot of otherwise useful boats and ferries far more quickly than if the tunnel had not been built. But in economics bygones are bygones. Once the capital expenditures on boats and ferries have already been made, they are, so to speak, irretrievably sunk and no longer count. The only economically sensible thing to do is to operate the boats and ferries as long as fares can be charged that cover their current operating costs.

On the other hand, it may be thought that we should add to the benefits, as calculated above, the saving that will be secured over time from not having to renew expenditures on boats and ferries as they become obsolete. But again this would be wrong. For although in these circumstances it is possible to use total current expenditures on boats and ferries as a *basis* for estimating the gross benefits of providing similar services by a tunnel, however the tunnel benefits are calculated, there is no more sense in adding to this estimate of benefits a sum equal to the saving of future capital outlays on boats and ferries than there would be in adding to such an estimate of benefits the capital outlays of an alternative tunnel or an alternative bridge.

This sort of double counting, among others, is treated at greater length in Chapter 12.

Chapter 6

COST-BENEFIT CAPACITY ADJUSTMENTS

1 Cost-benefit techniques are not confined to appraising complete investment projects but are employed, also, to determine whether the capacity of existing projects should be extended and, if so, by how much. In so far as the question is one of estimating the optimal amount of new capacity, or the optimal use of the existing capacity, the economist is explicitly concerned with conventional marginal analysis.

2 A popular example of the latter would be the taxing of vehicles on some existing road in order to realize an optimal traffic flow. As the flow of vehicles increases over a given stretch of highway there comes a point after which the average speed falls as the flow, or volume, of traffic increases. Simplifying some of the ideas and thinking in terms of a uniform type of vehicle, we can separate two sorts of costs which motorists, as a group, impose on themselves, and which grow as the volume of traffic grows: (a) the time of the trip and, therefore, since we can attribute a value to people's time, the cost of the trip, and (b) the direct costs of operating a vehicle, chiefly fuel.

Volume of traffic is measured along the horizontal axis of figure I.4, and cost per vehicle trip is measured vertically. The vertical distance between the horizontal axis and the A curve at any point, therefore, measures the average cost per vehicle trip for that volume of traffic—cost including (a) time and (b) fuel. The sum of these costs are represented as being constant up to traffic volume OQ_0, but increasing beyond that volume. Thus beyond OQ_0 not only does every additional motorist raise the composite cost to himself, by raising the average cost he also causes each of the motorists already using the road—the 'intra-marginal' motorists— to bear this additional cost. The sum of the *additional* costs borne by all the intra-marginal motorists, *plus* his own total cost, makes up the increment of total cost attributable to the

16

additional motorist. At any volume of traffic, the relation between the average cost per motorist and this corresponding increment of total cost caused by an additional vehicle is given, as every economics student knows, by the respective heights of the average curve and the curve marginal to it.

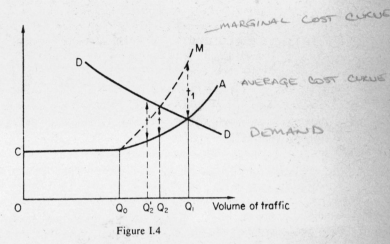

Figure I.4

In Figure I.4, the marginal cost curve M appears as a broken line that is marginal to the average cost curve A. Once the A curve begins to rise, as it does after traffic volume OQ_0, the marginal cost curve M also rises, but more steeply. The DD curve is the demand curve for trips along this stretch of highway, and can usefully be thought of as indicating, at any volume of traffic, the marginal value of the trip to the existing number of motorists. In the absence of any restriction the volume of traffic would tend to settle[1] at OQ_1. At this volume of traffic, each motorist finds the marginal value of his trip to be equal to, or no lower than, the cost (in terms of time and fuel) of his trip. Once the cost of his trip is revised to include the additional cost the motorist imposes on the intra-marginal vehicles, we have to be guided by marginal cost curve M. Employing the marginal cost principle of choosing as

---

[1] Strictly speaking, a statement about 'tending to settle' implies that the equilibrium volume of traffic at OQ_1 is stable. Since we are interested with optimality questions here, and not stability conditions, we shall continue to assume stability conditions are met unless otherwise indicated.

optimum the volume at which marginal cost is equal to marginal value, or price, volume OQ_2 is chosen—the point at which the M curve intersects the DD curve. This optimal flow of traffic, OQ_2, can be brought about by levying an optimal tax, t, on each vehicle using this highway—t being equal to the difference at Q_2 between the average and the marginal cost curve.

3 In order to calculate this tax it might seem necessary (1) to make some statistical estimate of the average cost curve in Figure I.4 and, therefore, of the cost of its two main components, time and fuel, and (2) to make some estimate of the demand curve DD for trips along this stretch of highway. With respect to (1), however, estimating the full range of the average cost curve is not necessary; only the portion of it between Q_2 and Q_1. Indeed, if one has estimates of the average cost in the vicinity of Q_2, there is enough information to calculate the 'point elasticity' of the A curve at Q_2—point elasticity being here defined, conventionally, as the percentage increase in the volume of traffic for a one per cent increase in average cost—which enables us to calculate the marginal cost at Q_2.

We could further simplify things by assuming that this point elasticity remains constant along the relevant range between Q_1 and Q_2—though Q_2 cannot be discovered until we have made an estimate of the demand curve DD. With respect to (2), and if we declare ourselves satisfied with a rough calculation of the optimal tax t, we could either assume the demand curve to have a unit elasticity at all points or we can omit consideration of the demand curve, at least provisionally. Let us follow this latter alternative. Provided we have the average cost and its corresponding point elasticity, for the existing volume of traffic at Q_1, the marginal cost at Q_1 can be derived by the familiar formula $M = A(1 + 1/E)$, where E is the point elasticity at Q_1 of the A curve, and M and A respectively are marginal and average cost.[2]

Now the tax per vehicle trip, or toll, t, must be set equal to the difference between average and marginal cost; i.e. $t = M - A$, or $t = (1 + 1/E)A - A$, or $t = (1/E)A$. Thus the required toll is got by

---

[2] Let total cost be $T = AQ$, where A is average cost and Q is total quantity. Define dT/dQ as marginal cost M, which $= d(AQ)/dQ = A + Q(dA/dQ)$. Therefore $M = A[1 + (Q/A)(dA/dQ)]$. But, by definition, $(dQ/dA)(A/Q)$ is point elasticity, E, of the average cost curve. Hence, $M = A(1 + 1/E)$.

multiplying the average cost of the journey at Q_1 by the inverse of the elasticity. If, for example, the average cost of the trip at Q_1 is \$2.50, and E is equal to 5, the toll is set at \$2.50 × 1/5, or at \$0.50.

This toll, equal to t_1 in Figure I.4, is clearly estimated for the existing volume of traffic OQ_1, which is somewhat greater than the toll t in the Figure that realizes the optimal traffic volume at OQ_2. If this toll t_1, somewhat larger than the 'ideal' toll t, were imposed, the volume of traffic would in fact be reduced to OQ'_2, somewhat below the optimal traffic volume OQ_2. It is manifest that the steeper is the demand curve DD the smaller is the difference between Q_2 and Q'_2. If the cost of estimating the relevant portion of the demand curve about Q_0Q_1 was high, and the error likely to be high also, the calculated toll t_1, and the output OQ'_2 resulting from its imposition may be judged satisfactory.

This toll can easily be converted to a fuel tax. By dividing the fifty cents toll by the number of miles of highway, say twenty-five, we obtain a tax of two cents per mile. If, on the average, there are fifteen miles to the gallon with the calculated optimal volume of traffic, the optimal fuel tax becomes thirty cents per gallon.

The complications we have avoided—traffic composition, variety of highway systems, daily patterns of traffic flow—are obvious enough. But this has enabled us to make the concept clear. A more complete calculation, even for the simple case we have been considering, would have required that the spillover effects of additional traffic on persons other than motorists be brought into the calculation.

4   The cost-benefit analysis of a road-widening scheme fits in well with the preceding construction. The relevant comparison is that between the optimal traffic volume OQ'_1 with the existing road system, at which, in Figure I.5, the marginal cost curve M_1 cuts the demand curve DD, on the one hand, and the optimal traffic volume OQ'_2, on the other, for some added width to the road.

If, for example, we double the width of the existing road—which allows the maximum volume of traffic at constant cost to double, let us say, from OQ_1 to OQ_2—we can compare the average and marginal curves, and the respective optimal volumes, OQ'_1 and OQ'_2. The shaded area represents the excess benefit; the excess additional motorists' valuations over the additional operational and congestion costs of moving from OQ'_1 optimal volume to OQ'_2 optimal volume.

This measure of excess benefit over all currently incurred costs would have to be projected over the future as a stream of benefits. The benefit stream may then be discounted to the present and compared with the initial capital costs of road widening.

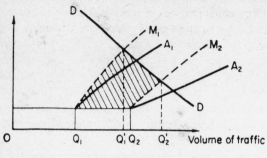

Figure I.5

If this investment were the only one available, we should—provided the rate of discount used was equal to the rate of return on investment in the private sector—continue investing in road widening until the discounted benefit–cost ratio were unity, or until the investible funds were exhausted, whichever took place first. If, however, a large number of roads could be widened to some extent and the funds available were limited, these funds should be spread among them as to maximize the total benefit-cost ratio.

5   A similar sort of analysis is at the base of the decision to increase the capacity of an electricity generating plant. Simplifying Williamson's (1966) treatment, we can suppose that additional electricity plant can be effectively supplied only in indivisible units.

In Figure I.6 we assume an unchanged demand over the period, with existing capacity equal to OQ_1. Thus marginal cost is constant up to output OQ_1 after which it becomes vertical. It therefore traces the reverse-L shaped line $C_1F_1M_1$. The overhead costs for the output OQ_1 is given by the rectangle $C_1C_2F_2F_1$. If the demand curve were to pass through F_2 (which it does *not* do in the Figure), it would not pay to install the additional indivisible unit of capacity generating an additional output Q_1Q_2; for the value of each additional unit of electricity, from Q_1 onwards, would be below the average inclusive cost (current cost plus overhead cost), OC_2. But with the demand curve DD, as shown in the Figure, it just pays to do so, since the social gain measured by the triangle A for the first Q_1M additional units exactly offsets the social loss measured by triangle B on the remaining MQ_2 units. If the demand curve were higher than DD shown in the Figure, the A triangle would exceed in area the B triangle, and there would be an excess of benefit over cost in extending generating capacity from OQ_1 to OQ_2.

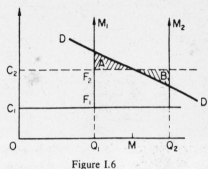

Figure I.6

No difference in principle arises if the demand for electricity fluctuates over the period in question, but the demand curve has to be shaped accordingly by an appropriate weighting system. If the highest price the community will pay for a given unit of electricity is $1 per hour for eight hours of the day (a maximum daily price of $24), and only fifty cents per hour (a maximum daily price of $12) for the remaining sixteen hours of the day, then over the twenty-four hours it would average $66\frac{2}{3}$ cents.

In this simple case of a division of the day into an eight-hour peak and a sixteen-hour off-peak period, the daily demand curve for the calculation would be the vertical sum of the two prices, each weighted by its fraction of the day. In general, if the peak price was p_1, the off-peak price p_2, the fraction of the day for peak usage w_1, and the fraction for off-peak usage w_2, then the composite daily price is $p_1w_1 + p_2w_2$. In the above case, therefore, it is $(\frac{1}{3} \times 1 \cdot 0) + (\frac{2}{3} \times 0 \cdot 50)$ or $66\frac{2}{3}$ cents, as stated.

Having derived the weighted demand curve by such methods, it is again necessary that the area of triangle A exceed that of B in order to justify the introduction of an additional generating plant.

21

PART II. ECONOMIC CONCEPTS OF COSTS AND BENEFITS

Chapter 7

CONSUMERS' SURPLUS

1   In economics, in 'normative' or allocative economics at least, the worth or value of a thing to a person is determined simply by what a person is willing to pay for it. If a man is ready to pay as much as $5 for a gallon of cider, it may be inferred that it is (in his own estimation) worth to him no less than $5.[1] If the gallon of cider is priced at $2, the purchase of one gallon of it provides with a consumer's surplus of $3 (i.e. $5 less $2).

2   This consumer's surplus is the most crucial concept in the measurement of social benefits in any social cost-benefit calculation. For all except marginal changes in the amount of a good, the market price prevailing in a perfectly competitive setting is an inadequate index of the value of the good. Using partial analysis, therefore, the economist engaged in a cost-benefit calculation has to go beyond a simple price *times* quantity measure of the benefits arising from the products or services of a project. Instead, he makes use of the area under the entire *ceteris paribus* demand curve. Even in the fairly common case, when an investment project is designed to save some part of the costs

---

[1] Although this simple view of the matter will suffice for the analysis in the following chapters, the reader might be interested in the theoretical refinements of Note *A*, Part VIII. These refinements can be important in some circumstances, as will be indicated in the treatment of external effects in Part III.

currently incurred in making use of existing facilities—an example would be a bridge built to replace an existing ferry service—the consumers' surplus concept is implicit in the cost-saving calculation. Indeed, the magnitude of this cost-saving is itself no more than a part, the major part it is true, of the horizontal segment of consumers' surplus that is measured by the fall in the price of the service. The remaining part is the triangular area, tacked on to right of the horizontal segment, arising from the additional services demanded at the lower price.

Since the *ceteris paribus* market demand curve explained in textbooks is the required construct, the reader does well to recall what things go into this *ceteris paribus* pound: population of given size, tastes, the prices of all other goods and productive services, and the distribution of society's assets among its members. As we shall see later, a change in any one of these things can alter the shape of the demand curve in question. Any resulting change in the measure of consumers' surplus will then require careful interpretation. For the present, however, the reader should bear in mind that the interpretation of consumers' surplus demands a reversal of the causal direction usually implied in the interpretation of the demand curve. Instead of the eye travelling horizontally, that is, from a given price to the maximum amount consumers are willing to buy at that price, the eye now moves vertically upward: that is, beginning from a given amount of the good offered on the market, the corresponding point on the demand curve indicates the maximum price the consumers are willing to pay for the last unit of that amount.

3 A simple yet workable definition of consumer's surplus (note the apostrophe after the *r*, indicating the surplus of a single consumer) is that it is the maximum sum of money a consumer would be willing to pay for a given amount of the good, less the amount he actually pays. We may extend the idea by thinking about asking a consumer the maximum sum per week he would be willing to pay for only one pint of milk, the maximum sum he will then pay for a second, the maximum for a third, and so on. These sums, which we can speak of as 'marginal valuations', are plotted as the heights of successive columns in Figure II.1. If a price per pint of milk is fixed at, say, twenty cents, he continues to buy additional pints of milk until his marginal valuation is equal to or below that price. Figure II.1

23

illustrates a case in which the man buys seven pints of milk at twenty cents, so spending $1.40 per week on milk. The area contained in the shaded parts of the columns above the price line is a sum of money equal to the man's consumer's surplus.

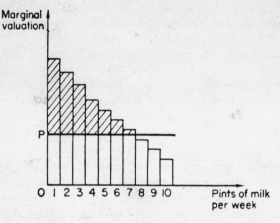

Figure II.1

4   Once perfect divisibility is assumed, the stepped outline of the columns gives way to a smooth demand curve. From a point on the vertical, or price axis, the horizontal distance to the curve measures the maximum amount of the good he will buy at that price. The *market* demand curve, being a horizontal summation of all the individual demand curves, can be regarded as the marginal valuation curve for society. For example, the height QR in Figure II.2, corresponding to output OQ, gives the maximum value some person in society is willing to pay for the Qth unit of the good—which, for that person, may be the first, second, or n^{th} unit of the good bought. But to each of the total number of units purchased, which total is measured as a distance along the quantity axis, there corresponds some individual's maximum valuation. The whole area under the demand curve, therefore, corresponds to society's maximum valuation for the quantity in question. If, say, OQ is bought, the maximum worth of OQ units to society is given by the trapezoid area $ODRQ$. Now the quantity OQ is bought by the market at price OP. Total expenditure by the buyers is, therefore, represented by the area $OPRQ$ (price OP *times* quantity OQ). Subtracting from the maximum worth of buyers ($ODRQ$) what they have

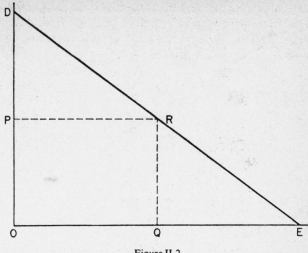

Figure II.2

to pay (*OPRQ*) leaves us with a total consumers' surplus equal to triangle *DRP*.

If an entirely new good *x* is introduced into the economy, and is made available to all and sundry free of charge, the area under the resulting demand curve, *ODE* (given that prices of all other goods are unaffected) is a good enough measure of the gain to the community in its capacity as consumer. The services provided by a new bridge, or a new park, would be familiar examples. Again, however, if a price, *OP*, for the service is introduced, the amount *OQ* will be bought, leaving the triangular area *PDR* in Figure II.2 as the consumers' surplus. Estimates of consumers' surplus, it need hardly be said, are to be entered as benefits in all cost-benefit calculations.

5 Any investment having the object of reducing the cost of a product or service is deemed to confer a benefit on the community, which benefit is often referred to as a 'cost-difference', or a 'cost-saving'. The benefit of a new motorway, or flyover, is estimated by reference to the expected savings of time, and of the cost of fuel, by all motorists who will make use of the new road or flyover. As already indicated, however, the concept of cost-saving is derived directly from the concept of consumers' surplus, as can be shown by reference to Figure II.3. Thus, prior to the introduction of, say, the new flyover in question,

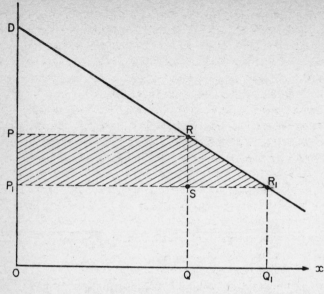

Figure II.3

the consumers' surplus from using this particular route (being the maximum sum motorists are willing to pay above the amount they currently spend on the journey—an average of OP per journey) is the triangle PDR. If the flyover halves the cost of the journey to them, from OP to OP_1, at which lower cost the number of journeys undertaken is increased from OQ to OQ_1, the consumers' surplus increases from PDR to P_1DR_1, an increase equal to the shaded strip PP_1R_1R.

This increase of consumers' surplus can be split up into two parts. There is, first, the cost-saving component, the rectangle PP_1SR, which is calculated as the saving per journey, PP_1, multiplied by the original number of journeys made, OQ. The other component, represented by the triangle SRR_1, is the consumers' surplus made on the additional journeys undertaken, QQ_1, either by the same motorists or by additional motorists. The cost-saving item that enters a cost-benefit calculation is, as indicated, no more than a portion of the increment of consumers' surplus from a fall in the cost of the good. Since it takes no account of the additional goods that will be bought in response to the fall in cost, the cost-saving rectangle alone can be accepted as a *minimum* estimate of the benefit.

26

We might call this explanation a casual account of the matter, though not a misleading one. Nothing need be said about *utility* since we are not going to translate our money magnitudes into utility terms: the area under the market demand curve, that is, does not become translated into a sum of individual utilities, but remains simply as a sum of their valuations. The extent of the collective improvement from the introduction of a good is, then, expressed in terms of a sum of money which is measured by a triangle of consumers' surplus, such as PDR in Figure II.2. Its interpretation is simply the maximum amount of money the group as a whole would offer in order to be able to buy OQ of this new good at price P. The extent of the collective improvement from a reduction in its price, however, is expressed as an increment of consumers' surplus, as for example the strip PP_1R_1R in Figure II.3. The strip can be interpreted as the maximum amount of money the group as a whole would offer in order to have the price reduced from OP to OP_1.

6 So far, the consumers' surplus analysis has had reference to the demand for a final good, say a clock, although it can also be extended to the derived demand for some input, or intermediate good, such as the steel that is used in the manufacture of clocks.

The appropriate consumers' surplus measure for steel, or steel of a particular kind, is obtained from the correctly *derived* demand curves for steel. Thus the short run demand curve for steel derived from the clock industry is obtained by subtracting from the marginal valuation of the nth clock the combined cost of all the other inputs that enter into the production of this n^{th} clock—assuming the prices of these other inputs to be fixed, and assuming that all the inputs are combined efficiently.[2] All such derived demand curves for this particular kind of steel can then be added together taking special care not to violate the *ceteris paribus* assumptions which in this instance requires that we introduce each of the relevant demand curves for the final steel-using products in sequence as will be explained in section 2 of the next chapter.

---

[2] The first order conditions for productive efficiency require that input rates of substitution be inverse to the ratio of input prices. The elasticity of the derived demand for an intermediate good such as steel varies *inter alia* with the elasticity of substitution between this intermediate good and others, and also with the elasticity of the demand for the final goods using the intermediate good.

Note, however, that the correctly derived short run demand curve for steel, arising, say, from the demand for clocks, is not always the same as the clock-producer's demand for steel. If the clock producer is a monopolist who sets output to equate marginal revenue to marginal cost, his demand curve for steel—as for each of his other inputs—will be derived from his marginal revenue curve, and not from the market demand curve for his clocks.

7   Something more has now to be said about this relationship between price and quantity. Beginning from a general equilibrium system, we could deduce that the amount of a good x that is bought depends not only on its own price but, in general, on the prices of all other goods and factors, also on tastes, on technical knowledge, and on the distribution of resource endowments. In statistical estimates of the price-demand curve for x, the relationship is much more restricted. We might, for example, try to gather enough data so as to derive a specific equation from the relationship $X = F(P_x, P_y, P_z, M)$, X being the maximum amount of good x demanded, P_x, P_y, P_z, being the prices respectively of the goods x, y, and z, and M being aggregate real income. Goods y and z could be chosen as being close and important substitutes for x, or else y could be a close substitute and z a close complement of x, the relative prices of all other goods being ignored. Sometimes the price of one or more factors are to be included in the function. If, for example, the good x is taken as being farm tractors, the income of the farm population would obviously be a significant variable in the demand for tractors. In any statistical estimate of the price-demand curve for X, the *ceteris paribus* clause will operate to hold constant only those variables, other than P_x, that are included in the function F. All those variables that are not included in the function F—an almost unlimited number of goods and factor prices—are assumed, provisionally at least, to be of negligible importance.

Although this procedure is fairly general, there has been some recent controversy about the M term.[3] If aggregate *real* income is held constant in constructing this *ceteris paribus* demand curve, we are left with a curve which summarizes the pure substitution effect of, say, a declining price. No income-effects are included, and the measure of

---

[3] A controversy started by Friedman (1949).

consumers' surplus derived therefrom will be conceptually accurate.[4]
If, on the other hand, aggregate *money* income is held constant, any fall
in the price of x raises the real value of an unchanged aggregate money
income and—if the income-effect on x is positive—results in some
further increases in the amount of x bought (along with changes in the
amounts bought of all other goods).[5] The resultant demand curve is
therefore a compound of substitution and income effects. In consequence, the measure of consumers' surplus derived from such a
demand curve can be no more than an approximation to the ideal
measure based on a pure substitution-effect demand curve, as proposed
by Friedman (1949). It will be less accurate according to whether the
income effect is more important.

However, the difference that arises from using constant *real* income,
as against constant *money* income, in the statistical derivation of a
demand curve for a single good, is likely to be too slight relative to the
usual order of statistical error to make the distinction significant in any
cost-benefit study. The emphasis in the *ceteris paribus* pound of the
market price-demand curve for x is to be placed, instead, on the
constancy of the prices of the goods closely related to x. Thus, the
amounts bought of all other goods in the economy, including those of y
and z, may alter as they please in response, say, to a decline in the price
of x.[6] The measure of the x consumers' surplus is not thereby affected.

---

[4] Moving along a demand curve for which real income is constant entails an unchanged
welfare—no shifting, that is, of the marginal valuation curve because of changes in
welfare (or real income). For elaboration of this point the reader is referred to Note A
of Part VIII.

[5] If a person is willing to pay, say, \$5 for the first pint of milk per week and, after paying
\$5 for the first pint is willing to pay \$4 for a second pint, then he would be willing to
pay more than \$4 for the second pint if he did *not* have to pay as much as \$5 for the first
pint, but some smaller sum, say \$2. For in that case he would be making a consumer's
surplus of \$3 on the first pint of milk bought, and to the extent that this makes him
better off he is willing to pay more (assuming his income-effect with respect to milk is
positive) for the second pint. The reader interested in these refinements is, again,
referred to Note A of Part VIII.

[6] If the demand curve for x has an elasticity greater than unity the amounts demanded
of other goods will fall and (assuming full employment) some of the factors released
from the production of these other goods will move into the production of x. If,
however, the demand for x is of less than unit elasticity, factors will move out of x and
into the production of other goods, the demand for which will, on balance, increase.

In the limiting case of unit elasticity of demand for x, there is no change in total cost
and total expenditure of x, and no change in total expenditure on all other goods taken
together.

(Only if alterations take place in the *prices* of the closely related goods y and z, following a fall or rise in the price of x, does the measure of x's consumers' surplus have to be qualified—as we shall see in the next chapter.) For the area under the demand curve for x is a valid measure of the gain to consumers only when the introduction of x, or a decline in its price, is accompanied by access to all other goods at unchanged prices.

Notwithstanding the above remarks, there is apparently so strong a temptation among those who become acquainted with the consumers' surplus concept to seek algebraic additions to an increase in the consumers' surplus for x in the consequent shifts of demand for goods related to x that I append a note to this chapter containing a simple example in order to reassure the reader that in measuring the consumers' surplus of a new good, or a good the price of which has changed, he should neglect the induced shifts of demand of related goods.

8 In the preceding paragraphs we have emphasized the propriety of ignoring the repercussions on the amounts of other goods bought whenever measuring the change of consumers' surplus arising from an alteration in the price of x alone. This injunction to ignore consequent shifts in the *ceteris paribus* demand curves for other goods does not, however, preclude an interpretation of the resulting areas under such demand curves. Assuming provisionally constant costs in the production of all goods in the economy, a fall in the price of x will cause a shift to the left of the *ceteris paribus* demand curve for good y which is, we assume, an important substitute for x. The now smaller area under this demand curve for y is the consumers' surplus enjoyed from the availability of y, at the unchanged price of y, when the price of x is lower than before. This smaller area of consumers' surplus for y accords with common sense, for with the fall in the price of its close substitute x the existing level of welfare will depend less on good y than before. Thus if y were now to be totally withdrawn from the market, the welfare loss suffered by society would be smaller simply because the substitute x has become available at a lower price than before.

To illustrate, in Figures II.4(x) and II.4(y), the initial *ceteris paribus* demand curve for each good is the solid line. $D_x E_x$ is the demand curve for x when the price of good y is held constant at p_y. $D_y E_y$ is the demand curve for y when the price of good x is held constant at p_{x1}. If now, as a result of some improved method of production, the price of x falls from p_{x1} to p_{x2} then the demand curve for y falls from D_yE_y to $D'_yE'_y$ as is shown in Figure II.4(y). At the unchanged price p_y, the smaller quantity of y, OB, is demanded instead of the quantity OC which was demanded before the fall in the price of x.

With a lower price of x consumers are obviously better off. They would, of course, be better off even if they had to buy exactly the same amounts of x and y as they did before the fall in the price of x. But they further improve their welfare by buying more of x and buying less of y. Once they have made these changes in their purchases of x and y, how do we interpret these consumers' surpluses? First, the measure of the gain in consumers' surplus is represented wholly by the shaded strip in Figure II.4(x) between the original price p_{x_1} and the new price p_{x_2}. Provided all other goods prices remain unchanged—and in particular that of the close substitute y—this shaded strip measures the most that consumers will pay to have the reduction in the price of x.

Second, the dotted triangle show in Figure II.4(y) represents the consumers' surplus in having a price p_y when the price of x is now p_{x_2}. This triangle is the difference between the most they would pay for OB of y (OD'_yRB) when x is priced at p_{x_2} and what they have to pay for OB of y (OP_yRB).

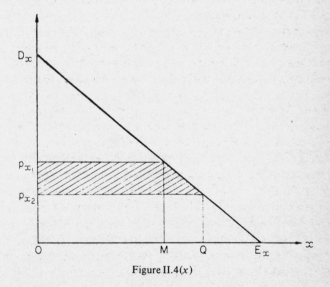

Figure II.4(x)

31

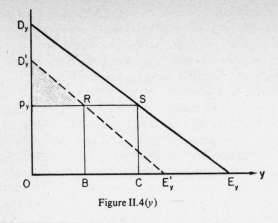

Figure II.4(y)

Note particularly the interpretation of this reduced triangle of consumers' surplus—that where the demand curve for y shifts inward in response to a fall in the price of x. The reduction of the *initial* area of consumers' surplus, $p_y D_y S$ (corresponding to the original price of x, p_{x_1}) to this smaller area of consumers' surplus $p_y D'_y R$ (corresponding to the lower price of x, p_{x_2})—a reduction in area equal to $D'_y D_y SR$—is *not* to be regarded as a loss of consumers' surplus consequent upon the fall in the price of x from p_{x_1} to p_{x_2}. This reduction in area is simply the consequence of consumers' bettering themselves by switching from good y to the new lower-priced good x. Provided supply prices are constant, and we assume they are, the *ceteris paribus* conditions are met, and the partial analysis depicts the consumers' gains wholly within the area of the demand curve of the good the price of which has fallen—irrespective, that is, of the resulting magnitude and direction of the shifts in demand for all other goods in the economy.

It follows that if we are focusing our attention on the consumers' surplus of the good x, and it appears to increase in response to a rise in the price of the substitute good y, this larger area under the demand curve for x is to be interpreted as the maximum amount of money that people are now willing to pay for having x available at its unchanged price when all other prices are given and the price of the substitute good y is higher. To be sure, consumers as a whole are worse off when the price of y alone is raised, but this larger area of consumers' surplus for the good x means that—given all prices. including the now higher price of y—the gain wholly associated with having x available at the same price is, in these circumstances, larger than before.

This proposition can be extended to cover a potential good x, one that can be introduced at a known cost and, indeed, will be introduced if the demand for it is large enough. Let the existing good y continue to rise in price and it will be socially profitable to introduce the good x at a price equal to its marginal variable cost when, at that price, the consumers' surplus is large enough to cover the capital costs incurred in the production of x.

9   The economist, examining the future course of the demand curve for x in order to calculate the magnitude of future benefits from its consumption, does *not* therefore need to distinguish between the rises in consumers' surplus for x that indicates an increase in society's welfare and the rises in consumers' surplus that are indicative of a loss in social welfare, the result, say, of price-rises or unavailabilities elsewhere in the economy. He accepts as data all the prices and goods over which he has no control, for they fall outside his domain of investigation. If the project is that of investing in an increased output of x, the magnitudes over the future of the consumers' surplus of the increased output of x are to count no matter how they arise.

No exception to this rule occurs if the rise in the price of a good y, or of any other good related to x, is a result of direct government intervention. If the government levies an excise tax on y, or adopts a policy of withdrawing y from the market, the economist is always at liberty to point out the lack of economic justification for such policies, and the consequences that are likely to follow from their implementation. But assuming these policies are to prevail over the relevant time period, he has no choice but to measure the changes in the consumers' surpluses of good x in the usual way.

Only if the economist is engaged in a cost-benefit study that encompasses a number of closely related goods is he in a position to pronounce on actions calculated to change other relevant prices from some generally acceptable pattern, say from that corresponding to marginal social costs. A transport economist, for example, would wish to point out that the apparent increase in the consumers' surplus of private traffic, which seems to warrant investment in road-widening schemes, is the result simply of a reduction in the availability of public transport, a reduction that is itself the result of traffic congestion on existing roads. The imposition of a traffic toll that produces an optimal flow of traffic will increase the efficiency of public transport, and may reduce private motorists' surplus to a magnitude that no longer warrants investment in road-widening. Such a solution is clearly the more efficient one, and that which, in the circumstances, the economist will propose. In contrast, if the economist is required to advise on road-widening schemes but is allowed no control whatsoever on the existing volume of private traffic (which may well be greatly in excess of an optimal flow) he has no choice but to accept such political constraints and to calculate the benefits of a road-widening scheme under the existing conditions.[7]

10 We have stated that in the construction of the demand curve for a good x the appropriate *ceteris paribus* pound contains all other product prices, all factor prices, tastes, technology, and resource endowments. Since changes in resource endowments can imply changes in distribution or in the size of population, and changes in technology can imply changes in real income per capita, the *ceteris paribus* clause can be expressed in an alternative form that requires constancy of product prices, population, per capita income, distribution, and tastes. We shall now go on to consider the treatment of consumers' surplus when each of these items is no longer held constant, beginning in the next chapter with the treatment of consumers' surplus when the prices of related goods are altered.

NOTE TO CHAPTER 7

Let us suppose, first, that a new good, x, is introduced into the economy since this necessarily implies smaller expenditures on other goods.[8] Now, as indicated in Chapter 7, the reader may suspect that if expenditure is withdrawn from other goods in the economy, losses are incurred there, and that these losses ought to be offset against the consumers' surplus for x as conventionally measured. Such a suspi-

---

[7] This theme is developed in Mishan (1967).

[8] If an existing good x were reduced in price, expenditure on it may remain constant—which is a necessary (though not sufficient) condition for the amounts bought of all other goods to remain unchanged.

cion is, in general, unwarranted—at least, under the usual assumption of maximizing behaviour. In order to convince the reader that this is so, we shall cook up an example which, at first, seems to bear out the belief that losses will be incurred elsewhere. We shall take as our example, then, an existing ferry service across a river that is to be replaced by a railway bridge. The ferry charges $2 per person, and manages to break even when carrying the existing number of passengers. The average cost of labour and maintenance is $1.50, the remaining fifty cents being the return on capital (the capital expenditure on the ferry-boat).

For simplicity we can suppose that people are quite indifferent as between the two ways of crossing the river. If the *inclusive* unit cost of the rail service (total variable cost plus total overheads *divided* by number of journeys) is expected to be also $2, no profit could be made above the normal return on capital. There would then be no incentive to undertake the building of the bridge. Indeed, there would be a negative incentive in view of the fact that capital had already been invested in the ferry service. For rather than lose passengers to the rail service, the ferry-owners would be ready to reduce fares below $2; any fare above $1.50 is in the nature of a quasi-rent, and contributes something to the owners of the ferry-boat who cannot extricate their investment.[9] if, however, the inclusive unit cost of the rail service is expected to be $1.20, it could introduce the service at, say, $1.40, make a profit (above normal return on capital), and put the ferry out of business. Now if we reckon the annual benefit of the investment in the bridge as consisting of this profit and, also, the consumer's surplus from reducing the fare from $2 to $1.40, then indeed, we should have to set against it the loss to the ferry-boat owners of fifty cents per unit. But this way of reckoning things is unnecessary: it offsets a gain of fifty cents to the passengers against a loss of fifty cents to the ferry-boat owners, which is only a transfer as between one group and another. It is simpler to reckon the benefits as a straight-forward cost-saving; the savings effected from reducing per unit current resource cost of $1.50 to per unit resource cost of $1.20, *plus* some area of surplus for any additional number of journeys taken in response to a reduction in the

---

[9] On the assumption that there is no alternative use, and no scrap value, for the ferry-boat. If there is, the minimum contemplated by the owners will be above $1.50.

price from $1.50 to $1.40. Let us be quite clear about the reduction in unit resource costs.

The relevant current cost of the ferry journey is, in total, $1.50, for the capital invested in the boat is irrecoverable (bygones are bygones in economics). The full costs of the resources required to maintain the ferry service are therefore $1.50, these being only the variable costs of operating the service. The relevant current cost of the rail-bridge service is, however, only $1.20. Since capital costs have not yet been incurred, this $1.20 per unit includes the capital cost (the return that capital would fetch if placed, instead, in some other use). It is the difference between these current resource costs of providing the existing service which is a measure of the minimum gain—any additional services, in consequence of setting the price lower than $2, adding some area of surplus as indicated in Figure II.5.

Let C_1 ($1.50) be the current cost of the ferry service, and P_1 ($2) the price it charges. Let C_2 ($1.20) be the expected current cost of the rail service, and P_2 the price contemplated ($1.40). With the ferry service, the consumers' surplus is equal to the triangle P_1DR_1, and the quasi-rent to the ferry-boat owners is the rectangle $P_1R_1S_1C_1$. With the rail service, the consumers' surplus will equal the triangle P_2DR_2, and profit (above normal return) equal to the rectangle $C_2P_2R_2S_2$. The

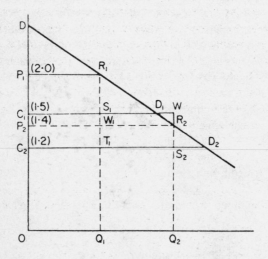

Figure II.5

36

difference in social benefit as between the two services, therefore, amounts to the cost difference on the *original* number of journeys, this being a sum equal to the rectangle $C_1C_2T_1S_1$ *plus* the additional gains to consumers from a reduction in the price from P_1 to P_2, which gains are equal to the triangle $R_1W_1R_2$, *plus* the profit (C_2P_2 per unit) on the additional number of journeys, Q_1Q_2, which is equal to $T_1W_1R_2S_2$.[10]

What is significant is that—assuming the variable resources to be perfectly mobile—the loss of quasi-rents by the ferry-boat owners will be wholly offset by the gains to consumers when the price falls from P_1 to P_2. Moreover, an estimate of the saving in costs as between the two services, when reckoned over the original amount demanded, will always be an underestimate of the benefit.

Moreover, in a perfectly competitive economy, where market prices can be taken to equal their average costs, we should need to compare only C_1 and C_2, which is much simpler. The benefit would be equal to the strip $C_1C_2D_2D_1$, which area can be broken into the cost-difference *times* the original amount sold, plus the triangle of consumers' surplus on the additional amount sold as a result of the reduction in price (equal cost).

Even if the new good that is introduced is not identical with the old good, whose sales are now reduced, the general conclusion follows. The strip of consumers' surplus may be taken as an estimate of the benefit in disregard of the reduction in sales of the old good. Similarly if x and y are substitutes a decline in the price of x, with the price of y remaining unchanged, will produce a benefit that is equal to the gain of consumers' surplus when this is measured with respect to the *ceteris paribus* demand curve for x. Problems of adjustment arise only when the price of y changes simultaneously, either exogenously or as a direct consequence of the reduction in the price of x, and to these problems we now turn.

---

[10] This is equal to the cost-difference on the amount of the service that will be taken at the P_2 price, which is equal to the rectangle $C_1C_2S_2W$, *less* the small dotted triangle D_1WR_2 *plus* the triangle $R_2S_1D_1$.

Clearly, if the price P_2 were reduced to the cost C_2, there would be an additional benefit equal to the triangle $R_2S_2D_2$, consumers thereby gaining an area $P_2C_2D_2R_2$, which exceeds by that triangle the loss to capital-owners (equal to the rectangle $C_2P_2R_2S_2$).

Chapter 8

CONSUMERS' SURPLUS WHEN OTHER PRICES CHANGE

1 This chapter is a simple exercise in partial equilibrium analysis: in the adding and subtracting of consumers' surpluses arising from sequential or simultaneous changes in the prices of two or more related goods.

2 Hicks (1956) has shown how the consumers' surplus on two or more substitute goods, say gas and electricity, that are introduced simultaneously can be measured. Suppose that gas is introduced at a given price p_g into an area which has no electricity. The shaded triangle of Figure II.6(g) can be taken as a measure of the resulting consumers' surplus. If, following this event, electricity is introduced at a price p_e, the demand curve for electricity D_eE_e is obviously smaller when gas is available at a fixed price p_g than it would be in the absence of gas. For already the consumers derive much benefit from gas, and the introduction of a fairly close substitute is not so great a boon as it would be if, instead, there had been no gas in the first place. The additional gain to consumers from introducing electricity into a gas-using area is given by the dotted triangle in Figure II.6(e). The sum of these two triangles together measures the consumers' surplus from providing both gas and electricity at prices p_g and p_e respectively.

Should the economist elect to measure the simultaneous introduction of gas and electricity using the same sequential device but in the reverse order (that is, first measuring the consumer surplus for introducing electricity when gas is assumed to be unavailable, and then measuring the consumer surplus for gas on the assumption that electricity is already available), the sum of these two component surpluses should, theoretically, be exactly the same.[1]

This method of adding consumers' surpluses can, of course, be extended to three or more goods, and is just as valid if the goods in question are complements rather than substitutes. If, for example, gas and electricity were complements—as they would be if the only use of electricity were the heating of electric pokers for lighting gas fires—a fall in the price of gas would raise the demand curve for electricity.

The analysis is of course symmetrical for simultaneous *withdrawal* of two or more goods. Thus, assuming again that gas and electricity are close substitutes, if electricity is first withdrawn from the market while gas remains readily available at its old price p_g, the loss of consumers' surplus is given by the dotted triangle in Figure II.6(e). Since gas is a substitute, the demand curve for gas shifts to the right following the withdrawal of electricity. The resulting consumers' surplus for gas then becomes the shaded triangle in Figure II.6(g), and

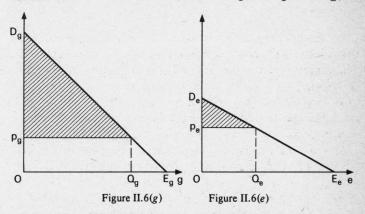

Figure II.6(g)   Figure II.6(e)

---

[1] The so-called path-dependence problem, which allows for differences in the result according to the order in which the changes are taken, is a mathematical theorem that has no relevance in this economic context. For it is one in which the consumer is held to be consistent in his choices. Therefore for any given set of simultaneous changes in goods availability and/or goods prices there must be a unique exact measure of consumer surplus (no matter which ordinal measure of consumer surplus is used).

Mathematically, the necessary and sufficient condition for path independence with respect to a change in any pair of prices, p_i and p_j, is that $\dfrac{\partial q_j}{\partial p_i} = \dfrac{\partial q_i}{\partial p_j}$ (where q_i and q_j are the corresponding quantities). This condition, however, is explicit in the Hicksian system (see Hicks, 1939, appendix). For a verbal elaboration of this point the reader is referred to Mishan (1980), pp. 192–3.

is the measure of the loss sustained if gas, previously available at p_g, is withdrawn from the market.

3 The further extension of the method to simultaneous *price* changes poses no problems. Suppose once more that electricity and gas are close substitutes and that the prices of both rise. The loss of consumers' surplus arising from the rise in the price of gas from p_{g_1} to p_{g_2}, the price of electricity being (provisionally) unchanged, is shown by the shaded strip in Figure II.7(g). As a direct result of the rise in the price of gas, the demand curve for electricity now moves outward from $D_e E_e$ to $D'_e E'_e$ in Figure II.7(e). If, following this adjustment, the price of electricity rises from p_{e_1} to p_{e_2}, the further loss of consumers' surplus is given by the shaded area in Figure II.7(e). It is hardly surprising,

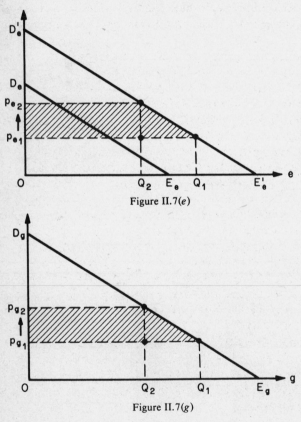

Figure II.7(e)

Figure II.7(g)

after all, that the loss of consumers' surplus from a rise in the price of electricity becomes greater according to whether the price of its substitute good has become higher or less available. The less available or the more expensive are substitute goods, the more it matters if the price of the good in question rises, and vice versa.

If, instead, gas and electricity happen to be complementary goods, a rise in the price of gas causes an inward shift of the demand curve for electricity. The additional loss of consumers' surplus of any concomitant rise in the price of electricity is then smaller than if the price of gas had not risen in the first place. This also makes good sense since an initial rise in the price of gas makes electricity *less* useful when it is complementary with gas—and not more useful as it will be when it is a substitute for gas.

The reader can soon convince himself that the analysis is symmetric for a sequential or simultaneous *fall* in the prices of two or more goods.

4 For expositional purposes we have so far held supply prices of all goods constant. By now removing this simplification we can see that the above analysis is applicable also to cases in which supply curves slope upward or downward. For if any good y is related to good x, the equilibrium price of y will also be affected if, in the first instance, there is an exogenous change in the price of x.

Let us restrict our attention to the two-good case in which the good having an exogenous fall in price, say electricity, has constant costs and the related good, say gas, which is a substitute for electricity, does not have constant costs.

Again, using the device of taking the price changes in sequence, the exogenous fall in the price of electricity from p_{e1} to p_{e2} first increases consumers' surplus in electricity by the shaded area in Figure II.8(*e*). But this fall in the price of electricity induces a leftward shift of the demand curve for gas from DD to $D'D'$ in Figure II.8(*g*). If we assume first that, as in Figure II.8(*g*), gas has an upward-sloping supply curve there will be a fall in the equilibrium price of gas from p_g to p'_g.

The total increment of welfare arising from the initial fall in the price of electricity *plus* the further induced fall in the equilibrium price of gas is calculated by adding to the shaded strip in Figure II.8(*e*) the shaded strip in Figure II.8(*g*). The interpretation of this procedure is straightforward enough.

41

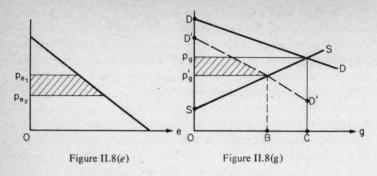

Figure II.8(e)   Figure II.8(g)

First, the shaded strip in Figure II.8(e) represents the increment of consumers' surplus arising from the fall in the price of electricity *with the price of gas at p_g*. Second, the shaded strip in Figure II.8(g) represents the further increment of consumers' surplus for a fall in the equilibrium price of gas from p_g to p'_g *with the price of electricity remaining at p_{e_2}*. The sum of these two areas then is a measure of the amount that consumers are willing to pay for reducing the price of electricity from p_{e_1} to p_{e_2} when, as a result, the price of gas to them will also fall from p_g to p'_g. An extension of the analysis reveals that if gas has, instead, a *downward* sloping supply curve, the leftward shift in its demand curve which is associated with the fall in the price of electricity, results in a higher equilibrium price for gas and therefore entails a *loss* of a strip of consumers' surplus—consequently a *subtraction* of that strip from the shaded area in Figure II.8(e). The resulting difference between the two areas is then a measure of the amount consumers are willing to pay when the price of electricity falls from p_{e_1} to p_{e_2} and, as a result, the price of gas is increased.

Symmetrical reasoning applies also to goods that are complements. If, for example, gas were now complementary with electricity, a fall in the price of electricity causes an *outward* shift in the demand curve for gas. If the supply curve of gas is upward-sloping its equilibrium price rises, and a loss of consumers' surplus in gas has to be subtracted from the gain in consumer's surplus arising from the fall in the price of electricity. If, on the other hand, the supply curve of gas is downward sloping, the outward shift in its demand curve implies a fall in its equilibrium price. To that extent there is an additional consumers' surplus in gas to be added to the increase in consumers' surplus from the fall in the price of electricity.[2]

To introduce a little more complication, if electricity itself has an upward-sloping supply curve, the induced change in the equilibrium price of gas will itself induce some further shift in the demand curve for electricity and, therefore, some change in its equilibrium price also. A further correction of consumers' surplus is then called for. One can continue in this way indefinitely, though, under plausible assumptions (related to familiar stability conditions), these repercussions become smaller and converge to new equilibrium prices for electricity and gas.

Since the errors in estimating the relevant demand curves over the future in any cost-benefit study are large enough to swamp the errors from ignoring these repercussions on the equilibrium prices of related goods, it is usual not to bother much about such refinements. In the

---

[2] These simultaneous price changes, or simultaneous introductions, of related goods can have particular importance when measuring the social costs of closely related discommodities (or disamenities) or, alternatively, the social benefit from their reduction. In order to put up with successive increments of some discommodity, say noise, a person would require increasingly larger sums. There is, of course, no market in the discommodity noise as there is, say, in the discommodity labour. But we can conceive of a downward-sloping marginal valuation curve for each person in the community indicating the maximum sums he would pay to be rid of successive decibels of some initial volume of noise.

If there are now two chief sources of noise, aircraft noise and automobile noise, each of such demand curves for reducing its own noise is constructed on the assumption that the amount of the other noise remains unchanged. Such demand curves are complementary, and the sum of their areas of consumers' surplus will *understate* the value to society of simultaneously reducing *both* sorts of noise. For if we first remove all aircraft noise—or, which comes to the same thing, if we set the price of reducing aircraft noise at zero—then the demand curve for reducing automobile noise rises. (This makes good sense since it may not be worth much to reduce automobile noise so long as aircraft noise remains undiminished.) Consequently the consumers' surplus to be gained from now removing all automobile noise is larger than it was when aircraft noise remained undiminished. The addition of this larger consumers' surplus from the abolition of automobile noise (when aircraft noise has already been reduced to zero) to the initial consumers' surplus from the abolition of aircraft noise (when automobile noise had *not* been reduced) measures the total benefit to society of reducing both sorts of noise simultaneously.

For simplicity of exposition, we have used the concept of a maximum sum the individual will pay to reduce a decibel of noise. However, a cost-benefit analysis that seeks to realize a potential Pareto improvement would instead use the concept of a minimum sum the individual should be paid to induce him to bear with the nth decibel of a given n decibels of noise, with the $(n-1)$th decibel, and so on. This way of constructing the schedule could make a sizeable difference to the calculation, as is explained in Part III (see especially Chapter 20).

preceding example of an initial fall in the price of electricity, attempts to calculate further additions or subtractions of consumers' surplus arising from the change in the equilibrium price of gas would be reasonable only if the change were large. Secondary repercussions (those falling on the equilibrium price of electricity itself) would almost certainly be ignored.

Chapter 9

CONSUMERS' SURPLUS WHEN FACTORS OTHER THAN PRICES CHANGE

1 We now consider the treatment of consumers' surpluses when changes occur in any of the following: population size, income distribution, per capita income, and tastes whether spontaneous or induced. The first three factors can be handled together.

2 When estimating the demand curves over the future for goods to be provided by new investment projects we have to make allowance for the growth in aggregate real income and its distribution.

Ignoring considerations of military or political power, a rise in population without any rise in real per capita income is not generally thought of today as conferring an increase in social welfare. Nonetheless, the resulting rise in demand for goods does operate to increase consumers' surplus as defined and, consequently, may eventually make economically feasible particular projects that would, in the absence of population growth, remain economically unfeasible.

In fact population growth and growth of per capita real income are the two components of aggregate economic growth, and together contribute over time to the apparent growth of social benefits arising from any investment project that is currently undertaken. Clearly the expectations of such growth-induced benefits have to be taken into account by the economist who is required to declare in advance the average rate, or future pattern, of aggregate economic growth on which his calculations are to be predicated. Having adopted some acceptable pattern over time of aggregate economic growth, he must then determine the way in which this economic growth will affect the magnitude of the benefits conferred by the goods that are to be produced by the investment project(s) under examination.

For example, in the *absence* of any expected growth in the economy, a hypothetical investment of 100 this year is expected to yield an annual stream of real benefits of 10, 10, 10, . . . , 10, ignoring the question of uncertainty. Allowing for an annual average growth rate of aggregate real income of 4 per cent, and assuming an income elasticity of unity for the goods produced by this investment, it becomes necessary to revise the annual stream of benefits to something like $10 \cdot 4$, $10 \cdot 8$, . . . , $10 (1.04)^n$, the nth year being the terminal year. Indeed, as indicated, the investment may prove to be economically unacceptable in the absence of such a rate of growth of aggregate demand.

This appears to be straightforward enough wherever a unique project is at issue such as a tunnel under the Severn river, a bridge over the Channel, or a new national park. For such projects will not, over the foreseeable future, be 'threatened' by rival projects of a like nature. In such cases growth in population alone (ignoring, that is, any increase in per capita income) will act to increase the demand for the services of such projects. The value of such services will grow, then, simply because the same service is being provided to more people. The bridge or tunnel or national park will accommodate an increasing number of travellers or visitors per annum—up to some point without an increase in current costs of upkeep.[1]

As for growth in per capita income in the absence of population growth, the increase in the usage of such newly created assets is less certain. For example, it may be the case that very few people will demand more park visits in response to a continuing rise in their incomes. Nevertheless, even if a person pays no more visits to a national park as he becomes richer, the value he places on the same number of visits will 'normally'—that is, if his income (or welfare) effect is positive—increase over time. This is not because his annual visits to the national park necessarily provide him with more utility as he becomes richer, but simply because the maximum sum he is prepared to pay for the same number of visits is higher when his real income is higher. Making our calculations on the basis of constant money prices over time, any rise in the value of benefits over time for all such reasons must be entered into the calculations.

---

[1] We are ignoring the eventual costs of congestion as numbers increase. These are adverse spillover effects, or external diseconomies, that fall on the users themselves of tunnels, bridges, and national parks, and they are discussed in some detail in Part III.

3 Where, however, there already exists one or more enterprises similar to that being contemplated, the returns to the already existing enterprise(s) are likely to be affected by the introduction of a new one. In what way, if any, should one allow for this?

Suppose the issue is that of building a bridge A, bearing in mind that another bridge B may be built a few years later. If this later bridge B will be built wholly in response to the growth in traffic—itself a result of the growth in population and in per capita income—there may be no reduction in the traffic using the older A bridge. But a problem will arise if the B bridge is to some extent competitive with the A bridge. The questions in issue are then two: first, whether the A bridge should be built at all if it is known in advance that a competitive, and possibly superior, bridge B is to be built at a later date; second, if it appears economically feasible to build the A bridge today notwithstanding the later introduction of a B bridge, *when*, if at all, should the B bridge be introduced?

Concerning the first question, the alternatives to be compared are those of introducing the A bridge today and a B bridge at some later date where the size of the two bridges can be varied as also can the date at which the B bridge is introduced. Since discrete variations in timing and in size of bridge can be large, there will be a large number of alternative possibilities. Each of such alternatives is to be regarded as a separate investment project. And the object of the exercise is to choose that investment project which, according to some investment criterion, is ranked highest.[2]

The answer to the second question is similar to the answer to the question of whether to take account of the repercussions on the *amounts* bought of other goods when the price of a good x alone has fallen.

Given the existence of the A bridge, the building of the B bridge is justified only if the future benefits from building it—as measured by the expected consumers' surplus from the use of the B bridge—exceeds its capital costs. It would not matter even if the traffic expected to use the B bridge (and to generate excess benefits sufficient to cover its capital costs) had the incidental effect of leaving the A bridge devoid of traffic. The A bridge has already been built: the capital sunk into it irrecoverable. We need then to compare only the capital cost of

---

[2] See Part V on investment criteria.

building the new *B* bridge and the resulting benefits, given that the *A* bridge already exists.[3] The demand schedule for the services of the *B* bridge provides us then with a measure of the *additional* benefits to be reaped from any additional capital expenditure. The area under the new demand curve, that is, provides us with a measure of the consumers' surplus with the existing *A* bridge in the *ceteris paribus* clause. This consumers' surplus is to be interpreted as the maximum sum that the potential users of this bridge are ready to pay *when already they have the* A *bridge at their disposal.*

4   Consider now a *spontaneous* shift in the demand from *x* to *y* that decreases the consumers' surplus of *x* and increases that of *y*, and would appear therefore to warrant reduced investment in *x* and increased investment in *y*. Once more the crucial question is whether the economist is asked about investment in *y* without his having any control or say in the matter of the output and pricing of *x*, or whether, instead, both *x* and *y* come under his surveillance.

To illustrate with a topical example, suppose there is a movement of population over time from London to the Brighton area. Increased investment in social capital, especially in public utilities, will be required in the Brighton area at the same time as existing social capital in London falls into disuse. If we suppose that, prior to the exodus, the amount of social capital was just right in both places, a prospective shortage of 100,000 houses in Brighton would be matched by a prospective vacancy of 100,000 houses in London. There would also be a need to extend schools, build roads, invest more in transport, electricity, gas, water, telephones, and provide additional distributional services in Brighton, all of which would require additional capital, while the equivalent capital investment in London would become superfluous. Clearly, it would have been more economical of society's scarce resources if the desire to move to Brighton had not occurred, for then the existing social capital stock would have sufficed.

---

[3] A private firm, having already built the *A* bridge, would not however also build a *B* bridge unless the (discounted value of) future expected revenues it could collect would not only cover the capital costs of the *B* bridge but, in addition, would cover any loss of revenue it would have to sustain on the old *A* bridge. If, on the other hand, the *B* bridge were to be built by some other private company, the company that built the *A* bridge would have had to take into account that the revenues they would be able to collect once the *B* bridge was built would be much smaller. In these circumstances it might not be profitable for them to build the *A* bridge.

But, once this change has occurred, the economist is concerned only with ways of meeting it efficiently.

Once social capital is irretrievably sunk in the London area, nothing can be done about it. In the light of existing demands unwanted capital facilities become useless. All that matters now is the economic feasibility of building new social capital in Brighton, where it is wanted. We have, therefore, to compare the additional capital outlays in Brighton with the magnitude of the expected benefits over the future as measured by the demand schedules for the extra services in question.

However, what the migrants into the Brighton area are willing to pay for the services will depend, among other things, on what they are compelled to pay for them in the London area. Only if they had to pay more than the marginal costs of public services in London could the amounts they would be willing to pay in Brighton be accepted as a correct measure of the benefits there. Indeed, an ideal allocative procedure would require that the managers of these service industries (public utilities, and the like) be ready at all times to reduce the charges for such services to no more than the current marginal costs of providing them, rather than lose a customer. If the economy actually worked in this way, the services of the economist could be dispensed with in such circumstances. But since it is difficult to discriminate between customers in this way, and since extending a reduction in charges made on behalf of one customer to all other customers involves the company in losses of revenue—such losses being, in effect, transfer payments from the company to its customers—the customary charges are generally maintained.

If this is so, however, it follows that the choice of moving from London to Brighton is being made on the wrong terms. For if, by reducing the charges of one or more of such public services until it is nearer to the marginal cost of its provision, a number of such 'emigrant' families can be induced to stay on in London, then a potential Pareto improvement can be effected: everyone concerned can be made better off as compared with the alternative situation in which such families move to Brighton.[4] The ideal experiment is not to allow any family to move from London to Brighton without first offering it the

---

[4] If the annual excess over the variable current costs of providing family A with electricity is $100, an effective bribe to family A of $60 would leave the London electricity company with $40 more revenue than it would earn if the A family moved. Both the A family and the company are therefore better off than if the A family moved to Brighton.

option of buying all such existing services at their marginal running costs. If when such terms are offered to potential migrants they are still willing to move, and to pay for all newly required public services prices which cover their inclusive costs, well and good.

Unless marginal cost pricing is already established in the public utility sector, such an ideal experiment—call it option 1—is likely to run into administrative and political objections. For the costs of discovering potential migrants, and of offering them special marginal cost terms without arousing the suspicion and hostility of other households can be prohibitive. If, however, option 1 is adopted, and all potential emigrants from the London area are presented with special permits enabling them buy public utility services at their marginal costs, their demand schedules for any such service, say electricity, in Brighton will be based on a *ceteris paribus* clause that includes a price for electricity in London equal to its marginal cost. In order to determine, in advance, whether there can be an excess of benefit over cost from installing an electricity-generating plant in Brighton to meet the requirements of potential migrants, the optimal output of such a plant must first be estimated by reference to this option 1 demand schedule. At this optimal output, it is necessary that the total revenue from the sale of electricity plus the consumer's surplus (on, say, an annual basis) together exceed the total operating and overhead costs. (It should be evident that the *apparent* losses of quasi-rent suffered by the London electricity authority, in consequence of its being obliged to offer to sell electricity to all potential emigrants at marginal cost, are in fact no more than transfers of benefit. Those potential emigrants that now decide to stay on will enjoy the transfer directly. Those that, notwithstanding the marginal cost offer, move to Brighton, make allowance for this potential bonus in their valuation of the worth of electricity in Brighton.) Such calculations do, indeed, pose statistical difficulties. But unless there is reason to believe that there is an excess of social benefit over cost under the hypothetical conditions of option 1, there can be no presumption that a potential Pareto improvement is realized by such an investment simply because there is an excess of benefit estimated by reference to the *uncorrected* demand schedule.

Option 2 consists of offering marginal cost prices for London's public utilities only *after* the migrant families have incurred expenses in moving to Brighton. Since they will now have to incur the additional expenses of returning to London in order to avail themselves of these privileges, their demand schedule for Brighton electricity will be somewhat higher than that under option 1. Yet if they have, indeed, already moved to Brighton, this option 2 demand schedule is the correct one to use in evaluating the electricity project. Clearly, if excess benefits are assured under the 1 option, they are *a fortiori* assured under the 2 option. On the other hand, if excess benefits are not possible under the 1 option, they may be possible under the 2 option. In that case, it may be inferred that although the potential migrants would not be willing fully to finance the additional electricity-generating capacity in Brighton if they were offered marginal cost prices *before* they left London, once they moved to Brighton (without knowing of the special offer) they might be prepared to cover the total costs of the additional capacity rather than incur the expenses of returning to London.

Finally, the economist may have to accept the administrative and political constraints that prevent either option 1 or option 2 being implemented. Even if there are low cost ways of obtaining reliable answers to hypothetical questions, which enable the economist to form an estimate of the option 1 demand curve and which, in turn, enables him to declare that the electricity project is uneconomic in that a potential Pareto improvement will not ensue, there may be nothing he can do to persuade families not to move to Brighton. In such circumstances, the avoidable losses of quasi-rents by the London electricity authority which have to be borne because of the 'unnecessary' emigration from London (of those families which, if offered marginal cost prices, would have stayed in the London area), and which may not be covered by the excess benefits of the Brighton electricity project when calculated by reference to an uncorrected demand schedule, have to be accepted as an inevitable consequence of the institutional constraints. In other words, since people are constrained to choose whether to stay on or move to Brighton on the 'wrong' terms, the possible losses are inevitable, and the economist has to regard them as bygones. By accepting a demand curve for electricity based on a *ceteris paribus* clause that includes the prevailing London price, and not its marginal cost there, he concludes that the project is economically feasible if his calculation reveals an excess of benefits over cost—that is, if benefits exceed costs after ignoring losses of quasi-rent arising from the institutional, or political, constraints (which, in this instance, serve to present the potential migrant with the 'wrong' terms).

51

Thus a spontaneous change in tastes, from some existing good x to another good y, would appear to involve society in a waste of resources—unavoidable perhaps, but a waste for all that. Some part, at least, of the capital invested in the production of x is, for no 'sensible' reason,[5] rendered useless and additional capital has to be built to meet the new demand for y—additional capital that could otherwise have been used in raising real incomes. In that sense society is worse off than it would have been had its tastes remained unchanged. This conclusion emerges with greater force if we suppose, first, a change from x to y, followed after an interval by a change in taste back from y to x again, with the cycle perhaps repeating itself. For in this cycle, or swing of fashion, capital is used up which could otherwise—had tastes remained unchanged—have been invested in useful additions to the capital stock.

5 What of induced changes in taste? Part, at least, of the expenses and enterprise of advertising agencies is directed into attempts to alter existing patterns of taste so as to favour the goods of their clients. The question that arises is about the benefits to society, if any, of employing resources for this purpose. We have argued above that in the presence of frequent though spontaneous changes in tastes resource-wastage is unavoidable. If, however, under its existing political institutions, society permits the use of scarce resources for the express purpose of inducing these changes in taste—including attempts to shift tastes from x to y, and later from y to x—the social waste can no longer be held to be unavoidable, a consequence only of exogenous factors. Even if the attempts to alter existing tastes are not always successful, one can point to a social loss of those resources that are used up by advertising agencies.[6] Moreover, if we are thinking in terms of a more dynamic

---

[5] Unless economists make judgements about tastes which, up to the present, they have been very wary of doing.

[6] I am concerned only with resources used to persuade people to change their tastes, not with resources used to provide information. I am aware that advertisers have long sought to convince the public that advertising is also entertaining and informative, and even (priced at zero) demanded by the public as a joint product. But there is no great difficulty in maintaining a distinction between the aim of providing partial information (as offered by commercial advertisers) and the aim of providing impartial information (as offered, say, by consumers' associations). Nor is much imagination needed to surmise that if all commercial advertising were to cease, newspapers, and other media, would give more space, and time, to providing information on the goods offered by industry.

economy, and the induced changes of tastes are from x to y, from y to z, from z to w, and so on, where y, z, w, are new sorts of goods which, without persuasion, would not have been wanted (or, at least, not in those quantities), then idle capacity is prematurely brought about in the production of each of these goods, and an unnecessary rate of obsolescence is 'artificially' induced. So long as the economist remains neutral as between tastes, avoidable waste can be said to be taking place. Such losses, if unexpectedly introduced, are borne by the owners of capital. But once the risk of rapid changes in taste are recognized, they are passed on to the country at large (along with the factor costs of advertising) through the higher prices needed to cover the higher costs of 'artificial' obsolescence.

An investment for the express purpose of changing tastes—as distinct from expenditures necessary to provide impartial information —such as that undertaken by an advertising agency, may be expected to generate a future stream of additional revenues to the producers. The factor costs of the investment in advertising are, of course, paid ultimately by the consumers of the advertised products. But whether this investment creates additional demand for existing or new goods, the additional revenues cannot be interpreted as social benefits. Furthermore, the resulting obsolescence of the plant and machinery, used in the production of these goods from which demand has been removed, can be interpreted as an avoidable social loss. Thus, so long as the economist has no means of ranking tastes, he cannot place any additional social value on the demand for goods generated in this way. The economist's calculations are based on the assumption that existing tastes remain unchanged for the period covered by the calculation. Only on such a condition can he make comparisons between alternative economic organizations.[7]

---

[7] Supposing that the problem of scarcity still exists (a moot point with respect to Western countries), there is a case for society's making provision for using resources in order to *avoid* spontaneous changes in tastes. and to maintain existing tastes; a better case. I should think, than could be made for the use of scarce resources in order to induce changes in tastes. so effectively reducing the available stock of capital, or its rate of growth.

Chapter 10

RENTS AND PRODUCERS' SURPLUSES

1 Rent may be defined as the difference between what the factors, or productive services, of a resource-owner earn in their current occupation and the minimum sum he is willing to accept to keep there.[1] It is then a measure of the resource-owner's gain from having the opportunity of placing his factors in the chosen occupation at the existing factor price, given the prices his factors would earn in all other occupations. It is the proper counterpart of consumer's surplus when this is regarded as measure of the consumer's gain from having the opportunity of buying a particular good at the existing price, where all other prices are given. And like a change in consumer's surplus, it is a measure of his change in welfare when the relevant prices facing him are altered. Whereas the increase of consumer's surplus is a measure of his welfare gain for a fall in one or more product prices, the increase in that person's rent is a measure of his welfare gain for a rise in price of one or more of his factors. (In either case, of course, new opportunities can be substituted for favourable price changes.)

Nevertheless, the area above the supply curve of a factor, say labour, does not provide so useful a measure of the labourer's rent as does the area below his demand curve provide a measure of his consumer's surplus. Let us see why.

2 Conventionally, a person's price-demand curve is drawn as sloping downward to the right, his price-supply curve as sloping upward to the right. If income effects are zero, the individual's demand curve must slope downward: it can slope upward—the characteristic of a so-called 'Giffen good'—only if the income effect is negative, and large relative to the substitution effect. Analogous remarks apply to

---

[1] For more refined measures of rent, the reader is referred to Note *A*, Part VIII.

the individual's supply curve. If the income-effect, or rather the 'welfare effect',[2] is zero, the individual supply curve must slope upward: it can slope downward, or become 'backward-bending', only if the welfare effect is *positive* and large relative to the substitution effect.[3]

In general, the smaller are these welfare effects that accompany price changes, the more accurate as an estimate of consumer's surplus, or rent, will be the relevant area derived, respectively, from the individual's demand, or supply, schedule. In the case of a person's demand curves, there is a presumption that the welfare effects are small. For a man's current expenditure, at least in the West, is commonly spread over a wide variety of goods each of which—with, perhaps, the exception of housing—absorbs only a small proportion of his total income. Indeed, as living standards rise, the variety of goods offered by the market increases along with the increase in a man's real income. One might surmise therefore that the welfare effect will become less important an ingredient in his price-demand curve for any single good.

The case is otherwise for the individual's supply curves, in parti-

---

[2] Assuming his *money* income constant, a fall in the price of a good, which makes a person better off, can be regarded as an increase in his real income. For there is some rise in his money income which (given all other prices constant) will be accepted by him as equivalent to a fall in the price of that good. Here, no difficulty arises in identifying the increase in his welfare with the income effect so measured.

In the case of his supplying a service to the market, however, his money income cannot be assumed constant, since, obviously, it varies with the amount of the service he elects to supply at the price offered. What is more, a rise or fall in the *resulting* money income does not necessarily correspond with a rise or fall in his welfare (or 'real' income). A rise in the wage-rate, for instance, may result in workers choosing so to reduce hours as to maintain money income constant, notwithstanding which his welfare has increased: for his income is the same while he enjoys additional leisure. A positive welfare effect, that is, can be associated with no change in his money income, or even with a reduction of his money income. For this reason, it is more sensible to talk of the 'welfare effect' resulting from a change in the supply price.

[3] An increase of welfare has a 'normal', or positive, welfare effect if the person offers *less* at any given price—if, that is, he keeps more of the good he is offering for himself. A worker who came into an inheritance would supply less labour (or take more leisure). Hence, if the price of the good a person supplies is raised, the substitution effect induces him to supply more while a positive welfare effect causes him to supply less. As distinct, then, from the income effect on the demand side, the 'welfare effect' on the supply side, if it is positive, or 'normal', works *against* the substitution effect.

cular for his supply of productive services, say the supply of labour, skilled or unskilled. If he supplies to the market only one sort of labour, the welfare effect arising from a change in the price of this labour falls entirely on this quantity. It then exerts a preponderant effect. Backward-bending supply curves for individual workers are not regarded as curiosa, a fact which would seem to make the measurement of economic rent rather awkward.

But there is a countervailing feature in connection with individual supply curves, which tends to restore measurability. Notwithstanding the mathematical convenience in postulating an economy in which each individual contributes, in general, to all goods in the economy, spreading his total effort among them—as he spreads his income among all goods—on the equi-marginal principle, this postulate is recognized as unrealistic. Nor is it a necessary condition for the model of perfect competition, which model is quite consistent with the more realistic assumption that the worker is constrained in his chosen employment to work a given number of hours, and between stated times. (He may, of course, be offered overtime work, though again it will be subject to constraints on the days and times.) For this reason, there is little point in conceiving of the worker's rent from his employment in precisely analogous terms as his consumer's surplus.

3 In picturing consumer's surplus, we think of the excess marginal valuation over price of the first unit bought, of the second unit bought, of the third, and so on until, with the purchase of the nth unit, the excess is zero. Explicitly ignoring welfare effects, the analogous procedure for rent would be the excess of the supply price over the marginal valuations, or minimal sums acceptable to the workers, for each of a number of successive units of labour offered until, again, for some m^{th} unit of labour offered, the excess became zero. But, as we have indicated in the preceding paragraph, the worker is not permitted to choose his hours of work on the equi-marginal principle. If, on the contrary, he were allowed, his rising marginal curve VV, in Figure II.9, would intersect the wage-rate line, W, at, say, 32 hours. His rent would then be the dotted area above VV and below the W line. If, however, the job offered a forty-hour week, and no less, he would be constrained to work eight hours longer than the thirty-two hours that he would choose in the absence of any constraint; and for these eight hours the wage offered is below his successive marginal

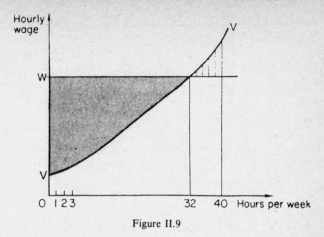

Figure II.9

valuations. On these eight unwanted hours extra he suffers a loss equal to the shaded triangle. His net rent is therefore the dotted area *minus* the shaded area. And, since he is offered the job as an all-or-nothing proposition, he will accept the job only if the difference between these two areas is positive.

Since all workers finding employment in this occupation will be obliged to work the forty-hour week, irrespective of whether they would prefer to work fewer or more hours, the net rent from working the forty-hour week is, for any one of them, the first area less the second area (if any). Letting the worker's weekly (disposable) pay be represented as the area of a unit column with height equal to this weekly wage, as in Figure II.10, the rent is the dotted rectangle measured from the top of the column.[4] By gradually raising the weekly wage and observing the numbers that enter the industry, in response to the higher wage, a supply curve of labour to the industry is generated, and from this we are able to identify the rent of those employed. Thus in Figure II.11, if at the lowest wage, W_1, seven men

---

[4] This minimal wage necessary to attract the worker into the industry or project will be greater, by the costs of movement (pecuniary and psychic), than the hypothetical minimum wage where movement costs are zero. *Per contra*, once the worker has moved into the industry, the minimal wage he will accept to remain there is equal to this hypothetical minimum wage *less* the full costs of movement.

In considering a possible introduction of a new project, however, it is the former minimal wage that is relevant.

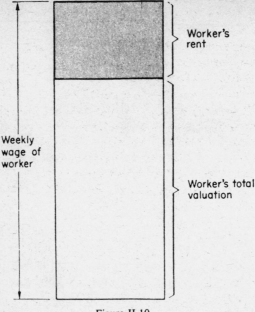

Figure II.10

just agreed to work, they make no rent. If now the wage rises to W_2 and, in response, another ten men are just willing to enter the industry, the first seven enjoy between them a rent equal to the dotted rectangle (W_2-W_1) *times* the distance 0–7. If the wage rises to W_3, and four more men enter, the first seven men between them make a rent equal to (W_3-W_1) *times* the distance 0–7, and the next ten men

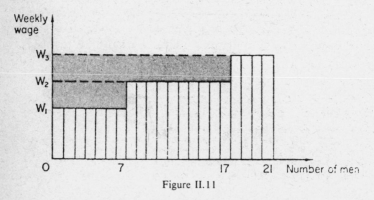

Figure II.11

58

between them make a rent equal to $(W_3 - W_2)$ *times* the distance 7-17, and so we could go on. We are enabled to do this simply because no worker is allowed to alter the number of hours he gives to the industry in response to changes in the wage.

Once large numbers of men are involved the stepped supply curve gives way to a smooth supply curve. The corresponding dotted area above this supply curve can then be used as an approximate measure of the aggregate rent enjoyed by those employed in the industry. Its magnitude can be interpreted as the largest sum they would be willing to pay to be in this occupation at the existing wage, given all the other opportunities open to them. An estimation of such rents would always be entered as a benefit into a cost-benefit analysis of a project if it were known that a wage lower than the existing wage (necessary to attract enough workers to operate the enterprise) would yet suffice to attract *some* workers.[5]

4 This area above the industry, or project, supply curve of a factor, which may be used as a measure of the rent of the factors employed there, is to be distinguished, in general, from the area above the supply curve of a firm or industry.

There are, nonetheless, particular circumstances in which the area above the supply curve for an industry, or firm, can be properly interpreted as a measure of rent. First, there is Ricardian rent in which labour and capital, both of them available in any amounts at constant prices, are applied in fixed proportions to a given quantity of land. The supply curve of the resulting product, say corn, rises, not because of any changes in the supply prices of the variable factors, labour and capital, since, as just stated, their supply prices remain unchanged. The supply curve of corn rises simply because the best land is limited in supply, and, as the price of corn rises with an expanding demand, it becomes worth while to bring inferior lands into cultivation. Even if there is only one quality of land, though limited in amount relative to demand, rent will accrue to it once the marginal cost of a bushel of corn rises above its average cost—as it eventually will, because of diminishing average returns to additional

---

[5] In estimating the rent of the industry's workers by such a supply curve of labour, it is not necessary that labour offered be equally efficient. If, as the industry expanded, the subsequent workers were less efficient than the original ones, costs to the industry would indeed rise. But the measure of workers' rent remains unaffected.

'doses' of labour and capital. In these circumstances, the area between such a supply curve and the price of the product provides a measure of the rent accruing to the owner of the fixed factor, land.[6] Increases in such rents arising from the introduction of an investment project are accordingly entered on the benefit side of the analysis.

Secondly, there is the case in which the area above the supply, or cost, curve has to be identified as, what Marshall (1925) called, *quasi-rent*. For over a short period, during which the capital employed by the industry, or firm, is in the specific form of plant or machinery, it is deemed to be fixed in amount, and to have no alternative use. In this short period, then, it partakes of the nature of land, and all its earnings above those necessary to induce it to remain in the occupation (zero in the strict Marshallian quasi-rent concept) are to be regarded as rent. In this short period, then, if the price of the product rises above the per unit variable cost of the product, the resulting excess receipts over the total of these variable costs are quasi-rents; such positive sums making a contribution to the industry's, or firm's, overheads or capital costs.

The above two instances are clear examples of economic rent to a scarce factor. They enter as part of the benefit of producing a given amount of goods during either a short or a long period. Thus, if a given piece of land is used to grow a new crop, or to site some new project, any rise in the rent of the land is to be entered on the benefit side of the scheme. If, within a short period, some investment in the industry, or firm, causes its variable costs to fall, the additional quasi-rents that result are also to be entered on the benefit side.

5   The case is quite different, however, when the long run supply curve of a good is produced by two or more factors, that are imperfect substitutes and may, indeed, be used in varying proportions. To appreciate the difference with the minimum of effort, let us follow the standard textbook procedure and, first, assume that all firms in the industry are of equal size and efficiency. In that case the rise in the supply price of the good reflects the growing scarcity of the factor that is intensive to the product. With only two factors, say labour and

---

[6] Increases in such rents, however, cannot generally be equated with a *net* increase of welfare to the community. For they can be offset to a greater or smaller extent by losses incurred by consumers arising from a resulting higher product price as output is expanded.

capital, the production of a larger amount of a good x will entail a rise in net price of capital relative to labour, where capital is used more intensively in x than it is in the production of other goods. Owing to the greater proportion of capital used in x as compared with its proportion, on the average, in other goods, the per unit cost of x rises relative to the unit costs of other goods.[7]

Any point along this rising supply price for the product indicates the minimum average (inclusive) cost for each of the firms in the industry and, therefore, the minimum average (inclusive) cost for that output. Thus at output Ox_1 in Figure II.12, the minimum average inclusive cost for all firms is given by x_1m_1. A typical long-period envelope curve for such a firm is represented as S_1S_1. At the larger output OX_2, the minimum average inclusive cost for the industry is given by x_2m_2, and the typical long-period envelope curve for the firm is represented by S_2S_2. Clearly then this long-period industry supply curve cannot be interpreted as a net gain by the producers of this particular good since each of them makes zero (Knightian) profit[8] in long-period equilibrium. It is in fact a curve of average cost *including* rent.

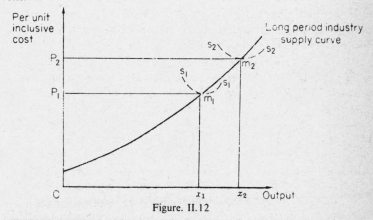

Figure. II.12

<hr>

[7] Put otherwise, if there are more than two goods in the economy, the expenditure on capital, as a per cent of total factor expenditure, is, for x, above the average per cent for the economy as a whole. x's increased proportional expenditure on the higher-priced factor, capital, results therefore in a higher-than-average rise in (relative) cost.

[8] Normal return on capital is not profit, any more than normal return on labour. In the long-period equilibrium, at any point on the industry supply curve, expenditure on factors (both labour and capital) is deemed to be just covered by revenue, leaving no profit, positive or negative, to induce firms to move into, or out of, the industry.

But if it is a curve of average cost *including* rent, is it also a curve of marginal cost *excluding* rent—as indeed is the supply curve in the case of Ricardian rent?[9] The answer is yes, in the sense that the sum of money represented by the area above this curve could be captured by a perfectly discriminating monopsonist,[10] albeit one that produces all the different products that make use of these two (or more) factors.

Since real rentals (the price of units of capital) rise and—unless there are increasing returns to scale—real wages fall as the output of x is expanded we are able, under particular monetary assumptions, to calculate the rise in the money rentals, and the fall in money wages, corresponding to increased amounts of capital and labour required by some given increase in the quantity of the product x. We can then associate the increase in the area above the supply curve of x with the increased amounts of the two factors employed in the x industry when each factor is multiplied by the increase, or decrease, of its income. More specifically, the addition to the area above the supply curve for x is made up of the gains of only those units of capital now employed in x *less* the losses of only those workers now employed there. These gains and losses in x are clearly only a part of the total gains and losses accruing to the factor classes as a whole since they are also employed in other industries.

It is certain therefore that any increase in the area above the supply curve for x is *not* to be associated with a net gain by either factor or by both factors taken together.

Thus, so far as shifts of demand curves are concerned, say from product y to product x, attempts to measure net benefits arising in the x industry—or, to be more ambitious, net benefits arising in all industries that use the two (or more) factors—are hardly practicable, especially where, as is likely, a larger number of factors are involved. Indeed, such a shift in demand implies no more than a movement from one part of the production boundary to another. It is a movement that, in general, raises the earnings of some factor classes and lowers those of others. But one need not infer that there are net gains to society as a whole.

If, on the other hand, the area above the supply curve of x

---

[9] See Ellis and Fellner (1943).
[10] I am indebted to Professor J. M. Currie for this observation.

increases solely in consequence of a downward shift in this curve, the result say of an improvement in technology, it need have no effect on factor prices. In this technically 'neutral' case, the increased area does indeed count as a benefit. In so far as the reduction in the cost of producing x is wholly passed on to consumers, the gain will be measured as an increase in consumers' surplus. In so far as some part of this gain is withheld by the producer, for a time at least, it partakes of monopoly rent.

6 The reader will have noticed that no mention has been made of the concept of 'producers' surplus', of which we used to hear a lot until recently. There is no call for it. The concept that is symmetric with consumers' surplus is that which is known as economic rent which we have examined in the earlier parts of this chapter.

True, some instances of economic rent—Ricardian rent and Marshallian quasi-rent—have occasionally been referred to as 'producers' surplus'. But the use of the term in this connection, or in any connection, has served only to confuse thinking. We shall continue then to use only the more generic term economic rent—either (a) *consumers'* rent, or consumers' surplus, in so far as the benefits accrue to members of society from a fall in product prices, or else (b) *factor* rents in so far as benefits accrue to some members of society from a rise in factor prices.

Chapter 11

OPPORTUNITY COST

1 Opportunity cost is one of the economist's key concepts. In general terms, the opportunity cost of the current use of some good or of some input is its worth in some alternative use. This definition, however, suggests a possible ambiguity wherever there is more than one alternative use. In such cases either the definition has reference to the alternative having the highest value for the individual, or else the particular alternative use is determined by the problem. Since the economist, evaluating the benefits and costs of a project, is subject to political constraints that narrow the range of choice, we shall usually be thinking of opportunity cost in terms of particular alternatives. Thus, in examining an investment project, the economist addresses himself to the question of whether its introduction will affect a potential Pareto improvement as compared with the existing situation. It is the uses to which materials and productive services would be put in the absence of the investment project that become, therefore, the relevant alternatives for the measurement of opportunity costs. There are, however, some minor complications arising from the variability of time and space which can be explained by a number of pertinent examples.

2 One of the required inputs for an investment project may have to come out of a fixed and non-augmentable stock of it. An example would be the total oil reserves in a country that cannot expect to import oil in the foreseeable future. The cost of the amount of oil required by the project is, in the first instance, the market value of the marginal units of oil to be withdrawn from existing or expected uses. If a lot of oil is to be used in the project, the value is not to be estimated as equal to expected price *times* quantity, but as equal to the area under the relevant portion of the demand curve for oil in its existing or expected uses.

These remarks apply as well if the required inputs come from a

64

constant flow, say, of the annual amount of water available in an area that cannot import water. In each year that the project uses up an amount of water, the cost of it is the value forgone that year in other uses, where the value is again estimated by reference to the demand curve for those uses.

If now the stock or flow of the required materials can be augmented by the employment of factors or by imports from other parts of the world economy, the additional stock or flow required by the project will come to have a lower cost the longer the period available for adjustment. This proposition follows the conventional Marshallian treatment in which no expansion is possible, by definition, in the shortest period; for all practical purposes, the stock of the material is fixed. Given more time, some factors can offer their services in augmenting supplies of the material, but other factors will remain fixed. During such a period the combination of factors will not be so efficient as it will be in a period long enough for all factors to move 'freely' into the production of this material—at factor prices that are no higher than those prevailing in the production of all other goods in the economy. In a short period, then, the cost of the material will be higher than in a long period. Consequently such materials will generally cost more for a project that requires them for only a year or two than they will for a project that will require them for many years.

It should be borne in mind, moreover, that the additional factors used in producing more of these materials for the investment project have to be costed by the economist not at their market prices but at their opportunity costs. Although these come to the same thing under conditions of universal perfect competition, in the real world of imperfect competition the divergences may sometimes be significant.

If we assume, provisionally, that factor-owners are indifferent as between alternative employment opportunities, and that costs of movement as between one employment or area and another are nil, then the opportunity costs of factors used in the project in question are equal to the market value produced by such factors in the uses from which they are to be withdrawn. And this market value is higher, the greater the degree of monopoly in such markets, the larger the excise taxes levied there, and the greater the incidence of positive spillovers, or external economies, that vary with output.

3   This concept of opportunity cost is easily extended to encompass the occupational preferences, costs of movement, and involuntary or disguised unemployment.

Consider, first, the limiting case in which there are no costs of movement and the factor-owner has no particular preferences as between alternative employment opportunities open to him. Let a worker be currently employed in the production of good x at a wage of $20 a day where the value of his marginal product happens to be $30. Although he is willing, under our simplifying assumptions, to move to a new enterprise y at $20 a day, his opportunity cost to the y enterprise is not the $20 wage he received in x (or is willing to receive in y), but the $30 of value a day that he could continue to produce if he remained in x.

Suppose now that our worker requires at least $25 a day to induce him to move to the y enterprise, the extra $5 being just enough to offset the costs of movement to y and/or having to take up a less attractive job there. The opportunity cost to y of his daily labour is now $35: to the value of his marginal product of $30 in x, there has now to be added the $5 which the labour requires to reconcile him to working in y rather than in x.

The logic of this position can be made plainer by considering what happens if, *contrary to the above argument*, the opportunity cost to y were reckoned *not* at $35, as indicated, but at $30. It would then seem that by selling the worker's product in y at $31 there should be a net social gain of $1. Economic efficiency, it would seem, is then met by transferring the worker from x to y. But if, as we have supposed, the worker is indifferent as between receiving $20 in x and $25 in y, there will be an excess benefit of ($30–$20), or $10, of employing him in x as compared with an excess benefit of only ($31–$25), or $6, of employing him in y. Therefore the movement of the worker from x to y will have resulted in a social loss. By setting the opportunity cost to y at $35, as argued above, the worker would not be transferred to y unless the value of his marginal product there is at least $35. Only when it is more than $35 in y, will there be a net social gain in transferring his labour from x to y.

In general then, in order to calculate the opportunity cost of a factor brought into a new project we should add to the marginal value of factor in its current use the sum that would exactly compensate the worker for all costs, subjective and objective, associated with moving into employment in the new enterprise. Of course, he may prefer the new enterprise, either for the type of work or for its location, above his present occupation, in which case he would be willing to move at a lower wage. If so, this premium he would pay has to be *subtracted* from the value of his marginal product in the existing occupation in order to arrive at the figure for his opportunity cost in the new enterprise.

4 The opportunity cost concept continues to be serviceable if the treatment of costs of movement or occupational preference is extended to involuntary unemployment. Thus in a less than fully employed economy, the opportunity cost of the labour of an unemployed worker is in the last resort equal to the value that the worker attaches to his 'idleness' or, more generally, to his non-market activities.

If an investment project has the effect of bringing into employment factors that would otherwise remain involuntarily unemployed, the opportunity cost to the project of using such factors will in general be less than their market prices. How much less depends upon the period of idleness which can be expected in the absence of the opportunities provided by the project, and the worth to factor-owners of their non-market activities. Idle land provides a familiar example. If the owner has no personal use for it, neither hunting on it or strolling on it, and deriving no pleasure from merely gazing at it in its unused state, its value to him, and therefore its opportunity cost to the economy, is nil. If some new enterprise can make use of this piece of land in the production of a good x, and (by discriminating exploitation[1] of the demand curve for x) could offer at most $10,000 for its use, the whole of this $10,000 becomes the measure of social benefit from bringing the land into economic use. Whether, after some bargaining by the landlord, the price of the land is set at $2,000, and the price of x is set so that consumers enjoy a surplus of, say, $5,000, leaving $3,000 to the owners of the business as excess profits, makes no difference to the measure of social benefit of $10,000 of bringing the land into use. Subsequent changes in the price offered for the land, and in the price charged for x, affect only the distribution of the $10,000 of social benefit.

The case is no different if the landowner enters into a contract with a private corporation or government agency giving it full rights over the

---

[1] The perfectly discriminating monopolist is a fictional character who, by discriminating among his consumers, charging each the maximum for successive units purchased, manages to appropriate to himself the whole of the consumers' surplus.

land for a fixed period. If, after a number of years, the private corporation or government agency finds no further use for the land and is ready to transfer the rights at the rent specified in the contract, or at a lower rent, the mere fact that the newly negotiated rent (between the corporation or government agency and the owners of the new enterprise) enters into the annual expenses of the new enterprise, does not admit them as costs in a social cost-benefit calculation. The opportunity cost of the piece of land to the economy is still nil, and as such it must be entered in a proper social evaluation. Only if an alternative use for this land is discovered, say that of growing potatoes, will its opportunity cost become positive. It will then be equal to the value it adds to the potato-growing activity.

It may be remarked, however, that the land and the landowner are separate entities whereas, in the case of labour, the services of the labourer and the labourer himself are not separable. This difference may have important philosophical and social implications. But in economics the distinction is itself of small significance. It may, however, produce a difference of degree. For there is a likelihood that workers will attach greater value to their 'idle' labour, or to their non-market activities, than will the landowner to the idleness of his land.

Thus if an unemployed type A labourer, whose services can be used in a new project, will otherwise remain unemployed for a period of about a year then a sum just large enough to compensate the labourer to forgo his 'idleness' or non-market activities for the period of about a year has to be entered as the opportunity cost to the new project of using his labour. Since it is supposed that after that year this A labourer can be employed elsewhere, the opportunity cost of continuing to use his labour in the project has then to be set equal to the value of its marginal product in that alternative employment—*less* his costs of movement there, and *less* a sum necessary to compensate for any preference for his existing employment (or *plus* such sum if he prefers the alternative employment).

5   The practice is not much different once we introduce unemployment benefits into the economy. What matters in a cost-benefit analysis is simply that the additional value produced by a hitherto unemployed worker exceeds his opportunity cost in his new employment. Where no costs of movement are involved, and where he has no preference, given any level of expenditure, as between being employed and being unem-

ployed, the opportunity cost of his moving into employment can be taken as equal to zero. It follows that if his labour can now be used to produce no more than $1 worth of output, society is to that extent better off. In such circumstances, his labour, wherever used, enters a cost-benefit calculation priced at zero.

If, as will be the case in general, the worker is not indifferent to non-pecuniary factors,[2] his opportunity cost to industry is not equal to zero. It is the compensating variation necessary to induce him to move from his 'unemployment activities' to a particular industry and, therefore, once more, it will vary according to his preference for working in the particular industry in question. Moreover, the compensating variation may be a negative sum if, on the whole, he resents being unemployed. For this means that, if necessary, he will pay up to some maximum weekly amount, say $10 from his savings rather than remain unemployed. In that case, the opportunity cost of his labour to the particular industry is *minus* $10.[3] If, on the contrary, he attaches some positive utility to his being unemployed, the compensating variation will be a positive sum. He must then be paid some minimum sum, say $20, before he will agree to move to some specific employment opportunity. In that case, the opportunity cost of his weekly labour to that industry is $20. Unless, then, he adds at least $20 worth of value by his efforts there, society is better off, on the Pareto principle, leaving him unemployed.

This bit of argument is straightforward enough. The only excuse for presenting it is that the financial aspects of unemployed benefit have been known to confuse matters.

Unemployment benefit, whether it is collected by the worker 'as of right' from an insurance scheme, or whether it is wholly or partly

---

[2] It is common in advanced Western economies to put the accent on *non-pecuniary* activities, as against the accent on *non-market* activities in less advanced economies. The distinction is of no importance for a cost-benefit analysis that is consistent in regarding the worker's compensating variation (for moving from his current occupation) as a necessary component of the opportunity cost of his labour in some new industry.

[3] If his wage in that industry is $50 and the value he adds to its product is $80, we can infer (i) the remaining members of society are better off by $30 ($80 of value added less the $50 paid to him), and (ii) the worker is better off by $60 (his $50 wage plus the $10 he is willing, but does not have, to give up). The total social gain is therefore $90. And this $90 is the excess of the value he creates over the opportunity cost: $80 *less* (− $10).

government relief, is to be regarded in economics as a transfer from the earning members of society to the non-earning beneficiary. Nor does it matter in this context whether the money paid to the unemployed worker is from taxes, from loans or from an issue of new money. What is pertinent in this connection is that this transfer to the unemployed worker is *not* a payment for his contribution to society's output of goods, since this contribution is assumed to be zero. But the money paid to him does enable him to consume a part of the aggregate product of the rest of society.

Should the worker now agree to enter into some particular employment, provided that the existing transfer payment to him continued to be paid, such payment is likely to be recorded as a wage. Yet the burden on the rest of society is no greater than before. And assuming that he is only just willing to work for that same transfer payment, the worker's welfare also remains unaltered. Consequently, the opportunity cost of whatever he produces is nil. If, however, he would not agree to enter the particular employment unless he were paid at least an additional $25, then clearly this $25 becomes his opportunity cost.

In so far, then, as the institution of unemployment or welfare benefits raises the worker's minimum acceptable wage above these transfer payments to him, the excess has to be reckoned as a positive opportunity cost. To illustrate: suppose the unemployed worker receives $75 a week as unemployment benefit, in consequence of which he will not undertake the particular employment for less than $100. It should be evident that this $100 is *not* the opportunity cost of his employment, since if the worker agrees to relinquish the transfer payment of $75 in order to take up employment at $100 a week, by assumption the worker himself is no better off (nor worse off). But the rest of society is made worse off by having to transfer to the worker (who is made no better off) an additional $25. It is this additional cost to society as a whole, which is necessary to induce the worker to take up the particular employment, that is the social opportunity cost. In order that a social net benefit results from his employment, it is, therefore, necessary that the worker's contribution be valued at above $25.

If, on the other hand, his return to productive employment has a positive utility for the worker entirely independent of the pay, he will be willing to take up the employment at a wage that is below the unemployment benefit he is receiving. He might, for example, be willing to take the job for as little as $60, which implies that he is willing to give up $15 a week from his $75 of unemployment benefit simply to be back at work. In that case, the opportunity cost is *minus* $15; his returning to work confers a gain on the rest of society equal to $15. Thus even if his marginal product in employment is negative (say, *minus* $5), there is a social net benefit of $10.

In sum, accepting the initial distribution of welfare as determined by the *status quo*, which involves, also, an acceptance of the existing rates of unemployment benefits to those currently unemployed, the compensating variation required by any unemployed worker to move him to a particular occupation—measured as the minimum wage he will accept for that job *less* the unemployment benefit—has to be regarded as the opportunity cost of his labour to that industry. In order to realize a potential Pareto improvement it is necessary only that the value of his product in that industry exceeds this opportunity cost.

Finally, unemployment benefit that runs for a limited period, or falls away gradually, or precipitately, after a certain length of time, introduces only an obvious qualification. If, for example, unemployment benefit runs for exactly six months, a man is likely to accept a lower wage after the elapse of five months than after the elapse of only five days. This eventuality, however, poses no conceptual problem. Economists have to accept the decision of any factor-owner concerning the minimum worth of his factors, and therefore his compensating variation, in whatever circumstances the factor-owner finds himself.[4]

6 The calculation of opportunity cost in conditions of disguised unemployment follows from the preceding analysis. The fact that the

---

[4] In the case of capital, however, occupational preferences can be disregarded, leaving opportunity costs to be determined by earning differentials alone. If, in a short period, existing machines are specific to their existing function, their value elsewhere is nil and, therefore, their opportunity costs are nil. If, on the other hand, the machines have a range of uses (as, for instance, lathes), they can, at some cost of conversion, produce a value in other uses. In that case opportunity costs are positive. In any cost-benefit calculation, an existing machine has to be valued at this opportunity cost. Where such a machine has a number of alternative uses, it is clearly to be valued at the highest of the alternative opportunity costs. Earnings above this *highest* opportunity cost (sometimes known as its transfer price) are defined as quasi-rents, and accrue to the owners of the machine. In a cost-benefit analysis, however, we need consider only the benefits in excess of the relevant opportunity cost.

marginal product of labour in agriculture is nil in some parts of Asia does not always warrant its being costed at nil in the evaluation of an industrial project there. It may be true that labour in the fields may be used until its marginal physical product is nil, and it is therefore true that if the labour were transferred elsewhere the apparent loss in terms of physical output or of the market value is also nil. Indeed, we are to suppose it is nil. Yet on the principle elaborated above, the opportunity cost of such labour in industry is its nil marginal product in agriculture *plus* the sum necessary to compensate him for the costs incurred in moving out of agriculture (excluding, however, any transfer payments received when in agriculture). Thus only in the purely hypothetical case where such costs are zero is the opportunity cost of such labour to be equated to zero.

The fact that the labourer in agriculture receives more than the marginal product of his labour, assumed here to be nil, does not modify these conclusions. For such payment to the labourer is in effect a transfer payment to him, no matter how it is regarded by the recipient or by the donors. To illustrate, in certain parts of Asia many small holdings are extended family affairs, and although the value of the marginal product of labour is nil, each worker receives a share of the proceeds equal, say, to the *average* product of labour. If this average product is valued at $3 a week then, ignoring costs of movement and occupational preferences, the worker will not move elsewhere unless he is offered at least $3. This $3 becomes the supply price of his labour to industry. Nonetheless the social opportunity cost of his labour to that industry is zero, this being equal to the minimum sum he will accept to go into industry above the transfer payment of $3. Put otherwise, against the compensating sum of $3 he requires, there has to be placed a gain of $3 to the remaining members of the extended family. Thus although it will be necessary to pay the worker $3 a week to get him into industry, this $3 could indeed be paid by the remaining members of the extended family without their being any worse off. (For total output does not fall when he leaves, and they save the $3 that was paid when there.)

The fact, say, that industry can afford to pay him a wage of $5 a week implies only that his marginal product in the industry is at least $5—not, of course, that his opportunity cost is above zero. There is therefore a clear economic case for his employment in that industry if the value of his marginal product is $1, or indeed, anything above zero.

However, the provisional assumption of zero costs of movement and of occupational indifference is obviously unrealistic. In general the opportunity cost of his labour to industry is equal to the zero marginal product in agriculture *plus* a sum to compensate him for his preference for the agricultural community *plus* the costs of movement (both physical and psychic). If each of these two items were valued at $2, the opportunity cost to industry would be $4. This sum of $4 can be seen to equal the compensation necessary to induce him to move to industry (equal also to the supply price of his labour to industry, which is $3 + $4, or $7) *less* the transfer payment of $3 he receives when he works in agriculture. Thus, in the absence of wage-setting or any restriction by labour unions, the opportunity cost of successive agricultural workers to industry can also be derived by subtracting from the industry supply curve (the curve of minimum payments necessary to attract successive agricultural workers) the transfer payments they received in agriculture.

Chapter 12

TRANSFER PAYMENTS AND DOUBLE COUNTING

1 The only transfer payments discussed so far are the (disguised) unemployment benefits which were treated in the preceding chapter in connection, with the calculation of opportunity costs. We now consider, first, other types of transfer payments for the purpose of distinguishing them from social benefits and losses.

2 The obverse of the benefits or direct subsidies received by unemployed persons are the direct taxes paid by employed persons and private firms. Although private firms properly assess the profits of their enterprises net of all the taxes they pay, the economist interested in *social* cost-benefit analysis—which is tacitly understood by the term cost-benefit analysis, unless prefixed by the *private*—values all benefits gross of tax. If, out of a $100,000 per annum benefit resulting from the construction of a dam, $35,000 is paid from the gross revenues as direct taxes to the government, this transfer of $35,000 to other nationals, via the central government, does not of itself entail a loss for society. If a number of people benefit from the dam to the tune of $100,000, after all costs are incurred, the fact that between them they transfer $35,000 to other members of society entails a spreading or redistribution of the benefit of $100,000, but not a reduction of it.

In contrast, however, the acceptance of the conventional nationalistic scope of cost-benefit analysis requires not only that estimates of consumers' surplus be excluded wherever this surplus accrues to foreign and not to domestic consumers. The benefits to the home country must also exclude all taxes on the gross proceeds that are levied by foreign governments. Moreover, these gross proceeds of a particular foreign investment can be reckoned as gross revenues to the home country *only* if that investment has no effect on the sales of goods produced by plant and equipment established abroad by previous investment from the home country. If, for example, a new investment in the foreign country B, by the nationals of the home country A, produces goods which are substitutes for those already being produced in B from previous investments made there by country A, any loss of profits sustained on these previous investments have to enter as part of the costs of the new investment.[1]

If, on the other hand, the new goods are complementary to those produced by plant and machinery already invested in country B by the nationals of country A, the additional profits earned by these older investments have to be added to the expected gross revenues of the new investment.

3 So far we have followed the convention of restricting the jurisdiction of a cost-benefit analysis to the citizens of the nation state. Within the nation's territory, that is, all transfer payments are disregarded in evaluating public investment projects. As indicated above, however, such transfers are not to be disregarded if they take place across national territories. A tariff on foreign imports may be held to benefit the tariff-imposing nation even though it inflicts a loss on foreigners that exceeds the gains of the tariff-imposing nation.

Although this convention is plain enough as between nations, problems can arise when political decisions taken within a country appear to impose jurisdictional constraints.

To illustrate, the central government may have agreed to give a bounty to any local authority undertaking to build a hospital, or a road, to certain specifications. In the absence of the bounty, we can suppose, none of the projects would be admitted as economically feasible, whereas each of them would be if the bounty were entered into the calculation as a net benefit, or as a contribution to the costs—as undoubtedly it would be by the local authority.

It may, of course, be argued that the bounty offered by the central government is, at least, equal to the net benefits enjoyed by the rest of the nation—which include all those people other than the local

---

[1] In the limiting case of a continuous demand curve in country B for a good *x* produced there as a result of previous investment goods from country A, the same investor in country A reckons his revenues not by reference to the price of *x* but by reference to *x*'s *marginal revenue*. In such a case, the economist follows suit.

citizens having direct access to the hospital, or road, and whose expected benefits have been entered into the calculation. But since the cost-benefit calculation should, in any case, take account of the benefits to be experienced by everyone in the nation, there is no economic justification for separately including the amount of the bounty on the benefit side. On a strict interpretation of the Pareto principle there is no warrant, then, for admitting a project that would, in the absence of the bounty, be regarded as economically unfeasible.

The bounty, it may then be alleged, is granted in consideration of some benefit to the nation at large that is difficult to quantify. A broader, or longer, highway than would otherwise be undertaken, or a hospital having underground facilities, may have a military value for the nation which the economist, or any one for the matter, will find difficulty in appraising. The economist may be able to salve his professional conscience by entering the value of the bounty as equal to the additional security provided for the nation by the project—leaving it open to experts, however, to argue that the same additional amount of security could be provided at smaller cost.

If, on the other hand, no such considerations are present, the bounty is no more than a transfer from the nation's taxpayers to the present and future inhabitants within the locality—notwithstanding which, government authorities may insist that the bounty be entered as a cost-saving item in evaluating the project. In such cases, the economist, as a practical matter at least, may have to comply; his calculations are, in effect, being subjected to political constraints. For all that, he should make it quite clear in his report that the calculation is subject to this political element and that, on a strictly economic calculation, the bounty cannot be treated as a benefit, or cost-saving, item.

This is not the first occasion in this volume, nor will it be the last, that political, or institutional, constraints will have to be considered. Wherever such constraints affect the outcome of the evaluation, in particular where, in their absence, the investment decision would be other than what is, the economist has the duty of making the fact abundantly clear. Not even majority opinion is to be treated by him as the considered opinion of the nation, the voice of the people in council. Political decisions may be poor decisions for a large number of reasons too tedious to recount.

Finally, the reader may be reminded that the economic criterion employed by the economist is one that is independent of voting procedures and, therefore, independent of the outcome of any particular political debate. In the last resort, the further information and analysis the economist can offer become a part of the contribution to a more informed debate which may occasionally reverse preceding political decision.

4 The error discussed above is that of counting transfer payments as costs or benefits. Another error is that of counting real costs or real benefits not once but twice, or more than twice.

Consider the rise in land values that results from economic growth or from population movements, either those arising spontaneously or those following the construction of a railway or road between two towns.

It is sometimes alleged that a rise in rents paid by restaurants, shops, gasoline stations, etc., in some new locality, or along some new route—which rents reflect the increased benefit derived from such facilities by migrating families, or by additional drivers or passengers—may be ignored inasmuch as rents elsewhere will have fallen. There is, it is argued, simply a shift in rents, a result of a shift in demand from one area to another, or from one route to another.

In the absence of economic growth, this can be true. But where it is true, it is a reflection of the belief that the *flow* of additional benefits in some areas is equal to the *flow* of additional losses in other areas. If economic growth is supposed, the flow of some additional benefits will exceed the corresponding flow of losses. What one has to guard against is counting the same benefit or loss twice; once as a flow, and again, later, as a change in asset-valuation derived of the flow.

The annual rent of a particular site is, in the first instance, a transfer to the landowner of the annual excess profits made by the owner of the business established on it. And these excess profits are, themselves, nothing more than a transfer to the owner of consumers' benefits from the services that are sold on the site. Provided that, in the case of people who transfer their custom to this business, the transfer was made on the proper terms (the services of the business from which they transferred their custom being offered at their marginal cost), any excess valuation above costs of these additional services furnished by this business should, in any case, be entered into the relevant cost-benefit calculation. If this site were to be sold, its market price would be the capitalized value of the now higher expected stream of rents. However, the rise in the stream of rents to this particular site—the result of the excess profit, arising from the increased demand (and increased consumer valuation) of such services—has been, or should have been, entered into the calculation of the flow of benefits. Since in any case benefit streams are to be discounted to the present in a cost-benefit calculation, in order to compare them with capital costs, we must not, in addition, include increased site valuations.

To illustrate, if the construction of a railroad from A to B raises the market value of those houses that are situated near the new railroad station in A, these capital gains are not to be brought separately into the calculation of benefits. The value of such houses rises simply because, once the railroad is built, their occupants have additional advantages either for job opportunities, shopping opportunities, or outings. The estimate of these advantages already have, or should have, been entered into the cost-benefit analysis of the railroad on an annual basis. Therefore to add their capital gains as well would amount to a clear case of double-counting. Needless to say, the same remarks apply to the capitalized stream of the value of and disadvantages that arise from the siting of the stations, or from the construction of the railroad.

5   Again, if this new railroad so reduces the time and increases the convenience of travel as to offer new job opportunities to a number of men, we ought *not* to include the measure of these new rents (a measure of the increase in their welfare from switching to the new jobs) as *additional* benefits. For such benefits are already subsumed in the (potential) consumers' surplus of the new railroad. Such a measure of consumers' surplus—approximated, say, by an estimate of the potential demand schedule for train journeys per annum—reveals the maximum sum each person will pay for a number of train journeys. And in determining this maximum sum, he will take into account the rents of the new job and, indeed, all other incidental utilities and disutilities accruing to him from the new railroad service.

The same *caveat* also applies where the consumers' surplus measure of benefit, which arises from reducing the cost of a good, comprehends the additional profits enjoyed by a number of inter-mediate agents that handle the good.

Consider, for example, an irrigation project that reduces the cost of grain production over an area. The benefit, to be placed against the costs of the project, is to be reckoned as the saving in costs of production on the existing output *plus* the area of the triangle of surplus (representing the excess of value over cost of the additional output demanded at a lower price, which price is equal to the new and lower cost). Once more, however, any rise in the profits of farmers, or of grain merchants, or of bankers, and so on, is *not* to be entered as benefits additional to this full cost-saving of the irrigation project. Such items are to be seen as transfers of part of this benefit from consumers to farmers and middle-men—at least during some period of adjustment in a competitive economy. Put more generally, the calculated benefit arising from the lower resource cost of grain is distributed among consumers, farmers, and middle-men, according to market forces and institutions.[2]

6 Existing enterprises, public or private, will sometimes have to be abandoned if the project in question is introduced. Another instance of double counting occurs when the capital and/or operating costs of these existing enterprises are included as items among the benefits of the project. This may be done on the argument if the project is introduced and produces goods that are substitutes for those pro-vided by the hitherto existing enterprises, a saving is effected through not having to renew their capital expenditure and/or their operating costs.

But the benefits of the project in question are to be calculated as the sums that the beneficiaries are willing to pay for the goods it provides, and these sums themselves are determined by reference to the prices of (and, therefore, by reference to the expenditures upon) the goods of these existing enterprises. It follows that the benefits of the project in question, calculated on the basis of willingness to pay

---

[2] It may be thought that additional sales, or processing, of grain should raise the profits of middle-men and millers since, at an unchanged mark-up, they handle a larger volume of grain. Yet inasmuch as it requires some additional services to handle an additional volume of grain, the rise in profits is to some extent a private rather than a social gain, for existing workers may have to work harder without a commensurate rise in earnings. To the extent this is not so, there can be short-period quasi-rents which disappear in the long period when additional factors are brought into grain distri-bution and processing so as to restore normal profits there.

for its goods, already reflects expenditures upon, and therefore the costs of, the alternative goods of those enterprises that will be displaced if the new project is introduced. Therefore to include as benefits of this project the capital or operating costs of enterprises that will be displaced is effectively to include them twice among its benefits.

Put differently, such a practice would be equivalent to that of including among the benefits of a new project A the capital and operating costs of an alternative new project B, and vice versa. The assumption, instead, that project B is already in existence makes no essential difference to the logic.

Should the reader, notwithstanding, still be a little uncertain of the implied double counting involved in the practice described, let him consider an example of a cost-benefit calculation being made for a project A (say, a large electricity-generating plant) that will, if adopted, displace existing enterprises B (say, a hundred smaller electricity generators). Consumers of electricity may reasonably be supposed to be indifferent as to whether they are supplied by A or B and would switch to A only if the price set by A were lower. For greater simplicity, we can assume that x units of electricity only will be used by the community, irrespective of the price. A correct calculation of the benefits of introducing the A project clearly amount to no more than the existing expenditure of the community on the x units of electricity currently being generated by the B enterprises, this sum being the maximum that people are willing to pay for x units generated by the A project. The expenditure on the x units being generated by B, however, depends upon the price set by B—which should certainly not be less than the unit operating cost. Let us assume, provisionally, that the price set by B is such that it exactly covers unit costs, inclusive of capital costs: in effect, B is in long-run equilibrium.

If, now, it turns out that the capital and operating costs of A are exactly the same as those of the existing enterprise B, there is clearly no case of introducing the A project. But if some wayward economist, after calculating the expected benefits of introducing the A project by reference to expected willingness to pay for x units of electricity, adds to that calculation of benefits the future saving, say, of capital costs of B enterprises (which will no longer operate if the A plant were installed), he will certainly discover that the benefits of

A exceed costs. Were the economist to include the saving in capital *and* operation costs when B is scrapped in consequence of the installation of A, he would have exactly doubled the calculation of the true benefits and would innocently conclude that project A was eminently desirable.

The logic of this argument is not essentially changed if—getting away from the electricity example—the goods provided by the A project are imperfect substitutes for those currently being provided by B. If the consumer of A goods believes that they are superior to B goods, an additional benefit of the A project is reflected in his willingness to spend more on A goods than on B goods (the reverse being true if he regards A goods as inferior in any respects). Nor is the argument different, although it will be extended, if project A provides, in addition, goods quite different from those provided by B.

In this connection, however, some correction will have to be made to the calculated benefits of A if existing enterprise B prices its products above current average operating costs. For in that case rents are accruing to B in either a short or a long period—that is, quasi-rents or monopoly rents respectively. Inasmuch as the abandonment of B production would entail an irrevocable loss of these rents, their (annual) amount would have to be subtracted from the A stream of benefits. Rents accruing to any factors in B that would also be irretrievably lost if B production were abandoned would also have to be subtracted from the A stream of benefits.

For the remaining factors once employed in B, the assumption is that they will find employment at current market prices in other firms and sectors of the economy. However, where costs are incurred in the movement of these factors to other employment, such costs must also be subtracted from the calculated benefits of the A project.

7 Finally, the stream of net benefits will not, in general, also include the rents of factors employed *within* the project wherever the net benefit is the result of subtracting the social opportunity costs of those factors from the social value that they contribute to the project. The interest in the rents enjoyed by, say, the workers in the project may be regarded as arising from concern with the distributional aspects. But to add rents to the net benefits (when calculated properly

as mentioned above) would be to add to net benefits an item that arises basically from transfer payments.

To illustrate, let the social opportunity cost of a particular worker in the project be $20 a week and the social value of his contribution $150 a week, as a result of which the net social benefit of his employment there is $130 a week. But, as indicated earlier, the wage actually paid to him is a transfer to him from the rest of the community. Such wage includes his rent, rent being reckoned as the excess of this wage above that minimum wage necessary to induce him to work in the project.

Assume, now, that he would, when unemployed, receive a transfer of $80 from the rest of the community. We may suppose that this minimum necessary wage rises to $100. If the actual wage paid to him is $100, his rent is zero. If, instead, the actual wage happens to be $130, his rent is $30. But since the rest of the community is worse off by the extra $30 that it has to transfer to him, there is no change to the net social benefit (which remains $130, as above). Similarly, if the actual wage paid is $350, as a result of which his rent is $250, this gain to him has to be offset exactly by the extra $250 taken from the rest of the community.

We conclude that rent, as a surplus to the worker or factor owner employed within the project, varies directly with actual factor payment, or transfer, and is not needed in the calculation of net social benefits.

Chapter 13

SHADOW PRICING (I)

1   Broadly speaking, a 'shadow' or 'accounting' price—the terms are
interchangeable—is the price the economist attributes to a good or
factor on the argument that it is more appropriate for the purpose of
economic calculation than its existing price, if any. There is nothing
very special about the notion of a shadow price. In evaluating any
project, the economist may effectively 'correct' a number of market
prices and, also, attribute prices to unpriced gains and losses that it is
expected to generate. He will for example, add to the cost of a factor,
or subtract from the cost of a good, in making allowance for some
external diseconomy. Wherever the amounts of a good. to be added to
or subtracted from the existing consumption, are large enough, the
economist will substitute for price the more discriminating measure of
benefit, consumers' surplus. Certain gains, or losses, to an enterprise he
will value as zero, since for the economy at large they are only transfer
payments. The cost of labour that would otherwise remain idle, he
must value at its opportunity cost; not at its wage; and so on.

Nonetheless, the term has been used more specifically in a number
of connections, and it will, perhaps, avoid confusion if these are briefly
indicated.

2   First, the term has long been used in mathematical programming,
a technique in which the value, at given prices, of an 'objective
function' is, say, maximized, subject to certain amounts of inputs and a
number of technologically feasible factor-combinations. From this
'primal' problem, a 'dual' problem can be derived having a corresponding objective function which is to be minimized. It transpires that, for a
wide class of problems, the variables in the dual solution can be
interpreted as shadow prices, or accounting prices, inasmuch as they
are the 'correct' input prices—being consistent with the maximum

value of the primal objective function.[2] We shall not, however, be using the term shadow price in connection with this technique.

Secondly, the term has been extended to estimates of social benefits, or social losses, that are either unpriced or not satisfactorily priced. Unpriced, or inadequately priced, benefits or losses may be valued either (a) by adopting the prices of similar things elsewhere, or (b) by calculating the price for a good, or a 'bad', that is *implicit* in government decisions to undertake particular projects, or (c) by calculating the spillover effects by reference to market prices, or by some other method. Consider each method in turn.

(a) The price adopted for some public good, or service, may be based on that at which it is sold in some other region of the country. Thus, the value of a public amenity such as a beach, a park, or a museum, to be established, say, in New York may be estimated by reference to the prices charged for similar beaches, parks, or museums, in other parts of the United States. Such prices, even when attempts are made to allow for differences in circumstances, are not very satisfactory. The prices that are set elsewhere for such things are not likely to be optimal prices, and are sometimes set arbitrarily or, rather, by reference only to political considerations. Since a correct measure of the benefit is the maximum that people would pay for the service rather than go without, one cannot hope for much from this device. At any rate, no generalization that is useful, and also not obvious, can be made with respect to this practice, and we need say no more about it here.

(b) Wherever there is an uncalculated benefit B associated with an authorized public project which, on a cost-benefit analysis that is confined to *measurable* benefits, reveals an excess of costs over benefits, ΔK, it can be argued that the implicit value, or shadow price, of this uncalculated benefit B is equal to ΔK—or, rather, that is at least equal to ΔK.[3] One of the difficulties of this argument is that one cannot hope for a deliberate and systematic criterion to be invoked in such a

---

[2] When these shadow prices are imputed to the given inputs, the value of the dual objective function is minimized. It can then be interpreted as the minimum input cost, subject to the constraints, and to the requirement that no profits (excess revenues) be made. These shadow prices are, therefore, no different from the factor prices that would emerge in a perfectly competitive equilibrium in which product prices are exogenously determined. An unusually clear introduction to the uses of mathematical programming is provided in Throsby's book (1970).

case. There can be, and there usually are, the widest discrepancies between these implicit valuations, though even if this were not the case the validity of this procedure is open to methodological criticism.[4]

(c) The existence of spillover effects requires that market prices be corrected *inter alia* for incidental losses and gains falling on persons other than the producers or users of goods. These incidental social losses or gains can sometimes be valued by reference to market prices, though not without difficulty. Prices of such goods, once corrected for the spillover effects they produce, are also spoken of as shadow prices. However, we shall defer the discussion of spillover effects to Part III.

Finally, and most commonly perhaps, shadow prices are associated with the calculation in those countries, often poorer countries, in which the costs of imports and the prices of exports do not properly reflect relative scarcities whether of finished goods or materials. The inadequacy of such prices as indicators of relative scarcity arises from a number of factors that interfere with the working of markets, both domestic and foreign. The domestic currency in such countries is frequently over-valued and is maintained at its existing level by exchange controls, import quotas, and other trade restrictions. The analysis in this chapter is restricted to this particular interpretation of shadow prices. To all intents and purposes, therefore, the shadow prices we are to investigate are no more than the opportunity costs of the materials that enter into international trade.

3 Since we shall be particularly interested in the shadow, or accounting, prices of imported goods, we shall assume that the official exchange rate of the domestic currency is set at a level other than that which would prevail in conditions of free international trade. If such countries intend to maintain their over-valued currencies through trade and exchange restrictions, in addition to short and long term foreign borrowing, shadow prices are, indeed, indispensable in evaluating projects there. In this connection, some of the largest poor countries

---

[3] If, instead, there happens to be an *uncalculated* social loss, D, arising from an authorized public project which shows an excess of measured benefit over measured cost ΔB, then, on the same argument, the implicit value, or shadow price, of this uncalculated loss D can be taken to equal ΔB—or, rather, as not greater than ΔB.

[4] For arguments tending to reject the validity of this procedure for deriving implicit valuations, the reader is referred to the chapters on 'Loss of Life and Limb' in Part VI.

come to mind: India, Pakistan, Brazil—although, under a system of fixed exchange rates, West European countries are occasionally prone to periods of trade imbalance which might warrant the introduction of shadow prices.

Assuming full employment and international free trade equilibrium, there is no problem in calculating the accounting price of traded goods. Ignoring transport costs etc., the foreign price of a ton of manganese imported into India is equal to its domestic price there which, in turn, is equal to the value of Indian exports necessary to pay for it. Given perfectly competitive factor and product markets, and the absence of external effects, Indian exports are priced at the opportunity cost of the factors used in their production. In that case the domestic price of a ton of imported manganese (or a unit of any other import) is equal, ultimately, to the opportunity cost of the Indian factors used in producing the goods to pay for it.

Removing the assumption of international free trade, the domestic costs of imports rise with the degree of protection provided. If there is, say, a 200 per cent *ad valorem* tariff on manganese, the domestic price will be three times the foreign or world price (assuming constant world supply price). The question arises, which price do we use—the domestic or the world price—as the relevant opportunity cost of the manganese imports to the Indian economy. The accounting price for Indian exports poses a similar problem. Do we use the world price of such exports or do we use the value of these exports to the domestic economy?

In developing the analysis by which such questions can be answered, it will simplify matters if we restrict ourselves provisionally to small changes. We then avoid the need to invoke consumers' surplus and rents. We may take market prices, in the assumed absence of all spillover effects, as indicators of per unit social values.

One might think, first, to come down in favour of using foreign, or world, prices, *not* domestic prices, on the grounds (i) that everything produced and consumed domestically has an effect (via the availabilities argument) on the balance of payments; (ii) that, because of substitution possibilities, we can compare one thing with another and, in particular, we can conveniently compare any good with foreign exchange; (iii) because world prices express their real cost. or benefit. to a country in terms of foreign exchange; and (iv) free foreign

86

exchange is a good yardstick because it can be used to satisfy almost any need.[5]

4   These considerations are, for the general case, not very compelling. There is no question but that if $1 million of foreign exchange can be used to purchase x tons of foreign steel, or y tons of foreign nickel, then, *in terms of exchange reserves,* x tons of foreign steel and y tons of foreign nickel are equally costly irrespective of the duties on each. The revenues from the tariffs can, of course, be regarded simply as internal transfer payments, whereas the cost (in terms of foreign exchange) to the country, as a consumer in the world economy, is simply the world price—assuming, always, that it is constant.[6]

One may concede all this, however, without concluding that in any cost-benefit study traded goods should be valued at world prices. On the contrary, there may be a stronger case to be made for valuing traded goods at domestic prices. We shall be in a better position to say so after some analysis of the conditions under which either sort of valuation is allocatively correct.

In general, the question of valuation depends on the relevant political constraints. The economist, as a rule, will accept the rate of exchange as a datum over the foreseeable future, and he will do so in full knowledge of the restrictions on trade and payments that the government deems necessary to maintain it. If, therefore, within the foreseeable future, there is small expectation of any change in existing policy, the economist does the best he can only by working within these apparently irremovable restrictions.[7]

---

[5] Such reasons are given by Little and Mirrlees (1969). They would be more acceptable if there were no excise taxes or tariffs, or else very low ones, or, possibly, under some very special conditions.

[6] If the foreign supply price is upward-sloping, the marginal import cost is above the foreign price. (Similarly, if the foreign demand for the country's exports is downward sloping, the country's marginal export revenue is below the foreign demand price.) But since we are concerned here with more fundamental issues, we may assume that over the relevant range world supply prices are constant unless otherwise stated.

[7] The economist may, indeed he should, urge on the authorities the need for a change to more 'rational' economic policies. But once he comes to making cost-benefit estimates, they are to be made with reference to those economic policies that are likely to prevail, not those that 'ought to' prevail.

We shall now compare the effects of quotas and tariffs on the prices of traded goods under two main assumptions; first (a) that the government cannot increase the total foreign currency available for imports, which implies that it can import more of some goods only by reducing other imports; and secondly (b) that it can increase its total imports by increasing its exports.

5 *Assumption* (*a*)—Suppose, first, a rigid quota system for manganese imports, having the result that the domestic market price is $3,000 a ton whereas the foreign purchase price is but $1,000 a ton.[8] Since domestic private firms value the manganese at $3,000 a ton, a public enterprise requiring annually 100 tons of manganese should be able to make a social gain from their use when they are costed at $3,000 a ton. If it could not do so, it may think to appropriate the 100 tons of manganese from the private sector and cost it at less than $3,000, say $1,000 a ton. Thus the manganese allocated by, say, government decree to this public project will be at the expense of the private sector. If we ignore all spillovers associated with the outputs of private goods, the resulting movement of a scarce material from existing uses in the private sector to a use in the public enterprise where it has imputed to it a lower value is allocatively a retrograde move: potential welfare is reduced.

If, then, no more imports of manganese into the country are permitted, we should allow the public enterprise to buy it from the domestic market only at the going price of $3,000 a ton which, in these circumstances, is to be entered as the opportunity cost of the manganese.

It is, however, quite possible for the government, while maintaining unchanged the *total* foreign exchange value of imports, to reduce some other kinds of imports which use up $100,000 of its limited receipts of foreign currency in order to enable the country to import an additional 100 tons of manganese. If asked to advise which kinds of current imports should be sacrificed so as to make available to the public enterprise this additional 100 tons of manganese, the economist would clearly choose to reduce the $100,000 worth of imports having the lowest *domestic* value—so minimizing the opportunity cost of these manganese imports.

---

[8] Since the exchange rate is taken to be fixed, dollar prices can be used in lieu of rupee prices.

The economist may not be consulted, however, in which case the domestic value of whatever kinds of imports are actually sacrificed for this purpose may well be higher than is necessary. Whatever the domestic value of these forgone imports—say $100,000 worth of English cutlery—such value may seem to be the opportunity cost of importing the 100 tons of manganese. However, since there is always the alternative of selling this manganese in the domestic market, their use instead in the project appears to imply another opportunity cost of the manganese. We should therefore pause here to reconsider the relevant concept of opportunity cost in this cost-benefit context.

If one defines opportunity cost of an input [9] to be used in the public project as the *highest* alternative social value to be forgone—either (a) from switching existing inputs from their current uses to the project or (b) from producing *additional* inputs by using factors that are engaged in doing other things or (c) a combination of (a) and (b)—it implies that in order for the social net benefit of the project to be positive, the project must yield social benefits *in excess of* any alternative social benefits that might be produced with the inputs. Thus, if all such calculations are subject to a political constraint (P), one requiring that no public project be introduced so long as the inputs needed in its construction or operation can be used elsewhere in the economy to produce a social value higher than that produced by the public project, then the above definition of opportunity cost is the appropriate one to use. But if there is no such political constraint, it may be assumed that the cost-benefit criterion to be met takes the form only of a potential Pareto improvement as compared with the existing situation. In such a case, the appropriate definition of opportunity cost of the relevant inputs are the social values that are *actually* forgone when these inputs are used in the public project. On such a definition, calculation of a positive net benefit implies that the project does indeed effect some potential Pareto improvement—even though it may not be the largest possible improvement in the circumstances.

To illustrate, let us suppose that the value of the domestic cutlery forgone, in order to import the required 100 tons of manganese, is $250,000. If the (P) political constraint prevails (and assuming no other constraints operate to prevent the additional manganese imports

---

[9] Where the input is a material goods, and not a productive service such as labour, we can ignore costs of movement and occupational preferences.

from being used by the private sector) the appropriate definition of the opportunity cost of the manganese inputs entails a sum equal to $300,000. For this $300,000, which exceeds $250,000, is what the 100 tons of manganese will fetch on the domestic market. And if the public project shows a negative net benefit when the manganese is costed at $300,000, we infer that its use in the private sector, where it is worth $300,000, will produce a yet higher social benefit than if it were used instead in the public project. If, however, the (P) constraint does not prevail, the economist will reckon the opportunity cost at $250,000, this being the value of the cutlery that is actually forgone in acquiring the manganese inputs.

Of course, the government may have made it clear that if the project is feasible it will pay for the additional 100 tons of manganese wholly by a reduction in the imports of transistors having a total domestic value of $350,000. In that case, and irrespective of the existence or otherwise of the (P) constraint, the opportunity cost of the 100 tons of manganese to the public project is clearly $350,000. For the fact is that, unless the project can meet the net benefit criterion with the 100 tons of manganese costed at £350,000, the alternative of not reducing the imports of transistors will yield a higher value to the economy.

6 *Assumption* (*b*)—Consideration of a flexible quota scheme enables us to introduce an alternative possibility: in any year included in the project's cost-benefit period India may *increase its exports* in order to pay for the additional 100 tons of manganese. Only if two conditions are met can we now justify using, as the opportunity cost of manganese, its world price of $1,000 per ton: (1) that the world demand for the Indian exports in question is infinitely elastic over the relevant range, and (2) that there is no purely domestic tax on the exported good.

The reader will recognize that, in the absence of the first condition, the demand price of the exportable will be forced down if more is offered on the world market so that, in general, India's marginal export revenue, rather than the existing demand price for her exports, should be used. If we ignore bilateral agreements, it may yet be possible, by discriminatory practices, to confine the reduction of export prices to *additional* exports only, in which case the additional export revenue will be greater than if the world price on all of that particular export has to be reduced in order to sell more.

If, however, such discriminatory practices are not economically feasible, we have to estimate the elasticity of foreign demand for the Indian export in question in order to calculate the amount of exports required and, therefore, the corresponding subtraction of domestic value that is necessary to bring in an additional $100,000 of foreign exchange to pay for the 100 tons of manganese. Thus, if the *domestic* market price of jute is $1 per pound but, because of the inelasticity of foreign demand, 250,000 pounds of it have to be exported in order to earn $100,000 of foreign exchange, then the domestic value forgone—at least on the assumption that the (P) constraint is in operation—is $250,000. For even if there were no need to subtract any jute from the domestic consumption (the 250,000 pounds of jute being additionally produced using hitherto unemployed or underemployed resources, and produced at a marginal resource cost of $1 or less per pound) the existing *highest* alternative value of an extra 250,000 pounds of jute is the $250,000 it is worth on the domestic market. Clearly the export of 250,000 pounds of newly produced jute entails a potential loss of domestic value equal to $250,000. In the absence of the (P) constraint, however, the social opportunity cost of the additional 250,000 pounds of jute destined for exports can be the true resource cost of its production to the economy—the net payment to all individuals affected that would just compensate to induce the required services of the resource-owners. And this may well be much below $250,000. However, it will simplify the exposition in the remainder of the chapter to assume that the appropriate opportunity cost of 250,000 pounds of jute is $250,000.

Of no less importance is the second condition. If, for instance, the first condition is met—the foreign demand price for jute is constant—and the required $100,000 of foreign exchange can be obtained simply by exporting 100,000 pounds of jute, the domestic value forgone is $100,000 *only* if there is no domestic tax on jute. If, however, there is, say, a 60 per cent *ad valorem* tax on domestic jute, the domestic value of jute is $1.60 per pound, and therefore the domestic value of the 100,000 pounds exported is $160,000. (Again, of course, in the absence of the (P) constraint—and in particular if there are underemployed resources—the opportunity cost of an additional production of 100,000 pounds of jute may be much less than $160,000.)

If neither of the two conditions is met, the opportunity cost of the 100 tons of manganese is, using the above figures, $400,000—

250,000 pounds of jute from the domestic market valued at $1.60 per pound.

Let us summarize under the assumption that the jute needed to pay for manganese imports is subtracted from domestic consumption. If, first, there is no excise tax on jute but, because of inelasticity of foreign demand, 250,000 pounds have to be exported, the loss of domestic value is $250,000. If, secondly, there is no inelasticity of foreign demand but there is an excise tax of 60 per cent, the loss of domestic value is $160,000. Thirdly, if there is both inelasticity and the tax, the loss of domestic value is $400,000. In this last case, the cost to the economy of 100 tons of manganese is unambiguously $400,000. In the preceding two cases, it will be $250,000 and $160,000 respectively, but only *in the absence of* the (P) constraint. If, however, the (P) constraint prevails, the resulting opportunity cost of 100 tons of manganese will be $300,000 (this $300,000 being the sum the 100 tons of manganese will fetch on the domestic market and, therefore, the potential value to be forgone when they are used in the public project).

Removing the assumption of constant world *supply* price can raise further the cost of 100 tons of manganese to the Indian economy. For example, let the elasticity of the world supply of manganese be so low that additional Indian imports of 100 tons per annum doubles its world price. The 100 tons will then require $200,000 of foreign exchange which in turn requires twice the volume of additional exports—500,000 pounds of jute rather than 250,000 pounds. In the third case of the preceding paragraph, for example, the effective cost of 100 tons of manganese to the Indian economy will be now $800,000 rather than $400,000.[10]

Finally, the reader may recall that our analysis has been simplified by maintaining the assumption that any changes required in the

---

[10] I have made no allowance in these proposals for the degree of monopoly in the production of the chosen exported good, say, jute. In so far as the domestic price (without tax) of jute is above the export price the argument in the text applies, the relevant price being the domestic price.

It is true that the greater the degree of monopoly (as measured, say, by the ratio of price to marginal cost) in the production of jute as compared with the production of other goods in the economy, the greater the scope for allocative improvements. Again, however, though the economist can recommend such improvements, in undertaking a cost-benefit study he has to accept the present and future prices of goods (corrected for spillover effects) as indicative of their value, at the margin, to the community.

amounts of domestically consumed imports or exportables are small enough to enable us to ignore the effect on their domestic prices. If this simplification is removed, the areas under the relevant portions of the demand curves have to be substituted as measures of social value for the approximate measures used in the text—domestic price *times* quantity.

Chapter 14

SHADOW PRICING (II)

1 Let us now shift our attention from quota schemes, or exchange controls (that directly ration either particular categories of imported goods or else imported goods in general), toward tariff schemes that ration imports by price. The essential arguments are unchanged. If there is a 200 per cent *ad valorem* tariff on manganese, a ton of manganese bought at $1,000 on the world market sells at a domestic price of $3,000. True, in the tariff case the government collects the revenue of $2,000 on each imported ton of manganese, whereas in the quota case this $2,000 becomes a windfall to the initial recipient of the quota who might well (if the government allows it) sell his quota-permit to others at a maximum price of $2,000 per permitted ton. But whether this 'monopoly rent' is received by the government, or by private persons or firms, is merely a distributional aspect which, of itself, provides no guidance in the determination of the accounting price of imported manganese. What is again significant, however, is the potential sacrifice of domestic value entailed in using an additional ton of manganese for this project. Where the country cannot, or will not, increase its exports, the opportunity cost of 100 tons of manganese is, as before, either the domestic value of manganese or else (if valued higher) the domestic value of those imported goods that are withdrawn from the market in order to make available the foreign exchange for the manganese imports, or finally, and in the event of political constraints preventing the sale of manganese to the private sector, the domestic value of the forgone imports even though this is less than $300,000.

Where the country is able, and chooses, to pay for the additional manganese by increasing its exports, its opportunity cost is the domestic value of those goods subtracted from the domestic economy in order to export them for additional foreign currency.[1]

More generally, the import of an additional 100 tons of manganese presents the country with a choice either of reducing other imports or of increasing exports, or of a combination of both.

It goes without saying that, accepting the existing trade restrictions, economic efficiency is promoted by keeping the opportunity costs of each method in line with the other. If the smallest loss of domestic value from reducing other kinds of imports were $300,000, and the smallest loss of domestic value from increasing exports were $350,000, the first method—import-reduction—is to be preferred each time until both methods (or any combination of the two methods) yield the same result. Again, however, the economist can only recommend such policies to the government. In so far as the government fails to implement them, the economist must derive his social costing from the actual, or expected, policies. If the government elects to pay for an additional 100 tons of manganese by additional exports of jute that subtract from the economy a domestic value of $400,000 when it might, instead, have raised the necessary foreign exchange by exports of raw cotton, which would have subtracted a domestic value of only $300,000, the actual accounting price of the 100 tons of manganese has to be set at $400,000 until such time as the government sees fit to revise its policy.

2 In order to clarify concepts in calculating shadow prices for imports, we have concentrated on reducing some quantity of either one kind of import or another, or of increasing some quantity of one export or another. It is, of course, entirely possible for the government to reduce the amounts of a number of imports and/or expand the amounts of a number of exports simultaneously in order to pay for the additional imports of manganese and of any other goods. Although the calculation would then take a little longer, the principle is the same: the opportunity cost of the additional imports is the sum of the losses of domestic value arising from the reduced amounts of a number of imports and/or from the reduced domestic availability of the amounts of those goods that are to be exported.

In a limiting though unrealistic case, we might suppose that on each

---

[1] Again assuming that changes in the amounts of imports are small enough to warrant the adopting of domestic price (rather than the area under the demand curve) as indicative of social value.

occasion, and irrespective of the kinds and quantities of additional imports required, the government chooses to reduce all imports and expand all exports in fixed proportions that do not change over time. In this hypothetical case we could formulate the shadow price of imports in terms of a 'national parameter' or shadow price of foreign exchange—a scalar that, for marginal changes in imports in which elasticities of demand and supply can be ignored, can be applied to any $1 of additional imports.[2]

3 So much for the calculation of accounting prices for *imports* used in public projects. What of the calculation of accounting prices for the *exported* outputs of these projects? It will be conceded that goods produced by the project, and exported, should be evaluated by reference to the same conceptual framework used in determining the accounting prices of imports. But the public project's imports, regarded as alternatives to the use of domestic inputs, are valued as opportunity costs,[3] whereas exports of the project's output, regarded as alternative to domestic consumption, are valued as social benefits. The measure of such benefits is the value to the domestic economy of the imports they make available to it.[4] In particular, the benefit measure of

---

[2] The formula for such a parameter takes the form of a weighted average of the ratios, for each import, of its domestic value to its world price *plus* a weighted average of the ratios, for each export, of its domestic value to its world price. Hence the formula given by Dasgupta. Marglin. and Sen (1972) p. 216:

$$P^F = \sum_{i=1}^{n} fi \frac{P_i^D}{P_i^{cif}} + \sum_{i=n+1}^{nth} Xi \frac{P_i^D}{P_i^{fob}} \quad \text{where} \quad \sum_{i=1}^{n} fi + \sum_{i=n+1}^{nth} Xi = 1$$

where P^F is the shadow price of foreign exchange. P_i^D is the domestic price of the ith import whose quantity is reduced or the ith home-produced good that is exported. P_i^{cif} is the *cif* price of the ith import that is reduced, and f_i its weight (as a fraction of the total reduction of domestic value of imports), while P_i^{fob} is the *fob* price of the ith good that is exported. and x_i its fractional weight.

Clearly there is nothing wrong with such a formula provided no one is misled by its presentation into the belief that the shadow price of foreign exchange can really be worked out once and for all.

[3] The costs of these imports can. if necessary. be compared directly with the benefit to be imputed to them from the sale of the outputs of the project—ultimately the addition to domestic social value.

[4] The benefits of the exports, so calculated. can also be compared directly with the costs of their production—ultimately their opportunity cost in terms of domestic value forgone.

the project's exports is the domestic value of the specific goods that will be imported from the additional foreign exchange made available. A rational procedure, in this connection, would be one that used the additional exchange reserves in purchasing imports having the largest domestic value—account being taken of external effects, if any. But, again, in any project evaluations the calculation of the expected benefits, arising from the project's exports, must depend on the economist's judgement of the additional imports the government will actually allow; if one million yards of cloth exported by a new textile project adds $1 million to the foreign exchange reserves, they should not be priced at $1 million but at the domestic value of the additional imports that are to be bought for the $1 million. Given, say, a rising foreign supply price for the imports in question (which reduces the buying power of the extra $1 million foreign exchange) and a high tariff on those imports, the domestic value of the additional imports, now made possible by these exports, could be, say, $2,500,000, which is then the social benefit, or accounting price, of the additional exports of cloth.[5]

In sum, the accounting prices both of additional imports and exports involved in any investment project—or the social opportunity cost of imports and the social benefits of exports—are to be calculated by reference respectively to the subtraction from, and addition to, the country's domestic value, not by reference to world prices of traded goods.

Admittedly the implementing of these proposals will present more difficulty than the use of world prices as accounting prices. For one thing, the practising economist cannot always be sure, in evaluating a project involving traded goods, which particular imports will be displaced, or which particular imports or exports will be increased. He

---

[5] It might seem reasonable to argue that the exportable part of the output of the project *also* has an *opportunity cost*, in that it could have been sold instead on the home market and added therefore to domestic value. Again, however, the resolution of the problem depends upon the constraints postulated. If the economist is to decide where all the project's outputs are to go, in particular which parts are to be exported and which retained for home use, he will regard them as alternative opportunities and, therefore, choose to place any output where it adds most to domestic value. In the text, however, we are assuming that the decision to export certain portions of the project's annual output is one that has already been made either by authority or custom, or possibly by the economist working within certain constraints.

has, perforce, to engage in some guesswork. But he is at least guessing at the magnitudes of the right things. And wherever the calculations that arise from using two alternative methods can be significantly different—as they certainly can be wherever substantial trade restrictions exist—it is advisable to place reliance upon rough estimates of the relevant concepts than on more exact estimates of irrelevant ones.

4 Let us consider, finally, the social benefits, if any, of introducing import substitutes—consumption or intermediate goods produced domestically that are expected to displace current imports in so far as they can be regarded as reasonable substitutes for those currently imported.

If the government is determined to prohibit some particular good currently imported, the economist has the straightforward task of undertaking a cost-benefit analysis in which the benefits of the proposed domestic substitute good, x, is reckoned by reference to the market demand curve for it *under the condition* that the import good y, which it is intended to displace, will no longer be available. Where, however, the government leaves open the question of whether or not to introduce the substitute good x, the question to be answered by the economist may take either of two forms: (a) should x be introduced when the imported y good remains available at its existing price, or at some other price? or (b) should x be introduced if there is to be the option of having only x or only y?

If the (a) question has to be answered there is no conceptual difficulty. The benefits of introducing x are calculated by reference to a demand curve for x that is to be estimated on the assumption that y will still be available either at the existing price or at some other price to be decreed by the government. If, instead, the (b) question has to be answered, since x and y are to be mutually exclusive, net benefits for either must begin from a hypothetical situation in which there is neither x nor y. Thus the calculated social *net* benefit, B_y, for the option of continuing with the existing imports of y, is to be reckoned as the maximum sum consumers are willing to pay to continue buying the quantity of y at the price in question (measured by reference to the demand curve for y when x is unavailable), *less* the opportunity costs of the exports that are used to pay for it. These opportunity costs are, as indicated earlier, measured as the domestic value of the goods withdrawn from the home market for this purpose.[6] The social *net* benefit, B_x, from introducing x at, say, a price equal to its marginal variable cost, in the absence of y is to be calculated by reference to the demand curve for x drawn on the assumption that y is unavailable. From such a demand curve we estimate the maximum sum consumers are prepared to pay for the 'optimal' amount (at which price is equal to marginal cost),[7] and we subtract from it the total opportunity costs of producing that much x. The criterion for introducing x rather than y requires simply that B_x exceed B_y.[8]

---

[6] Again the question of which particular export will depend upon political constraints. If the economist is informed that y is no longer to be imported, then on grounds of allocative efficiency he will advise a reduction of those exports having the lowest domestic value. But if, in the event, the government is expected to reduce some other exports, the economist is obliged to value the opportunity costs of y accordingly.

[7] If the government decides to set the price of x above its marginal variable cost, or to levy an excise tax on x, the economist has no choice but to estimate the maximum sum consumers will pay for the amount bought at this higher price.

[8] Although B_y is treated in the text as a flow of net benefits, one which may be expected to increase over the foreseeable future, such sums can be reduced to a present capitalized value by the use of an appropriate rate of discount and added, in the form of a capitalized opportunity cost, to the capital costs of the x project. (The methods available for comparing stocks and flows over time are treated in Part V on investment criteria.)

Chapter 15

THE PROBLEM OF SECOND BEST

1   Wherever the familiar optimum conditions are not met in the rest of the economy, one *cannot*, in general, justify employing the marginal cost pricing rule to determine ideal outputs in the remaining sectors. As for evaluating a particular project, it is no longer possible, in these circumstances, to enter the prices of factors as costs in the usual way. The problem of what is then to be done, what rules to employ, is the problem posed by the theory of second best.[1] Although account has been taken of a number of special cases in the preceding chapters, the subject warrants more explicit treatment for two reasons: first, because familiarity with allocative economics presupposes an understanding of the context in which the second best theorem is pertinent. In particular, the economist, tendering advice on investment projects, has to be aware of the limited conditions under which the usual allocative propositions are valid. Secondly, because cost-benefit analysis is specifically concerned with the proper pricing of factors, which prices enter into the costs of the projects. To an increasing extent, also, cost-benefit analysis is invoked to determine the optimal size of the plant to be established and, in a 'short period' the size of the optimal output of the existing plant.

2   It is a commonplace that optimal conditions are no more than first order, or necessary, conditions in maximizing a social welfare function subject to a production constraint.[2] The second best theorem does no

---

[1] Although this problem had been recognized and discussed previously, the attempt to formulate it explicitly, and in full generality, was first made by Lipsey and Lancaster (1957).

[2] The reader may wish to consult my *Survey* paper (1960), section II, which interprets and examines these optimal conditions.

more than point out that, if one or more additional constraints are imposed on this welfare function, the necessary conditions for a maximum are different from the usual ones and, in general, are more complex.[3] The obvious corollary follows that, in order to identify a maximum welfare position under these circumstances, it may be necessary to forsake those familiar optimal conditions that are strictly relevant to the simple case of a single constraint, the boundary of production possibilities.

Now in the simple case of no constraint additional to the production boundary, the more relevant set of necessary conditions is cast in the familiar form of setting the price of each good proportional to its corresponding marginal cost. Put otherwise, the ratio of the prices of any pair of goods has to be made equal to the ratio of their corresponding marginal costs. It follows, therefore, that if there is but one constraint additional to the production boundary, which takes the form, say, of the price in sector X being 40 per cent above its marginal cost, the above condition is met—and a general optimal position attained—simply by setting the prices in all the remaining sectors 40 per cent above their corresponding marginal costs.[4]

---

[3] The more general proof proceeds as follows: in order to maximize some function

$$F(x_1, x_2, \ldots, x_m)$$

subject to a single constraint

$$\phi(x_1, x_2, \ldots, x_m),$$

using the Langrangian method. maximize $W = F - \lambda\phi$. The necessary conditions will include $F_i = \lambda\phi_i$, or

$$F_i/F_j = \phi_i/\phi_j (i = 1, 2, \ldots, m).$$

However, if now an additional constraint is introduced. say $F_1/F_m = k\phi_1/\phi_m$, where $k \neq 1$. the Langrange method requires that we maximize the function

$$W' = F - \lambda\phi - \mu \ (F_1/F_m - k\phi_1/\phi_m),$$

and the necessary conditions become much more complex. See Lipsey and Lancaster (1957).

[4] It is occasionally asserted that the stricter condition, price *equals* marginal cost, is required. since it meets a further optimum condition which is not met in equiproportional case. as in the 40 per cent above cost instance in the text. This further

One cannot depend on the problem being that simple, however, and the economist has to face the question of determining a price and output for one or more industries in circumstances where he cannot hope to influence price and output policies in the rest of the economy. Since there is not the slightest prospect of his being able to obtain the necessary data to calculate an exact second best solution for the industry, or industries, in question, it is necessary to consider conditions under which he can, with some assurance, recommend either marginal cost pricing or some other simple rule.

The existence of varying degrees of monopoly in the economy at large does not, of itself, justify much concern over misallocation. Enterprises that continue to survive are able to cover their full costs and, in a fairly competitive economy, not many enterprises are likely to make revenues that vastly exceed their costs for any length of time. Thus, although it is not to be expected that the economy, at any moment of time, attains an optimum position, in its continuous

---

[1] (contd) condition is then identified as that ensuring equality between the marginal product of the factor in that use and the marginal (subjective) valuation to the factor-owner in alternative non-market uses (say leisure). If, for example, the hourly wage of a specific type of labour is $5, and the market value of its marginal product is 40 per cent more, or $7, then, it is argued, by allowing the worker to increase his number of hours, a net social gain will obtain. The worker, for instance, may agree to work an hour longer for $5.50, a further hour for $6, and so on. At the same time, as he produces more, the market value of the good declines. By allowing workers to extend their outputs until the market value of an hour's work is equal to the workers' subjective value of the hour, both worker and consumer can be made better off, or rather, as well off as possible.

This argument would be valid if, in perfect competition, each worker separately determines the number of hours he works in each job in each industry by reference to the wage offered to him. But whether he is paid by the hour or by what he accomplishes, this condition is never met in modern industry, no matter how competitive. Given the wage, or the rate for the job, he cannot adjust the number of hours to his own preferences. The worker has to accept, as a constraint, the hours of work per week (plus the specific overtime opportunities, if any) that go with the job. The modern worker is then faced with an all-or-nothing weekly agreement. He measures the wage offered against the full forty-hour week, say, and accepts or rejects. Marginal adjustments to output are, even in the absence of all intervention by labour unions, not by the hour, or by the piece, but only by the entrance, or exit, of additional workers; the marginal worker having zero rent.

Given these constraints, full employment and universal perfect competition imply that, in equilibrium, the opportunity cost of moving a worker from x to y is the same as his value in x; and no reshuffling of factors can result in a potential Pareto improvement. The economy is then in an optimal overall position, with the prices of all goods set m per cent above their corresponding marginal costs.

adjustment to changes in the conditions of demand and supply, it may not be too far from an overall optimal position for any prolonged period.[5]

The one factor that diminishes such hopes, however, even in a highly competitive economy, is the existence of significant spillover effects, since there is no necessary tendency here toward self-correction. The larger the spillover effects and the less uniform is their incidence throughout the economy, the smaller is the confidence that can be reposed in the presumption that a competitive economy tends to a tolerably good allocation.[6]

3 The above remarks do not afford much consolation, but, in certain circumstances, the economist can say something more definite. For what matters in determining the price and output of the good in question, say X, are the price or output policies followed in the production of closely related goods, say Y and Z, that are identified as the constrained sectors. If, in an otherwise perfectly competitive economy, the constrained Y and Z sectors were 'deviant', Y's price being 50 per cent above its marginal cost and Z's price being 10 per cent above its marginal cost, then—provided Y and Z were substitutes for X—the mark-up for the free sector, X, should obviously be something between 10 per cent and 50 per cent. This is intuitively plausible. For if, instead, we had set the mark-up for X at below 10 per cent or above 50 per cent, we should have widened the price-marginal cost ratios between the three substitute goods, thereby removing them further from an ideal position of equal price-marginal cost ratios.

Nor need we stop here. We could surmise that the excess price-marginal cost ratio, EPR, to be adopted in determining X's output,

---

[5] The scope for improvement in productive, or technological, efficiency may, however, be far more important than allocative efficiency of this overall sort. And if so, the question of whether to spend a given sum of money in seeking such allocative improvements or in seeking advances in productive efficiency is easily answered. But whether attempts at increasing productive efficiency are successful or not, the allocative problem still remains.

For the arguments that productivity improvements are, at present, more profitable than the usual allocative improvements, the reader is referred to Leibenstein's 1966 paper.

[6] Allocative and other aspects of spillovers, and their treatment in a cost-benefit analysis, are discussed at length in Part III.

would not be far removed from a correct second-best ratio if it were calculated as an average of the EPRs of the substitute goods Y and Z, when these EPRs are weighted by their respective total values. Clearly if the value of Y with its 50 per cent EPR were large relative to the value of Z with its 10 per cent EPR, this rule would provide an EPR for X closer to 50 per cent than to 10 per cent.

This rule, however, does assume that goods Y and Z are about equally good substitutes for X. If Y happens to be a closer substitute for X than Z is, the response of X's demand is more sensitive to a proportional change in the price of Y than it is to a proportional change in the price of Z. In consequence Y's weight, in determining the average EPR for X, has to be more than proportional to its total value. For the more sensitive is the demand for X to the price of a particular substitute, the greater is the departure from the correct second-best amount of X in response to a given movement from the correct second-best price of X. If we are concerned, as we are, with the second-best optimal *outputs* of the goods, it is more important to set the price of X, or rather the EPR of X, closer to that of the more sensitive substitute Y than to that of Z, other things equal.

If, however, either or both of Y and Z are complementary with X, the reasoning, though analogous, gives opposite results. Suppose X is bread and Y is butter, and imagine a situation in which both have the same price-marginal cost ratio of unity—an EPR of zero. Ignoring all other goods for the moment, there is then, as between X and Y, a correct allocation of factors. Now suppose a rise in the price of butter, Y, by 50 per cent. This does not raise the demand curve for X, and the value of X, as it would if X were a substitute. Being a complement, the demand curve for bread, X, and its value to people, fall. Its equilibrium output falls also. It follows that, comparing the X and Y outputs with their initially correct outputs, they are both too small relative to the outputs of all other goods. Clearly, an attempt to redress this subsequent 'allocative distortion' by responding to the exogenous rise in price of Y with a proportional rise in the price of X only aggravates the situation by reducing both outputs further. *Per contra*, responding to the exogenous rise in the price of Y by a reduction in the initial price of X—in this instance *below* its marginal cost—increases the outputs of both X and Y: the demand for X will increase directly following a reduction in its price, and, with a lower price for X, the marginal value of Y, and the demand curve for Y, the complementary good, will shift upward. The outputs of both X and Y are thereby increased by a lowering of X's price and the initial optimal position approached once more. If the only goods closely related to the free sector, X, are all complements, the required EPR for X would approximate a weighted average of their EPRs prefixed by a negative sign—with, again, those goods more closely complementary with X carrying more weight relative to their value.

The rule for setting the EPR for X when its related goods comprise both substitutes and complements follows accordingly. If the EPRs of all related goods are positive—which is very likely if the goods are produced by private enterprise—the EPR for X by this weighting rule will be positive for a predominance of substitutes, and negative for a predominance of complements.[7]

If the general belief, that the predominating relationship between goods is that of substitutes, is accepted, it is also possible to justify, in a rough and ready way, marginal cost pricing of the free sectors irrespective of the deviations from marginal cost pricing in the constrained sectors. Or, rather, the rule to be adopted in the free sectors is that prices should be set, as suggested by Farrel (1958), *no lower than* their corresponding marginal costs. They may, of course, be set a little higher: how much exactly can be roughly calculated or guessed at. But, in general, such prices are not to be set lower than marginal costs.

4   In addition to such guiding rules, one can visualize circumstances in which one can go ahead and use straightforward marginal cost pricing for a group of industries, or for all industries, within a geographical area, in disregard of what is happening in the constrained remainder of the economy. Thus, if changes in the prices, or outputs, of the industries within this area have negligible repercussions on the demand for goods outside this area of the economy, we can set the prices of the goods within this area equal to their corresponding marginal costs without fear of making things worse. For maximizing the value of the outputs within the area, by equalizing (through the marginal cost rule) the value of the marginal products there of each

---

[7] Mathematically exact rules for setting the prices of the free sector goods, given the price-marginal cost ratios of the constrained sectors, have been derived by Green (1961).

factor class, does not very much affect the value of the collection of goods produced in the remainder of the economy. Thus without doing any worse in the constrained rest of the economy, we do the best we can for this area by reshuffling factors as to maximize the value of the resulting product-mix there.

This last mentioned proposition, however, is not of much use to the economist unless he is required to offer advice to all industries within such a geographical area. For a single project, such a restrictive condition, enabling one to ignore the effects of the price to be set on the outputs of other goods, is not likely to be met. Nevertheless, the economist may occasionally find that an alternative condition can be met: that the factors used in the project in question are *specific* to that project. Such factors that spring to mind, a specific site, or specific machine, or a highly specialized type of labour, have been discussed in a previous chapter, and the reader will appreciate that a factor that is strictly specific in the production of X implies that it has a zero value in any alternative production over some period, long or short. The price of X should therefore be set low enough as to employ all of such specific factors. True, the lower the price of X is set the smaller will be the demand and outputs of the substitute goods for X in the constrained sector, and the larger, therefore, will be the outputs of other goods. But since the opportunity cost of the specific factors is nil, it is better that X be expanded at zero opportunity cost to the economy at the expense of its substitutes, letting the non-specific factors (which have a *positive* opportunity cost) move out of these substitute goods in order to add value elsewhere.

5　The reader is reminded at this juncture that this question of marginal cost pricing—either in the long run which determines the size of the plant, or in the short run which determines the output produced by the existing plant—has been discussed under the tacit assumption that any necessary changes in the tax structure do not, of themselves, have any allocative effects.

In the long period the optimal size of the plant is determined by the condition that demand price equals long period marginal cost. If, therefore, the demand curve cuts the long-period marginal cost curve at an output in the range of declining average cost—marginal cost, and therefore price, being below average cost—the plant size will be one for which average (inclusive) cost is below price. And if there is only one price, set to equal marginal cost, the enterprise cannot meet its total cost from its revenues. Similarly, if, in the short period, the demand is such that the output for which price equals marginal cost is one for which marginal cost is below average cost, the marginal cost pricing rule specifies an output at which, so priced, total revenues fall short of total factor costs.[8]

By discriminating monopoly pricing or, more practically, by the use of two- or multi-part tariffs, the marginal cost-pricing rule can, however, be made consistent with the aim of covering the full costs of the enterprise.[9] There may, however, be political or other constraints that rule out the possibility of two- or multi-part tariffs. If so, the alternative is either (a) that of producing a smaller than optimal output in order to cover costs—setting price equal, at least, to average cost (and, therefore, above marginal cost)—or else (b) that of subsidizing the enterprise so as to enable it to meet its factor payments when it sets a price equal to marginal cost (and, therefore, below average cost).

If there are no 'distortions' involved in raising taxes—as, in principle, there would not be if lump-sum taxes could be levied[10]—there can be no purely allocative objections to the (b) alternative, and, therefore, to financing a falling-cost service by means of a public subsidy. But raising additional taxes of the usual sort does involve the community in costs. Apart from additional administrative costs of altering the tax structure, and of collecting the taxes, the raising of taxes, other than lump-sum taxes, has incidental allocative effects. Income taxes, in particular, can have effects on effort, and can reduce the incentive to produce marketable goods or services while increasing

---

[8] The reader is reminded that the marginal cost pricing condition is a necessary, but not sufficient, condition. Confining ourselves to a partial analysis, it is required also that total benefit from the output exceeds total costs.

[9] A two-part tariff is usually one which exacts a fixed charge from the buyer unrelated to the amount of the good he takes at the price. The commonest examples are quarterly charges for telephone service and for electricity service, which charges are set independently of the consumption of the services. Such charges have the effect of transferring a portion of what would otherwise be the consumers' surplus to the service enterprises.

[10] Lump sum taxes are taken to mean taxes that are invariant to a person's earnings. Although, as a result of the wealth effect, such taxes will in general alter the supply of a person's productive services, they will not 'distort' the objective rate of substitution between factor and product. If, therefore, there are no other taxes in the economy, the introduction of lump-sum taxes does not infringe the factor-product optimal condition.

the incentive to spend more time and effort evading taxes. In view of these income-tax effects, there may be a case, after all, for setting price above marginal cost and equal to average cost. The consequent misallocation need not be serious if the prices of substitutes for this good are already set somewhat above their corresponding marginal costs and/or the demand for this good has a low elasticity.

There may, also, be political or social objections, which the economist has to accept, to pricing a good at its marginal cost in the long or short period, and financing the loss through public subsidies. If the good was consumed predominantly by wealthier groups, distributive arguments could be brought against the proposal to price at marginal cost and cover the losses from public revenues. On the other hand, even if the revenues raised by marginal cost pricing sufficed, or more than sufficed, to meet factor payments, there may also be objections to it on distributive grounds. It is not, for example, impractical to charge public transit passengers different fares for travelling at different times of the day. During peak-traffic hours, at least, higher fares could be charged to meet the higher marginal (congestion) costs. But, it may be objected, the passengers during peak hours have little choice in view of traditional business hours. In the circumstances, charging according to marginal costs would be charging lower income groups more for having to travel in discomfort, compared with those who have the choice and the leisure to travel more comfortably at other hours. This is so manifestly inequitable that it has not been seriously contemplated. In such cases then, political constraints translate marginal cost pricing into 'average' marginal cost pricing.[11] And if public subsidy is not forthcoming, there may be no choice but to resort to 'average' average cost pricing.

6   Finally, so long as the economist confines himself to estimating the cost of some specific project that is technically feasible, he need not be too inhibited by the second-best theorem. For no matter what the allocative condition of the economy at large, a Pareto improvement is effected if a factor is transferred from its existing employment to the specific project X where its value is higher—or, put more generally, if

---

[11] If vehicular traffic is believed to be subsidized, inasmuch as its current operational marginal costs do not include the spillover effects it generates, there is a case for setting the public transit fares below marginal costs.

the value of the marginal product of the factor to be employed in X exceeds its opportunity cost.[12]

REFERENCES AND BIBLIOGRAPHY FOR PART II

Balassa, B. 'Estimating the Shadow Price of Foreign Exchange in Project Evaluation', *Oxford Economic Papers*, 1974.

Blaug, M. 'The Rate of Return on Investment in Education in Great Britain', *Manchester School*, 1965.

Currie, J. M., Murphy, J. A. and Schmitz, A. 'The Concept of Economic Surplus and its Use in Economic Analysis', *Economic Journal*, 1971.

Dasgupta, P., Marglin, S. and Sen, A. *Guidelines for Project Evaluation*, United Nations, 1972.

Dorfman, R. (Ed.). *Measuring the Benefit of Government Investments*, Washington DC: Brookings Institution, 1965.

Ellis, H. S. and Fellner, W. 'External Economies and Diseconomies', *American Economic Review*, 1943.

Friedman, M. 'The Marshallian Demand Curve'. *Journal of Political Economy*, 1949.

Glaister, S. 'Generalised Consumer Surplus and Public Transport Pricing', *Economic Journal*, 1974.

Green, H. A. J. 'The Social Optimum in the Presence of Monopoly and Taxation', *Review of Economic Studies*, 1961.

Hansen, W. L. 'Total and Private Rates of Return to Investment in Schooling', *Journal of Political Economy*, 1963.

Harberger, A. C. 'On Measuring the Social Opportunity Cost of Labour', *International Economic Review*, 1971.

Hause, J. C. 'The Theory of Welfare Measurement', *Journal of Political Economy*, 1975.

Hicks, J. R. *Value and Capital*, Oxford: Clarendon Press, 1939 (1946).

— *A Revision of Demand Theory*, Oxford: Clarendon Press, 1956.

Leibenstein, H. 'Allocative Efficiency versus X-Efficiency', *American Economic Review*, 1966.

Lipsey, R. and Lancaster, K. 'The General Theory of Second Best', *Review of Economic Studies*, 1957.

Little, I. M. D. and Mirrlees, J. *Social Cost Benefit Analysis*, OECD, 1969.

Marglin, S. A. *Value and Price in Labour Surplus Economies*, New York, Oxford University Press, 1976.

---

[12] In general, any transfer of factors from one product to another affects the distribution of real earnings in the economy, and also the relative prices of the goods as between which factors are transferred, both of these consequences affecting the general pattern of demand, and, therefore, of the existing price-marginal cost ratios. The first feature in particular implies that the optimal position itself—uniquely determined only if there is a uniquely specified welfare function (which, in fact, is usually assumed in the treatment of second best theory)—alters in response to the factor movements which one would want to recommend by reference to the marginal cost price ratios of the existing situation. Nonetheless, in so far as the magnitudes of the factor movements are those pertinent to cost-benefit studies, the assumptions of partial analysis may be adopted. For the secondary repercussions on product prices arising from such relatively limited factor movements are likely to be negligible.

Mishan, E. J. 'Survey of Welfare Economics, 1939–1959', *Economic Journal*, 1960.

— 'Interpretation of the Benefits of Private Transport', *Journal of Transport Economics and Policy*, 1967.

— 'The Plain Truth about Consumer Surplus', *Zeitschrift für Nationalökonomie*, 1977.

— *Introduction to Normative Economics*, New York: Oxford University Press, 1980.

Pauwels, W. 'The Possible Perverse Behaviour of the Compensating Variation as a Welfare Ranking', *Zeitschrift für Nationalökonomie*, 1977.

Peters, G. H. *Cost-Benefit Analysis and Public Expenditure*, London: Institute of Economic Affairs, 1968.

Prest, A. R. and Turvey, R. 'Cost-Benefit Analysis: A Survey', *Economic Journal*, 1965.

Rothenberg, J. 'Urban Renewal Programs' in R. Dorfman (ed.), *Measuring the Benefits of Government Investment*, Washington DC: Brookings Institution, 1965.

Scott, M. F. G. 'How to Use and Estimate Shadow Exchange Rates', *Oxford Economic Papers*, 1974.

Silberberg, E. 'Duality and the Many Consumer's Surpluses', *American Economic Review*, 1972.

Throsby, D. *An Introduction to Mathematical Programming*, New York: Random House, 1970.

Weisbrod, B. A. *Economics of Public Health: Measuring the Impact of Diseases*, Philadelphia: University of Philadelphia Press, 1960.

Winch, D. M. *The Economics of Highway Planning*, Toronto: Toronto University Press, 1963.

PART III. EXTERNAL EFFECTS

Chapter 16

INTRODUCTION TO EXTERNAL EFFECTS

1 External effects, an abbreviation for external economies and diseconomies—sometimes referred to as 'externalities', more picturesquely as 'neighbourhood effects', somewhat vapidly as 'side effects', and more suggestively as 'spillover effects', or, briefly, 'spillovers'—first appear as 'external economies' in Alfred Marshall's *Principles* in connection with a competitive industry's downward-sloping supply curve. Marshall's argument is that, as industry expands by, say, an additional firm, any resulting reduction in the average costs of production accrues to *all* the firms in the industry. The total reduction of costs experienced by all the intra-marginal firms is to be attributed to the entry of the additional firm. The true or 'social' cost of the additional output produced by this marginal firm is not the total cost of it as calculated by that firm, but this cost *less* the total saving in costs by all the intra-marginal firms. This proposition is important in determining the 'correct' or 'optimal' output of the industry. For in practice the additional firm makes no allowance for the saving in costs it contributes to the rest of the industry. If, therefore, firms continue to enter the competitive industry until, at the going price of the product, the total cost of the firm is equal to its total revenue, the equilibrium size of the industry will be that at which the market demand price is equal to the average (inclusive) cost of the good in question. But the marginal cost, or total cost of the incremental firm, will be below average cost by the amount of the total cost-savings it confers on the intra-marginal firms. Therefore marginal cost will, to the same extent, be below the market price and, abiding by the marginal-cost pricing rule, output should be extended beyond the competitive equilibrium until marginal cost is equal to price. The existence of external economies in a competitive industry, Marshall concludes, entails an equilibrium output that is below optimal.

Constructing a curve marginal to the industry's supply curve, the point at which this marginal curve cuts the demand curve identifies the 'ideal', or optimal, output. This concept, and its corresponding construction, was extended in a symmetrical manner to external diseconomies, to reveal that the optimal output of a competitive industry was below the equilibrium output. These external effects were later remarked to have wide application, not only as between firms in determining the optimal size of the industry, but as between industries themselves. Nor are such effects confined to industry. They operate as between persons and groups, and as between firms and industries and persons.

2 Fairly standard examples of spillovers include the adverse effects on flora, fauna, rainfall, and soil, in cutting down the trees of a forest; or the effects on the mosquito population of creating artificial lakes, and other ecological repercussions that ultimately enter into the welfare of people. The pleasure given by the erection of a beautiful building or, more commonly alas, the offence given by the erection of a tasteless or incongruous structure, is an external effect. So also is the congestion suffered by all the traffic from additional vehicles coming onto the roads; or the noise and pollution arising from the operation of industry or of its products; or the loss of life consequent upon the increase in air or ground traffic.

From a little reflection on examples such as these, it emerges that one characteristic common to all of them is the incidental, or unintentional, nature of the effect produced. The person or industrial concern engaged, say, in logging may, or may not, have any idea of the consequences on the profits or welfare of others. But it is certain that they do not enter into his calculations. The factory owners, whose plant produces smoke as well as other things, are concerned only to produce the other things that can be sold on the market. They have no interest in producing the smoke, even though they may be fully aware of it. But so long as their own productivity does not suffer thereby, and they themselves are not penalized in any way, they will regard the smoke as an unfortunate by-product.

112

If these external effects are not deliberately produced, however, neither are they deliberately absorbed by others. Such effects may add to the enjoyment of life, as does the smell of fresh-cut grass, or else add to life's vexations as does the noise, stench, and danger of mounting automobile traffic. But they are not within the control of the persons who are absorbing them—at least not without their incurring expenses.[1] However, a definition of external effects that gives prominence to these aspects—that a person's welfare, or a firm's profits, depends upon things that are initially outside his control, which things are incidental to the activity of others—is by itself insufficient and may, indeed, lead to confusion. Let us see how.

3 The statement that a firm's or industry's outputs or profits, or a person's welfare, can be influenced by the activities of others is true, apparently, within the context of any general equilibrium system. In particular, it is true within a general equilibrium system that has no external effects of the sort illustrated above.[2] The familiar interdependent system of Leon Walras is a case in point. Among the set of equations posited are those for individuals regarded as consumers and owners of productive services. All the *variables* in each person's utility function—whether they refer to the amounts of finished goods bought or the amounts of productive services offered—are deemed to be entirely within his control. The parameters within each person's utility function, however, are the set of prices; and these are determined by the system as a whole.

Thus for each person, the quantities of the things that he is willing to buy or to sell depend, *inter alia,* on the set of market prices of these things. The amounts of goods supplied by perfectly competing firms also depend upon the market prices. These set of market prices can, in general, be altered by any changes in technology, in people's tastes, or in the accumulation and redistribution of assets. It follows that the activities of persons and firms, in response to these sorts of changes, have incidental effects on the welfare of others. If, to take a humble example, people start changing from tea to coffee, the price of tea will

---

[1] If an adverse spillover effect could be avoided without incurring any costs, it could hardly be called an adverse spillover. Certainly no problem would arise.

[2] The system is, of course, a *theoretical* construct only. Engineers affirm that in all input-output activities there is wastage, and therefore waste material is absorbed into the air, the earth or its waters, so creating the potential for external effects.

at first tend to fall and that of coffee to rise. The producers of tea will initially suffer and those of coffee benefit, while the consumers of tea will be better off and the consumers of coffee worse off.

But in this general equilibrium system, in the absence of all external effects as commonly understood, such interdependence operates indirectly, and through changes in market prices. Each and every exogenous change mentioned—a change in techniques, in tastes, or in factor endowment—entails a corresponding change in the equilibrium set of prices. Since, in general, every price is affected, every person's welfare is affected also, and this can be very important.[3] Nevertheless, given perfectly competitive markets and no external effects, each general equilibrium position meets the requirement of a Pareto optimum, viz. one in which it is not possible to make one or more persons better off without making at least one person worse off.[4] In contrast, the concern with external effects arises just because their existence implies that—unless special arrangements are made—the equilibrium solutions attainable may *not* be Pareto optimal.

We may, then, infer that external effects are effects on others that are conveyed directly, and not indirectly through prices. If we allow that these effects on people's welfare matter in principle no less than do the priced products and services, it follows that it is just because these external effects, these by-products of the activities of others, are not properly priced or not priced at all, that the equilibrium solution is not Pareto optimal. To illustrate, the competitive equilibrium price of steel spades is $10, price being equal to long-run average, and marginal cost. In their production, however, noise is produced, this being the only external effect in the economy. The noise created in producing the marginal spade would be tolerated without complaint only on receipt of, say, $7 by those disturbed by the noise. The net valuation of the marginal spade is, therefore, $10 minus $7, or $3 altogether. The marginal cost however is $10, and the equilibrium is not optimal. For if we produced one spade less to start with, the factors released would—assuming universal perfect competition—create $10 of goods

---

[3] For instance in appraising welfare criteria. See my 1957 paper.
[4] If every relevant effect in the economy is properly priced, the economy is in an optimal position. The reverse, however, is not true, since optimality can be consistent with unpriced spillovers. See the example in Chapter 19.

elsewhere. The accompanying loss in social value, however, is $3, as above. Society is better off to the extent of $7: some can be made better off (to the extent of $7) without anyone else being made worse off. As stated, therefore, the original position could not have been optimal.

If external effects could somehow be 'properly' priced like the other goods and 'bads' of the economic system—where the term 'bads' is occasionally used as an alternative expression to disutility, or 'diswelfare', or 'discommodity', of which, say, the provision of labour services could be taken as an example—then indeed any perfectly competitive equilibrium would, again, be optimal. One can go further: if each external effect were to be priced in a competitive market, along with other goods and bads, it would cease to be an external effect. Before elaborating this point, however, let us attempt a definition.

4   Write the equation

$$U^1 = U^1(x_1^1, x_2^1, x_3^1) \tag{1}$$

where U^1 is the utility, or welfare, of person 1, and x_1^1, x_2^1, x_3^1, are the amounts he has (flows, or stocks, according to the problem) of three of the goods, x_1, x_2, x_3, on which his utility, or welfare, depends. Equation (1) is no more than the statement that person 1's utility, or welfare, depends on the quantities he has of those goods. No external effects are implied by the equation. If, instead, we write his equation as

$$U^1 = U^1(x_i^2; x_1^1, x_2^1, x_3^1) \tag{1a}$$

the possibility of an external effect is implied. The term x_i^2 gives the additional information that person 1's utility, U', depends not only on his own quantities of a number of goods, but also on x_i^2, on person 2's quantities of x_i. If x_i were flowers, then person 1's welfare is affected not only by the flowers in his own garden but also by those in his neighbour's garden. We could also interpret equation (1a) as a production function, U^1 being the output of good 1, and the x's as the inputs used in the production of good 1. The equation (1a) is now interpreted as saying that the amount of good 1 depends directly on the inputs x_1, x_2, x_3, etc., used directly in the production of good 1, and depends also on the amount of input i used in the production of good 2. The amount of the ith input used in the production of good 2 (this amount being under the control of the producers of good 2—*not* of the producers of good 1) is therefore regarded as imposing external effects on the output

115

of good 1, and also, therefore, on the price of good 1 and the profits of the producers of good 1.

Such notational definitions are common enough in the literature. Another would be $\delta U^1 / \delta x_i^2 \neq 0$, which can be interpreted as saying that a small change in person 2's quantity of good i will not leave person 1's utility unchanged. For the external effect to *exist*, however, we should have to add the information that $x_i^2 \neq 0$. Thus $x_i^2 > 0$ implies that person 2 purchases some of the ith good; $x_i^2 < 0$ implies that he sells some of the ith good. If we write $\delta U^1 / \delta x_i^2 > 0$, then person 2's external effect is one that raises person 1's welfare, the converse being true for a reversal of the inequality sign. Notation of this sort is helpful, but there are limitations. Thus, if x_i^2 refers to person 2's purchase of, say, a lawn-mower, it is not possible to infer from the notation alone whether person 1's welfare is reduced (a) by his envy of person 2's new lawn-mower, (b) by its being a noise-nuisance, (c) by the extra smoke suffered by person 1 among others (including person 2) in conse-quence of the factory's production of an extra lawn-mower, or (d) by a combination of any or all of these. We return to these possibilities in the following section.

Again, the fact that person 1 reacts to the amount of good i taken, or produced, by person 2, without his being able to control person 2's consumption or production of good i—which information is imparted by the notation above—does not suffice to define an external effect in the economist's sense. My wealthy aunt's welfare (as well as my own) depends unambiguously on the amount of arsenic I put into her tea. If it was discovered that in my impatience to inherit her fortune I had used arsenic to accelerate the natural process of ageing, the coroner would be unlikely to refer to the results of my enterprise as an external effect. Yet, if person 1 be my aunt, person 2 be myself, x_i^2 be the amount of arsenic that I use, $\delta U^1 / \delta x_i^2 < 0$ expresses the proposition that my aunt's welfare varies inversely with the amount of arsenic that I use. It would therefore fit the situation just depicted. In contrast, the conven-tional interpretation of the external effect indicated by the same term $\delta U^1 / \delta x_i^2 < 0$ would be that of my good aunt suffering at the thought of my injudicious consumption of arsenic, in small doses, as a stimulant. In order, therefore, to comply with the conventional meaning of external effect, the x_i^2 notation is to be interpreted strictly as person 2's consumption, or production, of good x_i which is determined solely by reference to his own immediate interest, and in disregard of the effects

116

it may have on the welfare of others.

5   Once the reader has a clear idea of what an external effect is,[5] a little reflection will convince him that the number of external effects in the real world are virtually unlimited. If my wife is envious of her friend's new fur coat, her friend's wearing it in my wife's presence has an adverse external effect on at least one person. A cigar smoked in the presence of non-smokers has adverse external effects. Attractive short-skirted women may generate adverse external effects on other women and favourable external effects on men. A's promotion causes B to rejoice, and C to curse. And so one could go on.

Now if all the administrative costs, and all the associated expenses and efforts, involved in reaching mutually satisfactory arrangements were zero, the possibilities for mutual gain would be completely exhausted and, by definition, a Pareto optimum would prevail. Thinking along such lines, the utilitarian (in the narrow sense) would approve of measures designed to reduce the costs of reaching mutual agreements about external effects. If, for example, negligible time and effort are required for the non-smoker to bribe the smoker to desist from lighting his cigarette, both can be made better off by the arrangement. However, the potential gains of a vast number of such mutual arrangements are likely to be smaller than the minimal costs and efforts needed for such arrangements. They are uneconomic in the sense that once these costs and efforts enter the calculus the net potential benefits are negative.

But this is not all. Among those external effects for which some arrangements would reveal net potential benefits that are positive, not

---

[5] There are quite a number of economic phenomena—all, perhaps, relevant to considerations of optimality—masquerading in the literature as external effects which cannot be admitted on the interpretation in the text. Common among these are such developments as the pooling of risks, improved training facilities, and other cost-saving arrangements. Such arbitrary extensions of the original concept, and the consequent ambiguity generated, are discussed in my 1965 paper. A recent misapprehension arises in the case of a person who cannot be admitted into an already packed theatre, or who has to queue without certainty of entry. The consequent decline in his welfare, certainly related to the welfare of others, is not, however, an instance of external effects, but of non-optimal pricing. An ideal mechanism would choose a set of prices as to fill the theatre exactly (ignoring discontinuities), with no one being left out who would be willing to pay the price to get in. There are, of course, obvious practical difficulties in implementing such an 'optimal' set of prices; and these difficulties, not external effects, account for such frustrations.

all are socially acceptable. Economists, and society at large, might wish to distinguish, and in practice do distinguish, between external effects that are a source of 'legitimate' satisfaction or grievance, and those that are not. Among the latter is the resentment or envy felt by some people at the achievement or possessions of others.[6] But though such reactions may elicit sympathy, and qualify for psychiatry, they are unlikely to command moral approval. Once ethics are brought into external effects in this way, the question of which effects are to count and which not, must, in the last resort, depend upon a consensus in the particular society. Though such ethical distinctions will confine the application of Pareto improvements to 'legitimate' external effects, the economist would appear justified in accepting a distinction that society consistently makes. Though perhaps not formally embodied in legal documents, no economic policy that caters to these 'negative feelings' of people has ever been announced. In contrast, there is no lack of evidence that society does take seriously all tangible damage inflicted on people in the pursuit by others of pleasure or profit. Since adverse environmental effects provide, today, the most important instances of damage inadvertently inflicted on other people, they will feature prominently in our discussion of methods of evaluating them.

---

[6] These are sometimes referred to as 'interdependence effects', since they are conceived of as the utility of one person being dependent upon the utility of another person— either directly, or via the goods that enter into the other's utility function.

Chapter 17

INTERNALIZING EXTERNAL EFFECTS

1 The verbal description of an external effect—that is, a direct effect on another's profit or welfare arising as an incidental by-product of some other person's or firm's legitimate activity—would seem adequate to convey its meaning. Its nature is made yet clearer, however, by examining the notion of 'internalizing' the external effect. The basic idea is that of transforming the incidental by-product into a joint product that is priced on the market. I have been told by a number of Argentinians that before the turn of the century, cattle were slain on the ranches for their leather only. Their flayed carcasses were left to rot, but if found in time they could be used as fresh meat by the poor peasants. Apparently only the leather had a market price, the meat being a by-product, or external effect, of leather production—a favourable spillover of the leather industry for those peasants who happened to be in the vicinity.[1]

Suppose, however, that the human population began to multiply more rapidly than the cattle population, that the taste for meat grew, that meat began to be stored in refrigerators, and that, most important of all perhaps, the meat could be exported to distant markets. Domestic meat would become scarce and, therefore, a market for it would come into being. It would then cease to be a spillover, an unintended by-product in the process of obtaining hides for leather. It would take its place as a good in its own right, a joint product with leather. Whatever the separate demands for meat and leather are like, the long run competitive equilibrium output is optimal since the cattle population is

---

[1] Notwithstanding which the number of cattle slain could be optimal if, at the margin, the value of the meat was zero. We discuss this point further in the next chapter in terms of 'allocative significance'.

expanded to the point at which the sum of the market prices are equal to the marginal cost of cattle production. The external effect has been internalized into the pricing system.[2]

Internalizing spillover effects arises also in the case of external diseconomies that are internal to the industry. Common examples of the latter category are deep-sea fishing, in which any additional fishing boat above a certain number reduces the catch of each of the existing fishing boats in the fishing grounds; or traffic congestion, in which every additional vehicle above a certain number causes delay to each of the existing number of vehicles using a given highway system. Internalizing this sort of spillover would require that a positive market price be imputed to the currently unpriced though scarce resource—the area of the sea in the first case, the highway in the second. Once such a resource is priced, it will be used more economically. The analogy of scarce land used in the production of, say, corn is exact. If priced correctly, which implies that in a competitive industry the rent of this scarce resource be maximized, the competitive equilibrium output that emerges is also the optimal output.[3]

Another example, though one in which internal accounting prices are substituted for market prices, is that of two separately owned but adjacent factories, A and B. Factory A produces shoes and is powered by an old-fashioned coal engine which emits so much smoke as to seriously affect the output of the B factory, which produces chocolate bars. The manager of the B factory remonstrates with the A manager, but to no effect. The daughter of the owner of the A factory and the son

---

[2] It may seem unnecessary to remark that the possibility of internalizing an external effect (or, in the absence of internalization, correcting for optimal outputs) does not mean that the creation of an adverse external effect need not make things worse. Yet students do sometimes argue as though this is so; as though, so long as optimizing by one method or another takes place, the creation of adverse external effects may be viewed with equanimity. The introduction of an adverse external effect into the economy is a bad thing no matter how the economy adapts to it. By internalizing the bad, or by optimizing the output that produces the bad, we are doing no more than making the best of a bad job. We are certainly not as well off as we should be if this bad had not appeared on the economic scene.

[3] Assuming a period during which there is one scarce fixed factor and one factor that is variable in supply at a constant price, the average cost curve eventually slopes upward. A curve drawn marginal to this average cost curve cuts the demand curve at the optimal output. At this output, the difference between average cost and marginal cost *times* output gives the amount of the rent to the fixed factor—the maximum rent possible in a perfectly competitive market in which the price of the product is treated as a parameter.

of the owner of the B factory decide to get married, in consequence of which the two factories come under common ownership and control, and the couple live together happily ever after. The cost of the smoke, reckoned in terms of the damage inflicted on the output of the B factory, is no longer a spillover generated by A and suffered by B. It is now unambiguously a cost to the joint A–B enterprise, and as such ways and means of reducing it will be sought. Either anti-smoke devices will be installed in the A factory, or else, if cheaper (and assuming the smoke-damage to B's output varies directly with A's output) A's output will be reduced to the point at which the value of the marginal damage to B's output, added to the marginal cost of shoe-production in A, is equal to the market price of A's shoes. Thus the smoke ceases to become a spillover effect, but a properly costed item that is internalized into the costing system of the A–B merger.

2 The number of spillover effects that can be internalized into the pricing mechanism, or into the costing systems of firms is, however, limited. Among those that cannot easily be internalized through the market are many of the by-products of modern industry and of the hardware it produces. One thinks, in this connection, of traffic noise and various forms of pollution arising from the spread of sewage and garbage and radioactive wastes; also of the postwar phenomenal growth of diseases of the nerves, heart, and stomach, caused by high-tension living, the most ubiquitous by-product of sustained technological advance. Why cannot such spillovers be so internalized? The answer is simple: in order for a competitive market for such spillovers to emerge, certain conditions have to be met which, in the nature of the physical universe, cannot be met. First, the potential victim of these adverse spillover effects must have legal 'property rights' in, say, their ownership of some quantum of quiet and clean air which, if such rights were enjoyed, they could choose to sell to others. Secondly, in order for such rights to be enforceable, it would be necessary to demarcate a three-dimensional 'territory' about the person of each potential victim in order to identify the intrusions of others and take appropriate legal action. Thirdly, in order for a monopolistic situation not to arise, each of these three-dimensional properties within a given area, which can be rented for particular purposes (say, to accommodate the noise or pollution of someone's activity), must be a close substitute for the others.

The first condition could, of course, be met in the sense that all forms of pollution could be outlawed in the absence of specific agreements between the parties concerned. But because the second condition cannot be met in the world we inhabit, there is difficulty in demarcating each person's property, and a consequent difficulty in identifying the trespasser and the extent of the trespass. Nor can the third condition be met, for in this hypothetical scheme of things the right to use one man's 'territory', within some given area, is no substitute for that of another man. Each man within the area has his own three-dimensional territory and, since the noise to be created by the new activity enters in some degree into all of such territories, the enterprise has to reach agreement with each one of them. None can substitute for the other. Unless all agree, the permission of those who do is worthless.

If it were otherwise, if one territory could be substituted freely for another, as could plots of land in an agricultural area, an appropriate market price would arise from the competition of the sellers. The physical universe being what it is, however, each potential seller is in a completely monopolistic position. For without his particular consent the necessary arrangement for the whole of the affected area cannot be concluded. The reader will detect a similarity between this hypothetical problem, posed by the third condition, and that facing a railroad company having to buy every mile of land through which the track has to run. The cost of acquiring rights where a large number of land-owners are involved could be prohibitive were it not for legislation compelling the sale of rights on terms which the courts will decide are reasonable. Another instance, occasionally reported by the press, is that of a single householder, or small business, holding out against a property company that is attempting to buy up a specific area of land as part of some new development scheme.

We must, then, resign ourselves to the prospect of never being able to internalize these important environmental spillovers within the market economy; that is, of not being able to create a market for them—which is, of course, one of the reasons why cost-benefit methods are required to evaluate them.

3   Some further light is cast on the nature of spillover effects by briefly observing the connection between them and collective, or public, goods. Environmental spillovers usually affect a large number of people within an area. If the spillover effect is favourable, it can be regarded as a form of collective good; if unfavourable, as a form of collective bad. If the favourable spillover effect is to be distinguished from a collective good, it is simply on the grounds (1) that the spillover is only a by-product of some other market-oriented activity, whereas the collective good is itself the intended product, and (2) that an adverse spillover effect, at least, is commonly thought of as *unavoidable*, or avoidable only at a cost, whereas the collective good may well be avoidable. To illustrate (2), consider an instance of an avoidable collective good; each person living within a neighbourhood is free to spend his time gazing at the public fountain, or walking in the municipal park.[4] In contrast, a downfall of artificial rain, caused by seeding the clouds above a certain area of farmland, would be an example of an *unavoidable* collective good (or avoidable only at a cost). If, on the other hand, too much rain water was one of the *by-products* of the destruction of a forest by a lumber company, this adverse spillover could also be regarded as an unavoidable collective bad.

In connection with the deliberately produced collective project whose effects are unavoidable, or non-optional, it must be realized that some persons may, indeed, receive too much of it—which is to say that their marginal valuation of the benefit is negative. Too much artificial rain, for example, might damage the particular crops of certain farmers. One may, nevertheless, call it a collective good if the sum of the maximum amounts of those who, on balance, benefit from the unavoidable collective effect exceeds the minimum payments necessary to compensate those who, on balance, suffer losses.[5] As indicated, one has only to think of this rainfall as one of the incidental effects of some other deliberate activity (the felling of the trees of a forest, or regular airline flights) to place it within the category of spillover effects.

---

[4] There can, however, be a problem of congestion if the number of people increases relative to the number. or the size. of the facilities provided.

[5] Among those who *on balance* gain from the given artificial rainfall, there can be those farmers whose crops receive too much rain in the sense that the benefit to them of the marginal inch of rain is negative. The optimal condition. however. requires that rain be increased until the sum of the benefits and losses of the marginal inch of rain is equal to the cost of producing it.

Chapter 18

ON THE VALUATION OF SPILLOVERS

1 In principle, the method of valuing spillover effects for a cost-benefit analysis is straightforward. Any particular spillover effect associated with a given project is but one among any number of consequences affecting the welfare of different people in the community. We must consider, therefore, only the *difference* made to their welfare by the spillover effect in question. Any i^{th} person made better off on balance by the spillover effect would offer a maximum positive sum, V_i, rather than go without it. Any i^{th} person made worse off on balance would require some minimum sum V_i to induce him to put up with the spillover, such sum to be received being prefixed by a negative sign. These sums are known as compensating variations; for if paid by the former individual, or if received by the latter individual, his welfare will remain unchanged.

Assuming n persons are affected, if the condition $\sum_{i=1}^{n} V_i > 0$ is met— if, that is, the algebraic sum of the individual compensating variations is positive—we conclude that gainers can more than compensate losers, and the value of the excess gain over loss is the value to be attributed to the spillover effect in question. Wherever $\sum_{i=1}^{n} V_i < 0$, however, an excess of loss over gain is to be attributed to the spillover. There may well be cases where part, or all, of these compensatory variations are determined directly by reference to market prices. The cost of the extra laundry bills arising from industrial smoke is a popular example. Crop damage done by straying cattle is another. But, in the last resort, the value individually attributed to the spillover effect is subjective, and is to be conceived as the exact sum of money, to be paid or to be received, that restores a person's welfare to its original pre-spillover level.

In establishing a new project, any single associated spillover effect for which $\sum\limits_{i=1}^{n} V_i \neq 0$ has allocative significance, and must be considered in that project's evaluation. Wherever the type and size of the project is given to us by technology, the question of whether or not the project should be undertaken can be properly answered only by taking into account *all* the effects arising from the construction and operation of the project, all the costs and all the benefits and, therefore, all the spillover effects also. If, for example, building a dam for irrigational purposes has the following incidental consequences: (1) it creates an artificial lake in which people can swim or boat; (2) it spoils the fishing; (3) it provides a body of stagnant water which causes a rapid increase in the insect populations in the vicinity, the first is a positive spillover, the latter two are negative spillovers. Each is to be evaluated in the manner stated above, and added together algebraically to the excess benefits (positive or negative) of the project.

2   There will be occasions, however, when the economist is presented with a number of alternative projects that differ only in size of plant, and, therefore, in the volume of outputs produced. He then compares successively larger sizes of plant in order to discover the difference made to benefits and costs. Starting with some size of plant that yields excess benefits over costs, it should be obvious that so long as further increments of plant size confer more benefit than cost there is an advantage in increasing the plant size. And it goes without saying that the associated increments of spillover, positive or negative, should be added algebraically to the benefit side of the calculation. Some spillovers, however, may or may not vary with the size of the project. A small dam, for example, may destroy the fishing just as much as a large dam.

The size of these increments, in the limiting case, could be so small that for all practical purposes the changes in the plant size can be regarded as continuous. In this limiting case we are then in the familiar textbook world of continuous curves, comparing long-run marginal cost with long-run marginal benefit—except of course that for private goods each person's marginal benefit is coterminous with demand price, whereas for collective goods the marginal benefit is the aggregate of benefits conferred simultaneously on all persons by the marginal unit of the collective good.

It is not to be supposed for a moment, however, that cost-benefit analysis confines itself to evaluating collective goods. A railroad or hospital is not, strictly speaking, a collective good; the services produced by either can be separately allocated to each of a number of persons just as a loaf of bread can be allocated to a person for his own particular consumption. And for that matter, the construction of a bakery might warrant a cost-benefit analysis, with the initial size of the plant and, later on, the output to be produced, determined on the marginal cost pricing rule.

3 In the absence of all spillovers, the necessary rule requiring marginal valuation to the community to be equal to marginal cost of the good in question[1] is valid both for collective goods and single goods. For a single good, as distinct from a collective good, however, each person separately enjoys the amount of the good that he chooses: the consumption by person A of five loaves of bread a week is deemed to provide no satisfaction whatsoever to anyone else. Thus, as distinct from a collective good, the single good has to meet a stricter condition: namely, that the amounts chosen by each person are such that the marginal valuation of bread for each one of them is exactly the same.[2] This is not, in general, true of collective goods: the last foot of width to a bridge, or the last acre to a national park, being valued differently by different people. This stricter condition for single goods is met in perfectly competitive equilibrium since each person equates his own marginal valuation to the price of the good, which price is of course equal to marginal cost.[3]

---

[1] Although this marginal-cost rule rolls easily from the tongue, care must be exercised in its interpretation. Although each consumer equates his marginal valuation of a loaf to the market price of a loaf and, in perfect competition, therefore, to the marginal cost of a loaf, it does not follow that *each* of, say, n consumers has a marginal valuation equal to the marginal cost of producing loaves of bread. Supposing the marginal cost curve of producing loaves of bread to rise smoothly, the marginal *cost* is below the marginal valuation of each of the consumers save the nth (where any of the n consumers could be the nth consumer). For the remaining $n - 1$ consumers, the incremental unit cost of a loaf is, in varying degrees, below their marginal valuation of a loaf.

[2] If there is only one price for each single good on the market then the so-called exchange optimum condition is also met: further advantageous exchange of such goods as between persons is not possible.

[3] This is a necessary though not sufficient condition for optimal output in a partial setting. It is further required (1) that total conditions be met, i.e. that there be an excess of total benefit over total cost, and (2) that there be no other output which has a greater excess benefit over cost. (If these conditions are met, 'second order' conditions must also be met.)

This necessary rule, stated above, and valid both for collective and single goods, has to be modified in an obvious way, if, now, spillover effects accompany the production or consumption of the goods in question. Consider first a single good. If the bakery emits smoke which irritates people in the vicinity, and this irritating smoke varies directly with the number of loaves produced, smoke will be allocatively significant in determining the optimal output. The marginal valuation to society of the existing output of loaves is no longer just equal to the price that each and any of the n consumers is prepared to pay for his own marginal loaf of bread. For in order to meet the demand for any additional loaf the bakery must emit some additional smoke. From the value to society of an additional loaf one has therefore to subtract the sum of minimal compensatory payments, $\sum_{i=1}^{n} V_i$, which sum would be necessary to restore the welfare of the n smoke victims. Prior to any correction, the competitive equilibrium output would be one where the marginal valuation of loaves alone was equal to marginal cost, but where the marginal valuation of the joint loaf-and-smoke product was below its marginal cost. In order to meet the optimal condition for this joint product, the output has to be reduced below the competitive equilibrium (so raising the marginal valuation of loaves) until the marginal *social* valuation—that of the loaf and its associated spillovers—is positive, and equal to, marginal cost.[4] The alternative statement, that optimal output is determined at the point where the price of the good is set equal to its marginal *social* cost, is the result simply of transferring the calculated value of the associated spillovers to the other side of the equation. In this loaf example, instead of subtracting the calculated loss of the smoke damage from the value of the marginal

---

[4] In this calculation there is a tacit but plausible assumption: that the individual consumer of loaves is not himself aware of the connection between his own purchases of loaves and the smoke irritation he suffers in consequence of his own purchases. If this is granted, his resulting loss of welfare can be included with those of the remaining $n - 1$ consumers whose welfares decline with the purchase of his loaves. If, on the other hand, the spillover effect arises from his direct use of some good, say the noise from operating his lawn-mower, he can be assumed to subtract from his own satisfaction the value of any discomfort borne in operating the machine. In that case the uncosted spillovers, for which an adjustment has to be made, are those experienced by the remaining $n - 1$ people in the vicinity.

Where n is a large number, we lose little accuracy but much work by calculating the spillover effects for n people rather than for a different $(n - 1)$ set of people for each person's purchases.

loaf, the sum is added instead to the marginal cost of the loaf. Positive spillover effects, or, to be more precise, spillover effects that are on balance advantageous to society, are treated in the same manner, a positive sign for the compensatory sum substituting for the negative one above. Optimal output is therefore, in such cases, greater than competitive equilibrium output.

The same adjustment is required for collective goods. If some collective good, say a dam, has both positive and negative spillovers, say it provides boating but spoils the fishing, the net sums for all persons in the community are added algebraically, and the resulting total added algebraically to the marginal benefit of the collective good—or else subtracted, algebraically, from the marginal cost of the good.

4 A conscientious cost-benefit study, it is hardly necessary to remark, cannot ignore any spillover effect, positive or negative, that is of social concern. Although the value of some spillovers will be harder to estimate than others, the principle of evaluation indicated in this chapter may not be abandoned as a guide to the methods of calculation to be adopted. To adopt some other principle, such as deriving a value from the outcome of the political decision-making process, is to adopt a principle that is inconsistent with the Pareto criterion on which the estimates of the other, more measurable, items are based—on which, indeed, all allocative judgements are made in economics. A harsher judgement of this practice would regard it as tantamount to deception. For the economist is given his brief by a political authority in order to make an estimate according to independent *economic* principles; not in order to rationalize the political process. We shall have more to say about the tendency of economists to resort occasionally to this sort of subterfuge in a later chapter, on estimating the value to society of loss of life and limb, in Part VI.

Chapter 19

ENVIRONMENTAL SPILLOVERS

1 We now turn to a more detailed consideration of adverse environmental spillovers. The warrant for doing so does not derive simply from their rapid growth, especially in the postwar period, nor simply from their frequent neglect, but from the evaluative problems that arise whenever an adverse spillover effect has a *large* effect on the welfare of a number of people. If the judgement, that adverse environmental spillovers have become more important, since the war, than favourable spillovers, is questioned by the reader, he need not complain of bias. The analysis of favourable spillovers is quite symmetrical, and economy in exposition suggests that a thorough treatment of either type of spillover alone, favourable or unfavourable, will suffice to demonstrate the principles.

2 We have taken it for granted that spillovers have to be evaluated, ultimately, by reference to the subjective estimates of the victims of spillover effects. One can go further. One can argue for these compensatory sums being actually paid to the victims in the event of a project being introduced that generates adverse spillovers. Indeed, this view of the matter would seem to follow from the classical liberal doctrines as expounded by John Stuart Mill, in contradistinction to a Pareto economic decision based simply on the determination of a net balance of gain or loss, one in which the question of actual compensation is disregarded. *A fortiori,* the liberal doctrine would reject the 'social engineering' approach to the spillover problem, an approach that seeks to formulate 'tolerance levels' for society. True, the upper limit of the tolerable degree of, say, noise may be so chosen as to preclude ascertainable, physical damage or bodily hurt—given our present knowledge of the effects of noise on people and property. Yet noise below that limit can be highly irritating to a lot of people. If a man were subjected at regular intervals to the gentlest tap on the back of his head, his subsequent exasperation would hardly surprise us. Neither the fact that he emerged from the treatment without bruises, nor the affirmation that this head-tapping business was, in some mysterious way, an unavoidable by-product of the operation of modern industry and, indeed, could be counted on to promote exports, would assure us about its moral justification. And if the occasional, or frequent, bombarding of a man's ears with noise, as a consequence of other people's pursuit of pleasure or profit, can be said to differ from this imaginary case, it is only in our having over time become accustomed to it, and more obtuse as to the issues it raises. If the liberal economist rejects such social engineering norms as 'tolerance level', it is not merely because the choice of such a level for society is necessarily arbitrary, but because the adoption of such tolerance norms on behalf of all members of society runs counter to the doctrine that each man is deemed to be the best judge of his own interest, particularly in matters that affect him intimately.

3 It must be acknowledged however that economists have, as a rule, more eagerly defended this doctrine when man is regarded as a consumer of man-made goods than when he is regarded as a consumer of the goods provided by nature. The mere suggestion, say, that lace underwear should be withdrawn from production can be counted upon to provoke an outcry in the community, notwithstanding that lace underwear is not a requisite of the good life. Economists are usually well to the fore, though the issue be no more than that of offering the consumer a cheaper price for butter by removing import restrictions. Yet, when it comes to preventing avoidable suffering that accompanies the destruction of environmental amenity—something, it can be argued, that is a prerequisite of the good life—the response is all but perfunctory. The citizen can apparently be robbed of choice on those things—clean air, quiet, attractive surroundings—that critically affect his sense of well-being, without the public offering much resistance.[1] For far too long the public has been accepting the physical environment much as it has been accepting the weather; as a pheno-

---

[1] This was written in 1968. Since that time, much more prominence to environmental deterioration has been given by news media, and much more concern has been evinced by the public.

menon to which it can perhaps adapt but which, in itself, is outside the control of men.

Such an attitude, however, is not justifiable. Some framework of law is necessary if markets are to function in an orderly fashion, and if trade and enterprise are to flourish. But not all laws are equally effective in harmonizing the search for commercial gain with the welfare of society. The economist's interest in social welfare or, more simply, in extending the citizen's area of choice, can do more than offer suggestions to promote a smoother functioning of the existing economic mechanisms. At a time of rapid deterioration of the environment, he can suggest alterations in the legal framework itself as something that can make significant contributions to social welfare.

Already we have pointed out that the more significant environmental spillovers do not lend themselves easily to any method of internalization, and that, therefore, they can be very costly to avoid. If, in spite of this difficulty, some improvement is possible working within the existing system of laws, more yet can be done—it will be argued—by changing laws from being tolerant of spillovers to be intolerant of them. Before broaching this novel aspect of the problem, however, let us summarize three features of a popular doctrine still current among economists.[2]

4 (a) For any adverse spillover that varies with the output of a good x, the optimal output of x is uniquely determined. Given costless decision-making, this optimal output can be reached as well by levying an excise tax on good x as by offering an excise subsidy for reducing the output of x and as well by the manufacturer's being compelled to compensate the public for being associated, together with the spillover, with the optimal output as by the public's bribing the manufacturer to reduce output to optimal. One is supposed to conclude that the question of responsibility for the reduction of the spillover—the question of who compensates whom—in these cases of manifest conflict of interest has no bearing on the allocative problem of determining the optimal output. From such a conclusion it follows that differences in the ways by which this optimal output may be reached affect only the distribution of welfare in the community.

---

[2] Instrumental in initiating this doctrine was a rather long-winded paper by Coase (1960).

(b) Nor, apparently, can this question of who should compensate whom be settled by considerations of equity. If, for example, the smoke produced by a soap works can be said to damage the interests of the inhabitants living in the vicinity, so also can the required curtailment of the smoke-producing output (or the required installation of anti-smoke devices) be said to damage the interests of the manufacturers. The fact is simply that the interests of the two groups —the soap manufacturers (or beneficiaries from soap production) on the one hand and the victims of their smoke pollution on the other—are mutually opposed, and only a misuse of language can detract from the essential symmetry in respect of equity.[3]

(c) Finally, whatever the institutional framework, the party suffering from the spillovers in question has a clear interest in bribing the other party to reduce the initial (uncorrected) output in the direction of the optimal output. But recognition of the opportunity for mutual gain in moving to an optimal output leads to a consideration of the costs of negotiating an agreement between the two parties.

For instance, in the absence of such negotiating costs, the potential gain in reducing the output of x by successive units can be reckoned as the excess of the most the inhabitants will pay for the reduction of that particular unit of x less the minimum sum the manufacturer will accept for agreeing to the reduction. And if this potential gain is, say, $100, its division as between the two parties will depend upon their respective bargaining power.[4]

If, now, negotiating costs amount to $120, they will exceed the $100 of potential mutual gain. The contemplated reduction in the output of x is, therefore, no longer mutually advantageous. With this consideration in mind, an observed absence of negotiation to reduce the particular spillover is explained by the argument that the potential mutual gain in the movement towards an optimal output must be smaller than the costs of negotiating it. Since these negotiating costs

---

[3] This proposition gathers plausibility from habitual attention to the spillovers generated as between two firms or industries. The examples adduced by Coase (1960) are generally of this sort.

[4] The loss to the manufacturer from reducing the output of x by a unit is calculated as the profit forgone. Where, however, we are thinking in terms of the long-period supply curve of a competitive industry and ignore the costs of adjustment, the loss is calculated as that of a consumer surplus.

are real enough, involving as they do the use of scarce resources, they may be supposed frequently to swamp the (costless) mutual gains of a movement toward an optimum position.

By such reasoning some economists found themselves perilously close to an ultra-conservative doctrine that, in respect of spillovers at least, what is already in existence is best. And for the rest, one can do no more than await the advent of innovations, technical or institutional, that reduce the costs of preventive devices or the costs of negotiation and administration.[5]

5 This complacent, though fairly widespread, doctrine has been challenged in the literature on externalities.[6] But it has also to be challenged in the cost-benefit literature. It may be thought that whereas the externality literature is concerned primarily with optimal outputs, cost-benefit analysis addresses itself, in the main, to the question of the economic justification of a specific project taken as a whole (or the selection of several from a large number of technically feasible projects) and only in a secondary way to the question of optimal outputs of projects once they are established. But the arguments about optimal outputs summarized above, dealing as they do with compensatory payments, with equity and with negotiation costs—or transactions costs as they are more generally called—can just as well be extended to the issue of the acceptance or rejection of specific projects.

Having said this much to affirm the relevance of considerations (a), (b) and (c) to cost-benefit analysis, a brief word on each is appropriate before concluding the chapter.

(a) The alleged uniqueness of the optimal solution rests on the implied assumption of zero welfare effects. Once the assumption is

---

[5] Several minor propositions have appeared since 1960, all of them rather obvious.

(1) If, in response to an adverse spillover an optimal excise tax is imposed on the manufacturer's output, any subsequent mutual agreement reached between the spillover victims and the manufacturer will reduce output below optimal. See Turvey (1963).

(2) If the spillovers are 'overheads' (that is, unrelated to output) the firm responsible either closes down or continues to produce the same competitive output. See Davis & Whinston (1962), and Mishan (1965).

(3) Owing to the difficulties of calculating ideal excise taxes or subsidies for two firms inflicting spillovers on one another, especially in conditions of changing demand and supply, the merger solution is recommended. See Davis & Whinston (1967).

[6] The reader is referred to my papers of 1967 and 1971.

removed, as it has to be wherever the project in question has significant effects on welfare, optimality becomes ambiguous. This aspect of the problem is treated in some detail in Part IV.

(b) The freedom of one group to pursue its own interests or enjoyment, it is alleged, necessarily interferes with that of the other group once the externality situation is created. For example, the inhabitants of an area being polluted by the smoke emitted from a soap works suffer accordingly, but so also does the soap works (and its beneficiaries) if its operations are curtailed. The question, then, of which of the two parties should have the property rights in the airshed over the area—in effect, the question of which party has legally to compensate the other for forgoing some of the advantages it enjoyed before the externality appeared—may be settled by reference to the alternative distributional implications.

To be sure, distributional considerations ought properly to be taken into account in a social decision. But they are not the only considerations. Although such externality situations are indeed Pareto-symmetric, as described above, they are not, in general, symmetric with respect to ethical merit. In accordance with the classical liberal dictum, the freedom of a man to pursue his own interests has to be qualified in so far as it reduces the freedom or welfare of others. And the freedom of the soap manufacturer to spread smoke over the inhabitants of the area is not on all fours with the freedom of the inhabitants to continue to enjoy unpolluted air. For the mere action of the inhabitants in enjoying the unpolluted air does not *of itself* cause any damage to the soap works beneficiaries, whereas the action of the soap works, the emission of smoke, does *of itself* reduce the welfare of the inhabitants. The conflict, that is, is initiated directly by the action of the soap works: it is not initiated by the inhabitants breathing the unpolluted air. To take an extreme example, a conflict of interests between a householder A and a burglar B is indeed Pareto-symmetric and, of course, an optimal solution is possible. But the conflict of interests is clearly not ethically symmetric. The conflict is initiated by B's action and is manifestly culpable.

(c) The belief that the existence of negotiating costs, or transactions costs, militate in favour of the *status quo* is no longer tenable once we consider possible legal innovation, as we do in the following chapter.

134

Chapter 20

THE COSTS OF IMPLEMENTING POTENTIAL IMPROVEMENTS

1 Let us now turn to the costs of implementing potential Pareto improvements. Several ways of bringing about such movements are familiar to economists, and we concentrate first on those involving output reductions. If, on political grounds, they are all equally desirable, the choice of which to adopt can be decided by reference to cost alone.

(i) The tax-subsidy scheme[1] is perhaps, owing to the great work of Pigou (1946), the best-known method of inducing a firm or an industry to produce an optimal output. The difficulties of calculating the optimal excise tax, or subsidy, under conditions of changing tastes and techniques has been stressed recently.[2] Although the costs of calculating and administering the taxes are not likely to vary closely with the size of the expected revenues, they are likely to vary with the degree of accuracy aimed at. However, if the economist is not over-fastidious about realizing the exact optimal conditions, he will settle for a substantial improvement. It may not be troublesome to calculate an excise tax that reduces output to within 10 per cent or 20 per cent of the optimum, and it is certainly worth while since such a tax is likely to capture well over 90 per cent of the potential Pareto improvement. Indeed, if we assume the costs of calculating the required excise tax can be anticipated for any proportion of the potential Pareto improvement it makes possible, we can go on to formalize the conditions for an optimal degree of accuracy.

---

[1] Excise taxes are usually associated with adverse spillovers, and excise subsidies with favourable ones. But an excise subsidy could be used to curb outputs having adverse spillovers. Such a subsidy has, however, to be paid to the manufacturer for *reducing* his output below the profit maximizing output.

[2] For instance by Davis & Whinston (1967). Their model is confined to *reciprocal* spillovers as between two concerns and so appears to exaggerate the difficulties.

(ii) Government regulation of the volume of production—in so far as it is guided by optimality considerations—would seem to require more direct intervention than the collection of taxes. Since the same calculations have to be made of cost schedules, demand schedules, and spillover damage, government regulation is likely to cost more, and possibly to be more resented also, than the tax solution.

(iii) Direct prohibition of certain spillover effects can be justified in certain circumstances which we shall indicate shortly. Enforcement of such prohibitions are cheaper to implement than output-regulations or the levying of excises, but they are frowned upon as leading, generally, to non-optimal solutions.

2 (iv) Finally, potential Pareto improvements (whether those involving output reductions or those involving the installation of preventive devices or relocating industrial plant) can be negotiated by mutual bargaining between the producers and receivers of spillovers. This scheme deserves particular attention, since the case for non-intervention is sometimes defended on the argument that, if the costs of negotiating agreement between the parties are smaller than the maximum potential Pareto improvement, such negotiations will indeed take place. Thus, the fact that no such negotiations are initiated, it is held, can be accepted as *prima facie* evidence that the potential Pareto improvement is exceeded by the costs of negotiation and administration. In other words, if the total cost of the real resources involved in the necessary negotiations and administration is denoted by G, and the maximum potential Pareto improvement is denoted by ESB (Excess Social Benefit in the absence of all such negotiating and administration costs), the condition for negotiation to take place required that RSB, the *Residual* Social Benefit—defined as equal to (ESB—G)—be positive. Clearly, ESB can be positive while RSB is negative. But it is the RSB that measures the Pareto improvement (positive, or negative) in the wider sense that includes all the costs needed to implement the ESB. If it happens that, in moving to a new position, the RSB is negative then this *apparently* optimal situation (where ESB, alone, is positive) is in fact truly non-optimal; for it will not really be possible to make everyone better off by moving to this seeming optimal output once we include the G costs necessary to reach it.

These G costs—sometimes referred to as 'transaction costs'—can be broken down into sub-categories. Let G_1 stand for the costs of negotiating agreement between the parties having conflicting interests over adverse spillover effects. Let G_2 stand for the costs of administration and supervision that are necessary to *maintain* the mutually agreed solution. And let G_3 stand for the capital outlays, if any, required to implement the agreement in question.

The G_1 costs would appear to be the more significant of the three, and those more likely to vary with the law on legal liability—at least for the case of environmental spillovers suffered by the public at large. Under the existing L law these costs would include, for the public, (a) the costs associated with taking the initiative, plus the costs (b) of identifying the victims of the spillover effects in question, (c) of communicating with each of them, (d) of persuading enough of them to agree to the idea of making a joint offer to the spillover-generating industry, (e) of reaching agreement among themselves on the sums to be offered to that industry, and also on the contribution toward these sums to be made by each of them, and (f) the costs of negotiation with the industry.

Once the representatives of the public approach the industry, a favourable response will involve it in a parallel breakdown of expenses. Thus, there will be the costs (b′) of identifying the firms responsible, (c′) of communicating with each of them, (d′) of persuading the firms to consider accepting an offer from the public, (e′) of reaching agreement between the firms concerned about the sums acceptable for their cooperation, and also about the formula on which any agreed sum is to be shared among them, and (f′) of negotiation with the representatives of the public.

It would seem that such costs are much higher for the public than they are for the industry. For instance, the costs (b), (c), (d), and (e) for the public will increase rapidly with the numbers of spillover victims and with their dispersion over the affected area, whereas, for the industry, the costs (b′), (c′), (d′), and (e′) will not increase so rapidly with numbers. For the numbers are small (it may be only a single firm) in any case, and they tend to be concentrated within an area rather than dispersed over it. Moreover, reaching decisions on behalf of their stockholders is a routine matter for business executives.

3 This difference in the G_1 costs as between the public, on the one hand, and the spillover-generating industry on the other is, however, of incidental interest. The relevant question is whether these G_1 transactions costs are likely to be any lower if property rights in the environment are accorded to the members of society. If they are, the initiative has to be taken by the spillover-generating industry, and the sequence is reversed. The breakdown of the costs incurred by the industry in preparation for an approach to members of the public who are affected by the spillover is in the order (b'), (c'), (d') and (e'), and they now have reference to the industry's making an offer rather than to its accepting one. Once the public is approached by the industry, the public has to incur costs (b), (c), (d) and (e) before being ready to negotiate, this breakdown of costs now having reference to the acceptance of offers being made to them.

If we ignore the (a) costs—the costs of initiative—for the moment, it is hard to think of convincing reasons for expecting that any of these items should be markedly different when rights to environmental amenity are vested in the public at large, exception being made for item (d). The cost of persuading a large number of spillover victims to accept the idea of *making* a collective offer to the industry under the existing dispensation is sure to be much heavier than the cost of persuading them to accept the idea of *receiving* an offer from the industry under a constitution that ensures that the public receives full compensation for any reduction in environmental amenity. In contrast, for the (d') costs of persuading each firm under this new constitution to accept the idea of making a joint offer to the public is virtually nil, about the same as it is under the existing dispensation, for the firms' financial interests are to the fore in the minds of their business executives, and little persuasion is required to ensure receptivity to a scheme which may add to their profit, whatever be the existing law. If this argument is valid, the G_1 costs will be heavier with the existing legal framework than with one that guarantees compensation for any reduction of environmental amenity.

4   The question of initiative in (a) has been left to the last because of its crucial importance in determining the resultant allocation in the economy. If initiative were a productive service having a supply price, or at least a determinable cost, there could be no argument for intervention in the allocation thrown up by a competitive economy— so long as the existing law were accepted as a political datum. The mere fact that an economic rearrangement promising a potential Pareto improvement or, to use our notation, having a positive ESB, had not been negotiated could be regarded as *prima facie* evidence that the G costs were too high and, therefore, that the RSB would be negative. This notion of a supply price for initiative is, however, untenable, and the inference that, in the circumstance envisaged, the RSB must be negative is unwarranted.

In the first place, from the observation that an economic rearrangement having a positive ESB is not adopted, one cannot infer that the RSB is negative. For to infer, from the fact that mutual agreement has not been negotiated, that the RSB must be negative and in particular that the costs of initiative must be prohibitive, is invalid. Moreover, it is an inference that is not to be refuted by empirical evidence. Such inference precludes, that is, any independent evaluation of G costs, and in particular any independent enquiry into the costs of initiative. If such tautological statements are accepted, one is bound to support the *status quo*, and to argue that the absence of mutual agreement in the presence of schemes having a positive ESB indicates simply that the RSB must be negative. It is such reasoning that reinforces the reluctance of some economists to intervene in the competitive market solution.

The import of this way of thinking, which rationalizes the *status quo*, is to encourage complacency rather than to draw attention to methods whereby initiative might be made available at low cost by institutional changes. If, for example, a government agency were set up, empowered to investigate instances of public disamenity arising out of the activities of modern industry and its products, it might well discover a number of ways to lower all the other G_1 costs, from (b) to (f), to such an extent that, after allowance has been made for the costs of such an agency, optimal arrangements would be entered into which hitherto—in the absence of such an agency—would be quite impracticable.[3]

---

[3] Allowing that the idea of making an approach to the industry in question occurs to a private individual, or to a number of them, the risk of failure at any of the stages (b) to (f) grows with the numbers of the pollution victims and their dispersion. Apart from the sense of civic satisfaction, and the chance of gain from publicity, the benefit to the initiating party is no more than the difference between the maximum he (or they) will pay to reduce some of the spillover effects and the amount that he (or they) will actually pay, including a share of all the costs incurred in the hope of eventual agreement. This limited benefit, if positive, has to be set against the risk of irrecoverable loss of expenses plus the certain loss of time and effort until such time, if ever, as he (or they) succeed in setting up a representative organization which takes over subsequent risks and expenses.

In the presence of a constitutional guarantee of amenity rights, however, the necessary initiative would devolve upon the management of a firm or upon the executive body of an industry. Even if there were costs of initiative that could be identified, they would not be likely to add much to the routine costs of decision-making by these bodies. The risk of failure, which in any case would fall on the shareholders, would be smaller, since firms would not venture into a market without first having acquired reasonably reliable information about the extent of their legal liability for the spillovers that they generate.

Chapter 21

OPTIMAL METHODS OF CORRECTING SPILLOVERS

1 Prior to a discussion of the impact of the law on the costs of implementing potential Pareto improvements, let us look at several of the ways in which an existing competitive equilibrium output can be corrected for spillover effects. The exposition will be simplified by assuming, provisionally, that the welfare effects, or 'income' effects, on the public's spillover-valuation are zero. In terms of Figure III.1 below, this means that the cost of spillover curve EE_1 is uniquely determined. Thus in the absence of spillovers, the excess benefit curve BB_1 would determine the optimal output of x as that equal to OB_1, excess marginal benefit (or price *less* marginal cost) at B_1 being equal to zero.

There can be a number of ways, or combinations of ways, of dealing with spillovers. We illustrate three alternative methods.

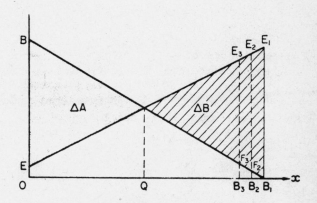

Figure III.1

141

2 *Method I.* If the only way of dealing with the spillover was to reduce the output of good x, we should want to reduce it to OQ, the optimal output. If the output were at OB_1, where it would be initially under the L law, the sum of the CVs (offered for eliminating the last, B_1^{th}, unit of noise) would be equal to B_1E_1, while the excess commercial[1] benefit over cost would, as mentioned, be zero. A social loss is, therefore, incurred in producing this final unit, since there is no commercial gain in its production while the noise-affected public is willing to spend up to B_1E_1 for its withdrawal. If the final unit is withdrawn, the measure of the improvement is the elimination of this loss, equal to the whole of B_1E_1. Further Pareto improvements are made by the eliminating of successive units up to the output OQ. Since further reductions of output would issue in potential losses—the collective CV gain of eliminating any additional unit of noise being exceeded by the loss of the excess commercial benefit, resulting from eliminating also the unit of $x - OQ$ is the optimal output. The measure of the Pareto improvement in reducing output from OB_1 to OQ is equal to the shaded triangular area, ΔB. If, instead, we had begun at zero output, the measure of the maximum pareto improvement in moving to output OQ is equal to the area of the dotted triangle ΔA. We shall find it useful to identify a triangular area such as ΔA with the *excess social benefit* (ESB) of producing the optimal amount of x as compared with an initial non-optimal output—in this instance with not producing any of it. This brief analysis follows the traditional approach which abstracts, implicitly or explicitly, from the impact of welfare effects on the spillover-valuation curve EE_1.

3 *Method II.* Rather than reduce output, one could concentrate wholly on preventive devices, such as anti-noise or anti-smoke devices. We shall suppose the effectiveness of these devices can be varied. For example, by spending an extra $\$1,000$, say, we can raise the effectiveness of noise-muffling on aircraft by the smallest discernible difference. The expenditure of this first $\$1,000$ does not reduce output[2] or, to

---

[1] The word *commercial* will be used as an adjective to describe calculations in which spillover effects are ignored.

[2] To be accurate, output remains unchanged if we ignore the extent to which, at least in perfectly competitive industry, such overhead expenditures on preventive technology raise long-period supply price and, therefore, reduce long-period equilibrium output.

continue with the aircraft example, the number of flights per week. It reduces the suffering of the victims directly. With a lower volume of noise created by each aircraft, the maximum sums that would be offered to eliminate each successive aircraft flight would, therefore, be somewhat smaller than the original amounts. We should therefore construct a new spillover-value curve, $E'E'_1$ in Figure III.1, that is below the original EE_1 curve. This is shown in Figure III.2, which is the same diagram as Figure III.1 except for having spillover-valuation curves below EE_1.

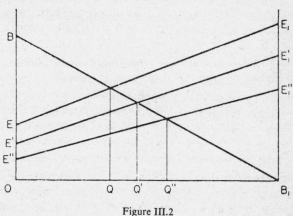

Figure III.2

The exact shape of the $E'E'_1$ curve is not at issue. If the \$1,000 were spent instead on wholly supressing the noise from a single plane, the nth plane, the new $E'E'_1$ curve would coincide with the old EE_1 curve except near B_1, where it would fall far below EE_1. If, as first assumed, the \$1,000 were spent on reducing the noise of all aircraft by a little, the $E'E'_1$ curve would, as drawn, lie everywhere below the EE_1 curve. The strip enclosed between these two curves, $EE_1E'_1E'$, would then represent the total value of the benefit experienced by the public from the spending of this \$1,000. Obviously this benefit must be worth more than \$1,000 if the introduction of this \$1,000 expenditure on noise-preventive devices is to be regarded as a Pareto improvement.

We can, of course, repeat this \$1,000 expenditure in order to secure the benefits of additional quiet, and draw the resulting curve $E'E''_1$ below the $E'E'_1$ curve. The additional benefits are represented by the area of the strip $E'E'_1E''_1E''$, and, again, can be justified only if they

143

exceed $1,000. Clearly, we can continue doing this until the value of the additional quiet is no greater than the additional $1,000 expenditure. In this way we maximize the Pareto improvement possible by means of this method alone while maintaining output at OB_1.

It should be clear, however, that if having gone as far as society can profitably[3] go in reducing noise directly by this second method, the resulting optimal output will have increased from OQ to some output greater than OQ, possibly greater than OQ'—the optimal output that corresponds to the expenditure of the second $1,000 on anti-noise devices. The more effective is this second method, the more can the original EE_1 curve be profitably lowered, and the closer to B_1 is the resulting optimal output.

4 *Method III* involves bribing the victims to move from an existing spillover locality. Under our provisional assumption of zero welfare effect, it makes no difference whether, under the L law, the victim discovers that it pays him to incur the costs of moving away from the airport zone or whether, under the $\overline{\text{L}}$ law, the airport authorities discover that it pays them to bribe him to move. Since the EE_1 curve is the vertical sum of the marginal loss curves for all noise-victims, the departure of any one of them reduces the width of the area OEE_1B_1 by a strip comparable with the $EE_1E'_1E'$ strip of Figure III.2. The resulting optimal output is then OQ'. As one after another depart, strip after strip is 'peeled off' the width of the original area OEE_1B_1, and the optimal output moves from OQ' to OQ'', and so on to OB_1. If all leave the vicinity, the spillover-valuation curve vanishes, and the resulting optimal output becomes OB_1.

Once more it should be apparent that unless the benefit from moving (the area of one of the strips) exceeds the cost of moving, there is no Pareto improvement in moving people from the locality. And, on the assumption that this is the only method of dealing with the spillover, the optimal number of emigrants from the area occurs when there is no person left in the vicinity whose migration would produce an excess benefit over the cost of moving, etc.[4]

---

[3] The word *profitable* in this context has reference to social gain, and is therefore a shorthand for Pareto-profitable.

[4] The reverse of this process, migration into the noisy vicinity, obviously reduces the optimal amount of activity. It may indeed occur to the reader that, if legal liability for

5 Now it need hardly be said that these three methods, among others that are possible, are all available at the same time—and not only singly, but in combination. We have therefore to pick out some optimal combination of them.

The diagram by which the 'optimal' pollution on the II method is commonly exhibited is that shown as Figure III.3. Along the horizontal axis, units of pollution are measured, and along the vertical axis is measured the marginal social value of the pollution damage and also the marginal opportunity cost of pollution abatement. Thus ON is the total pollution initially generated by the uncorrected OB_1 market output of X, and $OV'V$ is the marginal social damage curve. Up to OV' units, the pollution has no perceptible impact on people's welfare, after which successive increments of pollution entail increasing social loss (measured, say, by the maximum sum society is willing to pay to avoid that unit of pollution)—the Nth unit of pollution suffered being 'valued' at VN. Looking at the diagram instead from right to left, the $VV'O$ curve can be construed as the downward-sloping valuation or demand curve for pollution-reduction, and CC' as the upward-sloping marginal cost curve of pollution-reduction.

Figure III.3 clearly suggests that net social gain from reducing pollution is maximized by a reduction of NR pollution units, at which point the (falling) marginal gain from pollution reduction is equal to the (rising) marginal cost of pollution reduction. A tax of TN per unit of pollution would therefore be 'optimal' since—without knowledge of, or reference to, the VV' curve—the levying of such a tax will impel the industry to reduce pollution by NR. For up to the first NR units of pollution, it is cheaper to reduce pollution than pay the tax. After NR

---

4 (contd) spillovers were placed on the shoulders of the entrepreneur, there would be an incentive for people to migrate into the area.

But, like the case of introducing an optimal excise tax on output and *also* permitting subsequent mutual agreement between the opposing parties (which then reduces output *below* optimal), introducing legal liability for entrepreneurs, and *also* (after establishing a 'separate areas' situation, one in which there is a noisy area for industry and a quiet area for residential purposes) permitting people freely to migrate to the noisy area, reduces welfare below the optimum.

Given the establishment of separate areas—which, as has been shown in my 1967 paper, increases social welfare beyond that attainable by the optimal outcome within a single area—the maintenance of the right of any family to move into the industrial area *and claim adequate compensation* reduces social welfare. It makes the family no better off while raising the costs and reducing the outputs of goods in the industrial area.

units, the reverse is true. The 'optimal' pollution remaining is, there-fore, OR, and this is 'valued' at a sum that corresponds to the area of triangle $V'RW$.

Now by measuring along NO the distance in miles that the polluting X industry can be moved from the boundary of the inhabited area, we can interpret the CC' and VV' curves respectively as the marginal cost per mile of movement and the marginal social gain per mile of that movement arising from the associated reduction in pollution. We

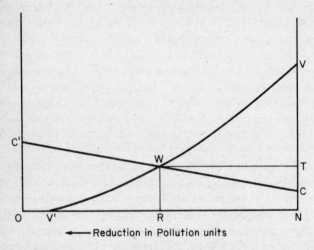

Figure III.3

should then conclude that NR is the 'optimal' distance to move the industry. However, since it will be convenient to represent this method III on the same axes as method II, we assume the possibility of a unique transformation of distance into units of pollution-reduction. Thus, in Figure III.4, the horizontal axis measures units of pollution, and the marginal cost curve for method III with respect to these units appears as $C_cC'_c$, which curve can now be directly compared with the marginal cost curve $C_bC'_b$ for method II which, like the marginal valuation curve VV', is the same as that in Figure III.3.

A similar marginal cost curve for method I can be shown as $C_aC'_a$ on the same diagram. This is, in effect, a marginal opportunity curve derived primarily from the forgoing of excess benefit (by reference to Excess Benefit curve BB_1 in Fig. III.1) as the output of the good X is reduced from OB_1 toward zero. Transforming reduced output of X into reduced pollution (simplified by assuming a fixed proportion between smoke and output) produces this required marginal cost curve of reducing pollution by method I with respect to polluting units.

In general the 'optimal' pollution levels when each one of the three methods is used alone will differ. In Figure III.4 they are OR_a, OR_b, and OR_c, respectively for methods I, II, and III. Their corresponding 'optimal' pollution taxes also differ. But if all three methods of reduc-

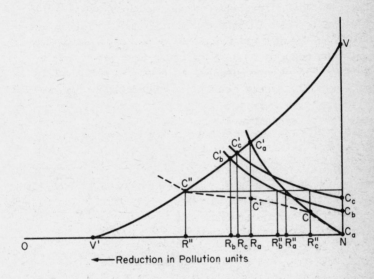

Figure III.4

ing pollution are to be simultaneously employed then economy requires that the amount reduced by each method is such that the marginal cost of each method is the same. This result follows from the idea of reducing the first, second, third, . . . n^{th} unit of pollution by whichever method is the cheapest for that unit, bearing in mind that eventually each of the methods is increasingly used. The succession of lowest incremental costs so derived forms a *composite* marginal cost curve, and the true optimal pollution-reduction is determined where this curve cuts the VV' curve at R''.

For simplicity of construction we assume the marginal cost curve of each of our three methods is independent of the costs, if any, incurred by the other two methods (an assumption that is unnecessary but facilitates the geometry). We can then construct the composite marginal cost curve for pollution reduction, $C_a C C' C''$, by 'horizontally adding together' the three separate marginal cost curves. From C_a to C on this composite curve, method I alone is used to reduce pollution. From C to C', some reduction is effected by both I and II methods. From C' onward, further reductions receive a contribution from each of the three methods.

The reader will at once observe that the composite optimal pollution that remains, $V'R''$, is smaller than the 'optimal' pollution determined by the employment of any one method alone. Consequently, the composite pollution tax $C''R''$ is also smaller than a pollution tax determined by reference to any single method of pollution reduction. Since the magnitude of the composite pollution tax is to be adopted by each of the three methods when they are used together, the pollution reduction contributed by each of the methods when they are used together is smaller than the 'optimal' pollution reduction effected by that method when it is used alone. Thus of the total pollution reduced jointly, NR'', methods I, II, and III are responsible respectively for amounts NR''_a, NR''_b, and NR''_c. Clearly each of these amounts is smaller than NR_a, NR_b, and NR_c, these being respectively the 'optimal' pollution reductions of methods I, II, and III, when each method is used alone.

Chapter 22

HORSE AND RABBIT STEW

1 As several conscientious economists have pointed out, the outcome of all too many cost-benefit studies follows that of the classic recipe for making horse and rabbit stew on a strictly fifty-fifty basis, one horse to one rabbit. No matter how carefully the scientific rabbit is chosen, the flavour of the resulting stew is sure to be swamped by the horseflesh. The horse, needless to say, represents those other considerations among which environmental spillover effects loom large. For all that, mention of environmental spillovers has until recently seldom taken up more space than a sentence or two in a footnote, or in the preamble to the expert's study which is, of course, the scientific rabbit, one having all the earmarks of professional competence.[1]

In our growth-fevered atmosphere there is always a strong temptation for the economist, as for other specialists, to come up with firm quantitative results. In order to be able to do so, however, he finds that he must ignore the less easily measured spillovers. In so far as the ignored spillover effects are adverse, this common response to the temptation imparts a bias toward favouring commercially viable projects, irrespective of their ability to withstand more searching criteria. As a matter of professional pride, and of obligation to the community he elects to serve, the economist should resist this temptation.

2 Yet, it may well be asked, until such time as more reliable methods are evolved to bring these spillovers into the calculus, what can the economist do? The least he can do is to reveal clearly the area of ignorance. After measuring all that can be measured with honesty, he

---

[1] This was written in 1968, at a time when economists were becoming more concerned to capture these spillovers. Volume VII of the *Commission for the Third London Airport* (the cost-benefit analysis put out by the Roskill Commission) was appreciative of the environmental damage a third airport would cause. But their quantitive methods fell short of the principles they adopted.

can provide a physical description of the spillovers and some idea of their significance. Secondly, he may offer a guess, or a range of guesses, of the value of damage to be expected. He will certainly want to avoid spurious quantification—spurious because based on invalid concepts.[2] Thirdly, and as a development of the preceding suggestion, he can have recourse to what I have called elsewhere (1969a) *contingency calculations*, these being the estimates of a critical magnitude for the spillovers which will just offset the excess benefits of a project that is calculated in disregard of the spillovers.

To illustrate, if the cost-benefit calculation of a new airport produces an excess benefit over cost of some $10 millions per annum for the next t years, but only by ignoring the aircraft noise it generates, the increased traffic congestion it causes, and the increased loss of life that is expected to follow, the economist can impress the authorities, and the public with the importance of these consequences by making hypothetical estimates of a critical *average* loss per person, or per family, based on rough calculations of the numbers of people likely to be affected. Thus (a), if it were reckoned that about half a million additional families would suffer in varying degrees as a result of the newly located airport, an annual compensatory sum averaging as little as $20 per family would wholly offset the excess benefit. Again (b), if the new airport becomes responsible for adding to the road congestion within the region of the airport, so as to cause an average delay of one hour a week to about one million motorists, this delay alone if valued at 20 cents an hour, would wholly offset the $10 million of excess benefits of the project. Similarly for loss of life, and any other remaining side effects.

Even though the estimate of the number of people affected is speculative, provided it is not altogether implausible, the resulting contingency calculations may well cast doubt as to the economic feasibility of the scheme—enough doubt, at least, to delay a decision until estimates of these less tangible, but socially important, features of the scheme can be made with greater assurance. On the other hand, there may be instances in which the per person, or per family, valuation of the spillover deriving from the contingency calculation will be so

---

[2] Worse, perhaps, than the attempts to measure the social cost of loss of life and limb by the present value of forgone earnings (which attempts are discussed in Chapter 45) is the attempt to measure noise or pollution costs by differences in property values (which is discussed in Chapters 47 and 48).

large as to place the economic infeasibility of the scheme beyond doubt.

3 Finally, there is nothing to prevent the economist from using the questionnaire method to secure information that is not thrown up, directly or indirectly, by the pricing system. True, economists have tended to scorn this source of data, and their scorn may be forgiven wherever more dependable information is to be had by observing what a man does rather than hearkening to what he says of himself. In particular, where behavioural relations are at issue, as they are in 'positive economics', there is everything to be said for this conservative practice: if the evidence does not suffice, we can always wait. But when it comes to evaluating spillover effects in a cost-benefit analysis, one cannot wait for more 'objective' information. Without some market mechanism by which people can express their attitudes to spillover effects, there may be no 'objective' way of measuring their costs. Indeed, the description of the nature of adverse environmental spillover effects, as unavoidable *collective* bads, itself suggests that the likelihood of a market mechanism being established for such effects is remote. Surveys based on the questionnaire method may be suspect for a number of reasons, but they are sometimes better than guesswork, and assuredly better than no information at all. The economist in earnest about making cost-benefit analysis a more discriminating technique will be giving plenty of thought to the measurement of environmental spillovers and, in consequence, plenty of thought also to the possibilities of evolving questionnaire techniques for eliciting critical information.[3]

REFERENCES AND BIBLIOGRAPHY FOR PART III

Baumol, W. J. 'On Taxation and the Control of Externalities', *American Economic Review*, 1972.
— 'External Economies and Second-Order Conditions', *American Economic Review*, 1964.
Bohm, Peter. *External Economies in Production*, Stockholm: Almquist & Wiksell, 1964.

[3] No matter how fastidious the recommendation of the economist it cannot, however, be depended upon to secure majority approval. By economic criteria, the economic policies adopted by majorities will generally be less than ideal. The sort of losses that can arise from existing political mechanisms have not been treated in these chapters. The reader interested in such problems should find stimulating reading in Buchanan's and Tullock's *Calculus of Consent* (1962).

Buchanan, J. M. 'An Economic Theory of Clubs', *Economica*, 1965.
— and Stubblebine, W. C. 'Externality', *Economica*, 1962.
— and Tullock, G. *The Calculus of Consent*, Michigan: University of Michigan Press, 1962.
Burrows, P. 'Nuisance: The Law and Economics', *Lloyd's Bank Review*, 1970.
— 'On External Cost and the Visible Arm of the Law', *Oxford Economic Papers*, 1970.
Coase, H. 'The Problems of Social Cost', *Journal of Law and Economics*, 1960.
Davis, O. A. and Whinston, A. B. 'Externality, Welfare and the Theory of Games', *Journal of Political Economy*, 1962.
— and Whinston, A. B. 'On the Distinction between Public and Private Goods', *American Economic Review*, 1967.
Devons, E. *Essays in Economics*, London: Allen & Unwin. 1961.
Dobb, M. *Welfare Economics and the Economics of Socialism*, Cambridge: Cambridge University Press, 1969.
Duesenberry, J. *Income, Saving and the Theory of Consumer Behaviour*, Cambridge, Mass.: Harvard University Press, 1949.
Eisner, R. and Strotz, R. H. 'Flight Insurance and the Theory of Choice', *Journal of Political Economy*, 1961.
Friedman, M. and Savage, L. J. 'Utility Analysis of Choices Involving Risks', *Journal of Political Economy*, 1948.
Graaff, J. de V. *Theoretical Welfare Economics*, Cambridge: Cambridge University Press, 1957.
Marglin, S. 'The Social Rate of Discount and the Optimal Rate of Investment', *Quarterly Journal of Economics*, 1963.
Margolis, J. 'A Comment on the Pure Theory of Public Expenditure', *Review of Economics and Statistics*, 1955.
Marshall, A. *Principles of Economics* (8th edn.), London: Macmillan, 1924.
McKean, R. *Efficiency in Government Through Systems Analysis with Emphasis on Water Resource Development*, New York: John Wiley & Sons, 1958.
Meade, J. E. 'External Economies and Diseconomies in a Competitive Situation', *Economic Journal*, 1962.
Mishan, E. J. 'A Reappraisal of the Principles of Resource Allocation', *Economica*, 1957.
— 'Rent as a Measure of Welfare Change', *American Economic Review*, 1959.
— 'Reflections on Recent Developments in the Concept of External Effects', *Canadian Journal of Economics and Political Science*, 1965.
— 'Pareto Optimality and the Law', *Oxford Economic Papers*, 1967.
— *Welfare Economics: An Assessment*, Amsterdam: North Holland Publishing Company, 1969(a).
— 'The Relationship between Joint Products, Collective Goods, and External Effects', *Journal of Political Economy*, 1969(b).
— 'The Postwar Literature on Externalities: An Interpretive Essay', *Journal of Economic Literature*, 1971.
— 'Choices Involving Risk: Simple Steps Toward an Ordinalist Analysis', *Economic Journal*, 1976.
Nath, S. K. *A Reappraisal of Welfare Economics*, London: Routledge & Kegan Paul, 1969.
Peskin, H. M. and Peskin, E. P. *Cost-Benefit Analysis and Water Pollution Policy*, Washington DC: Urban Institute, 1975.
Pigou, A. C. *Economics of Welfare* (4th edition), London: Macmillan, 1946.

REFERENCES

Ridker, R. G. *The Economic Costs of Air Pollution*, New York: F. A. Praeger, 1967.

Rothenberg, J. *The Measurement of Social Welfare*, New Jersey: Prentice Hall, 1961.

Samuelson, P. A. 'The Pure Theory of Public Expenditure', *Review of Economics and Statistics*, 1954.

— 'Aspects of Public Expenditure Theories', *Review of Economics and Statistics*, 1958.

Turvey, R. 'On Divergencies between Social Cost and Private Cost', *Economica*, 1963.

PART IV.   THE CHOICE OF A COST-BENEFIT CRITERION

Chapter 23

THE SOCIAL RATIONALE OF WELFARE ECONOMICS

1 Since cost-benefit is an application of the theory of resource allocation, itself a subject at the core of welfare economics, the rationale of such analysis, along with that of allocation theory, can be understood and vindicated only be reference to propositions at the centre of welfare economics. It is frequently alleged[1] that allocative recommendations that flow from welfare theorems are misleading, for without being explicit about them the economist makes recommendations that depend ultimately on his political predilections. It is argued, moreover, that even if his political predilections were shared by society, such recommendations would be unnecessary: the decisions on economic policy can, and should, be left to the political decision-making machinery. In particular, in a liberal democracy, in which the goals of economic policy are chosen by the people's elected representatives, the role of the economist is that of consultant only. His is the task of disclosing the implications of the policies being mooted and, perhaps, that also of suggesting alternative policies. By discharging these tasks, the economist enables the elected representatives to select policies having consequences that are consistent with one another, and that accord with the wishes of the majority of the electorate.

---

[1] Among others, by Graaff (1957), Nath (1969), Rothenburg (1961), and Tinbergen (1966).

One might add, in passing, that if this more restrictive role of the economist were accepted by the profession, and acted upon, the consequences would be more inhibitive than is generally recognized. For one thing, not only would cost-benefit analysis have to be rejected; other popular techniques, such as those used in traffic control and pricing, would also have to go. For another, economists would be hard put to justify their general approval of a competitive pricing solution. Thus, if the economists reject welfare economics, they may well have to reject also the economist's conventional presumption in favour of a competitive market.[2]

There can, moreover, be practical difficulties in the attempt to confine the economist to this more modest role of consultant, one whose task is only to reveal to decision-makers the implications of alternative economic policies. Allowing that the economist is both competent and honest, and produces a detailed list of all the 'economic' implications of each of the several policies under consideration, it is sure to baffle the ordinary politician. The economist can confidently anticipate a request that he, the economist, somehow 'organize' the raw data; that he provide some method by which the large variety of consequences expected from each policy be weighted in some way so as to enable the politician to compare the overall merits of the alternative policies. Such a request itself, however, places arbitrary powers in the hands of the so-called economic consultant—unless (which is more likely than not) he has recourse to the familiar propositions of resource allocation. We might well surmise that, in the absence of any other incentive, the need for politicians to assimilate an otherwise unmanageable mass of price-quantity data in order to reach decisions on economic policy would impel economists to formulate allocative propositions.

2   The uncomfortable consequences, or the practical difficulties, that would follow the repudiation of welfare economics do not of themselves, however, constitute a sufficient argument for its acceptance. It

---

[2] The economist could, of course, approve of the market for other than allocative reasons: for instance, on the grounds that it is a cheap and relatively non-political administrative institution for coordinating economic activity (where coordination implies no more than an absence of shortages or surpluses of goods at given prices). Such coordination is possible with a wide variety of patterns of price-cost relationships.

must be able to offer more positive merits. These emerge from a brief examination of the arrangement alternative to a market economy—that of making economic decisions entirely through the political process.

Decision-making through the political process, especially in a liberal democracy, is time-consuming. Even if the democratic process, alone and unaided, were somehow able to offer to each person the same opportunities and the same combination of goods that he already receives through the market, economists would have no difficulty in convincing people that the substitution of voting mechanisms for the pricing mechanism would take up an unconscionable amount of time and effort. And yet, prodigal though it would be in the use of time and effort, it is hardly conceivable that the political process will bring about an allocation of goods and resources as satisfactory as that brought about through the market. Whatever the outcome of the political process, it is highly unlikely then that such an outcome could not be materially improved by introducing pricing mechanisms. And, if some improvements can be effected by the introduction of such pricing mechanisms, they can also be effected by simple allocation rules which 'stimulate' the workings of the price mechanisms.

Nevertheless, allocation theory does not derive its justification from its being able to simulate the competitive market solutions—though this, no doubt, would suffice to commend it to many people. The reverse is rather the case: competitive markets are to be justified by reference to the propositions of welfare economics. And if so, it becomes necessary to understand the social basis of welfare economics; in particular, the nature of an allocative improvement. The attempt to do this begins with a consideration of value judgements.

Economists are not alone in being unimpressed by the workaday wisdom of majority rule in modern societies. Notwithstanding conventional safeguards, a majority in power is capable of irresponsible and even tyrannical behaviour towards individuals and minorities. There can be no reasonable expectation, in particular where legislation is influenced by party doctrine, that majority decisions will always respect minority interests, or even views that are widely held in society.

The consequences of these deficiencies in the working of democracy can be limited by decentralized institutions, and by constitutional restrictions that rest upon a broad consensus. The existence of either, that is, depends on near-unanimous acceptance of a number of ethical premises. Ideally such ethical premises could be formulated by the members of society only if none of them had any idea beforehand of the circumstances into which he was to be born. Though this is impossible, a sufficient degree of detachment might be realized in existing societies to ensure near-unanimous agreement on a number of provisions to be writ into a constitution.

In addition there may be a number of ethical propositions which, though they appear to command widespread assent, are not written into a constitution. Either the society has no written constitution or, if there is one, such ethical propositions appear to be too obvious to warrant mention. They can then be said to form part of a virtual constitution. And if, among these ethical propositions that comprise a virtual constitution, there are several on which a welfare economics can be raised then—provided always that the logical structure is flawless—its guiding rules can truthfully claim to rest on a widely accepted ethical base. Such rules, on any ethical ranking, would therefore transcend economic decisions reached by political processes, democratic or otherwise, even when they are neither ephemeral, opportunistic, or foolish. For decisions reached by the political process will almost always rest on a narrow basis of consent.

One might add, in passing, that even without the explicit concept of a virtual constitution, a theory of welfare economics might be developed from the democratic process. If the latter operates not as a majority-rule decision mechanism—justified on the cynical view that in the last resort it is better to count heads than to break them—but rather as a method of reaching agreement through informed debate, then indeed the principles by which broad categories of decisions are reached become relevant. For if consensus is reached through informed debate on certain sorts of issues, the existence of a common context of aspirations must be presumed. There is then likely to emerge a search for consistency in decision-taking on such issues, one that will tend to promote a common set of criteria. One such range of issues would comprehend certain kinds of economic problems, and the criteria sought for would be of an allocative nature. The incentive for discovering such criteria is, of course, economic. Once formulated, the implications of certain kinds of economic measures need not be debated at great length: they can be judged directly by reference to these allocative or 'welfare' criteria which, over time, will acquire a sort of constitutional status. In such an idealized democracy then, one might hope that time and intelligence would throw up those welfare propositions by which economists today seek to justify their prescriptive statements.

3   Now this notion of the welfare economist's ultimate appeal to a virtual constitution throws a clear light on the scope of welfare economics. For there appears, at first, to be only two propositions that would qualify for inclusion in such a constitution: (a) a Pareto improvement, and (b) a distributional improvement. A Pareto improvement takes place if some economic rearrangement makes one or more people better off without making anyone worse off. A distributional improvement takes place if there is near-unanimity that the distribution resulting from the economic rearrangement is an improvement.

This may seem modest enough in all conscience, but a little thought on the matter will reveal that neither proposition can be regarded as unambiguous until the economist has made a choice between the alternatives of grounding his welfare economics in utility or in ethics. If he chooses the former, the utility base, then every effect on the individual's utility is to count. If he chooses the latter, the ethical base, only those effects sanctioned by the constitution as valid are to be admitted into the economic calculus.

Adoption of the utility base may be defended on the ground that if, for any reason, we ignore one or more individuals' reactions to an economic change, the apparent 'Pareto improvement' which results may not, in fact, be a true Pareto improvement when such reactions are taken into account, or vice versa. In favour of the ethical base it can be argued that, if the concept of a Pareto improvement rests on an ethical consensus, this same ethical consensus may properly reject its validity unless it is restricted so as not to contravene other ethical judgements. Thus, notwithstanding that all members of society agree that an individual is the best judge of his own welfare, society may not wish to admit a Pareto improvement by reference to utility alone which otherwise affronts in any particular the moral sense of society.

The conflict between the utility and the ethical base of welfare economics can be observed most clearly in the generation of external, or spillover, effects, broadly defined. Outside the pricing mechanism, a person's welfare can be affected in an almost unlimited number of ways[3] by the actions of others. The ethical approach would admit as agenda only certain sorts of spillover effects. Among those to be excluded would be those external diseconomies sometimes referred to as interdependent utilities which, in more ordinary language, amount to the envy of any favourable chance in the fortunes of others.[4] External diseconomies which take the form of a loss of an individual's welfare from the mere knowledge of events that have no palpable impact on his circumstances might also be excluded. Such individual reactions are understandable, but they do not evoke social approval or encouragement. Unlike, say, environmental spillovers, they are not of a tangible nature, and need have no bearing on a person's style of living. If, for example, a person dislikes Welshmen, his resentment of the fact that a Welshman dwells within the vicinity of his home is not likely to be accepted in such a constitution as grounds for compensation—much less any displeasure he suffers from the mere knowledge that Welshmen dwell somewhere within the same region, or county, with small likelihood of his ever meeting any.[5] Nor for that matter

---

[3] Although a great number of such spillover effects are 'trivial' in the sense that the minimal costs of attending to them exceed any potential mutual benefit.

[4] If the 'interdependence' was positive, so that the person rejoices in the good fortune of others, society can approve, though without specifying that such responses enter the economic calculus.

[5] Such constitutional provisions do *not*, however, appear to argue against political activity motivated by considerations of race, colour, culture, religion, or nationality. The principle of nationalism, or of self-determination, or of racial homogeneity, derives its strength from the deep satisfaction of peoples in having a homeland among their own 'kith and kin', from pride in long traditions, from an abiding affection for their own institutions, customs, characteristics, attitudes, and ways of life; and, therefore also from a not irrational reluctance to suffer a risk of destruction, or possibly of dilution, of this social heritage, by having to share a common territory with a large number of people of altogether different origins and traditions.

Only fanatical addiction to a contrary ideal would unhesitatingly condemn those among a group, or race, or nation, who desire ardently to maintain their sense of continuity with the past, and who have no wish to alter their present ethnic mixture. Such aspirations, it can be argued, have no more to do with 'xenophobia', or 'chauvinism' than a strong preference for one's own home and family. They presuppose neither inhospitality to aliens, nor disrespect for the achievement of others. At the worst such aspirations are rooted in man's inner loneliness, insecurity perhaps, which translates itself into a desire for 'identification', and a need to belong.

Moreover, in a world where differences in national character, differences in race, class, dialect, culture, are being ironed out by rapid technological developments in transportation and in communication media, there is surely a particular case for viewing any counteracting movements to maintain differences, and to preserve some remnants of social variety in an increasingly anonymous universe, with more sympathy than is currently popular.

would such a constitution acknowledge the claims of a regular drinker that his enjoyment of life was somhow being reduced by the abstention of his companions, or the claims of a smoker who insisted the presence of non-smokers was offensive to him.

A virtual constitution, then, has also to determine the broad nature of the spillover effects that are to count as a matter of course in any economic calculus: expressed in more pedestrian discourse, what is to count and what is not, has to be decided by reference to what men of good will regard as reasonable.

There are, of course, borderline difficulties to be invoked on this as on every other issue under the sun. But in existing Western societies I do not imagine there will be much difficulty in deciding what sort of spillovers are to be included in the economic calculus and what sort are not to be included. Certainly environmental spillover effects would qualify for inclusion, and equally certainly 'psychic' spillover effects, such as envy, would be excluded. The reader may be able to amuse himself by thinking up some uncertain instances, but whether he manages to think of a few or many, the fact remains that if, instead, we base our welfare economics purely on utility, it will run into ethical objections and lose credibility.

4   Having opted for the ethical base, let us return to this question of the scope of welfare economics. It should be manifest at once that not all economic issues can resolve themselves into a Pareto and a distributional change. Some economic issues will raise other questions, such as that of striking a balance between a high level of employment and a high level of price stability, or that of choosing from a variety of time paths by which the economy can reach some predetermined level of output, or that posed by Adam Smith between defence and opulence. Each of these problems presents a variety of alternative choices, none of which stands out on any widely accepted body of principles as superior to the others. For instance, price stability alone, or high employment alone, is each accepted as a good thing. Near unanimity might be secured for the proposition that the more there is of each the better for society. Yet it is unlikely that any provision of the constitution, actual or virtual, will afford guidance where the chosen combination of these social goods involves quantitative adjustments as between opposing incommensurables—where the more of one social good, that is, can be enjoyed only at some sacrifice of a different sort of good;

where, for example, some increase in the stability of prices, which is an advantage to all, can be secured only at the expense of reducing the likelihood of everyone achieving gainful employment. It follows that there will be many issues in the formulation of economic policy which cannot call for guidance on a welfare economics that raises itself only on those ethical premises sanctioned by the virtual constitution.

5   To conclude, inasmuch as current allocation economics derives its rationale from welfare economics, the socially relevant part of that subject can have no affinity with the species of sophisticated games which economists can play with any ranking device that catches their fancy. As the term suggests, welfare economics is to be regarded as a study of the contribution economics can make to advancing the social welfare. As such it seeks general and conditional theorems, from which cost-benefit analysis and familiar optimizing techniques can be derived, all of them purporting to be independent of the current state of politics inasmuch as they take their sanction, ultimately, from the virtual constitution of the society for which they are intended.

However, since the relevant ethical premises are few—indeed, apart from those invoked to determine which effects are to count, only two would seem to qualify—it should be clear that while some issues of economic policy are fit subjects for welfare economics, it has little to contribute to other issues.

Chapter 24

THE ETHICAL LIMITATIONS OF A COST-BENEFIT ANALYSIS

1   The welfare economics that is to be raised on the ethical provisions of a virtual constitution ensure only a *partial* ordering of conceivable economic arrangements. In other words, if each conceivable economic arrangement is identified by a distinct collection of goods and a distinct distribution of it among the members of society, only some can be ranked as unambiguously better than others by a consistent dual welfare criterion, one comprising both the Pareto and the distribution improvement. Since these two provisions, each based on a social value judgement, are incommensurable, the welfare criterion is met only if neither provision is negated, and at least one is met. Such a criterion poses a number of problems which we need not stop to consider here,[1] for the simple reason that pure allocation theory and, therefore, cost-benefit analysis which is an application of this theory, is linked with but a single provision of the virtual constitution, a Pareto improvement. I say *linked with*, and not raised upon, simply because allocation theory is not raised on the actual Pareto-improvement provision, but rather on a 'diluted' version of it; what may be called a *potential* Pareto improvement. This can be defined as an economic rearrangement in which the gains *can* be so distributed as to make everyone in the community better off. So defined, the potential Pareto improvement will be recognized by some as a restatement of the familiar welfare test—that gainers be able to more than compensate losers—associated with the names of Kaldor (1939), Scitovsky (1941) and others, though in fact going back to Pigou (1932).

---

[1] The reader who would like to pursue the elusive issues connected with welfare criteria is referred to my 1965 paper. The insensitivity issue, however, is discussed briefly in the Note at the end of this chapter.

2   Granted that a cost-benefit analysis seeks to establish the presumption of a potential Pareto improvement, one must pass from the general concept to specific ways of estimating benefits and costs. The transition can be made by following the convention of the market economy, which regards people both as producers and consumers of goods. If *qua* producers, men are no worse off in consequence of some contemplated economic change, but are better off *qua* consumers then, on the whole, they are better off and a Pareto improvement is achieved. If they are all no worse off *qua* consumers, but better off *qua* producers, a Pareto improvement is also achieved. Similarly, if men are better off *qua* consumers and producers, there is a Pareto improvement.[2] Moreover, the value of goods and 'bads' to men, either as consumers or producers (factor-owners), is not worked out from scratch. Market prices can be deemed to provide these values in the first instance, following which they can be corrected for 'market failure'.

Except for marginal changes, in which case cost-benefit analysis is of little value, the notion of a surplus, or economic rent, is applicable. For measurement purposes this is customarily divided into consumers' surplus for changes in goods opportunities and rents for changes in factor opportunities. A common practice, however, is to accept factor costs as given, but to substitute some measure of consumers' surplus for changes in product prices.

This asymmetrical treatment is not wholly unwarranted in an economy in which factor groupings are few, but in which product groupings are many. A project that increases the output of a product or service may result in a large change in its price without appreciable effects on the relevant factor prices. The larger the change in that price, the more important it is to measure the gain, or loss, by consumers' surplus. Nonetheless, while there is some justification for paying more attention to consumer gains and losses than to the gains and losses of factor-owners, we have occasionally emphasized the importance of valuing factors at their opportunity costs in situations where they may differ markedly from their market prices.

Although it is seldom made explicit, the reader will do well to bear

---

[2] A person is no worse off *qua* consumer if product prices do not rise against him, and better off if, on the whole, they fall. A person is no worse off, or better off, *qua* producer, if, respectively, factor prices do not fall or, on the whole, rise in his favour.

in mind that all calculations that enter into a cost-benefit analysis, when reduced to a single point of time by acceptable methods, are to be interpreted as contributions, positive or negative, to the magnitude of some resulting potential Pareto improvement. What is to be concluded, then, from a cost-benefit analysis showing, say, an excess gain of $100,000 is *not* that everyone concerned *is* made better off in varying degrees; only that it is conceptually possible, by *costless* redistributions, to make everyone better off, in total by an amount equal to $100,000. And since economists have, from time to time, vented their dissatisfaction with the notion of a potential Pareto improvement as a criterion and measure of social gain, we can hardly employ cost-benefit techniques with a clear conscience without examining some of the criticisms to which the concept has been subjected.

3   First, the potential Pareto improvement test clearly ignores the resulting change in the distribution of incomes. Not only is it true that not everyone is made better off, it is also quite possible that those in the community who are made worse off are to be found largely among the lower-income groups. A change which makes the rich better off by $250,000 at the expense of the poor, who are made worse off by $150,000, still produces an excess gain of $100,000 for the community as a whole. As such, however, it is not likely to be accepted by all as an unexceptionable economic change—at least, not unless it is to be accompanied by redistributive measures which will make the poor no worse off than before, and possibly better off. A cost-benefit calculation may, indeed, be accompanied by observations on the resulting distribution, and even by recommendations in this respect. But the quantitative outcome of a cost-benefit calculation itself carries no distributional significance. It shows that the total of gains exceeds the total of losses, no more.

Moreover, the appeal of such a test is diminished by its hypothetical nature. A Pareto improvement which positively requires that when some are made better off, no one is made worse off, is assured of fairly wide acceptance. It does some good to some, and apparently does no harm to others. A *potential* Pareto improvement, which is consistent with a great many people actually being made worse off, has much less appeal. One factor, however, does make it easier to countenance. The spread over the last century of increasing wealth, and increasing electoral power, has made for egalitarian tendencies. The more progressive is the tax structure, and the more intensive is competition, the greater is the likelihood that a potential Pareto improvement will result in an actual Pareto improvement, or something close to it. In the limiting case of a system of taxes and subsidies designed to maintain complete equality of incomes, every potential Pareto improvement (allowing for sufficient divisibilities) is transformed into an actual Pareto improvement: via redistributive transfers, that is, everybody in fact becomes better off.

In the existing world, however, where projects can have distributionally regressive effects, the economist can, as indicated above, say something about the distribution resulting from the introduction of an otherwise feasible project. If the economist has reason to believe that it will be unambiguously regressive, his duty is to mention it. It may, in some cases, be practicable to combine the project with a distributional scheme. More often than not, the distributional effects on society as a whole are not large. Provided no spillover effects are involved, the *direct* local effects of a number of familiar sorts of project are apt to be progressive. One thinks in this connection of flood-control, electricity generation, irrigation, and the like. Once spillover effects are entered, however, the net impact on the local inhabitants can be distinctly regressive. The spillover effects of through-traffic highways, and of flyovers, constructed through working class neighbourhoods, provide familiar examples.

In order then for a mooted enterprise to be socially approved, it is not enough that the outcome of an ideal cost-benefit analysis be positive. It must be shown, among other things, that the resulting distributional changes are not perceptibly regressive and that no gross inequities are perpetrated.

NOTE TO CHAPTER 24

As a result of the connection between relative prices and the distribution of the collection of goods, it is possible that a movement from one collection of goods, Q_1 to another Q_2, which realizes a potential Pareto improvement, is compatible with the reverse movement, one from Q_2 to Q_1, *also* realizing a potential Pareto improvement.[1]

---

[1] This was first demonstrated, using the box diagram technique (involving two goods and two persons) by Scitovsky (1941), though the possibility of this 'paradox' was mentioned earlier, by Pigou (1932).

To illustrate, let I_1 in Figure IV.1 be the community indifference curve passing through the initial collection of goods Q_1 comprising Y_1 of good Y and X_1 of good X. This collection of goods can be thought of as being divided between two persons (or two groups of persons), A and B, in a manner indicated by point d_1 on the contract curve from O to Q_1 of the box diagram, $OY_1Q_1X_1$. The tangency of d_1 between A's indifference curve I_A and B's indifference curve I_B is, by construction, parallel to the tangency of the community curve I_1 at Q_1.[2] Since the alternative collection Q_2 is above the I_1 community indifference curve, it is possible to improve the welfare of everyone by moving to the Q_2 position (allowing, always, for sufficient divisibility). It is possible, that is, to make both A and B better off in the Q_2 than in the Q_1 position.

However, *having moved* to Q_2 on this recommendation,[3] the result-

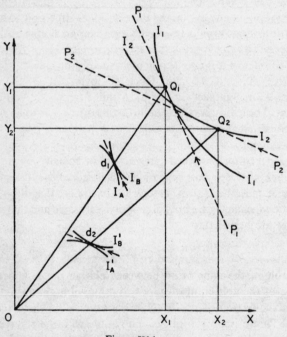

Figure IV.1

[2] A simple geometric technique for the construction of community indifference curves (that meet the optimal exchange condition) has been explained in my 1957 paper.
[3] Though *without* intervening in the resulting distribution so as, by transfer payments, actually to make both A and B better off.

ing distribution of this Q_2 collection might be one such as is represented by point d_2 on the OQ_2 contract curve of the box diagram $OY_2Q_2X_2$, A's welfare (greater than it was in the Q_1 position) being represented by A's I_A' indifference curve, and B's welfare (less than it was in the Q_1 position) being represented by B's I_B' indifference curve. Again, the slope of the mutual tangency of I_A' and I_B' is, by construction, parallel with the tangent of the community indifference curve I_2 passing through Q_2. With this distribution resulting from the movement from Q_1 to Q_2, the slope at Q_2 is such that the I_2 curve passes below Q_1. And from this we infer that a movement from Q_2 to Q_1 realizes a potential Pareto improvement: beginning with the d_2 distribution of Q_2, that is, a movement to Q_1 can make both A and B better off. [4]

The same apparent paradox results if, instead of community indifference curves, we make use of the relative prices arising from the respective distributions of the two collections of goods. The relative prices for Q_1 is represented by the slope of the line P_1P_1 tangent to the I_1 curve at Q_1, and at these relative prices it is clear that Q_2, being to the right of this price-line, is valued more highly than the Q_1 collection of goods. Once the community has moved to Q_2, however, the resulting relative prices are represented by the line P_2P_2 tangent to the I_2 curve at Q_2. At these relative prices it is equally clear that Q_1 being above the P_2P_2 line passing through Q_2, is valued more highly than the Q_2 collection of goods.

This apparent paradox is obviously a disconcerting theoretical possibility. It has to be taken seriously in attempts to prove some general propositions, for instance that some international trade is better for a country than no international trade. The possibility of such a reversal actually occurring in the real world, where there are a large number of goods and people, is much smaller, however, than the impression conveyed by a two-good two-person diagram. Moreover, no matter how likely we rate the possibility, it diminishes as the focus of our analysis narrows, and the effects both of distributional changes

---

[4] If, instead, we constructed Figure IV.1 so that I_1 passed *above* Q_2 and I_2 passed *above* Q_1, the reverse paradox is illustrated: that Q_2 is potentially Pareto inferior to Q_1, and also that Q_1 is potentially Pareto inferior to Q_2. However, this sort of paradox can be resolved by showing that for all such cases there is a unique hypothetical collection of goods, two distributions of which correspond respectively to the welfare combinations associated with Q_1 and Q_2 (See my 1973 *Econ. Journal* paper).

on relative product prices and of compositional changes on relative factor prices, become smaller. Nearly all cost-benefit calculations can be regarded as exercises in very partial analysis. Thus, all prices, outside those pertaining to the project, may be reasonably assumed constant.

Chapter 25
ECONOMIC MEASURES OF EXACT COMPENSATION

1 In discussing the alleged uniqueness of an optimal output in the presence of spillovers, economists have recently made explicit the assumption that, in estimating the potential mutual gain in costlessly moving to an optimal output, the so-called income effects—or 'welfare effects' as it is more accurate to call them—are to be ignored. The impression conveyed is that any impact these welfare effects have on the magnitude of compensatory payments, or on the resulting measure of the potential gain in moving to an optimal output, is best ignored: taking them into account would, apparently, clutter up the analysis without adding to it anything of practical value.

2 We now remove the assumption of zero welfare effects in order to consider those spillovers in which substantial changes in people's welfare are involved—important enough, at any rate, to make the question of whether a Pareto improvement is possible or not dependent directly upon the law's favouring one party's interest as against that of the other. In evaluating those projects having significant environmental spillovers, these welfare effects cannot be neglected.

There can be any number of ways of measuring exact compensation, but in all familiar circumstances only two of them need concern us. Their treatment is simplified by assuming that all welfare effects are positive, or 'normal',[1] which is to say, that a rise in a person's welfare raises the amount demanded of a good. This proposition in turn implies that the maximum sum he will pay for a given amount of it—or

---

[1] Although 'normal' welfare effects are plausible for the major spillovers suffered by the public, the significance of the analysis, or, indeed, of the general conclusions reached in the following chapters, do not in the least depend upon this particular assumption.

alternatively the minimum sum he will accept to forgo some amount of it—rises with an increase in his welfare.

In Chapter 18, on the valuation of spillovers, we used the term V_i to indicate the ith individual's compensatory payment, positive or negative—respectively a payment *from* the individual and a payment *to* him—and then *defined* it to coincide with the compensating variation (CV), a concept that has to be distinguished from the other exact measure, the equivalent variation (EV). The CV will now be defined, more generally as a measure of the money transfer necessary, following some economic change, to maintain the individual's welfare at its *original* level. If the price of one or more of the goods he buys rises, or if the price of the service he sells falls, or if the air he breathes becomes more contaminated, his welfare falls, and some minimum payment to him is necessary to restore his welfare to its original level. *Per contra*, if one or several of the goods that he buys falls in price, or if the price of his labour rises, or if a by-pass is constructed that reduces the flow of traffic past his private residence, his welfare is increased. It is then restored to its original level by exacting from him some maximum sum of money.

The EV, on the other hand, is defined more generally as a measure of the money transfer which, *in the absence of* the contemplated change, affords the individual an exactly equivalent change in his welfare. If, therefore, the price of a good he buys rises, or the price of his labour falls, or his environment becomes noisier, his welfare declines. But in the absence of any of these adverse circumstances, his welfare could be made to decline to an equivalent extent by exacting from him a sum of money. *Per contra*, if one or more of the goods he buys falls in price, or the price of his labour rises, or the airport near his home is abandoned, his welfare, we assume, rises. But in the absence of any one of these favourable events, his welfare can be raised to the equivalent level by paying him a certain sum of money.

3 In the remainder of this chapter, and also in the following chapter, we shall spell out the relationships between CV and EV in considering both the change from one economic position, say I, to another economic position, say II, and the reverse change from II to I, in preparation for Chapter 26, where the implications of alternative cost-benefit criteria are compared.

Although a glance through the formalized literature on the subject tends to give the impression of subtlety and elusiveness, the relationships between CV and EV are, in reality, strikingly obvious. All that is required of the reader is care in identifying the symmetries when applying the CV and EV definitions to the two sorts of change being considered, from I to II and from II to I. In fact, the study of these relationships is a prime example of those many cases in economics in which the reader is able to grasp the essential logic of the resulting propositions far more easily if he works through the exercises himself, using simple examples, than if he reads another person's formalized account of them. For this reason, rather than formalize the relationships, I shall invent numbers for a few simple examples for the brief contemplation of the reader, who will thereby easily perceive the essential logic involved.

Throughout this and the following chapter we shall, unless otherwise stated, assume that the relevant welfare effects are all positive, which is to say that according as each person's welfare rises, his valuation of the good in question increases. In so far as we are concerned primarily with environmental goods, this assumption is highly plausible. It has the necessary implication that the most a person will pay for a good is less than the least sum he would accept to forgo it. For in determining the sum v_0, the most he will pay for the good, he has regard to w_0, his current level of welfare. Thus if he has to pay the full amount v_0, he will be left at his initial level of welfare, w_0. By contrast, in determining the minimum sum he would accept to forgo the good, a sum equal to v_1, he must have regard to the level of welfare, w_1, that he would have reached with the good. Should he receive this sum v_1 instead of the good, he will indeed reach this higher level of welfare w_1.

The reader should note also that no matter how much higher is w_1 than w_0, the maximum sum v_0 that the person will pay for the good is always finite, if only because of the limits of his budget. By contrast, the sum v_1 can be infinite. To illustrate with an extreme example, if his current state of welfare, w_0, corresponded to that in which he was stricken with a fatal disease, whereas the welfare level w_1 was one involving a complete cure, the most the person could pay to move from w_0 to w_1, which is v_0, is a finite sum, no matter how wealthy he is. But there may be no sum v_1 large enough to persuade him to forgo moving from w_0 to w_1.

4 With respect to the opportunity of acquiring a particular good, there are then, in general, two alternative sums to be considered: a maximum sum he will pay to have the good and a minimum sum he will accept to forgo it. And it makes no difference if we are measuring the value of a bad rather than a good, inasmuch as forging a bad is formally the same as acquiring a good, and acquiring a bad is formally the same as forgoing a good.

Let us abbreviate the maximum sum that a person or a group will pay for a good as (max) and the minimal sum that a person or group will accept to forgo that good as (min), and then let us compare the sums (max) and (min) with respect to a movement from situation I to situation II.

We may suppose the I situation to be the existing situation, one in which, say, a given area is free of all smoke pollution (above some accepted amenity standard). The alternative situation, II, is that which will prevail if the B industry is permitted to establish itself in that area, which will then suffer from smoke pollution.

The most a certain person living in the area is willing to pay for the good, identified as the existing, unpolluted air—which can also be expressed as the most he will pay to avoid the bad, or smoke pollution, associated with the II situation—is, say, $80 a week. The least he will accept to forgo the good, or to put up with the bad associated with the II situation, is, say, $110 per week. But, of course, he is only one of a group of persons who live in that area and must anticipate the smoke pollution if the B industry is established there. By adding together the maximal sums of each person in that group, say group A, we have one value of the worth to it of preserving the area from smoke pollution. We suppose this A group (max) is $80 million. If we now asked each member of the A group to name the minimum amount he would accept as compensation for the anticipated smoke pollution by the B industry, the aggregate (min) value, let us suppose, would be $110 million.

Against these two values we have now to place an analogous pair for the B group that expects to benefit from the change to the II situation, which group will have to include consumers of the B industry's products.[2] Let the (max) and (min) figures for the B

---

[2] It is far from impossible that a resident of the area will both lose in so far as air quality is concerned and gain from buying the products of the B industry. Such a person will be placed in the A group if, on balance, he is worse off in situation II and in the B group if he is, on balance, better off.

group be $10 million and $12 million respectively. These figures of (max) and (min) for each of the two groups, A and B, are the basic data from which, in our first case, the relations between CV and EV can be deduced both for the movement from I to II and for the reverse movement from II to I.

5 In the light of these figures, invented to illustrate the most straightforward case, let us consider first the movement from I to II and ask ourselves what the CV for each group is and, therefore, the aggregate for the two groups taken together which, in this example, represent society.

The movement from I to II is a good for group B. By reference to the definitions at the beginning of the chapter, therefore, the aggregate CV for members of the B group is their (max), $10 million. To be tediously explicit, this $10 million is the sum which, if paid by members of the B group, would restore their welfare to its original level, as in situation I.

This same movement from I to II is, however, a bad for members of the A group. Again, by reference to the definitions at the beginning of the chapter, the CV for the A group is the (min) figure. To be tediously explicit once more, this $110 million is the sum which, if received by the A group in the II situation, would suffice to restore each member to the welfare he enjoyed in the I situation.

The aggregate CV for the members of both groups in the movement from I to II is therefore (+ $10 million − $110 million) or − $100 million. This *minus* figure for the algebraic aggregate of the two groups indicates a *negative* 'social net benefit', the gains of the B group falling short of the losses suffered by the A group by $100 million.

The result that the algebraic aggregate of the CVs is negative can be expressed by the inequality (1):

$$\Sigma CV\ (\text{I}\rightarrow\text{II}) < 0 \qquad (1)$$

Since a potential Pareto improvement in the movement from I to II requires that the gains in the movement be more than enough to offset the losses, this Pareto criterion is obviously not met in the case above.[3] Only if the figures were such that the algebraic sum of the

---

[3] By conventional use of jargon, the statement, 'The movement from I to II entails a *potential* Pareto improvement' is equivalent to the statement 'The movement from I to II meets the Pareto criterion.'

CVs were positive, reversing the inequality sign in (1), would the Pareto criterion be met.

6 By reference, again, to the definitions at the beginning of the chapter, we return to our (max) and (min) figures for each group in order to calculate the algebraic sum of the EVs in the movement from I to II.

The EV of this change for the B group is its (min) value, $12 million (the minimum sum the members of this group would accept to forgo this movement to II, which improves their welfare, since they would then be as well off as they would have been had they actually moved to II).

To members of the A group, by contrast, the movement from I to II is a bad. The aggregate EV to group A of the change is its (max) value, $80 million (since if the members of the A group were spared the movement to II on condition they paid $80 million, they would be exactly as well off as they would have been in II).

The aggregate EV for the members of both groups, A and B, in the movement from I to II is therefore (+ $80 million − $12 million) or + $68 million. This algebraic aggregate being positive, we may write:

$$\Sigma EV \ (I \rightarrow II) > 0 \qquad (2)$$

Seen from the perspective of the EV definition, the gainers from the movement to II, the B group, would require at least $12 million to forgo the change, whereas the losers from the change to II, group A, would be willing to pay as much as $80 million to avoid having to make it.

The rationale of inequality (2) above seems, therefore, clearly to favour situation I. For if the movement to II were indeed undertaken, there would be a potential Pareto improvement in *returning* to I: group A, being willing to pay as much as $80 million to have I rather than II, would easily be able to give group B the sum of $12 million that would reconcile group B to remaining with the I situation.

In this straightforward case the EV test follows the CV test in rejecting the movement from I to II.

7 Before ending the chapter it is necessary to make clear the symmetry of the CV and EV measures in relation to the movements from I to II and from II to I.

The reader will have noted the rationale above of the inequality (2) in rejecting the movement from I to II—namely, that if the movement to II had been undertaken, there would have been a potential Pareto improvement in returning to I. In the return movement, then, group A would be willing to pay as much as \$80 million, whereas group B would be satisfied to receive as little as \$12 million—a social net benefit of \$68 million in the movement from II to I. But these two figures, the $+\$80$ million for group A and the $-\$12$ million for group B, will be seen at once to coincide with the CV definition for a movement from II to I. That is to say:

$$\Sigma CV(II \rightarrow I) \equiv \Sigma EV(I \rightarrow II) \tag{3}$$

As we should expect from the structure of the symmetry, it transpires also that:

$$\Sigma CV(I \rightarrow II) \equiv \Sigma EV(II \rightarrow I) \tag{4}$$

This should, in any case, be manifest to the reader if he returns to the remarks preceding inequality (1). There it was stated that the B group, which gains in the movement from I to II, would pay as much as \$10 million for the change to II, whereas the A group would require at least \$110 million in compensation, implying a social net loss of \$100 million for the movement from I to II. Hence $CV(I \rightarrow II) = +\$100$ million.

If, however, the movement to II had already been made, then in a return movement to I group A would gain and group B would lose. According to our definitions, however, the EV for a movement from II to I is, for group A (the gainers) \$110 million, since such a sum, transferred to it, would just suffice to induce it to forgo the movement to I. As for group B, the EV for a movement from II to I is the sum \$10 million, this being the most the members would pay rather than return to situation I.[4]

---

[4] The reader will notice that if in the $\Sigma CV(I \rightarrow II)$ measure it is stated that a person or group B will pay at most 10 *in order to move to II*, and if in the counterpart $\Sigma EV(II \rightarrow I)$ measure it is stated that B will pay at most 10 *in order to avoid returning to I*, the two statements are, in fact, logically identical. They both express the same proposition: that B will pay 10 for having the II situation *rather than* the I situation. (Similarly, since B will have to be paid 12 to accept the I situation rather than II, $\Sigma CV(II \rightarrow I) \equiv \Sigma EV(I \rightarrow II) = +12$).

8 Since we know that $\Sigma CV(I \rightarrow II) > 0$ indicates that a potential Pareto improvement is met in the movement from I to II, it necessarily follows from (4) that the expression $\Sigma EV(II \rightarrow I) > 0$ indicates exactly the same thing. Either expression tells us, that is, that the Pareto criterion is met in a movement from I to II.

Per contra, since $\Sigma CV(I \rightarrow II) < 0$ indicates that a potential Pareto improvement cannot be realized in the movement from I to II, it follows from (4) that $\Sigma EV(II \rightarrow I) < 0$ indicates exactly the same thing. Either expression tells us that the Pareto criterion cannot be met in a movement from I to II.

Finally, since $CV(II \rightarrow I) > 0$ indicates a potential Pareto improvement met in the movement from II to I, it follows from (3) that $EV(I \rightarrow II)$ must also indicate that a potential Pareto improvement is met in the movement from II to I. On this Pareto criterion, then, whether it is expressed in the $\Sigma CV(lI \rightarrow I)$ form or in the $\Sigma EV(I \rightarrow II)$ form, situation I is ranked above situation II.

Per contra, since $\Sigma CV(II \rightarrow I) < 0$ indicates that a Pareto improvement is not met in the movement from II to I, it follows from (3) that $\Sigma EV(I \rightarrow II) < 0$ indicates exactly the same thing. Therefore on the Pareto criterion situation I cannot be ranked above II.

9 The preceding elaboration, admittedly a little humdrum, serves the purpose of clearing the way for the following chapter on alternative valuation criteria in cost-benefit analysis, In particular, it makes plain that it is not really necessary to use both a CV and an EV criterion, since the latter can always be expressed in terms of the former. Thus rather than talk of the $\Sigma CV(I \rightarrow II)$ criterion and the $\Sigma EV(I \rightarrow II)$ criterion, we can express the latter less esoterically as the $\Sigma CV(II \rightarrow I)$ criterion.

Chapter 26

ALTERNATIVE VALUATION CRITERIA IN COST-BENEFIT ANALYSIS

1 Let me remind the reader again that the context of a cost-benefit analysis is that of partial equilibrium analysis, one in which we concentrate on the valuation of several items on the assumption that the effects of consequent changes in the prices of all but the most closely related goods or bads may be neglected as we vary the amounts or introduce any one of these several items. For environmental goods being valued by a cost-benefit analysis, the effect on people's welfare may be significant. And if so, since we assume that the welfare effects are positive, the *direction of change* implied by the criterion—from I to II or, alternatively, from II to I—may make a substantial difference to the magnitude of the cost-benefit valuation. Indeed, it may also determine whether or not the criterion adopted is met.

As in the preceding chapter, the initial or existing situation is referred to as situation I, and the alternative being contemplated—the investment project that is to be the subject of a cost-benefit analysis—is referred to as situation II. It will simplify the exposition if we continue for a little longer to think of the existing situation, I, as that favoured by the environmental group A, and to think of situation II as differing from situation I only in its introduction of an industry that favours group B but incidentally pollutes the air, so reducing the welfare of the A group.

The alternatives that merit our attention in the choice of an economic criterion either for evaluating or for allocating the entire area under dispute or any part of it are five in number:

(a) auction of rights to the highest bidder;

177

(b) the CV test;

(c) the EV test (which, as indicated, can be expressed as the CV(II→I) test);

(d) both the CV and the EV test;

(c) the allocation of property rights and value accordingly.

2 The auction criterion (a) is effectively a comparison of the maximum sums that each person is willing to pay to possess rights to the good in question—in this case, let us say, the airshed that will be polluted if the new industry is located in the particular area. This allocative device is commonly justified on the grounds that in auctioning some scarce resource it will become the property of the person or group for which it has the highest value, a result that is thought to accord with an efficient allocation of resources.[1]

This device, however, may result in a solution that does not meet the standard Pareto criterion, as can be illustrated by the following example, in which, again, the move from I to II harms group A but favours group B. This B group will bid up to $100 million for the rights to the airshed (in order to move from situation I to situation II), whereas the environmental group A cannot bid more than $90 million (in order to remain in the I situation). In such an auction the rights will go to the B group and, eventually, the airshed will be polluted up to the legal limit. But for the Pareto criterion to be met it is necessary that the gains by the B group in moving to the II situation should more than suffice to compensate for the losses suffered by the A group in moving to II. If the minimum compensation acceptable to the A group exceeds $100 million, then clearly the Pareto criterion is not met. Since the A group's (min) sum will exceed its (max) sum according to the extent of the positive welfare effect, it is entirely possible that the (min) sum will exceed $100 million. Such a possibility is so far from being a *curiosum* as to cast serious doubt on the allocative virtue of the auctioning device—at least where the good in question has value as an environmental resource.

It might be suggested in this connection that instead of comparing

---

[1] The legal enforcement of the kinds and levels of pollution permitted over an area does not alter the argument, since each party will then offer some (maximum) amount for rights to the airshed, bearing in mind the pollution limits to which a potential pollutor will be subjected.

the (max) sums of the contending parties, their (min) sums should be compared and the rights to the airshed awarded to the party having the largest (min) sum.[2] If this were undertaken in our example, the rights might be awarded to group A rather than group B—as would be the case if B's (min) were $110 million and A's (min) sum were $125 million. But this proposal—which, if adopted in addition to the auctioning device, might act to deter the implementation of the auctioning solution—would not, of itself, meet a Pareto criterion either. Moreover, a comparison of (min) sums might just as well *confirm* the results of the auction—as would be the case if, instead of the above figures, B's (min) were $115 million and A's (min) were $105 million (though even in this case the Pareto criterion would not be met).

Reasoning along the lines of the above argument would also reveal that allocation of some part of the airshed to group A and some part to group B, according to their respective bidding for successive increments, would differ, again, from the allocation that is consistent with the Pareto criterion. For a simple demonstration of this proposition the reader is referred to the Note at the end of this chapter.

3 There is an expositional advantage in examining the next three criteria in the order (c), (d) and (b) and in letting the A and B groups vary from case to case.

Thus we consider first (c), the EV test alone, which is deemed to favour the project, or the movement from I to II, whenever $\Sigma EV(I \rightarrow II) < 0$ (else the movement to II is rejected).

As we know from equation (3) of the preceding chapter, however, $\Sigma EV(I \rightarrow II)$ is equivalent to $\Sigma CV(II \rightarrow I)$. Therefore the proposed test favours the movement to II if, beginning from situation II, we cannot justify a return to I on the Pareto criterion.

On first thoughts, the EV test does not, perhaps, seem to have as clear a justification for favouring a movement from I to II as does the CV test. But bearing in mind that we are using 'strong' ordering

---

[2] Such a proposal may not be practical, however. While it is not too costly to arrange an auction in which the highest bidder is almost sure to be the party placing the largest value on the rights to a resource, an arrangement elaborate enough to elicit information on the largest minimal sum each party would accept to forgo the rights to the resource is likely to be costly.

that excludes the possibility of 'I indifferent to II'—one which, in this instance, implies that if a particular test does *not* rank I above II, it necessarily ranks II above I—the EV test has to be regarded as being as valid as the CV test.[3]

4 Since the notion of employing (d), both the CV test and the EV test as a dual criterion, stems from a desire to reveal possible ambiguities and to avoid inconsistencies, it will be useful to lay out all four conceivable cases when the two tests are taken together. Instead of writing $\Sigma EV(I \rightarrow II)$, however, it will be easier to follow the argument if we write instead the equivalent expression $\Sigma CV(II \rightarrow I)$ in each case—though reminding ourselves, when necessary, that this is the import of the EV test.

There are, first, the two obvious cases in which the two tests yield the same result:

(1) $\Sigma CV(I \rightarrow II) > 0$ and $\Sigma CV(II \rightarrow I) < 0$, and
(2) $\Sigma CV(I \rightarrow II) < 0$ and $\Sigma CV(II \rightarrow I) > 0$.

There are, in addition, two conceivably ambiguous cases:

(3) $\Sigma CV(I \rightarrow II) < 0$, yet $\Sigma CV(II \rightarrow I) < 0$, and
(4) $\Sigma CV(I \rightarrow II) > 0$, yet $\Sigma CV(II \rightarrow I) > 0$.

If the figures are such as to accord with case (1), as they do in the self-explanatory Table IV.1,[4] a potential Pareto improvement equal to 20 is realized in the movement from I to II, whereas in the reverse movement, from II to I, a potential Pareto loss of 35 is effected. Therefore the dual CV–EV criterion unambiguously favours the movement from I to II.

TABLE IV.1

	Group A	Group B	Net Social Value
$\Sigma CV(I \rightarrow II)$	+100	−80	+20
$\Sigma CV(II \rightarrow I)$	−110	+75	−35

[3] In the preceding auction example in which it is shown that, despite B's (max) exceeding A's (max), it is possible for $\Sigma CV(I \rightarrow II) < 0$, indicating that the Pareto criterion is *not* met in a movement from I to II, this movement to II is rejected as a result of which the test is deemed necessarily to favour remaining with the existing I situation.
[4] The reader is reminded that a + sign before a figure indicates the maximum sum the group is willing to pay for the movement, and a − sign before a figure the minimum it will accept in compensation for the movement, the movement always being a good for one group and a bad for the other.

If the figures, instead, accord with case (2), as they do in Table IV.2, a potential Pareto loss of 70 is effected in the movement from I to II, whereas in the movement from II to I a potential Pareto improvement of 20 is effected. In this case, the dual CV–EV criterion unambiguously ranks I above II.

TABLE IV.2

	Group A	Group B	Net Social Value
$\Sigma CV(I \to II)$	+80	−150	−70
$\Sigma CV(II \to I)$	−100	+120	+20

The ambiguous case (3) is illustrated by the figures in Table IV.3. In the movement from I to II the Pareto criterion is not met, there being a net social loss of 10. But then neither is the Pareto criterion met in the movement from II to I, the net social loss from that movement being 25. In this case, the CV–EV dual criterion finds in favour of neither II or I. The convention in such cases is not to undertake the change—which amounts to choosing to stay with situation I whenever the dual criterion reveals an ambiguity of this kind.

TABLE IV.3

	Group A	Group B	Net Social Value
$\Sigma CV(I \to II)$	−110	+100	−10
$\Sigma CV(II \to I)$	+90	−115	−25

5 The last case (4), however, is just not possible for positive welfare effects.[5] The reader can easily convince himself of this simply by referring to the first row of figures in Table IV.1, where $\Sigma CV(I \to II)$ is positive, being equal to 20. Inasmuch as the welfare effects are positive, the (max) sum for a particular group will always, as indicated earlier, be smaller than the (min) sum. Since group A's (max) sum for moving from I to II is given by +100 (in the top row

---

[5] If welfare effects were in fact negative, then case (4) would be entirely possible, whereas case (3) would be impossible, and the conclusions reached in the text would have to be amended in fairly obvious ways, a task the fastidious reader may wish to undertake. Since the logical structure is clear enough, I have no compunction in sparing the reader such excursions into implausible regions.

of Table IV.1), its (min) sum for the movement from I to II must exceed 100 in absolute terms (as it does in the bottom row of Table IV.1, where it is equal to -110). Again, since group B's (min) sum for moving from I to II is given by -80 (in the top row of Table IV.1), its (max) sum must be smaller than that in absolute terms (as it is in the bottom row of Table IV.1, where it is equal to $+75$).

Now, if in the bottom row the negative figure for one group is larger (in absolute terms) than the positive figure above it, and the positive figure for the other group is smaller (in absolute terms) than the negative figure above it, the resulting negative aggregate in the bottom row must be larger (in absolute terms) than the positive aggregate above it. Thus in the example given in Table IV.1 the net social value of the movement from I to II is given in the top row as $+20$. In the bottom row it is given as -35.

Only in the limiting case of zero welfare effects, when the (max) and (min) figures are the same for each group, will the absolute value of the net social benefit be no greater in the bottom row than in the top. We may conclude, therefore, that in this context a finding of $\Sigma CV(I \rightarrow II) > 0$ entails *a fortiori* that $\Sigma CV(II \rightarrow I) > 0$ or *a fortiori* that $\Sigma EV(I \rightarrow II) > 0$. In sum, if the CV test ranks II above I, so, necessarily, will the EV test.

6 We have just ruled out the possibility of an ambiguous case (4): as concluded above, if the CV test in the movement from I to II is met, then *a fortiori* so is the EV test. As for the two unambiguous cases (1) and (2), a dual criterion is clearly unnecessary, inasmuch as the dual criterion will give the same ranking as the CV test alone. The interesting case left to consider is case (3), where the movement to II is rejected on the CV test and accepted on the EV test. This is the case illustrated in Table IV.3, where both $\Sigma CV(I \rightarrow II) < 0$ and $\Sigma CV(II \rightarrow I) < 0$: the Pareto criterion is *not* met for the movement from I to II which, on strong ordering, ranks I above II, and again the Pareto criterion is *not* met in the movement from II to I which, on strong ordering, ranks II above I. The ambiguity of the dual CV–EV criterion in this case is manifest.

Wherever a decision criterion yields an ambiguous result, as does the dual CV–EV criterion in the above case, the economist has no mandate to recommend a course of action. In particular, he cannot recommend a movement from the existing situation I to the II situation that is being mooted. But if he cannot recommend a movement to II, he is effectively finding in favour of the existing situation I.

Such an outcome may be thought to imply a bias in favour of the *status quo*. But any change from the *status quo* entails some costs, even if these are largely the psychological costs of adjustment—which tell in favour of the economist's adopting as an operative requirement a cost-benefit ratio well above unity. At all events, the convention of remaining with the I situation when the decision criterion is ambiguous may be regarded as a more sensible reaction to, say, that of tossing a coin to determine whether to recommend the existing I situation or the II situation.

Be that as it may, it is a current fact of life that whenever application of the decision criterion produces an ambiguous result, as it does in case (3), the economist does *not* recommend the change in question—with the practical effect that he finds in favour of remaining with the existing situation I.

It is for this reason that the use of a dual CV–EV criterion is unnecessary: operationally speaking, that is, the use of the CV test alone produces exactly the same results as the dual CV–EV criterion for all three possible cases. In particular, in the ambiguous case (3), where application of the CV–EV criterion cannot recommend the move from I to II, neither can the use of the CV test alone.

7 The legal endowment of property rights that favour either group A or group B arises from society's discrimination in favour of the relevant activities or aspirations of group A or B. For the implication of such property rights for valuation purposes is the attribution to the favoured group of the larger or (min) figure that it places on the good, irrespective of whether it would lose or gain the good in the movement from I to II. The consequence is that if the favoured group loses in the change from I to II, the CV test alone is used. If, instead, the favoured group gains in the change from I to II, the EV test alone is used.

The conferring of these property rights on either of the groups can make no more difference to the unambiguous cases (1) and (2) than the use of the CV test alone, or the EV test alone, or the use of a dual CV–EV criterion. For example, whether we use the top row of figures or the bottom row of figures in each of Tables IV.1 and IV.2, the outcome is the same: move to II in Table IV.1, and remain with I in Table IV.2.

For the ambiguous case (3) exemplified in Table IV.3, however, the conferring of property rights may make a difference as compared with the use of either test alone or of the dual CV–EV criterion. In particular, it may make a difference to the outcome as compared with the use of the CV test alone, which, as we have seen, is operationally a sufficient criterion in the absence of the legal endowment of property rights.

True, if we had a predilection in favour of environmental amenity, the application of the CV test alone in a proposed movement to II that involved environmental *deterioration* would require the (min) figure for the environmental group (say, group A). Therefore in the ambiguous case (3), illustrated in Table IV.3, the CV test alone would satisfy us, since the movement to II could not be justified. But if instead the movement to II involved an *improved* environment, the CV test alone in the ambiguous case (3) would again act against moving to II, whereas the conferring of property rights on the environmental group, implying the use of the (min) figure of that group, would favour the move to II.

This latter result can be illustrated by the numbers in Table IV.3a below, in which the two rows in Table IV.3 are reversed.

TABLE IV.3a

	Group A	Group B	Net Social Value
$\Sigma CV(I \rightarrow II)$	+90	−115	−25
$\Sigma CV(II \rightarrow I)$	−110	+100	−10

Since the net social value of the movement to II, in the first row, is equal to −25, the CV test discountenances the move to II, as, therefore, will the dual CV–EV criterion.

Suppose, now, that the law changes from an L law, permissive of environmental destruction, to an L̄ law, conferring rights in respect of specific environmental amenities and requiring adoption of the (min) figure for the environmental change in any project evaluation. In that event the bottom row of figures in Table IV.3′ has to be used, the relevant figure for the environmental group A being the minimal compensation of 110 to induce it to forgo the environmental improvement involved in the change to II. This bottom row is, of course, the $\Sigma CV(II \rightarrow I)$ test which is identical to the $\Sigma EV(I \rightarrow II)$ test.

184

It follows, therefore, that the introduction of an $\bar{L}$ law favouring the environmental group A implies that the CV test alone continues to be used when the change to II is one involving environmental disamenity. When the change to II is one involving an improvement of the environment, however, the introduction of an $\bar{L}$ law implies the use of the EV test alone. And this makes a difference to the adoption of the CV test alone only in the ambiguous case (3) and there only for a change involving an environmental improvement, as exemplified in Table IV.3'.[6]

Until such time as an $\bar{L}$ law is established, however, the economist has no warrant to evaluate projects as though such a consensus already existed. Granted the plausibility of positive (or, at least, non-negative) welfare effects in all familiar circumstances, the continued employment of the CV test alone as the basic criterion for cost-benefit analysis is vindicated.

8 Before concluding , it is necessary to give some brief consideration to an alleged blemish of the CV measure as a ranking criterion wherever there are two or more alternatives to the existing I situation.

It has been pointed out that where two or more price changes are involved in comparing an existing situation I with alternatives II and III, the use of the CV measure (as distinct from the EV measure) can rank II above III where the individual's utility function ranks III above II.[7] This possibility seems, at first blush, to be counter-intuitive—until we remember that a comparison of the movement to

---

[6] We need not labour the less likely case that would arise if property rights in the environment were instead vested in the commercial group B, since it is symmetric, in all relevant respects, with that discussed. Where the movement to II involved environmental damage the EV test alone would be used, and the CV test alone where the movement to II involved environmental improvement.

[7] So far as I can ascertain, this possibility was first pointed out by Foster and Neueberger (1974), and was later demonstrated by Hause (1975) in a two-good indifference map context, one of the goods being treated also as the *numéraire* in which the CV is measured. Later (1978) produced a numerical example of this phenomenon involving two goods and money.

Boadway's (1974) allegation that the use of the CV measure as a criterion can produce a contradiction falls into the familiar category of general equilibrium models of the variety described in my Note to Chapter 24. Boadway's demonstration that the use of the CV test yields contradictory ordering within an exchange economy limited to fixed amounts of goods is erroneous, however, as I pointed out in my 1976 paper. The possibility he tried to demonstrate cannot in fact arise in the exchange economy he postulated.

II with the movement to III may involve changes in the value of the *numéraire* in which the CV is measured.[8]

The reader should note, however, that the apparent absence of blemish in the EV measure arises simply because in the literature on the subject the comparison of each of the alternatives II and III is taken with respect to the existing I situation. The parallel pair of budget planes in the change from I to II and in the change from I to III are, therefore, parallel to the initial budget plane identifying the I situation. This would no longer be the case if, instead, we compared the change from I to II with the change from II to III and so on. In such comparisons, the blemish associated with the CV measure extends also to the EV measure.

It should also be borne in mind that the conditions necessary for this perverse (though conceivable) result to arise have not yet been made explicit—although it is apparent that the changes in welfare involved in the movement to II and III must be substantial. It is not possible as yet, therefore, to assess the plausibility of the occurrence of so perverse a result.

We need not, however, be unduly ruffled about this possibility, for two reasons. First, in the context in which price changes of goods are to be evaluated in a cost-benefit analysis, the effect on aggregate welfare is unlikely to be large. In any case, a cost-benefit measure of, say, the social gain from a fall in price of one or two goods or from the introduction of one or two goods is never measured with more sophistication than as a strip of, or area under, the market demand curve. A theoretically accurate *ceteris paribus* demand curve lies between the two compensated demand curves associated with the CV and EV measure respectively. Yet the statistical errors in measuring the demand curve makes it impossible to say whether the estimated gain is closer to the theoretically exact CV measure or to the theoretically exact EV measure.

Secondly, where the alternative changes being contemplated

---

[8] Thinking visually, in terms of an indifference map, the reference budget plane by means of which the CV measure is taken will be that resulting from the change in the prices. In contrast, the reference budget plane by means of which the EV measures are made is in fact the initial budget plane irrespective of the price changes. With the CV measure, therefore, the reference plane differs, in general, for each of the new price situations being compared, whereas with the EV measure the reference plane remains constant.

involve not changes in the prices of existing items but changes in the amount or quality of unpriced public goods—a frequent problem in cost-benefit analysis—the perverse possibility referred to does not even arise theoretically. Each person's CV or EV ranking of alternative situations II, III, . . ., necessarily coincides with his welfare ranking of them.

NOTE TO CHAPTER 26

The allocation of some given territory, hitherto left undeveloped, as between an environmental group A and a commercial group B through the auctioning of successive small parcels of land results in the amount of land measured as the horizontal distance $O_B Q_1$ in Figure IV.2 being owned by the B group and the amount $O_A Q_1$ being owned by the A group. The downward-sloping curve BB' is the valuation curve of this land for group B, as measured by the maximum sums of money it would pay for successive units, whereas the AA' curve is the marginal valuation curve for group A, as measured (from right to left) by the maximum sums of money it also would pay for successive units of land.

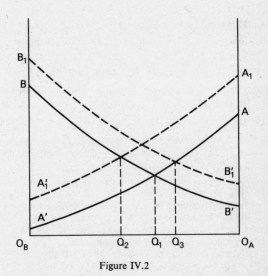

Figure IV.2

187

This Q_1 division of the land between the two groups does not, however, accord with one sanctioned by the Pareto criterion—at least, not if we continue to assume positive welfare effects. An allocation consistent with that criterion emerges when we contruct the curve $A_1 A_1'$ above the AA' curve. As we move leftward from point A_1', the height of this new curve is interpreted as the minimum sum acceptable to the A group for ceding a marginal unit of land to the B group. Clearly, this first marginal unit of land accrues to group B under the Pareto criterion, as the maximum sum group B will pay for it is equal to height $O_B B$, which exceeds $O_B A_1'$, the minimal sum acceptable to the A group. Proceeding in this way, the allocation sanctioned by the Pareto criterion results in $O_B Q_2$ going to the B group, the remainder going to the A group.

In the less likely case of group B's owning the land in the first place, the relevant curve for group B would be its (min) marginal valuation curve $B_1' B_1$ which intersects group A's (max) marginal valuation curve $A'A$ at a point directly above Q_3 in the figure. As a result, the Pareto criterion would sanction only $O_A Q_3$ of the total land being allocated to group A.

In the case in which neither of the interested groups A and B has had prior access to the territory put up for auction, it is no longer the case that a transfer of any parcel of the land entails a loss only to one particular group (the prior beneficiaries of the land) and a gain only to the other group. In this third case *either* group suffers an opportunity loss for any unit of new land that is allocated to the other group: if the unit goes to A, A's gain is accompanied by a loss for B and vice versa. Therefore both the (min) and (max) marginal valuation curves for each group are needed. Application of the Pareto criterion allocates $O_B Q_2$ of the land to group B and $O_A Q_3$ of the land to group A. The remaining land, $Q_2 Q_3$, cannot be allocated to either group on the Pareto criterion.[1]

---

[1] In a cost-benefit analysis undertaken to determine which of two groups, A and B, should have exclusive rights to a hitherto unused and indivisible area of land, its allocation to the B group should be regarded as one alternative situation (say II) and its allocation to the A group as another alternative (III). Should both movements to II and to III meet the Pareto criterion, one could be ranked above the other by reference to their net social benefits. Should neither movement meet the Pareto criterion, we have a case that corresponds with any point along the Pareto-indeterminate gap, $Q_1 Q_3$ in the figure.

Chapter 27

CONSISTENCY IN PROJECT EVALUATION (I)

1 In this chapter we shall examine a number of recent proposals which, if adopted in connection with cost-benefit analysis, would entail a departure from the Pareto criterion. These proposals arise in connection with equity and distribution, and in the treatment of so-called merit goods, intangibles, and the social rate of time preference.

2 *Equity and distribution.* The impact of large investment projects on the distribution of welfare has, of late, attracted some attention.

One form of response to this concern has been an attempt to incorporate distributional effects into a cost-benefit calculation by effectively expressing gains and losses in terms of utility rather than in terms of money. For each dollar of gain or loss to a specified income group there corresponds a particular marginal utility: the higher the income group the lower the marginal utility of a dollar gain or loss. Having transformed all *CV*s into utility terms, the cost-benefit criterion is met when the gains in terms of total utility exceed the losses. Clearly a cost-benefit criterion that is not met in money terms may be met when translated into utility terms, and vice versa.

The particular weighting systems that have been proposed are of necessity somewhat arbitrary and all assume diminishing marginal utility of income. One method is that of positing a particular form of the utility-income relation. If, for example, one adopts a function that results in a constant elasticity of *minus* 2 with respect to income, a 1 per cent increase in income is to be associated with a fall of 2 per cent in the level of the utility indicator. Alternatively the weighting system can be made dependent upon political decisions taken in the recent past. One way of doing this, proposed by Weisbrod (1968), rests on the assumption that all public projects that were adopted, notwithstanding their failure to meet cost-benefit criteria, were adopted as a

189

result of an implicit set of utility weights attaching to the earnings of different groups. By comparing a number of such projects these utility weights can be made explicit and, perhaps, become incorporated into the economist's cost-benefit criterion. Another method of weighting, that of calculating a set of weights from the marginal rates of income tax, derives from the premise that the object of a progressive income tax is to share the 'real' burden of any increment of tax equally among all income groups. Thus, if on the marginal dollar of income, the 'rich' (say those in the $100,000 to $500,000 bracket) pay 80 cents, and the 'not so rich' (say those in the $10,000 to $25,000 bracket) pay 10 cents, it may be inferred that 80 cents for the rich has a utility that is equal to 10 cents for the not-so-rich—or that an additional dollar to the rich is worth only $\frac{1}{8}$ as much as an additional dollar is worth to the not-so-rich.[1]

There can, however, be a number of objections to any method of incorporating differential utility weights into a cost-benefit analysis. First, there is the obvious difficulty of securing widespread acceptance of a given set of distributional or other social weights.[2] Secondly, the proposed utility-weighted criteria are at variance with the allocative principles by which the perfectly competitive economy is vindicated. It is sometimes argued that the conventional cost-benefit analysis carries an implicit weighting system; namely that one dollar is equal to one 'util' irrespective of who gains or loses the dollar, or that a dollar gained or lost has the same value for both poor and rich. But the rationale of the conventional cost-benefit analysis is not to be interpreted as having any affinity with a social goal of maximizing or increasing aggregate utility. No interpersonal comparisons of utility are to be invoked. As frequently indicated, cost-benefit methods derive their rationale from the concept of a potential Pareto improvement— the social value of output being so increased that (by costless redistributions of net gains) everyone *can* be made better off by the change in question.

If this much is allowed, cost-benefit analysis can be regarded as an extension of an efficient price system, one that enables us to select only those enterprises that are expected to produce an excess of social value

---

[1] For an application of distributional weights based on marginal rates of income tax to the figures produced by the Roskill Commission, see Nwaneri (1970).

[2] In this connection see the objections to Weisbrod's proposals (1968).

over resource cost. Once cost-benefit criteria depart from the traditional Pareto-based allocative criteria, then clearly public investment projects may be admitted even though the social value they produce falls below the value of the resource costs incurred, so that, indeed, everyone may be made worse off by their introduction. The introduction of some utility-corrected projects therefore implies a departure from the norms of allocative efficiency inasmuch as factors can be shifted from current uses into uses having a smaller value.[3]

Thirdly, no matter how accurate, or acceptable, are the set of utility-weights proposed, their incorporation into a cost-benefit analysis does not, in general, serve the purpose for which they are presumably designed—to promote equity, or at least to guard against projects that are distributionally regressive. For whatever the set of weights employed, the resulting utility-weighted cost-benefit criterion could still admit projects that make the rich richer and the poor poorer, especially if the rich persons affected by the project are numerous or are made very much richer.

Although the device of incorporating utility weights into a cost-benefit analysis as a means of enforcing the claims of equity or distribution is evidently unsatisfactory, distributional and other social goals have to be respected by the economist who offers advice to society. The least he should do is to point up the distributional implications wherever they appear significant. And since he need not affect to be so unworldly as to be in ignorance of society's commitment to greater equality, or to its declared aversion to measures that harden the lot of the poor, the economist can afford, on occasion, to be more emphatic. In particular, wherever an investment project that appears to be advantageous by ordinary cost-benefit criteria causes particular hardship to some groups, the economist should consider the practical possibilities of adequate compensation.

3 *Merit Goods.* It can be argued that cost-benefit analysis or, for that matter, the competitive price system, ignores considerations of 'social-merit'. To some extent, alleged omissions of such considerations in

---

[3] To this departure from traditional allocative norms, and to the implied inconsistency of procedure for the economy as a whole, private and public, there is the further consideration that such a method would aggravate the perennial Second Best problem— at least if we continue to be concerned at all with allocative efficiency.

specific cost-benefit studies can be ascribed to the existing difficulties of evaluation.[4] If the benefit of such 'good' things as better health, improved education, expanded recreational facilities, etc., could be satisfactorily measured, the impact of an investment project on these things would indeed be incorporated in the cost-benefit calculation. On the other hand, other social goods such as more civic participation, better community relations, or the alleviation of poverty, though they might notionally be brought into relation with the calculus, are likely to elude attempts to translate them into money values.

Socially desirable goods of this nature may be roughly, and to some extent arbitrarily, measured by what have come to be known as social indicators. The complex of units employed for this purpose will vary from one social indicator to another. Health, for instance, could include longevity, infant mortality, per cent reduction in a number of diseases, the sale of medical goods and services, and so on. The measurement of poverty might include such indices as the proportion of the population living below some chosen 'real' income, or living on what is deemed to be an inadequate diet, or in what is deemed to be sub-standard housing. The alleviation of poverty would therefore be measured by the per cent reduction in such an indicator.

Granted the difficulties of evaluation, wherever investment projects are expected to have perceptible effects on social goods that may be measured only by such indicators, a number of physical measures will in effect be used as indices of benefit and used supplementary to the evaluated benefits.

These social indicators are only just being constructed and are not discussed in this volume. Despite any contribution they will make in the future to our knowledge of the nation's welfare, they will not of themselves entail any alteration of the principles and methods of cost-benefit analysis as treated here.

4 *Intangibles*. There may be occasions, however, when the absence of data prevents the economists from putting a value on certain effects resulting from the project. Very often such effects are spillovers, which do not register on the market mechanism. Ignoring envy and other

---

[4] Although, as argued in the text, omissions in the valuation of any relevant items ought always to be made explicit by the economist.

inadmissible external effects, such spillovers can in principle be brought 'into relationship with the measuring rod of money', as Pigou (1932) put it. But although the spillover can be measured 'in principle', there are likely to be difficulties 'in practice' of putting reliable figures on them. What can be done in the circumstances has been discussed in Part III on external effects. When apparently nothing can be done, the effects may be described in some detail, and entered into the final table of costs and benefits. There is a temptation to go further than this, however, and leave a space opposite such unmeasurable effects for the so-called decision-maker to fill in.

Recourse to this practice is unsatisfactory. A cost-benefit analysis is raised on a single criterion, that of a potential Pareto improvement, which criterion is deemed related to a provision of the virtual constitution. Even if a political decision were made, say, to build a dam, a cost-benefit analysis of the dam that revealed a net loss would be properly regarded as a valid criticism of that political decision—which decision could be defended only by invoking *other* considerations, say equity, or national defence. The determination of the value of a project, or of any part or effect of that project, by the political process itself is either (economically) arbitrary, or else, if it arises from any other consistent body of principles, is in conflict with the allocative criterion on which a cost-benefit calculation proceeds. To add figures derived on one principle to figures obtained on some other principle produces an aggregate figure that carries no coherent interpretation.

The economist, as well as the decision-making body, should be aware of this. If a political decision has been to place the evaluation of the project in the hands of the economist, the economist is under obligation to base his calculations on a purely economic criterion. By covertly handing back some items included in the cost-benefit calculation for implicit, or explicit, evaluation by the decision-making body or its agents, and to do so after the political decision-making body has already agreed that the project is to be *evaluated* on an economic criterion—one which, as I have argued in Chapter 23, derives its rationale from a virtual constitution—is to effect a species of deception. It amounts to a sacrifice of meaning on the altar of quantification in order to save face. If the unmeasurable effect is completely beyond his range of reasonable guesses, so that a decision cannot be reached by the economist on the basis of the measurable data and reasonable guesswork, he serves the public better by confessing the truth: that, with the existing techniques and information, he is unable to discharge his task.

As indicated earlier, however, although the economist is unable to place a valuation on some critical magnitude he should provide the public with whatever information about it that he has (including informed guesses on any aspect of it). Indeed, he should let the public know exactly the sort of question he is trying to answer. What the economist must *not* do in these circumstances is to equate the eventual *political* outcome with the outcome of a *cost-benefit* analysis. As with any sort of (part) political decision, he reserves a right of independent professional criticism.

5 *The Social Rate of Time Preference.* As we shall observe in Chapters 35–36, there are substantial difficulties in discovering the rate at which society as a whole discounts the future. The difficulties arise not because society comprises a large group of people, or because of large differences between them in respect of tastes or wealth. Such features do not of themselves prevent the market prices of other goods from being regarded as equal to the corresponding marginal valuations of these goods for society. Nor, for that matter, does the fact that there is not a single rate of return on loans but, at any moment of time, a large number of rates each reflecting different time periods and different degrees of risk. Provided no coercion is employed, such lending and borrowing in capital markets that cover a wide variety of securities would produce mutually beneficial effects. It may be that, owing to some imperfection in capital markets—in particular, owing to an absence of institutions that might encourage lending and borrowing by persons and businesses of more modest means—some opportunities for social gain are not fully exploited. But it does not follow from this consideration that any improvement can be effected by attempting to alter the existing rates of interest.

The difficulty arises because the raising of investible funds by taxation involves (for the individual) coercive powers. The rate of return, net of income tax, will differ at the margin for people with different incomes wherever progressive income tax is in operation. The amounts saved and invested therefore differ from those which would obtain if the rates of return, net of income tax, were the same for everyone in any given securities' market and, of course, differ again from those which would obtain if there were no income tax. Given the vast number of taxpayers, and the wide variation in their estate, it is not easy to discover what the appropriate social rate of time preference should be. In the absence of countervailing considerations, however, one could infer only that it would be lower than that suggested by yields on existing securities.

Now there is much to be said for the economist's confessing his ignorance while trying to discover some useful proxy for the social rate of time preference. But there is no more to be said for the economist's support of the idea that a government, even the most democratic government, should itself decide the social rate of time preference than for his support of the idea that the government should decide any other price. And where the so-called policy maker, invoked by some economists, will turn out in practice to be little more than a bureaucrat, though perhaps a humane bureaucrat, the idea of empowering him to set crucial prices or, specifically, the social rate of time preference, has even less social warrant. In poor countries, for instance, the bureaucrat is likely to be one among the group imbued with 'Western ideas' of the desirability of rapid economic growth. He is likely to think of himself as the custodian of future generations, charged with the sacred task of transforming a 'backward' economy into a 'modern' economy in the face of the resentment, inertia, and 'superstition' of the masses. In the endeavour to achieve a faster rate of economic growth than that which would accord with existing behaviour patterns in the mass of people, the 'policy maker' will be prone to adopt a social rate of time preference for the guidance of economic decisions that is appreciably lower than that which is in realistic relation to people's actual time preference, or to the rates of return that would emerge under ideal economic institutions.

The economist who is prepared to accept the idea that society should be guided in its economic activity by prices that are set by or through the political process, and makes use of such prices in his cost-benefit analysis,[5] can always plead that he is simply following the wishes of those elected to take social decisions. But if so, he overlooks

---

[5] Accepting political *constraints* is by no means the same as accepting political *prices*. In the former case, the economist calculates whether a potential Pareto improvement can be met or not, given the political constraints that are likely to exist. In the latter case, however, and irrespective of political constraints, the economist is in fact *unable* to calculate whether or not a potential Pareto improvement can be made. In order to do so he must make use of *economic* prices, those arising from people's preference maps.

the fact that once he accepts from the political process prices or 'weights' that are arbitrary in that they do not correspond, in the last resort, to the subjective valuations of the members of society, not only is he unable to offer the public an independent *economic* appraisal of any plan or project (independent, that is, of the existing policies and preferences of the government of the day), he is no longer able to provide a coherent interpretation of his resulting calculations, nor to offer a vindication of any recommendations based on them.

Chapter 28

CONSISTENCY IN PROJECT EVALUATION (II)

1 If the arguments of the preceding chapters are accepted, there can be no place in an economic criterion, and more specifically a cost-benefit criterion, for the use of so-called 'national parameters' to supplement market data or, more broadly speaking, subjective valuation—at least in so far as such parameters are not offered as estimates of people's valuations but are derived instead directly, or indirectly, from political mechanisms. Such *politically*-determined national parameters include the social rate of discount, the weights to be attached to merit or 'demerit' goods (as distinct from 'ordinary' goods), and the weights to be attached to the gains and losses of the various income groups, or to the gains and losses of different regions.

There can, however, be other national parameters that are *economically* determined. Thus the parameter attached to a dollar spent on public investment—in other words, the social opportunity cost or 'shadow price' of a dollar spent on public investment—can depend solely on economic factors; on the marginal productivity of capital in the private sector, on the economic determinants of the social rate of time preference, and on representative economic behaviour of private individuals.[1] Again, the parameter that is attached to a dollar of expenditure on foreign exchange can be determined wholly by reference to the differences between the domestic prices of goods and their world prices, as indicated in Chapter 14.

While politically-determined prices or parameters have no place in any criterion of economic efficiency (based, as it should be, wholly on

---

[1] If the shadow price of investment exceeds unity, and the proportion of income saved varies with the income group, the weight to be attached to every dollar of outlay and to every dollar of benefit will depend upon the expected composition of the income group employed by, or receiving benefits from, the specific investment project.

individual valuations), the incidence of political *constraints* can hardly be avoided in a cost-benefit calculation. Moreover, no inconsistencies arise in acknowledging them. Political constraints as such do not offer to the economist arbitrary, or non-economic, valuations of goods. They act only to circumscribe the range of choices open to the economist. Such constraints in effect are to be construed as information on how the government is expected to act or react. The government may not act wisely: it may habitually violate traditional economic canons. Yet in undertaking a cost-benefit analysis under such conditions, the economist does not endorse government action. Indeed, he may go on record as opposing it. In taking into account the expected actions and reactions of the government, the economist is seeking to discover whether, in these particular circumstances, the introduction of the mooted project will yet realize a potential Pareto improvement.

Thus the economist, in evaluating a project, does not claim to be achieving optimal results. He is not claiming that nothing better can be done. On the contrary, he will readily agree that better can be done (for the economy at large as well as for the outcome of the project he is concerned with) if certain political or administrative constraints were to be modified or removed. But by making provision in his cost-benefit calculations for the constraints that are expected to prevail over the project's lifetime, the economist is addressing himself specifically to the question: what difference does it make to the economy if, under the constraints likely to be operative over the relevant time period, this specific investment project is introduced? In particular, does the project, under these conditions, bring about a potential Pareto improvement?

2 It cannot be too often stressed, however, that cost-benefit analysis as traditionally practised is no more than a useful technique in the service of social decisions. Indeed, the acceptance of the more rigorous and limited concept of a cost-benefit analysis put forward above, clearly implies that the outcome of a cost-benefit analysis alone is not socially decisive. It does not meet even conventional economic welfare criteria in so far as such criteria embody distributional provisos. It is certainly not to be thought of as a part of, or a substitute for, economic policy. A cost-benefit analysis neglects distributional effects. It neglects equity. It may have to ignore intangible spillover effects (though the economist should make this explicit). Of the occasional influence of a project on broad social goals, it can only draw public attention to the fact. In sum, a well-conducted cost-benefit study can be only a part, though an important part, of the data necessary for informed collective decisions.

Attempts to work more into the technique of cost-benefit analysis, to endow it with greater self-sufficiency for policy purposes by recourse to distributional weights or national parameters formulated by reference to political decisions or, at any rate, by reference to non-economic considerations, are to be resisted by economists in that they entail the following disadvantages:

(a) If the weights are to be chosen by the economist, they are arbitrary. They will vary with the political climate and are likely to cause squabbles among economists themselves, and between economists and the public. Since some projects will be accepted on one set of weights and rejected on another, one may anticipate continued political in-fighting over the weights to be adopted. To the extent economists did not reject the principle of employing such weights but participated in the struggle to establish one set of weights rather than another, cost-benefit analysis as a technique could become discredited.

(b) If the weights are chosen through the political process, they will also vary from year to year, and from one country to another, according to the composition of legislatures, political fashions, and the exigencies of bureaucrats. These variations could be such as, again, to bring the methods of cost-benefit analysis into disrepute.

(c) Once political valuations are believed pertinent for some items, there is no clear case for limiting the extent of political intervention for that purpose. If decision-makers can attach weights to merit goods, why not to ordinary goods also on the argument that, as among ordinary goods, some have smaller social merit than others? If they can attach a valuation to accidents or loss of life, why not also to a wide range of spillover effects? And if so much can be justified, there seems to be no logical reason against going further and having political decisions override all market prices and subjective valuations. Indeed, there is no reason why each and every investment project should not be approved or rejected directly by the political process, democratic or otherwise. With such a dispensation the economist could entertain the public by cleverly explicating the implicit prices or weights that could justify any particular investment decision so that it could compare them with those corresponding to some other investment decision.

There could not, however, be any independent economic critique, at this stage, of such political decisions.[2]

(d) Even if it were conceivably possible to secure permanent agreement within one country on the set of distributional weights to be attached to the benefits and losses of different income groups, it could not, as already indicated, be counted on to prevent the introduction of projects having markedly regressive distributional effects. Projects that would meet a weighted cost-benefit criterion could be such as to make the rich richer and the poor poorer if the beneficiaries were rich and many and the losers were poor and few. This possibility can be avoided only by a separation of these distributional effects from the Pareto effects of the traditional cost-benefit analysis.

(e) Last but not least is the question of consistency. Methods of project evaluation that can claim no virtue other than 'marshalling data systematically, putting them in quantitative terms, and rendering them commensurable' have nothing to commend them if, in the process, fundamentally different criteria are used in producing a single figure.

To illustrate, in having recourse to distributional weights, we are in effect employing a criterion that requires that the aggregate sum of all *util* changes be positive.[3] This criterion might easily accept an investment project that would be rejected by the traditional cost-benefit criterion, and vice versa. Moreover, as suggested earlier, a project accepted on this utility criterion might well realize a worse allocation of resources or realize a potential Pareto loss. The case is no simpler if we introduce into a cost-benefit technique both individual subjective valuations for some things and majority-determined social valuations for other things.

In general, when two or more criteria are jointly employed, problems arise. Allowing that each criterion taken singly has merit enough for it to be widely accepted, the application of either alone to an evaluation problem can yield different and possibly contradictory results to the application of the other. One can employ two criteria in

---

[2] The economist may want to point out that the weights shift about from one political investment decision to another. But a demonstration that political decisions can involve inconsistencies (who doubts it!) does not of itself establish the primacy of economic criteria.

[3] A money gain or loss, weighted by the util index appropriate to the level of income of the gainer or loser, provides a 'corrected' aggregate figure for all gains and losses which can be expressed in utils. The 'corrected' cost-benefit analysis is met if the excess of utils is positive.

project evaluation only (i) if there is general agreement on some higher principle to which both can be referred and which demarcates in advance the area of application of each criterion, and (ii) if the single resulting figure has a clear interpretation and a clear social rationale. Those who have proposed varieties of weighting systems or the use of national (politically-determined) parameters, have not as yet recognized, much less faced up to, these difficulties.

3 Finally, although the analysis in this volume purports to be appropriate for a cost-benefit criterion based on the concept of a potential Pareto improvement, we should be fully aware that—apart from its deficiency as a policy directive—such a criterion, as indeed any criterion of allocative efficiency in general, may conflict from time to time with law or popular opinion. Thus, the law might well forbid the undertaking of certain enterprises that can realize a potential or even an actual Pareto improvement. For example, gladiatorial contests, public exhibitions of obscenity, the sale of hallucinatory drugs, might be forbidden by laws expressive of public opinion even though every person directly affected might freely choose to participate.

The reverse is no less likely: the law may enact measures that do not realize a potential Pareto improvement. Issues over which feelings run high, and about which there is no financial complexity, can sometimes be more satisfactorily resolved by conventional voting procedures than by cost-benefit analysis. In addition, such political decisions modify the legal framework within which economic behaviour is circumscribed: in particular it can determine which of the two opposing groups in any conflict of interests—which arises with adverse spillovers—has the legal obligation to compensate the other.

REFERENCES AND BIBLIOGRAPHY FOR PART IV

Boadway, R. W. 'The Welfare Foundations of Cost-Benefit Analysis', *Economic Journal*, 1974.

Buchanan, J. and Tulloch, G. *The Calculus of Consent*, Michigan: University of Michigan Press, 1962.

Dasgupta, P., Marglin, S. and Sen, A. K. *Guidelines for Project Evaluation*, New York: UN, 1972.

Dobb, M. *Welfare Economics and the Economics of Socialism*, Cambridge: Cambridge University Press, 1969.

Foster, C. D. and Neueberger, H. L. 'The Ambiguity of the Consumer's Surplus Measure of Welfare Change', *Oxford Economic Papers*, 1974.

Graaff, J. de V. *Theoretical Welfare Economics*, Cambridge: Cambridge University Press, 1957.

Harberger, A. C. 'Three Basic Postulates for Applied Welfare Economics', *Journal of Economic Literature*, 1971.

Hause, J. C. 'The Theory of Welfare Measurement', *Journal of Political Economy*, 1975.

Irvin, G. *Modern Cost-Benefit Methods*, London: Macmillan, 1978.

Kaldor, N. 'Welfare Propositions in Economics', *Economic Journal*, 1939.

Little, I. M. D. *A Critique of Welfare Economics* (2nd edn.), Oxford: Oxford University Press, 1957.

Little, I. M. D. and Mirrlees, J. A. *Project Appraisal and Planning for Developing Countries*, New York: Basic Books, 1974.

Marshall, A. *Principles of Economics* (8th edn.), London: Macmillan, 1924.

Mishan, E. J. 'A Reappraisal of the Principles of Resource Allocation', *Economica*, 1957.

— 'The Postwar Literature on Externalities: An Interpretive Essay', *Journal of Economic Literature*, 1971.

— 'The Recent Debate on Welfare Criteria', *Oxford Economic Papers*, 1965.

— 'Welfare Criteria: Resolution of a Paradox', *Economic Journal*, 1973.

— 'The Uses of CV and EV in Cost-Benefit Analysis', *Economica*, 1976.

— *Introduction to Normative Economics*, New York: Oxford University Press, 1980.

— 'The New Controversy about the Foundations of Economic Calculations', *Journal of Economic Issues*, 1982.

Nash, C., Pearce, D. and Stanley, J. 'An Evaluation of Cost-Benefit Analysis Criteria', *Scottish Journal of Political Economy*, 1975.

Nath, S. *A Reappraisal of Welfare Economics*, London: Routledge & Kegan Paul, 1969.

Nwaneri, V. C. 'Equity in Cost-Benefit Analysis', *Journal of Transport Economics and Policy*, 1970.

Pearce, D. M. (ed.) *The Valuation of Social Cost*, London: Allen & Unwin, 1978.

Pigou, A. C. *The Economics of Welfare* (4th edn.), London: Macmillan, 1932.

Rothenberg, J. *The Measurement of Social Welfare*, New Jersey: Prentice-Hall, 1961.

Samuelson, P. A. *Foundations of Economic Analysis* (2nd edn.), Cambridge, Mass.: Harvard University Press, 1963.

Scitovsky, T. 'A Note on Welfare Propositions in Economics', *Review of Economic Studies*, 1941.

Sugden, R. and Williams, A. *The Principles of Practical Cost-Benefit Analysis*, Oxford: Oxford University Press, 1978.

Tinbergen, J. *Economic Policy, Principles and Design*, Amsterdam, 1966.

Toward a Social Report. US Dept. of Health, Education, and Welfare. Washington, DC, 1969.

Weisbrod, B. A. 'Income Redistribution Effects & Benefit-Cost Analysis', in Chase, S. B. Jr. (ed.). *Problems in Public Expenditure Analysis*, Washington, DC: Brookings Institution, 1968.

PART V. INVESTMENT CRITERIA

Chapter 29

INTRODUCTION TO INVESTMENT CRITERIA

1 The social benefits of an investment project come to fruition over the future. Some of the costs incurred by undertaking the investment project may also take place over the future. In general, then, there is a distinct time profile of benefits and costs corresponding to each of the investment projects under consideration.

We can ask any one of three related questions about such projects:

(a) What is the present social value of the stream of benefits, or of the stream of costs, or of the excess of benefits over costs?

(b) How should we rank a number of alternative investment projects? In other words, if we had to undertake any one, any two, any three, . . ., or all but one, of the n projects under consideration, which one, two, three, . . ., or $(n-1)$ of the projects should be chosen?

(c) Given funds sufficient for the financing of a specific project, or some or all of a number of projects, which of these projects, if any, should society adopt?

This last question, which is the crucial one, and the one to which we shall eventually turn our attention, will require a consideration of the social opportunity cost of the specific investment project; a consideration, that is, of the alternative social benefits necessarily, though implicitly, forgone by the private or public sectors in choosing to adopt a particular public investment project.

2 Let us first be clear about the nature of these costs and benefits. Investment in, say, a railroad requires an initial outlay of capital spread over the first one or two years. These expenditures are clearly costs. So also are the anticipated outlays at future periods of time, whether for repairs, maintenance, or for adding equipment, though their magnitudes are usually smaller than the initial outlays. Benefits are understood in the most comprehensive sense to include all additions to social welfare that can, in Pigou's words, 'be brought into relation with the measuring rod of money'.

Benefits should therefore include not only expected *receipts* over time since the services produced may not in fact be sold to the public but provided free, or sold at a price below its cost (rail travel could, for instance, be made free). Even if the good produced is sold at a price that covers its cost the revenue collected is almost always less than the full amounts people would be willing to pay rather than go without. For, as indicated earlier, an estimate of the full benefit to the buyers of the good is roughly equal to the area under the market demand curve. Again there are positive and negative spillover effects to be evaluated and added, algebraically, to the benefits of the direct recipients of the goods purposely produced by the project. The very existence of the railroad is a form of insurance even to those who use other means of transport, a form of insurance for which they would presumably be willing to pay something. Such sums, the estimated value of indirect benefits, are to be added to the direct benefits. On the other hand, any compensatory sums called for by those people whose assets or whose welfare decline as a result of the noise or pollution, or any other disamenity associated with the railroad service, are to be subtracted from the benefits.

We remind ourselves in passing that if we correct the benefit calculation for all spillover effects in order to come up with a net figure for *social benefits,* we *cannot* also invoke the concept of *social costs*— else we should be entering the same spillover effects *twice*, i.e. on the cost side as well as on the benefit side. By convention, therefore, outlays will be calculated as the actual money disbursements; the sums spent on the project at any time during its life. All the incidental effects on society that arise either in the building or in the operation of the project are to be added to, or subtracted from, the social benefits at the time they appear.

3 A distinction is sometimes made between 'capital costs' and 'operating costs', the former being the sums needed to build the project, the plant, machinery, and the like, the latter being the sums disbursed at regular intervals so as to maintain the flow of products or services. These latter or operating costs can be met from a 'revolving fund', which can take the form of a line of credit from the bank to be drawn on in order to meet the weekly wage bill, repairs, salaries and payments for materials. The indebtedness to the bank is limited by continual repayments either from the sale of goods or from government revenues. It is possible then to ignore all these operating costs and include in the benefit-cost stream outlays only for capital expenditures and interest-payments to the banks. In that case one has to be careful to subtract from gross receipts all expenditure on wages, salaries, materials, etc., leaving only a stream of net benefits or, more narrowly, net revenues.

In principle, however, it is simpler to disregard the distinction between capital costs and operating costs and enter *all* payments as costs, in which case *all* receipts (or 'gross receipts') (taken together with a net figure for the algebraic sum of all other *indirect* gains and losses) are entered as benefits. By subtracting, in each period, all the costs from all the benefits, we end up with a succession of net benefits (some negative, some positive or zero) to which we can conveniently apply any adopted investment criterion.

The advantages of setting out, initially, the gross figures in full may be illustrated by a simple example. Since the continuous flow of future benefits and costs is, in practice, broken up into discrete periods, frequently years, we can suppose a capital outlay of 100 today, or in year zero, is followed by an outlay on labour and materials of 130 during the next year, year one, and by sales of the resultant output, valued at 150, in year two. The series generated would then begin as $-100, -130, 150, \ldots$, and so on. If, however, one were to use the revolving fund concept, and omit setting down payments for labour and materials, the series might look like $-100, 0, 14$, the last figure being reached by subtracting from the sales of 150 both the value of labour and material inputs of 130 and also the interest payments of 6 on borrowing 130 for about a year. This figure of 14 clearly depends on the rate of interest at which the bank lends. For private businesses that seek to maximize profit the rate at which they expect to be able to borrow will indeed feature as no more than an unavoidable expense. But for public investment, the criterion to be used calls either for a special rate of discount, which in general differs from the actual borrowing rate, or else for a calculation of the internal rate of return, which is a product of the stream of net benefits *in the absence of* any discounting or compounding.[1]

For this reason it is advisable to set out in the first instance the gross figures as they appear period by period. Having decided the length of the period, we can subtract all outlays from all benefits only for the period within which they both occur. If, for example, we have the following stream of benefits and outlays:

Benefits	0	0	150	160
Outlays	100	130	135	0

it can be written as $(0-100), (0-130), (150-135), (160-0), \ldots$, or taking the algebraic sum in each of the brackets as equal to the net benefits (or excess benefits), $-100, -130, 15, 160, \ldots$.

In general, then, we can summarize the stream of expected benefits and costs as $(b_0-k_0), (b_1-k_1), (b_2-k_2), \ldots, (b_n-k_n)$, where b_0 and k_0 are the gross benefits and gross costs, respectively, in the initial period, b_1 and k_1 the gross benefits and gross costs, respectively, of the following period, and so on, the subscript referring always to the period, or year. If we now define the *net*, or excess, benefit in any t^{th} period, or year, B_t as equal to (b_t-n_t), we can write the above as a stream of *net* benefits, $B_0, B_1, B_2, \ldots, B_n$, where the Bs can, of course, be either negative, zero, or positive.

4. The choice of the size of the discrete periods into which a given length of time is to be divided is arbitrary. The year is customarily chosen for obvious reasons and, unless otherwise stated, we shall abide by the custom in the following chapters. For a comparison of very short investment streams, the breakdown into six-monthly, quarterly, or even monthly periods may be desirable.[2] There may not appear to be much to choose from as between two investment streams each running to three years. Broken into quarterly periods—and using quarterly rates of return and discount—one may be easily superior to the other.

---

[1] It might be thought that if we are given the rate of discount to be adopted, we could charge interest on móney borrowed (for labour and material payments) at that rate throughout the lifetime of the project. But this procedure would be valid only if all the opportunities for reinvesting future returns were those yielding a rate equal to that rate of discount, which in general is too restrictive an assumption.

[2] Indeed, for theoretical purposes at least, there is a mathematical convenience in postulating a *continuous* time-profile of net benefits.

It is perhaps unnecessary to remark that, since we are concerned with *social* benefits and not business profits net of tax,[3] our task is simplified somewhat. Neither corporation tax, income tax, nor excise tax for that matter is to be subtracted in the estimate of social benefits. Whether or not the government collects such taxes from the public enterprise in question, the value of such taxes is part of the social benefit.

---

[3] Given an annual progressive income tax, a business concern would not necessarily prefer a stream 30, −10, 10 to a stream 10, 10, 10, inasmuch as the former will pay more tax over the three-year period. After tax, for example, the former stream might be 20, −10, 8, and the latter 8, 8, 8. Unless the discount rate was very high, the latter would be preferred.

Chapter 30

CRUDE INVESTMENT
CRITERIA

1 Suppose we are faced with a choice of four investment options having the net benefits shown in Table V.1 below. Which, if any, do we choose if our budget is limited to 100?

TABLE V.1

	0	1	2	3	4
A_1	−100	115	0	0	0
A_2	−100	20	30	50	170
A_3	−100	100	110	−50	0
A_4	−100	80	110	−50	−10

If we had to choose *only one* from the four, we could be sure that it would never be A_4, irrespective of the criterion used. For A_3 is as good as, or better than, A_4 period for period. In the jargon, investment option A_3 'dominates' A_4. Thus if we subtract A_4's net benefit stream from that of A_3 the difference is a series, 0, 20, 10, 0, 10, these figures showing the amounts by which A_3's net benefits exceed those of A_4 in successive periods. In no period is A_3's net benefit less than that of A_4.[1]

Let us now consider three rather crude investment criteria, which however are commonly employed in the business sector, especially where the venture contemplated is risky.

---

[1] If, on the other hand, we had funds enabling us to choose two or more of these investment options, we might choose both A_3 and A_4. But we should never include A_4 while rejecting A_3.

2 *Cut-off period.* This is perhaps the crudest possible criterion that is used in business in order to decide whether or not to invest in a project. A suitable period is chosen over which the money invested must be fully recouped. The period could be ten years, though usually a shorter period such as five years, or even less, is chosen. Such a criterion may be justified in cases of innovation in products, or methods, that cannot be protected by a patent, and which innovations are likely to be copied by competing firms within two or three years. A cut-off period of three years, for instance, may be chosen in the belief that after three years further profits are uncertain, and increasingly unlikely. Glancing down the Table, it is clear that a cut-off period of three years *after* the initial outlay would admit the A_1 investment option. Indeed, more than the initial 100 is recouped in the first year after the outlay. The A_2 option only just scrapes home. A_3 would be able to recoup as much as 160 in the three years, while A_4 would recoup 130 (which, however, would be 120 if the outlay of 10 in the fourth year were certain).

The shortcomings of this criterion are easy to perceive. If the returns were not expected to accrue mainly in the first few years but mainly after the first few years, worthwhile projects would be rejected. A stream $-100, 0, 0, 20, 40, 60, 80, 120, \ldots$ would be rejected. So also would a stream $-100, 20, 20, 20, 20, 20, 20, \ldots$.

3 *Pay-off period.* Instead of choosing an arbitrary cut-off period, we may rank the investment options according to the number of years necessary to recoup the initial outlay. Clearly the A_1 project would be ranked first since its pay-off period is less than a year. For the A_2 project it is exactly three years. If we ignore subsequent *outlays* in the last two projects, it is one year for A_3 and more than one year for A_4.

The pay-off period rate of return is but another way of expressing the above results. It is obtained simply by dividing 100 by the number of years in the pay-off period. Since the A_1 investment option pays off the initial outlay in less than a year, we divide 100 by something less than a year which yields a pay-off period rate of return of more than 100 per cent. For the A_2 project, the pay-off period rate of return is equal to 100 divided by three, or $33\frac{1}{3}$ per cent. For the A_3 project it is exactly 100 per cent, and for the A_4 project, it is somewhat less than 100 per cent.

The justification for either form of this ranking device is similar to that for the cut-off period. When imitation by competitors, or rapid obsolescence is anticipated, or in circumstances of political uncertainty, one of the overriding considerations is safety. One looks for quick returns and prepares for a hasty exit. A project such as A_1, which pays 115 within a year of 100 being invested, is likely, in such circumstances, to be looked on with greater favour than option A_2 which would not show any profit until the fourth year.

In the complete absence of uncertainty, however, it would be impossible to justify either of the above rules-of-thumb. If interest rates happened to be low, A_2 would be far more profitable than A_1, and more profitable than A_3 for that matter.

4 *The average rate of return* is the simplest way of taking account of all the figures in the investment stream. Just because all the figures are taken at face value in calculating the average rate of return, there is an implied assumption that all the figures have been corrected for uncertainty.

For all investment options having only an initial outlay of 100, such as A_1 and A_2 in Table V.1, there is no ambiguity in the method. One simply adds together all the subsequent positive net benefits, divides this sum by the number of years, and expresses the resulting figure as a percentage of the initial investment outlay. For the A_1 option, the sum of positive benefits is 115. This sum divided by one gives an average sum of 115 per annum, and expressed as percentage of the outlay of 100, is 115 per cent. For A_2 the sum over four years of the positive benefits is 270. This sum divided by 4 gives an annual average return of $67\frac{1}{2}$ and, expressed as a percentage of the original outlay of 100, is $67\frac{1}{2}$ per cent.

The weakness of this method is apparent at once. For it is by no means evident to anyone thinking of investing 100 that A_1 with an average of return of 115 per cent, is superior to A_2. It might be added in passing, however, that the weakness is not particular to this method, but arises also in the more sophisticated internal-rate-of-return method which will be treated later.

For investment options A_3 and A_4 having outlays in later years, we could add together all the figures, both positive and negative, after the initial outlay and proceed as before. For A_3, the algebraic sum of 100, 110, and -50, is 160. This sum divided by 3 yields an average of $53\frac{1}{3}$ per cent per annum. Similarly for A_4 which yields an average return of $32\frac{1}{2}$ per cent per annum.

5 *Net average rate of return.* The above results can be regarded as 'gross' average yields since they are derived from adding together only the positive net *benefit* figures. An obvious modification is to calculate a 'net' average yield in the same way except that the outlays are to be subtracted from the sum of the benefits before dividing by the number of years. In A_1, for instance, we should first subtract the outlay of 100 from 115, to give 15, this being 15 per cent of the 100 outlay. In A_2 we subtract the outlay of 100 from the positive sum of benefits of 270 before dividing by 4. Hence a net average rate of return of $42\frac{1}{2}$ per cent. Similarly, the algebraic sum for A_3 is 60. The returns being spread over three years, the net average rate of return is 20 per cent. The algebraic sum for A_4 is 40 and, spread over 4 years, offers a net average rate of return of 10 per cent. The comparison between the four projects looks a lot more plausible on this 'net' average method than on the 'gross' average method.

Under conditions of certainty at least, the net average rate of return, though clearly superior to the other investment rules, is unsatisfactory for two reasons.

(1) It depends upon the number of years chosen. To choose the length of the investment stream by reference to the number of consecutive years showing a positive net benefit is arbitrary. For example if project A_1 in Table V.1 yielded the slightest positive net benefit in year two—say, a return of $0 \cdot 1$—the average rate of return would result from dividing the total benefits, $115 + 0 \cdot 1$, *less* the initial outlay of 100, by 2 instead of one, giving $7 \cdot 51$, which on this method has to be accepted as the net average rate of return per annum on the 100 investment. This slight addition to the net benefit of the A_1 investment option makes it look, on this calculation, a very much less attractive proposition, a paradoxical result which could obviously cause a lot of trouble.

(2) A less apparent but not less serious defect is that the method takes no cognizance of the *pattern* or *profile* of the net benefits over time. Given the total amount of the net benefits, say 300, arising over a number of consecutive years, whether the net benefits are bunched together over the first years, spread evenly over the years, or bunched toward the end of the period, makes not the slightest difference to the net average rate of return. An investment stream of $-100, 5, 20, 25, 250$ is to be valued as highly as one of $-100, 250, 25, 20, 5$; or, for that matter, we should on this calculation be indifferent as between an

211

investment option having the stream −100, 1, 1, 1, 297, and one having the stream −100, 297, 1, 1, 1. But which person would not prefer the latter to the former? For people do take notice of the timing of benefits. They are not, that is, perfectly indifferent as between receiving $10,000 in ten years' time and receiving $10,000 today. Once we take into account the time dimension, we are impelled to move away from these rather primitive investment criteria to those more familiar to economists.

6 These more sophisticated investment criteria are all based on the common procedure of reducing a stream of net benefits (some negative, some positive) to a single value at a point of time. This is done by using some rate of interest as a weighting device through time. The more familiar fall into two categories: (1) those which determine the *value* of an investment stream at an arbitrary point of time by reference to a given rate of interest—the more popular procedure being that of determining a *present* value of the investment stream;[2] (2) those which determine an average *rate of return* by reference to the condition that the value be reduced to zero at the initial point of time. The more popular criterion in this connection is that known as the internal rate of return.

These two popular investment criteria, the present discounted value criterion and the internal rate of return criterion, will be compared in the following two chapters.

---

[2] Although, as I shall indicate later, there are manifest advantages in comparing investment streams by their terminal values.

Chapter 31

THE PRESENT DISCOUNTED VALUE CRITERION

1 If we have an investment stream such as $-100, 50, 150$, and we are given a rate of interest (or discount rate) of 10 per cent per annum, the present discounted value of the stream of benefits alone—50 after the first year, 150 after the second year—is given by the calculation

$$\frac{50}{(1 + 0 \cdot 1)} + \frac{150}{(1 + 0 \cdot 1)}2 = 169 \cdot 4$$

The present value of the outlay of 100 is also 100, since the 100 is, in these examples, supposed to be incurred right at the beginning, at year zero; that is, at the *beginning* of the first year or, for the sake of conformity, at the end of the zero[th] year. It is incurred just at the point of time to which we are reducing all subsequent net benefits or net outlays, and therefore does not require discounting to that point of time.

The *Net* Present Discounted Value of the investment stream above, being the present value of the benefits less the present value of the costs, is $166 \cdot 5 - 100$, or $66 \cdot 5$. If we wish to regard outlays as negative net benefits, the net present discounted value of an investment stream is simply the sum of all the net benefits when discounted to their present value.

In more general terms, given a stream of net benefits, $B_0, B_1, B_2, \ldots, B_n$, where the Bs are positive, zero, or negative, the net present discounted value is given by

$$B_0 + \frac{B_1}{(1 + r)} + \frac{B_2}{(1 + r)}2 + \ldots + \frac{B_n}{(1 + r)}n$$

or, more briefly,

$$\sum_{t=0}^{t=n} \frac{B_t}{(1 + r)}t$$

where *r* is the rate of discount.

The necessary instrument in this criterion is the appropriate rate of interest or rate of discount by which the net benefit at any point of time is weighted. It is commonly assumed that the correct rate of interest is that which reflects society's rate of time preference. (If, for example, society is taken to be indifferent between having $100 million today and $106 million next year, the *social* rate of time preference is 6 per cent per annum.) We shall, for the present, go along with this assumption though later on it will be argued that it is correct only under special conditions. In a Crusoe economy, if 120 bushels of corn next year are deemed by Crusoe to be equivalent in satisfaction to 100 bushels of corn today—by which is meant that he is perfectly indifferent to having either 100 bushels of corn today or 120 bushels of corn in a year's time—Crusoe's rate of discount is 20 per cent per annum. Until Man Friday arrives, and has some say in the decision, Crusoe's individual rate of discount can also be thought of as the social rate of discount.

2   To be more accurate, however, Crusoe's reaction to the choice presented to him gives us no more than the social rate of discount for the one year and, for that matter, is strictly valid only for 100 bushels of corn this year, not for more or for less. If, indeed, the same rate of discount did hold for successive years, then Crusoe would be indifferent as between 100 today, 120 next year, 144 in the year following that, and so on. It is, however, quite possible that his discount rate rises with the passage of time. Instead of being indifferent as between 100 today and 144 in two years' time, he might specify 150 in two years' time. This would mean that for the first year his rate of discount is 20 per cent, but for the second year he uses a discount rate of roughly 25 per cent per annum.

Again, even if we confine ourselves to the one year, it is not true that the same rate of discount holds for *any* amount of corn. If Crusoe agrees, though only just, to postpone consumption of 100 bushels of corn this year in order to have an additional 120 bushels next year, it does not follow that he will be prepared to forgo another 100 bushels of corn this year in exchange for another additional 120 bushels next year. It is more plausible to suppose that he should want more than an additional 120 bushels next year to persuade him to forgo this year the consumption of yet another 100 bushels; say an additional 140 bushels next year. We could say that Crusoe's marginal willingness to sacrifice 100 today for 120 next year reflects a discount rate of 20 per cent per annum, while his marginal willingness to sacrifice 200 today for 260 tomorrow reflects a discount rate of 30 per cent over-all. Put otherwise, we could say that for the first 100 bushels the marginal discount rate was 20 per cent, and that the marginal discount rate for another 100 bushels was 40 per cent.

These possibilities are to be noted before passing on. For it is also the case in society at large that, however the social rate of discount is determined, it is invariant neither with respect to the magnitudes of the intertemporal exchange of goods nor to the length of time involved. If we have information about the variation of the rate of discount with respect either to magnitudes or time, however, there is no difficulty, in principle, in adapting our chosen investment criterion accordingly. In the meantime, our task will be simplified by assuming but a single social rate of discount. Moreover, since we are to examine this concept in Chapter 33, we shall also assume that this social rate of discount is known to us. If the reader prefers, he can suppose, provisionally, that it has arisen from the interplay of market forces plus, perhaps, some form of government intervention that has the object of ensuring that the resulting rate of interest in the economy correctly reveals society's preference as between present and future goods. If, for instance, the social rate of discount is 10 per cent per annum, we shall take it that society as a whole is indifferent as between 100 today, 110 in a year's time, 121 in two years' time, and so on. And that, therefore, the *present* value of 110 in one year's time, or 121 in two years' time, is exactly 100.

3 Having made these provisional simplifications, let us go on to consider the following three propositions, all of them commonplace in the literature on the subject.

(1) The Net Present Value[1]—or Excess of Present Value over Cost—of a particular investment stream depends upon the rate of discount used. If, for instance, the stream of net benefits is −100, 0, 150, the net present value of the stream would be a little less than 48 if

---

[1] The term 'Net Present Value' will be used occasionally as an abbreviation of 'Net Present *Discounted* Value', or 'Net *Discounted* Present Value'.

the discount rate were 1 per cent. If, instead, the discount rate were 50 per cent, the next present value would be $-33\frac{1}{3}$.

(2) Which of a number of investment streams yields the largest net present value depends, in general, on the rate of discount used. If two investment streams are, respectively, -50, 20, 80, and -60, 20, 70, then the first, being 'dominant', will have a larger net present value irrespective of the rate of discount employed. If instead there is an A stream of -100, 0, 180, and a B stream of -100, 165, 0, a discount rate of 0·01, or 1 per cent, ranks A, with a net present value of about 76, above B, which has a net present value of about 63. If, however, the appropriate rate of discount is 0·5, or 50 per cent, the net present value of the A stream is -20 and is therefore ranked *below* the B stream, which has a net present value of 10. From these two examples, it should be manifest that there is a particular social rate of discount—between 1 per cent and 50 per cent—for which the two streams have exactly the same present value. Let us call this social rate of discount r^*. Then r^* is easily determined by equating the net present value formulae for the two streams, i.e. we set

$$-100 + \frac{180}{(1 + r^*)}2 = -100 + \frac{165}{(1 + r^*)}$$

and solve for r^*, which turns out to be about 9 per cent.

In general we can determine a net present value of a particular investment stream, say A, for each conceivable rate of discount. The resulting relationship can be plotted in Figure V.1 where the vertical axis measures PV_r, or net present value of the investment stream in question, and the horizontal axis measures r, the social rate of discount. The net present value of the A stream becomes smaller the larger is the rate of discount r; hence the negative slope of the A curve. It will be noted that the negative slope crosses the horizontal axis and continues below it into the south-east quadrant. This indicates that at discount rates above some critical rate of discount the net present value of the stream becomes negative (for example, at a 50 per cent discount rate, the stream -100, 0, 180, has a net present value of -20). A similar relationship can be plotted for the B investment stream.

If one of these two investment streams were dominant, it would lie above the other at all rates of discount. In the absence of dominance the A and B curves will intersect, either in the positive quadrant, as in the Figure, or else in the negative quadrant (not shown). For all con-

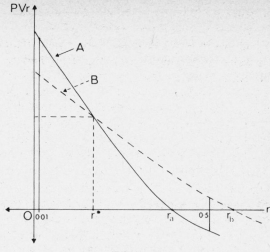

Figure V.1

ceivable (positive) discount rates—save one, r^*—the present values of the two streams differ. At discount rates below r^* the A stream has a higher net present value than the B stream, the reverse being true for discount rates above r^*. Only at r^* do both streams have the same net present value. It is obvious that if the rate of discount, from being a little above r^*, fell to a figure below r^*, the net present value of the A stream would change from being less than that of the B stream to being greater than it.

It may be observed finally, that there is a discount rate corresponding to each investment stream, r_a and r_b respectively, for which the net present values of the A and B streams are both zero.[2]

4 (3) As a corollary of the preceding proposition, it is simple to show that given the growth-path of an asset, the optimal 'gestation period'—that period giving the maximum net present value—is also determined by the rate of discount. Such a growth path is represented in Figure V.2, time, in years, being measured along the horizontal

---

[2] As will be explained in the following chapter, this property implies that r_a and r_b are the 'internal rates of return' respectively of the A and B streams.

217

axis. Total real value at any point of time is measured vertically and, therefore, at time zero total present value is measured. Common examples of growth curves are those of the growth in value of timber and wine. If a tree is planted, the value of the tree increases proportionally with the growth of the tree (assuming the price of timber constant). As for a bottle or barrel of wine, its value increases with time (up to a point) because of the improvement in its flavour. Let us consider the timber example.

A continuous growth path is represented by $G_0 G$ in Figure V.2. At time zero, total costs OC (measured along the vertical axis OV) are incurred in purchasing the sapling and in employing the labour to plant it. Although the sapling may begin to grow immediately after planting, its wood will be worth nothing until the end of the second year, from which point of time it grows in value—at first more rapidly—to a maximum after which it declines. The net value of the timber at any point of time is given by the vertical distance from the point of time measured along the horizontal axis to the $G_0 G$ curve.

In order to appreciate better the connection between this growth curve and the preceding Figure V.1, along with its examples, we could split the time axis into discrete units of a year, and measure vertically the total volume, and value, of timber at the end of each year. Instead of a continuous growth path we should then have a succession of vertical lines increasing in height up to point M. The heights of these vertical lines should then be regarded as the value of *alternative* investment streams. For instance, the vertical line above 4 on the horizontal axis could measure exactly 100. If OC measured an initial cost of 50, the investment option corresponding to $t = 4$ would be $-50, 0, 0, 0, 100$. The investment option corresponding to $t = 5$ could be $-50, 0, 0, 0, 0, 112$. The investment option corresponding to $t = 6$ could be $-50, 0, 0, 0, 0, 0, 120$, and so on for $t = 7, 8, 9, \ldots, n$.[3] Which of all the investment options would we choose? Bearing in mind the preceding proposition, we need have no hesitation in affirming that, in general, it will depend upon the social rate of discount.

If, then, we are given the social discount rate r, we can construct any number of *discount curves*, each different from the other by an

---

[3] For expository convenience we are ignoring the costs of tending the tree while growing. If these were constant at, say, 10 each year, the investment option corresponding to $t = 4$ would be $-50, -10, -10, -10, 100$.

increment of present value. Suppose the social discount rate is 5 per cent, one such discount curve V_1V_1 would measure, say, 80 at time zero along the vertical axis. At a point above $t = 1$ the height would be 84, at $t = 2$ the height would be 88·2, and so on, the height at the end of each successive year being 5 per cent more than that of the preceding year. Society is deemed indifferent to being anywhere along such a curve, any increase in time being exactly compensated by an increase in value. V_2V_2 can be drawn measuring, say, 90, along the vertical axis; V_3V_3 measuring, say, 100, and so on. Conceptually, these VV curves are infinitely dense, and we should select the highest among them that touches the growth curve. In the Figure, V_2V_2 is represented as the highest VV curve, touching the growth curve at Q, a point that corresponds to $t = 6·2$. We should conclude that the maximum *present* value of the net benefits at a 5 per cent discount rate is given by the height OV_2. The gestation period is 6·2 years, and *net* present value is OV_2 minus OC. It will be correctly surmised by the reader that the point Q is one of *tangency* between the discount curve and the growth curve. If there is any doubt about it, this property can be inferred by approaching the gestation period by a slightly different route.

The growth path G_0G, when looked at as a succession of vertical lines, or alternative investment options, is so shaped as to place these alternative investment options, eventually, in order of increasing value.[4] We need then only consider the increment by which the value of each investment option exceeds the one preceding it by a year, and compare the resulting increment in value with the given discount rate. There is always a social gain to be obtained provided the increment of value by waiting a year exceeds the social rate of interest. Postponing the cutting down of the tree from the fourth year to the fifth year will result in an increase in value from 100 to 112. Since society is indifferent as between 100 in the fourth year and 105 in the fifth year, there is a social gain of 7 (in the fifth year) from postponing the cutting down of the tree by a year. If we postpone the cutting for another year, the value of the timber rises by a further 8, to 120 altogether. But society is indifferent as between 112 in the fifth year and 105 per cent

---

[4] Initially, the annual *rate* of growth increases, but while it does this there is no sense in stopping the process. Only when the *rate* of growth begins to decline does the time arrive for comparing the increment of value with premium required to induce society to wait for this increment of value.

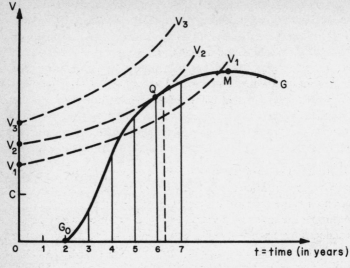

Figure V.2

of 112, or about 118, in the sixth year, so there is a further gain of 2 (in the sixth year) by postponing the cutting to the sixth year. Postponing the cutting to the seventh year would increase the value of the wood to 125. Society, however, would require a minimum of 126 in year seven to induce it to give up 120 in year six. If therefore it did postpone the cutting until the seventh year, a social *loss* of one (in the seventh year) would be incurred. We conclude the tree should be cut down some time between the sixth and the seventh year.

Once we return to the assumption of a *continuous* growth curve, however, the successive periods of time can be made as small as we like. In the limit, the increment of growth and the necessary time premium are equalized at a point of time. Visually, there is a mutual tangency at this point of time between the growth curve and one of the 5 per cent discount curves.

Chapter 32

THE INTERNAL RATE OF RETURN

1   The internal rate of return is a more respectable form of the average rate of return mentioned in Chapter 30 in that, like the present discounted value method, it takes account of time.

A simple example will illustrate how the internal rate of return is calculated. If we have a stream of net benefits, $-100, 50, 86 \cdot 4$, we can discount each of these net benefits to the present, $t = 0$, using a discount rate of 20 per cent. The present value of the net benefit of 50 in year one, when discounted at 20 per cent, is $50/(1 + 0 \cdot 2)$, or 40, while the present value of 86.4 in year two, when discounted at 20 per cent, is $86 \cdot 4/(1 + 0 \cdot 2)^2$, or 60. The present value of both 50 in year one and $86 \cdot 4$ in year two is, therefore, $40 + 60$, or 100; which is exactly equal to the initial *negative* net benefit, or net outlay, of 100. This 20 per cent discount, just because it equates the present value of the positive net benefits to the present value of the net outlay, is taken to be the internal rate of return of the above stream of net benefits.

We can, for the present, simplify the terminology a little by referring to *positive* net benefits simply as *benefits*, and by referring to *negative* net benefits simply as *costs* or *outlays*. The internal rate of return is, then, the rate of discount which makes the present value of the benefits exactly equal to the present value of the costs. Put otherwise, the internal rate of return is that rate of discount which makes the present value of the entire stream—benefits and costs—exactly equal to zero. Thus, if we have an investment stream,

$$B_0, B_1, B_2, \ldots, B_n \qquad (B_i \geqslant 0, \qquad \text{for} \quad i = 0, 1, 2, \ldots, n)$$

then the internal rate of return λ, is that for which the sum

$$\frac{B_0}{(1 + \lambda)} 0 + \frac{B_1}{(1 + \lambda)} 1 + \frac{B_2}{(1 + \lambda)} 2^2 + \ldots + \frac{B_n}{(1 + \lambda)} n = 0$$

or, more briefly, that for which

$$\sum_{t=0}^{n} \frac{B_t}{(1 + \lambda)} t = 0.$$

The sense in which the internal rate of return, so defined, is an average over time is conveyed by the example of a man investing, say, 100 for five years. If the internal rate of return of some given investment stream were 25 per cent per annum, the man would have in mind an *equivalent*, though simpler, investment in which his 100 in the present grows by 25 per cent each year. He sees his 100 in the present becoming 125 by the end of the first year, $156\frac{1}{4}$ by the end of the second year, and so on, to reach $100(1 + 0 \cdot 25)^5$ by the end of the fifth year. More generally, if the investment stream in question were -100, B_1, B_2, B_3, B_4, B_5, where the Bs are any pattern of benefits, and the internal rate of return were known to be 25 per cent, then an *equivalent* investment stream would be $-100, 0, 0, 0, 0, 100[(1 + 0 \cdot 25)^5]$. For this given investment stream, when discounted to its present value at 25 per cent, is, by assumption, equal to zero, and so also is the equivalent stream. Consequently, if a man is told that the internal rate of an investment stream over n years is equal to λ, he is justified in thinking of the investment as equivalent to one in which his initial outlay is compounded forward at the rate of λ per annum for n years.

Thinking of the internal rate of return in this way, the man will want to compare any such investment with the opportunities for putting his money into other securities, either equities or government bonds. If the only alternative open to him, or the only alternative he will consider, is long-term government bonds, perpetuities say, yielding 6 per cent per annum,[1] then an investment yielding a rate of return of more than 6 per cent (always assuming certainty or, at least, equal certainty) will be preferred to the purchase of these 6 per cent government bonds.

2   Let us now return briefly to the growth curve of the preceding chapter, depicted here in Figure V.3. The reader will recall that using the tangency condition between the growth curve, $G_0 G$, and the highest

---

[1] In the modern economy there is, of course, a wide diversity of government bonds even if we restrict ourselves to long-term issues. We simplify the treatment, for the time being, by assuming there is only one type of long-term government bond, say 'perpetuities', i.e. interest-bearing bonds having no redemption date, such as British Consols.

5 per cent discount curve at Q determined the optimal gestation, or investment, period. We have, however, here followed the convention of drawing the discount curve as straight lines by measuring the *logarithms* of the values along the vertical axis—thus successive x per cent differences appear along it as equal distances.

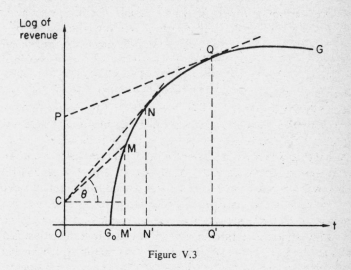

Figure V.3

If the highest present value, OP, at the given social rate of discount (which we continue to suppose is 5 per cent) determines the optimal period OQ', do we obtain the same result using, instead, the internal rate of return? We should hardly expect so, since this optimal OQ' period itself will vary with the particular magnitude of the rate of discount adopted, being longer the lower the rate of discount.

But first, how do we represent the internal rate of return on this diagram? The answer is that it can be represented by the slope of a straight line from C to any point of the growth curve, say M. For this slope is determined by $\tan\theta$, which is equal to the *excess* benefit EM at time M'—that is, total benefit $M'M$ *less* the cost OC at time zero— divided by time OM' in years. This fraction given by $\tan\theta$ must be the internal rate of return simply because, as required by definition, it is the rate of interest which reduces the total future benefit $M'M$ to a present value that is equal to the initial cost OC.

223

Now the highest internal rate of return possible is, on this construction, determined by the slope of the straight line from C that just touches the growth curve G_0G at the point N, there being no straight lines from C steeper than CN that can also just touch this growth curve.

If the optimal investment period is now defined as that yielding the highest internal rate of return, this will be a period equal to ON'. This optimal internal-rate-of-return period is clearly shorter than OQ', the optimal period on the net present value criterion. So which is it to be? Do we let the tree grow for a period OQ' or do we cut it down after ON' years? This is not the only sort of problem in which the results obtained by using these two investment criteria differ. We shall defer the resolution of this apparent discrepancy, however, until we have illustrated similar discrepancies in other investment problems.[2]

---

[2] A hint may be allowed the impatient reader, however. If, after time ON', the proceeds NN' could be reinvested in an identical tree-growing project, there would be a loss by letting the tree continue to grow to $Q'Q$. What is at issue, then, are the reinvestment possibilities whenever the tree is cut down. This reinvestment aspect of the problem is treated in some detail in later chapters on the 'normalization' procedure.

Chapter 33

THE ALLEGED SUPERIORITY OF THE DISCOUNTED PRESENT VALUE CRITERION

1 Consider the three alternative investment streams, A, B and C, listed in Table V.2. The undiscounted net benefit ratio, $(B-K)/K$, where B represents the benefits in the first year, and the only year in which benefits accrue, and K represents the initial capital outlay, would rank C greater than A. Why the *undiscounted* net benefit ratio? Since any rate of discount affects each of the benefits at t_1 in exactly the same proportion, we may infer that whatever be the discount rate, the resulting discounted net benefit ratio would give the same ranking as the undiscounted ratio.

This conclusion is valid, however, only for a two-period investment in which the outlay appears in the first period, and the benefit in the second. Add but one more period, and the ranking will in general depend upon the discount rate. For instance a stream -100, 10, 100, cannot be ranked in relation to the stream -100, 90, 10, without knowing the discount rate. If this were 1 per cent, the first would clearly yield a larger net benefit ratio than the second. If, however, the discount rate were 50 per cent, the second would yield a larger net benefit ratio than the first.

The two-period investment stream has also another property: the ranking of investment streams by their internal rates of return, as shown in the last column of Table V.2, is equal to the undiscounted net benefit ratio, $(B-K)/K$, and therefore produces the same ranking. There is no mystery about this: the excess benefit, $B-K$, as a fraction of the capital cost, K, is equivalent to one year's growth of the initial capital, K. Thus the capital of 100 in A will have been perceived to grow by 5 per cent, and in C by 25 per cent. A discount rate of that same per cent—5 per cent for A and 25 per cent for C— will therefore reduce the magnitude of the benefit so as to equal the original cost; which result follows the conventional definition of the internal rate of return.

For such two-period investment streams only, then, is the ranking unambiguous. Whatever the rate of discount, that is whether zero or any positive or negative figure, the ranking remains unchanged, and indeed gives exactly the same order as a ranking based on the internal rate of return.

TABLE V.2

	t_0	t_1	$(B-K)/K$	Internal rate of return
A	-100	105	5/100	5 %
B	-100	115	15/100	15 %
C	-20	25	25/100	25 %

2 This harmony between the present value criterion and the internal rate of return criterion will, however, as the reader probably suspects, break down if any of the investment streams being compared contains more than two periods. Indeed, this implication accords with the proposition exemplified above: that for investment streams in excess of two periods the ranking will vary with the rate of discount used. The internal-rate-of-return ranking does not, however, at all depend on the adopted rate of discount, but is independently determined. If it then so happens that at the ruling discount rate a number of investment streams show the same ranking by the two criteria, an alteration of the discount rate, which changes the present-value ranking of the investment projects, will also produce a discrepancy between this new present-value ranking and the ranking by internal rates of return.

The two three-period investment streams, A and B in Table V.3, illustrate this simple inference. Both investment streams are ranked equally by the internal rate of return criterion, each yielding 10 per cent. Not surprisingly, if the rate of discount were 10 per cent, the $(B-K)/K$ ratio, which is now to be interpreted as the *discounted* net benefit ratio would be zero in each case, and they would be ranked equally. If the rate of discount were 1 per cent, however, investment stream B would show a higher discounted net benefit ratio, 19/100, compared with that for A, 9/100. The reverse ranking is produced if

TABLE V.3

	t_0	t_1	t_2	Internal rate of return	$(B-K)/K$ at 1 %	$(B-K)/K$ at 10 %	$(B-K)/K$ at 20 %
A	−100	110	0	10 %	9/100	0	−8/100
B	−100	0	121	10 %	19/100	0	−16/100

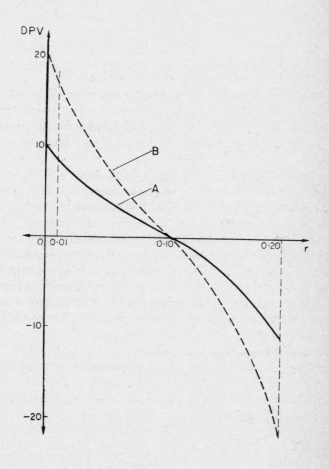

Figure V.4

227

the discount rate were changed to 20 per cent—B's net benefit ratio being $-16/100$ compared with $-8/100$ for A. A diagrammatic representation of these results appears in Figure V.4. The discounted present value (DPV) of the investment streams, measured vertically, and therefore also the discounted net benefit *ratio* of each investment stream A and B, varies inversely with the rate of discount r which is measured horizontally. At a 10 per cent rate of discount the two investment streams have the same present value, which is zero. Since a 10 per cent rate of discount reduces each of these investment streams to zero, their internal rates of return are, by definition, equal to zero. For discount rates of less than 10 per cent, at which the net present values of both streams are equal,[1] B's present value exceeds that of A, the reverse being true for rates in excess of 10 per cent.

3 In spite of this discrepancy between the two criteria, the internal rate of return has been recommended in some circumstances, particularly as a method of allocating a given capital budget among a number of potential investment projects. Thus one might select a number of public investment streams, subject to a budget, provided that the internal rate of return on each investment stream that is chosen exceeds the adopted rate of discount. The scheme is illustrated in Table V.4, which shows five investment streams in declining order of internal rate of return. The discounted present value of the net benefit ratio is also given for a discount rate equal to 3 per cent.

If the capital budget were 1,000, on this selection criterion only 350 of it would be spent. We should admit A, B, C and D. But we should not admit E. Only the first four projects have an internal rate of return in excess of the 3 per cent discount rate. Project E has an internal rate of return of only 2 per cent, which is below the 3 per cent discount rate. The reader will doubtless observe that the ranking by present discounted values (at 3 per cent) of the four selected investment options differs from the ranking produced by their internal

---

[1] Irving Fisher has defined the term *rate of return over cost* as the discount rate at which the $[PV_r(B) - K]/K$ ratio of two alternative investment streams are equal. In general this rate of return over cost is *not* equal to zero, as in the example above, and as depicted in Figure V.3. It is usually taken to be positive, as r^* in Figure V.1 of Chapter 31. The significance of this rate-of-return-over-cost figure is simply that of revealing the discount rate at which ranking reversal takes place.

TABLE V.4

	t_0	t_1	t_2	Internal rate of return	$PV_r(B-K)/K$ (for $r = 0.03$)
A	−100	110	0	10 %	7/100
B	−100	0	115	7 %	8/100
C	−100	106	0	6 %	3/100
D	−50	52	0	4 %	1/100
E	−200	2	208	2 %	−2/100

rates of return. But this is no matter, since the same four investment options would be admitted also, and the E project excluded, on the present value criterion.

If the capital available were only 200, the internal-rate-of-return criterion would select A and B, a choice which would be confirmed by the present-value criterion. However, let the capital available be only 100, and we are, again, faced with a problem. The internal-rate-of-return criterion chooses the A investment option. The present-value criterion chooses instead the B investment option.[2] Again, the reader may be inclined to put his faith in the present value method. If the rate of discount that is operative is 3 per cent, he will choose the B stream since he can exchange it for a net profit of 8 today, whereas the A stream can be exchanged for a net profit of only 7 today.

4 A further consideration also seems to tell against the use of the internal-rate-of-return criterion: more than a single rate of return may correspond to a given investment stream. A necessary, though not sufficient, condition for more than one internal rate of return to correspond with an investment stream is that not all the costs be incurred in the initial period: there will have to be net disbursement at later periods.

A simple example of such an investment stream, H, would be −100, 350, −400, which yields two internal rates of return, λ_1 of 46 per cent, and λ_2 of 174 per cent, since the use of either of these rates as a discount rate would reduce the present value of this

---

[2] The problem would arise even with a capital budget of 300 or more if the A and B investment were *mutually exclusive*, i.e. if, in any list of investment projects, we could include either A or B, but not both.

stream to zero, as required by the definition of the internal rate of return.[3]

Figure V.5 depicts the curve relating the net present value of the H stream to the rate of discount, r. The curve will be seen to cut the horizontal axis, not once (as does each of the investment streams in Figure V.4), but twice; once at the point where r is 0·46, and once where r is 1·74. Since either of these two discount rates reduces the present value of the H stream to zero, they are identified as the two internal rates of return, λ_1 and λ_2.

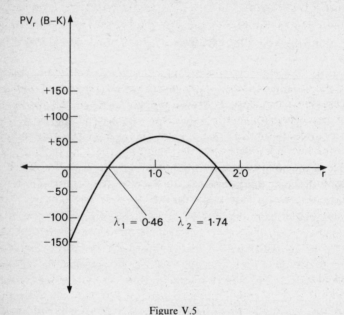

Figure V.5

---

[3] From the definition of the internal rate of return, say λ, we require a λ for which

$$-100 + \frac{350}{(1 + \lambda)} - \frac{400}{(1 + \lambda)^2} = 0.$$

The reader will recognize the expression as a quadratic equation with two solutions for λ, 0·46 and 1·74. On this definition a single capital outlay is *sufficient* to yield a single magnitude for the internal rate of return. This is not a *necessary* condition for a single internal rate of return, however. If, for example, there were a later outlay that was small enough, a unique internal rate of return would still result. An example would be the stream -100, 121, -1, which has an internal rate of return of a little over 20 per cent.

Of course, the reader might think that of these two internal rates of return, λ_1 (46 per cent) is the more reasonable. If he were obliged to adopt an internal rate of return for such a stream, he would probably choose 46 per cent. But he would find it difficult to justify such a choice, if he were not allowed to draw on intuition. Moreover, even if the reader did feel confident about the 46 per cent internal rate of return for the H stream, this example of two internal rates of return is only a special case. For one can devise investment streams to yield three, four, or indeed, any number of internal rates of return.[4] However open-minded the reader may wish to remain, he cannot deny that the case for preferring the present-value criterion above the internal-rate-of-return criterion looks very strong.

5 If, provisionally, we accept the present-value criterion, there is still the question of whether we are to rank investment streams by excess benefit over cost, by the ratio of benefit to cost, or by the ratio of *excess* benefit (or *net* benefit) to cost (which we used in Table V.4). These three alternative present-value criteria are worked out in Table V.5 for two investment streams, A and C, where K' is the present value of the outlays, and B' is the present value of the benefits both discounted, say, at 10 per cent. In the $(B' - K')$ column, A, having excess benefit over cost of 50, is ranked above C which has an excess benefit over cost of only 30. In the next, B'/K' column, however, C, having a ratio of benefit to cost of 2·5, is ranked above A which has a ratio of benefit to cost of only 1·5. In the final column showing $(B' - K')/K'$, the ratio of *excess* benefit to cost continues to show C ranked above A. A glance at the last two columns will assure the reader that B'/K' and $(B' - K')/K'$ will give the same ranking, since the latter ratio is derived from the former simply by subtracting unity from it. We can, then, ignore the B'/K' ratio and compare $B' - K'$ with $(B' - K')K'$.

Now if there is a capital budget of exactly 100, it may seem reasonable to be guided by the $(B' - K')/K'$ ratio ranking, and there-

---

[4] Determining the values of the internal rates of return corresponding to any investment stream implies solving for the roots of a polynomial. Any investment stream having n periods can be transformed into a polynomial having a maximum of $n - 1$ different roots, each being a possible internal rate of return. Only those that are positive will matter for investment criteria. Negative internal rates of return make sense, but are not usually of much importance. Complex roots do not appear to make sense in this context.

TABLE IV.5

	K'	B'	$(B'-K')$	B'/K'	$(B'-K')/K'$
A	100	150	50	1·5	0·5
C	20	50	30	2·5	1·5

fore to choose C rather than A. This is rational enough if it is established that he can have either A alone or, instead, five of the C streams. The outlay for five of the C streams uses up exactly the budget of 100, and produces a discounted present value of five times 50, or 250—which is 100 more than can be got by choosing to invest the budget of 100 in A. But suppose, now, that there is an opportunity for only a single C investment, what then? We should have 80 left over after putting 20 of the capital into C. If we could use this 80 left over in A (the A investment stream being divisible) it would be better to invest 20 in C and the remaining 80 in A, than to put the whole 100 in A; for, in the former case, the present value of the benefits would be $[(0\cdot8 \times 150) + 50]$, or 170, while in the latter case the present value of the benefits is only 150. But just as it may not be possible to increase the C investment, the A investment stream may not be divisible. In that case we have a choice; all the A stream, or all the C stream. If there were no other opportunities for the 80 left over from choosing the C stream, we should choose the A investment stream. Even if the funds left over from a choice of C did not have to be returned, but could be used to invest in the private investment sector of the economy at, say, 10 per cent, the A stream would still be chosen. For the adoption of 10 per cent as the discount rate ensures that the outlay of 80 invested in the private sector at 10 per cent per annum in perpetuity has a present value of no more than 80. There is, then, no excess benefit from using the 80 left over in the private sector if C were chosen: the excess benefit resulting from this course of action would still be 30—just as little as it would be if, instead, the 80 were returned to the government.

It is apparent that, under these conditions, investment stream A should be chosen. And if such conditions did prevail we should use the $(B'-K')$, or excess benefit, method of ranking which would place A, having an excess benefit of 50, above C having an excess benefit of only 30. It is no less apparent that if any multiple of the C investment stream were technically feasible, we should be maximizing the excess benefit of the given capital funds of 100 by opting for C rather than A. Under those conditions, the $(B' - K')/K'$, or excess benefit over cost ratio, method is the correct one to employ. Put differently, if we adopt the $(B' - K')$ method of ranking, we tacitly suppose that the alternative investment streams are of exactly the size given: no increase is possible. If, however, we adopt the $(B' - K')/K'$ method of ranking, we tacitly suppose the opposite; that either stream can be increased in any proportion. Where neither of these suppositions is true, we should not repose confidence in either method of ranking. We should then want to compare the present value of the benefits from using the given 100 of funds in each of the feasible number of ways.

Chapter 34

INVESTMENT CRITERIA IN AN IDEAL ECONOMY

1 Investment criteria, whether based on present discounted value or internal rate of return, are devised so as to enable us to choose between alternative uses of investible funds. If there are two or more alternative investment options each has to be compared with the others.[1] If there is only one investment project under consideration, the alternatives are either to use the funds for private expenditures, or for buying government securities. The latter course of action may be thought of as a financial transaction that does not of itself result in any new investment. Initially it is but a purchase of government bonds on the open market: a transfer of cash from the individual to the government. For society as a whole, however, and certainly for public investment, we must transcend all financial transactions and, in the last resort, consider at least two alternatives: either consumption or else investment in this particular project. If there is only one rate of interest on the market, which we are assuming to be the case for the present, it will be generally used as the relevant rate of discount in the present value criterion, provided that this market rate reflects society's rate of time preference. A rate of interest of 5 per cent that reflects society's time preference implies that society is indifferent as between $1 today and $1.05 in a year's time. If therefore one removes $1 worth of consumption today and returns $1.06 worth of goods next year, society is

---

[1] It is just possible that the reader may be wondering why we have continuously ignored mention of depreciation in the treatment of investment criteria. The short answer is that the principles which guide the rate of *amortization* are unrelated to those that arise in *selecting investments*. There is nothing mysterious about this. All investment criteria, whether based on present discounted value or internal rate of return, implicitly make allowance for the maintenance of capital through the requirement that the outlays on the investment project be (more than) covered by the present discounted value of its expected future benefits.

deemed to gain by the transaction. If, instead, one returns $1.04 in a year's time, society is deemed to be worse off from having postponed consumption. Consequently if a particular investment yields more than 5 per cent in a year's time, society is deemed better off from switching resources from the production of consumption goods to this particular investment good, and vice versa.

In circumstances where the only two alternatives open to the use of present resources are either investment today in a specific project or else consumption today, the investment project will be chosen if its internal rate of return *exceeds* the 5 per cent social rate of time preference. As for the net present discounted value of this investment project, it is sure to be positive (since, by definition of the internal rate of return, the net present value of this investment stream will be zero when discounted by a rate *higher* than 5 per cent), and is therefore admissible also on the present value criterion. A positive net present value, given the rate of discount equal to the social rate of time preference, indicates that the present value equivalence of the future benefit stream—as valued by society at its own rate of time preference—exceeds the present value produced by the same resources if, instead, they are used to produce consumption goods. Society is therefore better off by investing these resources and consuming the future products than by consuming their product today. In sum, undertaking *any* investment project that has a higher internal rate of return than the 5 per cent social discount rate, and therefore one that yields a net present discounted value greater than zero, makes society better off than it would be using the resources instead for present consumption.

2 In an ideal market economy, in which the existing rate of interest reflects the social rate of time preference, the economy is in equilibrium. If this rate of interest is 5 per cent, the marginal product of the existing capital stock is also equal to 5 per cent and, indeed, the internal rate of return on the current volume of investment—the so-called marginal efficiency of investment—is also equal to 5 per cent. In such an ideal economy, at the moment of equilibrium, any new investment opportunity having an internal rate of return above 5 per cent—or a net present value above zero when discounted at 5 per cent—will add to social welfare, as indicated above, and will be undertaken. Such investments will also appear immediately profitable to private persons and corporations. For, in a perfect capital market, they can sell the prospect of the future stream of returns (expected with certainty) for a present value that is larger than the initial outlay. The difference between the initial outlay and the present value so calculated is an immediate profit. If the investment stream is—100, 63, 66, the value of the benefits, 63 in year one and 66 in year two, when discounted to the present at 5 per cent discount, is 120. Once these subsequent benefits are assured by spending an initial outlay of 100, he can sell them on the market for a present sum of 120, the difference, 20, being pure profit.

In this long run equilibrium, with social rate of time preference equal to the existing (riskless) rate of return on investment, a straight-forward application of the present discounted value formula, or the internal rate of return formula, as already outlined, will suffice for an investment criterion. If, however, the rate of return on investment is above the social rate of time preference, for any of a number of reasons which we shall mention presently, investment criteria become less simple and, indeed, there are controversies about the 'correct' criterion which we shall have to examine. What seems to complicate the issue further is that, even in the absence of such deficiencies, the long run equilibrium rate of interest that would emerge is not uniquely determined by the interaction of individual's preferences and investment opportunities but may be varied through monetary and fiscal managements. We shall face these several difficulties in the following chapters.

Chapter 35

THE RATE OF DISCOUNT AND THE SOCIAL RATE OF TIME PREFERENCE (I)

1 The assumptions we have been working with—a perfectly competitive economy and, therefore, a perfectly competitive capital market dealing in a single long term government bond—may appear pretty stringent. A perfectly competitive capital market, for instance, could be taken to imply that every person is able to borrow, for any purpose and for any length of time, on exactly the same terms as any other person. Alternatively, we could envisage a capital market that is composed of a large number of markets that specialize according to the length of time of the loan and according to the type of investment for which the money is raised. All such markets could be conceived to be working perfectly if all men were equally eligible to trade, in any amounts they wished, in any of the markets.

There are however one or two implications of such constructs that are so far from being satisfactory as to make them appear unworldly and impractical. If a man were permitted to borrow any sum from one of such markets at the going rate, he could borrow a large sum for any period, say ten years, and could repay the loan on maturity simply by borrowing a larger sum, repeating the operation, if necessary, to the end of his life so that in fact the loan would not be repaid. For such a perfect capital market to promote optimal economic arrangements then, it would be necessary to have a population of perfectly honest men. But even this requirement would not suffice, for although all men were perfectly honest, they are yet likely to make errors of judgement or become the victims of untoward events. The wealthier a person is, however, the better placed he is to weather any adversity arising from misjudgment or misfortune. Given that differences in wealth are substantial, it would be irrational for lenders to be willing to lend as

237

much to the impecunious as to the richer members of society, or to lend the same amounts on the same terms to each. In order to make perfect capital markets a plausible assumption, we should have to require not only that men are perfectly honest but also that they are equally wealthy and wise, or alternatively, that there is perfect foresight in respect of the outcomes of all investment projects and repayments.

In a more realistic economy in which men can borrow at different rates of interest, according to their credit-worthiness, and in which they can increase their borrowing only by offering higher rates of interest, their marginal rates of time preference will differ. If person A's marginal rate of time preference is 10 per cent and person B's marginal rate of time preference is 20 per cent, and it is known that A will be called upon to finance 30 per cent of a given project with person B financing 70 per cent of it, then the *social* rate of time preference for this two-person economy may be calculated as $(0 \cdot 3 \times 10\%) + (0 \cdot 7 \times 20\%)$, or 17%. If now the rate of return on this specific project is expected to be greater than 17%, then both A and B can be made better off by undertaking the investment. In effect, a *potential* Pareto improvement is met no matter how the returns from this investment are in fact distributed between the two persons. In general, if there are n persons in the economy, and their marginal rates of time preference are $r_1, r_2, \ldots, r_n$ the social rate of time preference will be r, where $r = \sum_{i=1}^{n} x_i r_i$, where x_i is the share of the project that the ith person will be called upon to contribute to the finance of the project, and $\sum_{i 1}^{n} x_i = 1$.

This is what we are after at least, even though there are a large number of capital markets, and not everyone borrows either for personal consumption or for investment in current projects. However, it cannot be supposed that actual markets will reflect such requirements, and it would be virtually impossible to calculate this ideal social rate of time preference. Nevertheless, considerations of what is required should not impel us to discard the notion of a perfectly competitive capital market producing a single rate of interest, at least not at this stage of the argument. For though, admittedly, the conditions under which a single perfectly competitive capital market operates are far removed from circumstances that ever existed or are ever likely to exist, the problems that we want now to examine more closely would arise no less if there were a large number of capital markets, if the differences in risk were of the greatest importance, and if, in consequence, all such markets were highly imperfect. Nothing of economic significance is lost, in fact, but unnecessary complication by proceeding for some time with the fiction of a single perfect capital market, one trading in a single long-term government bond. This yield on government bonds we shall call the market rate of interest r.

2   Under what conditions can such a market rate of interest r be regarded also as the social rate of time preference?

In the modern economy, the market for the existing stock of securities is so large relative to new issues required to finance current investment projects that—provided there is a strong sense of the normal yield (which implies that price-stabilizing expectations prevail)—the prices at which securities as a whole are bought and sold are not much influenced by the volume of new issues. This state of affairs accords with the common 'Keynesian' assumption that the price of long term bonds is highly stabilized. Starting from any underemployment equilibrium for the economy, an exogenous increase of investment, entailing an excess current supply of bonds over the current demand for them (the current demand for bonds being equal to current saving) cannot then restore equilibrium in the bond market by raising the interest rate (lowering bond prices). If the rate of interest is perfectly stabilized, the excess of current investment over saving causes a rise in income and employment until, in a new employment equilibrium, saving again equals investment and therefore the bond market is in equilibrium at the perfectly stabilized rate of interest. The converse operation is assumed to take place if there is an exogenous decline in investment. More generally, however, the rate of interest is taken to be *imperfectly* stabilized, as reflected in the inelasticity of the so-called liquidity preference function. In that case, an exogenous increase in current investment results in a new equilibrium level of employment having a somewhat higher rate of interest, and vice versa. We should therefore have to conclude that, in general, the rate of interest varies positively with the equilibrium level of output and employment.

We might get around this problem, however, by arguing that what is wanted is a rate of interest that is consistent with full employment and price stability. Such a rate of interest could be taken to reflect the interaction between a fully employed society's current saving schedule and its current investment opportunities. No matter what a person's time preference pattern is like, he is able to borrow and lend all he wishes at the resultant market rate of interest. Each person's rate of time preference is therefore equated at the margin to the market rate of interest; which means that, in equilibrium, everyone has the same rate of time preference. For this reason it may be called the social rate of time preference and adopted as the social rate of discount in any investment criterion.

But a problem can arise if aggregate current saving, and possibly aggregate current investment also, depend not only on the rate of interest and income, as it can in a simple 'classical' or 'Keynesian' economy, but also on the community's accumulated wealth. If, for instance, people save less as their real wealth grows, then the apparently unique full-employment rate of interest, which we hoped to adopt as the social rate of discount, no longer obtains. Imagine the government, beginning now from a position of full employment with stable prices and a stable interest rate, deliberately lowering the interest rate by continued open-market purchases of bonds. At a lower interest rate, the resulting excess investment over saving and, therefore, excess aggregate demand, causes a rise in the general level of prices. The price level will, we know, continue to rise until real saving is increased to the extent necessary to restore equilibrium. However, the increase in real saving cannot come through changes in real income, or output, for the economy is already at full employment. We must have recourse to some other mechanism, in this case the wealth-saving effect: the rise in the level of prices causes both the stock of fiat money and the stock of government bonds held by the public to decline in real value. This apparent decline in wealth need have no effect on government expenditure, but it does cause people to save more. Prices therefore continue to rise until the saving-investment equilibrium is restored. The outcome of the government's open-market policy in lowering the interest rates turns out to be a new equilibrium at a lower rate of interest, but at a higher level of prices. If this mechanism is accepted, it follows that by use of open market operations, the government can ultimately establish any full employment equilibrium rate of interest over a wide range, leaving prices to find their own level. There is, therefore, no longer a unique rate of interest corresponding to the full-employment economy.

How important is this possibility if we intend to use the equilibrium rate of interest in a full-employment economy as the social rate of discount? It is generally conceded that if real income, or real wealth, increases autonomously, or if other exogenous changes take place, such as a change in tastes or in technological opportunities, the equilibrium rate of interest would also alter. We should not think of repudiating the use of the market of interest on that account. Why then should we feel uneasy if it is supposed that an alteration of the market rate of interest can result also from a believed change in the value of money and bonds held by the public? Whatever people's beliefs are about the current value of their assets, and however the government's actions have influenced this belief, it is not misleading to state that the resulting rate of interest provides the terms on which everyone is ready to forgo consumption today for consumption tomorrow. Thus, although the determination of the rate of interest may now be said to depend upon an additional factor, wealth (indirectly manipulated by the government in setting this rate of interest), it is nonetheless as valid an expression of the social rate of time preference in any new equilibrium as in the old.

3 It should be mentioned in passing, however, that if the real value of the public debt varies with the price-level, via the above mechanism, it is simply because the public debt is what is sometimes called 'deadweight' debt—indicating that, at some time in the past, the government sold bonds to the public and used the revenues, not for investment in real assets, but simply to meet current expenditures. Interest payments on such deadweight debt are, therefore, not met from the yields of real assets, since these do not exist, but from additional taxes raised for this purpose. To the public it may be a matter of indifference whether the government securities are backed by real assets or not. But when the price level changes it does make a difference. For if the government does hold real assets, they rise or fall in price along with the general level of prices, and the public's holding of real wealth does not alter.[1] It

---

[1] Nevertheless, where a government has used the proceeds of a sale of bonds to the public in order to buy *real* assets, a doubling, say, of all prices will enable it to double the nominal interest payments simply because the nominal return from the real assets it has acquired will also have doubled. Since debtors are not, however, required to pay out any more than the fixed nominal interest payments, the government gains to exactly the extent that its bondholders lose. Though it may be said that the community as a whole is no worse or better off as a result of this redistribution of income in favour

is, then, only when the government securities have no 'real' backing, when the 'wealth' they represent is in effect illusory, that a rise in the price level creates the illusion of a fall in real wealth, and vice versa. If somehow the community recognized that it was no better or worse off in consequence of its internal ownership of the public debt (including fiat money) and therefore valued it correctly at zero, the relationship between the rate of interest and the price level described above would not exist.[2] Once more the full-employment rate of interest would be uniquely determined.

---

[1] (contd) of debtors and against creditors, it is far from impossible that it will not affect aggregate expenditure. But we follow tradition here in mentioning the possibility, while disregarding the distribution effects on aggregate expenditure. We are left, then, only with the wealth-illusion expenditure-effects of movements in the price level.

[2] If people were all perfectly informed and rational, they would indeed perceive the connection between the interest on such bonds and the additional taxes required to meet the interest payments. In that case the community *as a whole* could not regard itself as having increased its wealth by buying such bonds. If then the price-level rose, their *tax payments* to meet interest on the deadweight debt would fall in real terms, and by exactly the same amount in real terms as their *interest-receipts* from these deadweight bonds. They would be neither better off nor worse off. Apart from possible distribution effects—operative when there is any price-change in the economy—their real saving would not alter. In such a situation the full-employment interest rate is indeed uniquely determined.

Chapter 36

THE RATE OF DISCOUNT AND THE SOCIAL RATE OF TIME PREFERENCE (II)

1 Even if we suppose the full-employment rate of interest to be uniquely determined, there may be other reasons for rejecting the market rate of interest as an expression of the social rate of time preference. If they are valid, we cannot use the market rate of interest as the social rate of discount in investment criteria. It may be the case that people suffer from an absence of 'telescopic faculties' which causes them to discount their future wants too heavily. They would then tend to save less than they would if they were not afflicted with this defective vision. Put otherwise, their rate of time preference tends to be 'too high', and they tend to save and invest less than they would if they were, in some sense, perfectly rational beings. The case for government intervention might be strengthened by regarding the state as custodian of the future, responsible for the welfare of future generations. In order to correct the imperfection of vision and/or of institutions, and to give more weight to the future, investment decisions should be guided by a 'true' social rate of time preference, one that is below the rate of interest thrown up by the market. But this argument presents difficulties.

A politically determined social rate of time preference or, for that matter, any other politically determined shadow price that, at best, can be rationalized by reference to the liberal democratic process, is not consistent with the strictly economic criterion to be adopted in a cost-benefit analysis. More precisely, a politically-determined social rate of time preference, or a politically-determined social discount rate, cannot be vindicated by the allocative requirement that the algebraic sum of the compensation variations be positive—the conditions for a potential Pareto improvement. In fact there is no consistent economic criterion by which both politically determined prices and economic determined prices can be justified and, bearing in mind the different mechanisms by which political prices and economic prices are determined, there is little likelihood of their coinciding.

This is not to say that there may not happen to be good economic reasons for a politically-determined rate of interest being below the rate of interest yielded by the market. The distribution of wealth would, in general, affect the equilibrium market rate of interest, as indeed it would affect any price in the economy, though it would not necessarily affect the rate of interest as determined by the voting mechanism. A politically-determined rate of interest is more likely to be influenced by the existing proportion of borrowers to that of lenders; numbers would count more than the distribution of financial power. Be that as it may, if democracy agreed to be guided in the formation of the rate of interest, as indeed in the formation of any other price, by the Pareto principle, no political opposition to the equilibrium rate of interest, produced in a perfectly competitive economy, could be justified—*provided there were no external effects*. And this indeed is how Marglin (1963b) proposes to justify the notion of adopting a social rate of discount below the equilibrium rate of interest thrown up by a competitive economy. The explanation draws on a particular type of external effect, one arising from the experience of welfare at the thought of additional consumption of future generations. It is possible that, quite apart from being concerned with the real income of his heirs, and the heirs of his friends and relations, a man is not completely indifferent to the prospective real income of future generations. If he is not indifferent, then the prospect of an additional one dollar of income to be enjoyed, say, by the next generation adds to or subtracts something from his present satisfaction.

2   Suppose it is known that a contribution today of $1 to an investment fund for future generations will realize $2, in real terms, in thirty years' time, which additional $2 will then be at the disposal of the future generation, how will a man react? He may be prepared to pay, at most, 20 cents today to be certain that the future generation enjoys an additional $2. But 20 cents falls short of the $1 necessary to bring this about. However, there may be a number of other people who also have a soft spot for the generation yet to be born, and derive some satisfaction from the thought that they will inherit more than the provision

currently being made for them by the economic system. The maximum sum each of such persons will be willing to pay now, in order that the future generation has an additional $2, is his compensating variation (CV). Clearly, if the sum of the CVs taken over all of such people exceeds the dollar of investment that is necessary to produce $2 in thirty years' time, there is a net gain to society from investing the extra $1. If, say, there are fifteen people altogether, each willing to give, at most, 20 cents today to the 'Posterity Fund' for the satisfaction of knowing that posterity will receive $2, then, by contributing 20 cents each, all fifteen of them are made better off. Altogether they contribute $3 today which, when invested, produces a sum of $6 for posterity, which obviously affords these fifteen people more satisfaction than if only $2 were made available to posterity.

In general every person in the community can have different feelings about posterity, and the welfare of a number of persons may fall if an additional $2 is made available to future generations by the Posterity Fund. For such persons the CV is negative. However, so long as the *algebraic* sum of the CVs of all people today is positive and exceeds the sum of $1, there is a case for the state investing an additional $1. Clearly, additional dollars today should be invested beyond the market volume of investment so long as there continues to be a potential Pareto gain. The volume of extra-market investment, that is, should continue to the point where the algebraic sum of all CVs of the future $2 is exactly equal to the $1 of investment necessary to produce it.

There can be, then, a case for assuming that, accepting people's preferences as ultimate data, the equilibrium rate of interest is too high, and that a careful calculation of people's CVs would reveal that the volume of current investment should be increased to a given optimal amount. This optimal amount of investment would be realized by the market if the rate of interest were set below the equilibrium at some predetermined figure. This lower rate of interest should then be regarded as the true rate of society's time preference and, for investment criteria, should be adopted as the social rate of discount.

3   What does this sort of analysis amount to? If, in a perfectly competitive capital market, 10 per cent becomes the market rate of interest at which some volume of current investment is undertaken, this resultant volume of investment will be too low because the relevant external economies have not been taken into account. An indirect way of making allowance for these external economies and, therefore, of producing the optimal volume of investment, is for the government to set the rate of interest that much below the 10 per cent equilibrium rate thrown up by the perfect capital market.

There can be two objections to this conclusion, the first a minor one. (1) Although the formal logic of the argument is sound enough, the notion that on balance people today would like to see consumption reduced in order to provide more consumption for posterity appears to be at variance with the familiar distributional judgements which favours transferring income from rich to poor within, and as between, communities. If society survives the hazards that science and technology have made possible then it is plausible to believe, and indeed it is generally believed, that—in the wealthier countries at least—our grandchildren will be far better off in terms of man-made goods (though they are likely to be much worse off in terms of resources of natural beauty) than we are today. This would still be so even if the rate of net investment were to fall to zero provided technological innovation, which is chiefly responsible for per capita growth in economically advanced countries, continued into the future.

To suggest, therefore, that real income be transferred from the relatively poorer generations of today in order to add yet more to the higher standards of consumption of the generations of tomorrow is to suppose that, when properly questioned, people would reveal notions of distributional propriety that are the opposite of those conventionally adopted by most people, including economists, and indeed adopted by all governments. Such a finding cannot be ruled out *a priori*, but no reliable evidence has been adduced to support it.

4 (2) More important, the question whether on balance external economies or external diseconomies arise in current investment, though relevant to economic policy, is ancillary to a consideration of the social rate of time preference *in the absence of external effects*.

There is little difficulty about the concept of a single individual's time preference. In the absence of a market rate of interest at which he can borrow or lend, the individual's rate of time preference varies, at any point of time, with his existing wealth, with the profile of his expected future income stream and the degree of its uncertainty, and with his 'impatience'. If, at any moment of time, a 10 per cent rate of time preference is universal we are justified in valuing 100 next year at about 91 today, and 100 the year after at about 83 today. But are we justified in valuing 100 in 50 years' time as equivalent to 100 $(1 \cdot 10)^{-50}$? Not if the 100 in 50 years' time will accrue to different people. If in 50 years' time the 100 accrues to a person B of a new generation, the enjoyment he derives therefrom might be every bit as great as that derived from it now by a person A of the existing generation. Person A would therefore have no business in evaluating the future worth of 100 by discounting it for 50 years at 10 per cent when he himself is not, in any case, going to receive it; when in fact person B is going to receive it. Whenever inter-generation comparisons are involved, as they may be in determining the rate of depletion or destruction of a non-renewable asset, it is as well to recognize that there is no satisfactory way of determining social worth at different points of time.

The employment of a discount rate, say the social rate of time preference to a stream of costs and benefits extending over generational time does, indeed, when used correctly, meet some criterion. But it transpires that the criterion met—if it is met—is not the familiar Pareto criterion, a criterion that we already know (from the preceding chapter) is met when the appropriate discount rate is applied to benefits and costs occurring within the lifetimes of members of a given generation. Examination of this issue, however, is postponed to Chapter 40. We shall therefore continue to suppose in the next three chapters that all the benefits and costs associated with the projects under discussion occur within a time span during which all those affected by the projects are alive.

5 Given these assumptions, we have now to consider more critically the various methods proposed for attributing a single value to a given stream of benefits and costs over time. And we continue to observe the convention of supposing that the market rate of return on private investment is also equal to the *social* rate of return on private investment, say ρ, and that this rate ρ is above society's rate of time preference, r, in conditions of certainty. One reason why the supposition is plausible, even in the complete absence of externalities of investment, is that income and corporation taxes have to be paid on returns from investment income. If the time preference of individuals also reflects society's rate of time preference, r, then individuals can ensure a return of r only by requiring a gross yield ρ

that is larger than r. For example a person who will not lend unless he receives a net return of 10 per cent per annum will in fact require a return of $16\frac{2}{3}$ per cent on his money if direct taxes on his gross return from investment amount to 40 per cent.[1]

Even in the absence of direct taxes, however, the excess of ρ over r could be explained as existing in a short period during which the volume of investment is below optimal. So long as current investment is *below* the optimal level, social welfare will be increased for every $1 taken out of current consumption and invested in the private sector, there to yield an annual return equal to ρ. For $1 consumed today is equal, according to society's rate of time preference, to $1(1 + r)$ tomorrow, whereas $1 invested today becomes equal tomorrow to a larger sum, $1(1 + \rho)$.

Clearly if there are no limits on the amounts the government can raise from the public for investment purposes, it should continue, in the interests of maximizing welfare, to reduce consumption in favour of investment (even if there are no opportunities other than those in the private investment sector) until the difference between ρ and r has vanished. In a short period, however, there are political constraints on the amounts the government can use for investment. And though whatever investment is undertaken in the short period will act to lower the market rate of return, ρ, for simplicity of exposition we can always choose a period so short as to make the decline in ρ negligible.

Maintaining the fiction of a perfect capital market, each person (in the *absence* of any direct taxes) must have a time preference equal to ρ, the certain market yield on private investment, this private time preference being in contrast with, and below, the 'true' or social rate of time preference r. Under these conditions, how is the discounted present value formula to be used in choosing between investment options?

---

[1] If 40% of his gross return, ρ, is taxed, then the remaining 60% of ρ has to be equal to the required 10% per annum. Therefore 100% of ρ must equal $100/60 \times 10\%$, or $16\frac{2}{3}\%$ per annum.

Chapter 37

A GENERAL CRITIQUE OF THE USE OF DPV IN PUBLIC INVESTMENT CRITERIA[1]

1 All the well-known criteria proposed for evaluating public investment streams embody a DPV procedure.[2] A crucial distinction, however, has to be made between (a) the older type of criterion, which simply applies what is thought to be an appropriate discount rate to the stream of benefits (positive or negative) in question, and (b) a newer type of criterion, in which provision is made for the allocation of the resulting benefits of a project as between consumption and further investment and within which category there can be differences as between behavioural, institutional and political assumptions.

The differences within the (a) category are elucidated in a comparison of formulations (1) to (4) which follow. Those within the (b) category are basically less controversial and may be represented by formulation (5) alone. The latter differences, as we shall see, arise only from the degree of elaboration thought to be appropriate and deserve only passing mention.

2 In order to economize on inessential elaboration of the analysis, the practice common in the literature, of ignoring (initially at least) uncertainty in order to focus on a critical part of the logic of investment criteria, is followed here. Again the assumption of 'full employ-

---

[1] This critique, incidentally, applies as well to the usual DPV methods employed by private corporations for evaluating alternative investment streams.
[2] My proposed normalization procedure (1967) being an exception, further reflection about which has resulted in the present critique.

ment' is maintained throughout the chapter,[3] as is the fiction that the market values of goods are equal to their social values, in particular that an outlay K on the public project is equal to its opportunity cost. The convention that voluntary changes in current saving entail equal changes in private investment is also followed in the text.

Let r be the rate of time preference common to all n individuals affected by the public project, and let ρ be the yield on private investment. Although there can be many different r's and ρ's (r_i for $i = 1, \ldots, n$, and ρ_j for $j = 1, \ldots, s$), and each r_i, ρ_j, can also be dated $t = o, \ldots, T$, an analysis conducted in terms of such generality adds only elegant complexity which may obscure the main lines of the argument. We shall therefore continue to regard r and ρ as single magnitudes, and not as vectors or matrices, except to comment on the proposals of others.

Writing $PV_a(B)$, then, as a shorthand for the present value of the stream of benefits (some of which can be net outlays, or negative benefits) when discounted at rate a, the four type (a) criteria to be reviewed are as follows:

(1) $PV_r(B) > K$

(2) $PV_p(B) > K$

(3) $PV_p(B) > K$ where $p = \sum\limits_{i=1}^{n} w_i r_i + \sum\limits_{j=1}^{s} w_j \rho_j$ and $\sum\limits^{n+s} w_{i,j} = 1$

(4) $PV_q(B) > K$ $\rho > q > r$

3 Criterion (1), the staple of textbook instruction, is superficially plausible enough. If r is the common rate of time preference, then the community is indifferent as between receiving the stream of benefits $(B), = B_o, \ldots, B_T$, and receiving its present value $PV_r(B)$. It is then convenient to rank the community's preference between any set of alternative investment streams, $B^1, B^2, \ldots B^g$, each of which results from an initial outlay K, according to the relative magnitudes of $PV_r(B^1), PV_r(B^2), \ldots, PV_r(B^g)$. In particular, any project having a benefit stream that meets the (1) criterion tells us that the present

---

[3] The financial outlay necessary for a public project can be many times the project's opportunity cost if unemployment is so high that a large proportion of the labour used in the project would have otherwise remained unemployed. For empirical calculations of the opportunity cost of a dollar of outlay under a wide range of employment conditions, see Haveman and Krutilla (1968).

value of that stream of benefits exceeds the present value of its costs and therefore represents a potential Pareto improvement for the community.

The rationale for criterion (2) is no less plausible. It suggests that if funds equal to K are to be spent on a public project, the average yield from the project should be no less than the ρ per annum that the sum K could fetch if it were placed instead in the private investment sector. If, over the period, the benefit stream yields on the average more than ρ, then the $PV_p(B) > K$ criterion is met, and there is a net gain from adopting the investment project.

Clearly, the (3) criterion is a generalization of (1) and (2) extended to cover all the different r's and ρ's in the economy. Since the weights, the w's, are the fractions of K contributed by the separable components of reduced consumption and of reduced private investment, the resultant weighted rate of return represents society's actual opportunity yield per dollar of investing a sum K in a public project. In general, then, p will vary according as whether K is raised by tax finance, loan finance, or as a mixture of both. Although (3) was originally proposed by Krutilla and Eckstein (1958), it was advanced again by Harberger (1968) in connection with a rise in interest rates in response to government borrowing[4] which is supposed to check both private investment and consumption.[5] With such a weighted discount rate, Harberger (1968) claimed (erroneously as we shall see) that 'the so-called reinvestment problem disappears' (p. 308).[6]

---

[4] Not surprisingly, Chicago School economists favour loan finance of public investments. Others favour tax finance either on the grounds (see Musgrave, 1969) that it tends to reduce the volume of private investment less than does loan finance, or else on the grounds (see Nichols, 1969) that loan finance entails future tax levies in order to service the debt.

[5] However, Drèze (1974, p. 60) asks if government borrowing does affect the rate of interest and, if so, whether a higher rate of interest increases current saving. His answer is simply that 'there undoubtedly exist cases where government borrowing does not affect the rate of interest, but is simply offset by rationing of private investment.'

Drèze compares his view with that of Arrow (1966), who argues that the divergence between 'the rate of interest implicit in consumption decisions and any market rate is so great that it must be accepted that savings are largely independent of the latter' and then goes on to say that the issue is 'to decide whether some consumers do react, at least, for some forms of consumption'.

[6] The conclusion reached by Sandmo and Drèze (1971), that for a closed economy 'the public sector's discount rate should be a weighted average of the rates facing consumers and the tax-distorted rates used by firms', is similar to that of Ramsey (1969) and much the same as the proposal put forward by Harberger (1968).

The well-known Arrow–Lind paper of 1970 produces criterion (4) as a modification of the popular (2) criterion, $PV_\rho(B) > K$ when, for their analysis, ρ can be taken as the highest actuarial rate of return corresponding, say, to the riskiest private investment. Accepting without criticism their argument that the risks associated with public projects, when divided among a large population of taxpayers, are felt by each taxpayer to be negligible—in contrast to the sense of risk apprehended by the private investor—a risk premium of $(\rho - q)$ can be attributed to the private investor. Inasmuch then as the investor is indifferent between the riskiest private investment at ρ and a virtual certain return of q on his money, a potential Pareto improvement is effected if funds are removed from this private investment, so forgoing ρ, and placed instead in public investment at a yield greater than q. Hence the proposed criterion $PV_q(B) > K$.

However, as they acknowledge in their reply (Arrow & Lind, 1972) to critical comments, the crucial assumption on which their criterion rested—that the set of public investment projects exclude opportunities in the private investment sector—did not receive explicit emphasis. And if the assumption is lifted, and the government, permitted to undertake private-sector investment, can avail itself again of the yield ρ, the $PV_\rho(B) > K$ criterion comes into its own again.

Although the (4) criterion is an interesting variation on the type (a) criterion, in other respects it is, as it stands, subject to a fundamental criticism of this sort of criterion.

4 Since the demonstration that follows applies to any of the four criteria, we can use $PV_p(B) > K$ to represent the generic type.

Given the stream of benefits $B_0, B_1, \ldots, B_T$, the above criterion is explicated as

$$\sum_{t=0}^{T} \frac{B_t}{(1+p)^t} > K \ldots \quad (1)$$

By multiplying through by a scalar $(1+p)^T$, we obtain the equivalent inequality.

$$\sum_{t=0}^{T} B_t(1+p)^{T-t} > K(1+p)^T \ldots \quad (2)$$

which can be summarized as $TV_p(B) > (K_p1$, where $TV_p(B)$ stands for the terminal value of the stream of benefits when compounded forward to T at the rate p, and $(K)_p$ stands for the terminal value of the outlay K when it is also compounded forward to T at rate p.

If and only if $PV_p(B) > K$ does $TV_p(B) > (K)_p$: one form of the criterion, that is, entails the other. But the latter form is more revealing, for it makes clear that in order for the criterion to be met, the sum of each of the benefits, B_0, B_1, . . , B_t, . ., *when wholly invested* and *reinvested to time* T *at rate* p must exceed a sum equal to K when wholly and continually reinvested at p to time T. Such a criterion is clearly applicable when in fact both the benefits and the outlays are to be used in exactly this way. If, however, they are not to be used in this way—and it is unlikely that they will be—then a criterion based on such a supposition can seriously mislead. Certainly, this $PV_p(B) > K$ criterion is misleading when it is applied to public investment projects without information in each case about the disposal of the returns to the project, and without information about the uses to which the sum K would have been put were it not used as initial outlay for the project.

5　To illustrate, suppose it to be the case that the outlay K required by a particular public investment is to be drawn *entirely* from the private investment sector, where it would otherwise have been reinvested at p to reach the terminal value $(K)_p$ at time T, whereas the project's benefits are to be wholly consumed as they emerge over time. The value of such benefits will therefore grow in value over time only at the rate r, this being the community's rate of time preference, reaching a total value indicated by $TV_r(B)$ at time T. Now if this sum $TV_r(B)$ happens to be smaller than the terminal value of K, or $(K)_p$, the project has to be rejected on a Pareto criterion: society, that is, would be better off leaving the amount K in the private sector (there to be continually reinvested at p) rather than removing K in order to pay for the public project.

Let us assume this to be the case and notice now that since $p > r$, it is possible that a terminal value of the benefits of the project calculated (erroneously in this example) as $TV_p(B)$, which necessarily exceeds $TV_r(B)$, may well exceed $(K)_p$ also. And if so, the public project would be approved by adopting (erroneously) the $PV_p(B) > K$ criterion (exactly equivalent to the $TV_p(B) > (K)_p$

criterion), although it would be rejected by the Pareto criterion.

6 We return now to the criterion $PV_r(B) > K$, regarded as a limiting case of the generic $PV_p(B) > K$ criterion. Its transformation into the $TV_r(B) > K_r$ form, however, enables us to appreciate immediately the sufficient conditions required for its valid application; namely, that all the returns from the project be *wholly consumed* as they occur and that the sum K be raised entirely from current consumption. Similarly, transforming the other limiting case $PV_\rho(B) > K$, into the form $TV_\rho(B) > (K)_\rho$ enables us also to appreciate at once that its Pareto validity is assured if, in fact, it is applied to a case in which the benefits, as they occur, are wholly invested and reinvested in the private investment sector at prevailing yield ρ until the terminal date T, and if the sum K raised from the private sector would have been wholly invested and reinvested also at yield ρ until T.

Put otherwise, the *correct* terminal value of a project's benefit stream and the *correct* terminal value of the opportunity cost of its outlay are both functions, in the simplest possible case, of three variables, r, ρ, and Θ, where Θ is the fraction of any income or investment return that is reinvested in the private sector. In contrast, a criterion $PV_p(B) > K$ makes the terminal value both of the benefit stream and the outlay a function only of p, whether p is equal to r, or to ρ, or to a weighted sum of r and ρ.[7]

Such simplifications are very agreeable. But one can go further. For in the procedure I propose there is no need to discount at all. As will be seen soon, all that matters are the relevant rates at which returns arising from an initial outlay K—whether invested in a public project or left in the private sector—are to be compounded forward

---

[7] See note 11 for conditions justifying the use of the $PV_r(B) > K$ criterion even when reinvestment effects are taken into account. As for the conditions justifying the use of the $PV_\rho(B) > K$, Feldstein (1972) alleges that it is based on an ambiguity in the notion of opportunity cost. For the purpose of investment criteria, opportunity cost should relate not to the best alternative use to which the resource *could* be put but to the alternative use to which it *would* be put.

I agree it should be the latter, but there is more to be said. For Feldstein ignores the question of political constraint. To illustrate: if the public investment authority is invested with powers to make the best possible use of funds that are otherwise available for particular public projects, then the use of ρ as discount rate is indeed justified, since in that case the best alternative opportunity open to such funds may well be that of investing and reinvesting them in the private investment sector at ρ.

to the terminal date T. Indeed, once this is done, the terminal values being compared can be discounted at rate r, ρ or p (or at any conceivable rate) without in any way altering their ranking.

7 In order to complete the critique of the (a) category of DPV criteria, we must also examine the criterion based on the standard IRR, or internal rate of return. There is a seeming advantage in being able to use the IRR for ranking projects without reference to the prevailing yields or interest rates in the economy. Nonetheless, it is not possible to accept or reject projects on the basis of IRR alone. For this purpose, the IRR has to be compared with whatever is believed to be the relevant opportunity rate.

In fact, letting λ stand for the IRR, the internal-rate of return criteria corresponding to the DPV criteria (1) through (4) are

$(1')$ $\lambda > r$, $(2')$ $\lambda > \rho$, $(3')$ $\lambda > p$, and $(4')$ $\lambda > q$.

As a ranking device, the IRR has fallen into disfavour among economists, chiefly because there can, in general, be more than one IRR for a given investment stream.[8] However, this is the less important reason. The more important reason is that, even in the common case in which all benefits are positive, the unique IRR calculated for an investment stream does not accord with the true average rate of return over time of the value of that stream. In fact, as conventionally defined, the IRR, when used as a criterion, has the same defect as the DPV criterion; namely, that a reinvestment rate is entailed that has no necessary relation to the actual rates involved in the particular case.

This defect follows from the standard definition of the IRR as that λ for which $\sum\limits_{t=o}^{T} \dfrac{B_t}{(1+\lambda)^t} = K$. For multiplying through by $(1+\lambda)^T$

we obtain $\sum\limits_{t=o}^{T} B_t(1+\lambda)^{T-t} = K(1+\lambda)^T$ . . . .   (3)

So explicated, (3) reveals the IRR to be defined as the rate which, when used to compound the benefits forward to T, produces a terminal value equal to outlay K when this is also compounded

---

[8] The reader is reminded that a necessary though insufficient condition for the IRR (according to the conventional definition) to have more than one value is that one or more of the net benefits, $B_1, \ldots, B_T$, be negative, a contingency not often encountered.

forward at that rate. The resulting terminal value of the benefits is therefore calculated on the implicit assumption that they are wholly invested and reinvested to T at the rate λ—irrespective, that is, of whether this calculated λ is less than r or greater than ρ. Since in any actual project, the disposal of the benefits depend upon behavioural and institutional factors, the actual terminal value of the benefit stream is, again in the simplest case, a function of r, ρ, and Θ and not, in general, of λ alone. In other words, before we can calculate λ as an average rate of growth of the initial investment K over the period to T, we must be able to calculate independently the actual terminal value of the benefit stream by reference to r, ρ, and Θ.

8 Recent recognition by several economists of the reinvestment problem has led to formulations of the (b)-type criterion, which can be represented by the requirement

(5) $PV_r(B) > AK$

where A is a symbol for the ratio of the social opportunity costs both of the public project and of the alternative use of the outlay K. To these two social opportunity costs we now turn.

Marglin's treatment, in his classic article of 1963, assumes that the required sum K is raised from tax revenue, and that of every dollar so raised a fraction, Θ_1 comes from an initial reduction in private investment having yield ρ, the remaining fraction $(1-\Theta_1)$ coming from a reduction in current consumption.[9] In addition, Θ_2 is the fraction of each dollar of any return that is placed in the private investment sector. Under these conditions, an amount K left in the private sector of the economy would generate a stream of consumption over the future which, when discounted at r, would converge to aK, a greater than unity.[10] This aK is the 'social opportunity cost' of a project requiring a nominal outlay of K.

However, the employment now of a criterion $PV_r(B) > aK$ can be justified only if the stream of benefits are entirely consumed as they

---

[9] In fact, Marglin produces three models in this paper. His third model introduces alternative and less plausible behaviour assumptions, while his first model is little more than a stepping stone to the second model, which is treated above as *the* Marglin model.

[10] In order for the infinite stream of consumption thus generated to converge, when discounted at r, to a finite sum, Marglin assumes that $\Theta_2\rho > r$.

occur. If, instead, the fraction $(1-\Theta_2)$ of each of the benefits is consumed as it occurs, the remainder being invested in the private sector at ρ, and the returns to these investment components treated in the same way, the consumption stream so generated can be discounted at r to a present value of $\alpha PV_r(B)$, α greater than unity. The corrected criterion, $\alpha PV_r(B) > aK$, can then be written as

$$PV_r(B) > AK\left(A = \frac{a}{\alpha}\right).^{11}$$

Later contributions that explicitly recognized the reinvestment problem produced models which, though interesting in themselves, reproduced the same essential features of the Marglin model. Feldstein's two papers (1964 and 1972), for instance, extend the formulation to cover other behavioural and institutional parameters. Bradford's 1975 paper is of the same family, and though he begins somewhat differently, his results conform to the same basic formula as Marglin's.[12] Since there is no fundamental novelty of conception in the later papers adopting this approach, remarks on the Marglin model are applicable also to their analyses.

Without doubt, the introduction of the type (b) criteria, which face up to the reinvestment problem, is an important step forward in the art of project evaluation, and goes far to remedy the defect inherent in the older DPV formulae. Yet the insight that inspired the innovation was channelled into the conventional mould. In the light

---

[11] In a limiting case, where $\Theta_1 = \Theta_2$, $a = \alpha$, and $PV_r(B) > A$ reduces to $PV_r(B) > K$. (In Bradford's 1975 model Θ_1 and Θ_2 are denoted respectively as a_t and α_{t+1} and when these are equal his criterion also reduces to $PV_r(B) > K$.)

[12] Bradford's 1975 paper, in some ways a development of his earlier paper of 1970, constructs a model which closely resembles that of Marglin. This resemblance is easier to appreciate by comparing Marglin's equation (8), condensed and cast in discrete form, with Bradford's equation (15), using a common notation.

Marglin's criterion then appears as $\displaystyle\sum_{t=0}^{\infty} \alpha B_t \delta_t - aK_o > 0$

while Bradford's takes the form $\displaystyle\sum_{t=0}^{T} \alpha_t B_t \delta_t - \sum a_t K_t \delta_t > 0$

where B_t is the tth benefit from the public project and K_t the tth net outlay, a_t is the shadow price of a dollar of the tth net outlay. The discount factor to be applied to B_t and K_t is δ_t.

Bradford's public investment benefit stream is finite (and not infinite as is Marglin's), and his shadow prices a_t and a_r vary with t.

For the special case $\alpha_t = a_t$, both reduce to the general form $PV_r(B - K) > 0$ which form includes the possibility also of a stream of net outlays.

of the new perspective provided, however, it is possible to break out of the traditional mould; to adopt instead a *terminal value* procedure that depends upon the application of simple rules rather than on elaborate formulae. Since my criticism of the new type (b) criteria is made only by way of comparison with this proposed procedure, its broad outlines are etched in the following section.

9 This procedure is one designed to transform an initial investment stream, $-K, B_0, B_1, B_2, \ldots, B_T$, into a stream $-K, O, O, O, \ldots TV(B)$. Of the initial return B_0, the proportion that is consumed is compounded forward at the relevant rate of time preference, say r, to the terminal date T. The remaining amount of B_0 that is unconsumed, being divided among different investment opportunities actually anticipated, each component is compounded at its yield to the following year, producing in aggregate an amount ΔR_1. Thus at time $t = 1$, we have returns $B_1 + \Delta R_1$ to allocate. Again, the proportion of this total $(B_1 + \Delta R_1)$ that is *consumed* at $t = 1$ is compounded to T at rate r, the remainder being allocated among the various investment opportunities anticipated in consequence of the existing political and/or administrative constraints. Continuing in this way until T, the original benefit stream is transformed into its terminal value $TV(B)$ at T.[13]

A valid ranking of, say, two mutually exclusive projects, X and Y, both of which may be rejected however, requires not only a common terminal date T, but also a common initial outlay K. This requirement is not restrictive. If, say, Y's initial outlay is 20 less than that of X, the 20 left over from the Y investment can be treated as generating a stream of returns in the private sector of the economy having a terminal value that is to be added to that of the Y stream of benefits.

As for the social opportunity cost of K itself, this is allowed for simply by treating the stream of returns it would generate if left in the private sector, on a par with projects X and Y. For identification,

---

[13] If, instead, behaviour and political constraints are such that the annual *return* on the investment component of the preceding year is taken as the basis for consumption and reinvestment of the current year, the rules are different. In that case, ΘB_0, the amount invested in the private sector out of the initial return B_0, is added immediately to the terminal value of the investment stream, while the annual return q_1, $= \rho(\Theta B_0)$, on this ΘB_0, continues to appear annually at $t = 1, 2, \ldots, T$. At $t = 1$, this q_1 is added to B_1', the aggregate return now being $(B_1 + q_1)$, of which a proportion Θ is placed in the private investment sector and the remainder consumed.

we refer to this alternative as the Z stream. Using the same rules, it compounds to terminal value $TV(Z)$.

In this way, we end up with three terminal values, $TV(X)$, $TV(Y)$ and $TV(Z)$ from which to choose, all generated by initial outlay K. No further operation is required for ranking purposes. If both $TV(X)$ and $TV(Y)$ are less than $TV(Z)$, neither public project is acceptable on a Pareto criterion. If instead, say $TV(X) > TV(Y) > TV(Z)$, then $TV(X)$ is chosen on the Pareto criterion. Any further operation that is acceptable, say, reducing the terminal values to present social values, to present benefit-cost ratios, or to internal rates of return, cannot alter this basic ranking.

Thus, corresponding present values for X, Y and Z are obtained simply by multiplying each of their terminal values by a scalar, $(1+r)^{-T}$. Corresponding benefit-cost ratios are obtained by multiplying them by a scalar $(1+r)^{-T}/K$. As for the corresponding IRRs, when defined in accordance with the basic concept of an average rate of increase over time of the initial investment K and therefore as that unique value of λ for which $\dfrac{TV(B)}{(1+\lambda)^T} = K$, the resulting equations

$$\frac{TV(X)}{(1+\lambda_x)^T} = \frac{TV(Y)}{(1+\lambda_y)^T} = \frac{TV(Z)}{(1+\lambda_z)^T} = K \text{ entails the ranking } \lambda_x > \lambda_y > \lambda_z.$$

10 Compared with this proposed terminal value procedure, the (b)-type investment criteria have a number of disadvantages. A minor objection to them is their employment of an infinite time horizon, an assumption that has obvious mathematical convenience in making fairly simple their required calculation of the shadow price of a dollar of private investment—provided that bounds are placed on the relative magnitudes of the parameters. Yet there is a finite time horizon for the expected benefit stream of all actual projects. Indeed, as mentioned earlier, if the method of project evaluation is to have strict Pareto justification, the time limit cannot exceed a certain period. Certainly, if the particular time horizon adopted is short, the application of criteria based on an infinite time horizon can seriously mislead.

A more important consideration is that of economy of time and effort. There is, at present, unlimited scope for further elaboration of (b)-type formulae. Differences between them can arise (i) because of differences in individual behaviour, especially with respect to saving and consumption, (ii) because of differences in institutional postulates, especially those describing the collection and disposal of tax revenues and, possibly also, the balance-of-payments effects, and (iii) because of differences in administrative and political constraints, especially with reference to the various methods of raising funds for public projects and to the directions for the sale and distribution of the benefits.[14] And since there is no limit to the degree of refinement involved in decomposing aggregates into smaller groups, or in distinguishing institutional factors, unless we break with old habits, there is every reason to expect a proliferation of unwieldy public investment criteria over the future.

Given the clearer perception of the issues conferred by these new investment criteria, the need for increased flexibility in actual project evaluation suggests we turn away from our habitual temptations to elaborate sophisticated formulae. Instead we should avail ourselves of the facilities provided by high-speed computers in producing a valid terminal-value ranking guided only by simple rules appropriate to the occasion. For although the instruction to the computer for any particular project will vary according to the factors mentioned in (i), (ii), and (iii) above, and according to the degree of refinement sought, the simple rules in question follow the same basic principle: a dividing of the aggregate returns at each time t into consumption and investment opportunities, and then a compounding of each component forward either to T or to $t+1$, respectively.

The proposed procedure also has the obvious advantage of conceiving the exercise in terms of a chronological movement forward through time, rather than the reverse. Thus the instructions for the two-period sequence, t and $t+1$, are explicit and easy to check. Moreover, the procedure is flexible enough to accommodate itself, if necessary, to political constraints that are expected to alter over time or are scheduled to take effect at later points in time, such as the provision of special investment opportunities in the public sector for the returns expected from the project in question.

---

[14] Thus, in addition to raising an initial outlay K by any mixture of tax finance and loan finance, a part can also be raised by using the funds that otherwise go to replacing the capital of existing public enterprises, a possibility mentioned by Steiner (1959) and by Mishan (1967).

Chapter 38

A NORMALIZATION PROCEDURE FOR PUBLIC INVESTMENT—AN APPLIED EXAMPLE

1 Let us now apply the normalization technique to the data given in Table V.6 below, adopting first the I political constraint that permits the public agency the alternative of using the funds K wholly in the private investment sector, and permits it also to invest wholly in the private sector the cash part of the benefits generated by a public project. We shall adopt as the common outlay K at time zero the sum of 100, this being the initial capital required for the B investment project. Since the project A requires a sum of only 20, the requirements of a common initial outlay of 100 can be met if the A stream can be multiplied by 5; if, that is, 5 of such projects can be implemented without affecting the values of the benefit streams. If, however, there is room for only one A project, which we shall suppose to be the case, the surplus of 80 will, in accordance with political constraint I, be left to grow at rate ρ in the private investment sector until the end of the common terminal period. As for project C, we shall defer consideration of its outlay until later.

Turning to the determination of a common terminal period, the adoption of the I political constraint, plus the particular assumption that the primary benefits to all three public projects are wholly encashable, ensures that ρ is the appropriate rate of reinvestment for all of the benefits of each project. We could therefore choose as the common terminal date t_3, at which time the last—and as it so happens, the only—primary benefit of 160 accrues to project B, there being no primary benefits from the other projects later than t_3. But for illustrative purposes let us assume that a specific investment option is open to project B which will transform a sum of 160 in t_3 to a single benefit of 210 in t_4. In that case, the common terminal period has to be revised to t_4. Inasmuch as there are to be no further specific public reinvestment opportunities open to any of these three projects after t_4, the normalized terminal values of the three projects at t_4 can be compounded forward, if politically directed, only at a rate ρ which will not alter the ranking.

2 Having chosen a common initial outlay of 100 and a common terminal period of t_4, we turn now the reinvestments of primary benefits assuming that the social rate of time preference, r, is 10 per cent, and the constant yield in the private investment sector ρ, is 20 per cent. The Z project is the use that can be made of this initial common outlay 100 alternative to any of the three public projects which, under political constraint I, becomes the investment of 100 in the private investment sector to the terminal date t_4. Since ρ is 20 per cent, the Z stream is $-100, 0, 0, 0, 100(1+0.2)^4$. This is shown along the Z row in the left half of Table V.7. Since $100(1+0.2)^4$, or 207·4 is the terminal value of the benefits from investing 100 in the private sector for four years, this 207·4 is placed under the (1) column headed $TV^n(B)$, which stands for the normalized terminal value of the benefits of the particular project. With respect to this Z project, this normalized terminal value of an initial outlay of K left in the private sector is, as indicated earlier, denoted by K'. IRR^n under column (2) stands for normalized internal rate of return, λ', of the project. For the Z project this is obviously ρ, or 20 per cent, being the rate at which we should have to discount K', or 207·4, in order to obtain 100 at time zero.

TABLE V.6

	t_0	t_1	t_2	t_3	(1) B	(2) K	(3) $(B-K)$	(4) $(B-K)/K$	(5) λ
A	-20	15	16	0	27·5	20	7·5	0·375	0·34
B	-100	0	0	160	120·2	100	20·2	0·202	0·17
C	-100	-250	-144	0	227·3	219	8·3	0·038	$\left.\begin{array}{c} 0·61 \\ -0·107 \end{array}\right\}$

3 The A public investment stream appears immediately below the Z stream as $-100, 15, 16, 0, 80(1+0.2)^4$. The last figure is the compounded terminal value of the 80 left over in the initial period and

TABLE V.7

	t_0	t_1	t_2	t_3	t_4	(1) $TV''(B)$	(2) IRR'' (λ'')	(3) $B'_i - K'$	(4) $\dfrac{B'_i - K'}{K'}$	(5) $\lambda'_i - p$	(6) $\dfrac{\lambda_i - p}{p}$
Z	−100	0	0	0	$100(1 + 0 \cdot 2)^4$	207·4	0·2	0	0	0	0
A	−100	15	16	0	$80(1 + 0 \cdot 2)^4$	214·9	0·211	7·5	$\dfrac{7 \cdot 5}{207 \cdot 4}$	0·011	$\dfrac{1 \cdot 1}{20}$
B	−100	0	0	0	210	210	0·204	2·6	$\dfrac{2 \cdot 6}{207 \cdot 4}$	0·004	$\dfrac{0 \cdot 4}{20}$
C	−100	130	0	0	0	224.6	0·225	17·2	$\dfrac{17 \cdot 2}{207 \cdot 4}$	0·025	$\dfrac{2 \cdot 5}{20}$

placed in the private investment sector for four years. To this terminal sum has to be added the 15 occurring in t_1 which is then compounded at ρ for three years, and the benefit of 16 occurring in t_2 which is to be compounded forward at ρ for two years. The initial A stream, with the 80 added to bring it an initial outlay of 100, is then transformed into the normalized stream, $-100,0,0,0$, $[80(1+0\cdot2)^4 + 15(1+0\cdot2)^3 + 16(1+0\cdot2)^2]$. This last item. the normalized terminal value of the A project, sums to $214\cdot9$ and is entered under (1). The normalized internal rate of return, being the λ' for which $214\cdot9/(1+\lambda')^4 = 100$, is $21\cdot1$ per cent and is entered as such in the (2) column.

Turning to the B project, the public agency will of course avail itself of the special opportunity to transform the benefit of 160 at t_3 into 210 at t_4 since 210 is larger than $160(1+0\cdot2)$, which is what 160 would fetch if left for the extra year in the private investment sector. The normalized B stream is therefore $-100, 0, 0, 0, 210$. This figure of 210 appears then as the normalized terminal value of the B stream in column (1), and the corresponding normalized internal rate of return appears as $20\cdot4$ per cent in column (2).

The last four columns, headed (3), (4), (5) and (6), indicate alternative investment criteria, and are derived from the figures in the first two columns. The reader should bear in mind, first, that the $TV^n(B)$ of the Z project, $207\cdot4$, is the *terminal* social opportunity cost, K', for each of the public investment projects, and that B_i' is the normalized terminal value of the ith public investment project; second, that the IRR^n of the Z project, 20 per cent, is the social opportunity yield p for each of the public projects. Because of the political constraint we have adopted, p happens to be equal to ρ, the yield in the private investment sector. (Under the II political constraint of course, it can be smaller than ρ.)

For the A public project, the entry in column (3) is $(214\cdot9 - 207\cdot4)$ or $7\cdot5$ as in the Table. The entry in column (4) is therefore $7\cdot5/207\cdot4$ as in the Table. The entry in column (5) is the normalized internal rate of return to project A less the social opportunity internal rate of return ρ yielded by the Z project. It is then $21\cdot1$ per cent less 20 per cent, or $1\cdot1$ per cent, this being the *excess* average per annum rate of growth from placing the 100 initial outlay in the A project rather than in the Z project. In column (6) the entry for the A project is $1\cdot1/20$, or $5\cdot5$ per cent, which ratio tells us that the per annum growth rate of 100 in the A project is $5\cdot5$ per cent higher than it is in the Z project.

The corresponding figures in these four columns for the B projects are $2 \cdot 6$, $2 \cdot 6 / 207 \cdot 4$, $0 \cdot 4$ per cent, and $0 \cdot 4 / 20$ or 2 per cent.

Using the criterion $B'_i > K'$, it is clear that both A and B projects qualify, with A ranking above B. Expressing the normalized terminal benefit of each project as a fraction having the common denominator K', as in the heading of column (4), clearly makes no difference to the positive sign or to the ranking. In column (5) the criterion $(\lambda' - p)$ is again met for both A and B projects and, again, A is ranked above B. Sign and ranking are clearly unchanged if, as in the last column, we express the *excess* normalized internal rates of return of projects A and B as a percent of the social opportunity internal rate of return, p.

4 Let us now normalize the investment stream of project C which is given in Table V.6 as -100, 250, -144. We can deal with -144 in two alternative ways; (a) we could attempt to raise an additional 100 at time t_0 since if it were invested in the private sector at a ρ of 20 per cent it would amount to 144 by t_2, a sum which could then be used to pay off the required outlay of 144. In that case the C stream would be converted into -200, 250, having an internal rate of return for the one year of 25 per cent. Using the alternative method (b) we could pay off the 144 at time t_2, by setting aside at time t_1, 120 of the return of 250, an arrangement which results in a stream -100, 130, and produces an internal rate of return for the one year of 30 per cent. If the constraints are such that the public agency can have no more than an initial outlay of 100 we shall have to adopt the (b) method which, however, also happens to give a better internal rate of return.[1]

Normalization requires, however, that the benefit of 130 at t_1 be now compounded forward at p, which is here equal to ρ or 20 per cent, to become $130(1 + 0 \cdot 2)^3$, or $224 \cdot 6$, at t_4, this figure being entered in column (1). The normalized internal rate of return for this stream

---

[1] Both methods give the same result only if the benefit of the initial C stream at t_1 were 240. In that case the investment stream -100, 240, -144, converts to -200, 240, by the (a) method, and to -100, 120 by the (b) method, the internal rate of return for both methods being 20 per cent, and equal to ρ. If the benefit at t_1 exceeds 240, the (b) method gives a higher internal rate of return; if less than 240, the (a) method gives the higher internal rate of return. This is because the (a) method effectively produces an internal rate of return that is an *average* of the internal rate of return of the (b) method and of the ρ of 20 per cent [the extra 100, borrowed on the (a) method, implies a 200 initial outlay, of which 100 produces the original return at t_1 and the extra 100 produces 120, or $100(1 + \rho)$, at t_1].

$-100, 0, 0, 0, 224 \cdot 6$, is that λ' for which $100(1 + \lambda') = 224 \cdot 6$. This is $22 \cdot 5$ per cent, which differs greatly from the two conventionally calculated internal rates of return of $60 \cdot 1$ and and $-10 \cdot 7$ per cent. Once columns (3) to (6) are filled for the C project, we observe that there is a perfectly consistent ranking of the three projects, C, A, B, whichever of the four investment criteria are used.[2]

It should also be apparent that the *conventionally* calculated internal rates of return are invalid not only for project C but also for projects A and B each of which produces only one such internal rate. In the A project, the conventional method calculates an internal rate of return of 34 per cent for the two periods only, thus ignoring what the benefits (15 at t_1 and 16 at t_2) would become by reinvesting them in the private sector at ρ up to the terminal date t_4. Even if the terminal date were t_2, the conventional calculation would be invalid since the 15 at t_1 actually becomes $15(1 + 0 \cdot 2)$ at t_2—*not* $15(1 + 0 \cdot 34)$ at t_2, as is implied by the conventional internal rate of return. Similarly, the B stream's conventional internal rate of return of 17 per cent, though correct for a 3-year terminal period, would be incorrect for a 4-year terminal period even if it did *not* happen to have a specific opportunity for converting its 160 in t_3 into 210 in t_4. For under the given constraints, a 4-year terminal period would require the 160 in t_3 to be reinvested at ρ for a year in the private sector to emerge as $160(1 + 0 \cdot 2)$ in the fourth year, and this would clearly produce an internal rate of return that is higher than 17 per cent.

The two conventional internal rates of return for project C are even more obviously wrong. The negative rate of $-10 \cdot 7$ per cent implies a negative average rate of growth, or annual loss of $10 \cdot 7$ per cent, for any capital placed in the C project. Yet it is manifest that, as already indicated, by placing in the private investment sector 120 of the 250 benefit received at t_1 in order to cancel the debt of 144 incurred in t_2, a

---

[2] If the C stream were, instead, $-100, 100, -144, 300$, we should be unable to make full provision for meeting the outlay of 144 at t_2 by investing the return of 100 at t_1 for a year at a ρ of 20 per cent, since this would transform the 100 at t_1 into no more than 120 at t_2—the transformed stream then being $-100, 0, -24, 300$.

We should then have to increase the initial outlay of 100 at t_0 by an amount equal to $24/(1 \cdot 2)^2$, or about 16, which latter sum when compounded forward two years at 20 per cent would yield about 24, so meeting the remainder of the t_2 outlay of 24. The transformed stream would then be $-116, 0, 0, 300$.

Unless such an investment stream were sufficiently divisible to be scaled down by $1 \cdot 16$, the common outlay condition would require that the A and B investment streams be scaled up by $1 \cdot 16$.

person can count on a stream -100, 130, which gives a net gain of 30 over the year. The other conventional internal rate of return of 60·1 per cent is also wrong. An investment today of 100 in C will just *not* grow to 160·1 in a year, or to 259·5 in two years. There is no way, that is, of converting it to a stream -100, 0, 259·5.

5 The normalized terminal value criteria of columns (3) and (4) can be converted into normalized present value criteria using any discount rate i without altering their validity as criteria, and without altering the ranking of the investment projects. For instance, since the $(B'_i - K')$ criterion is positive for the three projects, C, A, B, being respectively 17·2, 7·5, and 2·6, present discounted values are derived simply by multiplying each of these magnitudes by the same scalar $1/(1+i)^4$, which transformation obviously retains their rank order, and indeed their proportion. This result may seem puzzling to the reader since, on our assumptions, the various normalized investment criteria, and therefore the ranking of the public projects, seem to have been devised without recourse to the social rate of time preference, r, about which everything is usually supposed to hinge.

The social rate of time preference r does, however, continue to play an essential role in an economy having a private sector rate of growth of p (in the above example, ρ) that is above r. For only when the social rate of time preference, r, is used to discount the normalized terminal value of the benefit stream does the resulting figure represent the *equivalent* present value to society—that is to say, the present value as between which and the normalized terminal value society is deemed to be indifferent.

But this social rate of time preference r has another normative function. It provides a lower limit to the opportunity rate p at which the benefits can be compounded forward. Primary and secondary benefits are on no account to be reinvested at a rate below r. For example, the reinvesting of 16 of benefit today at a rate i, below r, would yield but $16(1+i)^t$ in t years' time whereas 16 today should not be surrendered for less than the larger sum $16(1+r)^t$ in t years' time, this being the exact sum that would compensate society t years' hence for giving up 16 today. Since in our example the opportunity rate in the private sector turns out to be ρ, which is assumed greater than r, no reinvestment of benefits at yields below ρ need be contemplated.

6 We may, finally, touch briefly upon the kind of changes that would be required if we alter the assumptions from those so far adopted in this chapter. Suppose the political constraint II, instead, were appropriate—so that if the public agency does not introduce any of the public investment projects it has to return the funds to the private sector of the economy where $(1-\theta)$ of every additional dollar is consumed and the remainder, θ, is invested—then the p_1 or p_2 social opportunity yield would apply (according as behaviour assumption (1) or (2) is relevant), and K', the terminal social opportunity cost of the public projects, would be smaller than it is in Table V.7. Inasmuch as the benefits accrue to the public as they occur (unless they are directed by the public authority to be wholly or partly reinvested in the private sector at ρ, which we are *not* assuming here) project A's benefit of 15 at t_1, 16 at t_2, and the 80 left over at t_0 are all to be compounded forward to the terminal date t_4 at p_1 or p_2, as is also the C benefit of 130 at t_1.

To introduce an extreme kind of behaviour, hinted at earlier in a footnote, if all the benefits were in kind, and individual behaviour were such that the receipt of such benefits led wholly to an increase in consumption, such benefits would have to be compounded forward at the social rate of time preference r. The initial capital outlay, K, on the other hand, would be compounded forward at the appropriate social opportunity yield p. For a terminal period of n years set initially equal to a particular investment stream of m years, the normalized terminal value of the benefits of the project may well exceed the terminal social opportunity cost K'. Yet if the period is extended long enough beyond the mth year, the terminal value of the initial outlay K will eventually exceed the terminal value of the project's benefits, since the benefits themselves are compounded only at r while K is compounded at some p that is higher than r. It would seem to follow that in such special cases, no matter how large are the benefits in kind, no public investment should be undertaken.[3]

Such a result depends, however, upon our assumption of no uncertainty. When uncertainty is introduced, it acts to shorten the terminal period. There are a number of ways of allowing for uncertainty which will be discussed in Part VII. One method, usually supplementary to

---

[3] Unless such benefits in kind may be sold on the market, so transforming them into cash returns which are then paid out to the public.

others, is to limit the common investment period on the grounds that after such a date the addition made to the present social value of increasingly distant and uncertain returns is negligible. In view of the pace of technological innovation, and of continual changes in taste and fashion, and in view also of the small present social worth of a dollar expected to be received in, say, 50 years' time,[4] a common period of more than 30 years would generally be regarded as exceptional.

7 The rules for the timing of a public investment project can be formalized in a number of ways, all of which, however, tend to the same transparent logic. No matter what investment criterion is used, the project should be introduced in that year which produces for it the largest return or value—subject always to the relevant political constraints. If the time profile of an investment stream is expected to be the same no matter when the investment is introduced then, seen from today, it should be introduced as early as possible. For the same excess terminal benefit in year m will have a higher *present* social value—granted that $r > 0$—than it will have in some later year n. The postponing of a project is justified only if, by postponement, the excess terminal value is expected to rise. If E is the normalized excess terminal benefit over cost in year n of introducing the project today, and E' is the larger excess benefit in year $n + 1$ of introducing the project in the following year, then society will be indifferent whether it be introduced now or next year if $E/(1+r)^n = E'/(1+r)^{n+1}$, and, therefore, if $E' = E(1+r)$. In general, postponing the introduction of the project by q years is justified only if its normalized excess terminal value increases over the q years at an average rate that is greater than r. The reasons why excess benefits may be expected to increase over time arise from the possibility of technological improvements over time and of rising demand for the goods produced by the project.

The above remarks, however, are valid if there are funds available only for this one specific project, after which no more funds will be available for similar projects. Such conditions are not very realistic. If funds are expected to become available in later years for similar projects in that area, there is less justification for delaying economi-

---

[4] At a rate of discount of 5 per cent, a dollar expected with certainty in 50 years' time is worth (to the same person) today about 7 cents. At a rate of discount of 10 per cent, it is worth less than $\frac{3}{4}$ of a cent. Such calculations, however, imply unwarranted inter-generation comparisons.

cally feasible projects. For as replacements are required, technically more efficient equipment can be introduced and extensions made to meet a growing demand. Such possibilities over the foreseeable future can be formalized into long term alternative investment options, the choice among which is to be determined by the largest normalized excess benefit at the end of a long run of time.

8 Let us conclude. The two special cases in the normalization procedure that make for great simplification require an initial outlay of K and no public special reinvestment opportunities. The first case is that in which the political constraint I applies, and in which all the benefits accrue as cash. Here the initial outlay K is compounded forward at ρ to become K' in the nth year, and the benefits of the projects are all wholly reinvested at ρ to the nth year. This is the case for which we could also use ρ as the discount rate in the criterion $PV\rho(B) > K$.

The second case is that in which political constraint II is operative and economic behaviour is such that $(1-\theta)$ of additional income from any source received by the private sector is consumed, the remaining θ being invested in the private investment sector at ρ. Here, the initial outlay K, and all the primary benefits, are compounded forward to the nth year at the rate p_1.

For all other cases in which political constraints are less simple or stable, in which benefits in kind generate no additional saving, in which the parameter θ varies as between groups, as between areas, and/or over time, the year by year compounding associated with the normalization technique provides the necessary flexibility and control over the data.

In order not to obscure the exposition, taxation refinements and international borrowing have been ignored. A brief word on each.

If the government raises $1 million by taxes from the public, the citizens suffer a reduction of $1 million of their disposable incomes, and consequently reduce their current consumption by $(1-\theta)$ $1 million. If, however, the benefit B_t of a public project is $1 million, this $1 million is received by citizens as an increment of gross income. Since they are required to pay taxes on it, the increment of *disposable* income will be $(1-t)$ $1 million, where t is the average tax yield on every dollar of gross income. Consequently, the increment of current consumption is equal to $(1-t)(1-\theta)$ $1 million. The t. $1 million of the benefit B_t collected by the government will be partly or wholly consumed or invested. And we should require information of the government's behaviour in this regard in order to calculate the rate at which to compound the projects' benefits forward to the terminal year.

In the case that a country raises a loan from abroad at some given rate of interest i, the loan being conditional upon its being used in a specific project, it is simply required that the normalized terminal value of the project's benefits (under the existing political constraints and economic behaviour) exceed $K(1+i)^n$. If no conditions are attached to the use of the loan, then clearly the project having the largest normalized terminal value of benefits has to be selected from all those whose terminal values exceed $K(1+i)^n$.

Finally, the reader is reminded that there can be a divergence between the actual market rate of return on private investment and the *social* rate of return on private investment. The ρ we have been using in the preceding chapters is, of course, assumed to be the latter, the 'true' or social rate of return on private investment, since it is the basis of the social opportunity yield and social opportunity cost.

In so far as external diseconomies remain uncorrected in the activities set up by the additional private investments, the use of the market yield in our calculations will overstate the social yield ρ. *Per contra*, in so far as social benefits are underestimated in the activities set up by the additional private investments,[5] the market yield on investment understates the social yield ρ. One cannot expect, *a priori*, that these opposing factors will cancel out however, and the economist may think it necessary to calculate an approximation to ρ that is above or below the actual market rate of return on private investment. Nevertheless, the use of the market rate of return on private investment, rather than the social rate ρ, though it will of course affect the magnitudes of the terminal (or present) values, is not very likely to make any difference to the resultant ranking of the public projects. Given the normalization procedure, in particular the

---

[5] The value placed by firms on the additional outputs produced by private investments may well exceed the competitive market price *times* quantity of the outputs. But since perfectly discriminating monopolists do not exist in the real world, the total revenue of a private monopolist will still fall short of the social value of the additional outputs (inasmuch as the latter is measured by the area under the relevant segment of the demand curve). To that extent the market rate of return in the private investment sector will understate the social rate of return to increments of private investment.

common terminal period and the compounding forward of the returns of alternative investment streams (including the Z stream) at a common rate p, the alternative investment profiles would have to be markedly different, and the divergence between the ideal ρ and the market rate of return on private investment would have to be quite startling, for the use of the market rate of return to generate a different ranking of public projects than that which would result from the use of ρ.

Chapter 39

SELECTING A SET OF INVESTMENT PROJECTS

1 We now take the final step in exploring the uses of investment criteria: that of selecting, from a large number, a set of investment projects subject to a budget constraint. The methods proposed here build on the normalization technique elucidated in the preceding chapters. In other respects, however, they will depart only in limited ways from the more familiar methods put forward in the last decade or so.[1]

The general features of this problem are, first, that there are several objectives or purposes, single or multiple, to be served, such as pest-control, flood-control, irrigation, electricity provision, or flood-control plus irrigation, or flood-control plus irrigation plus electricity, in one or in several regions. Second, that for each of these single or multiple objectives in a given region there is a number of alternative investment projects, all of which are technically feasible. Given the same competitive full-employment economy, with ρ greater than r, the problem is that of choosing, from among all the technically feasible investment projects, one project for each of some number of specific purposes—within the limits of the finances available. The set of investment projects chosen must be an optimum in the sense that society would prefer the capital budget to be used for this set of projects rather than for any other set.

2 Since we have argued, in previous chapters, that in general the use of r as a discount rate in calculating the present value of an investment stream is defective, and since we have also argued in the preceding chapter that normalized terminal values of both benefits and outlays

---

[1] I have in mind the contribution of Steiner (1959), among others.

are the components of a correct investment criterion, and that (except in special cases) no advantage derives from transforming them either into normalized internal rates of return or discounted present value criteria, we shall describe a method of investment selection based on the method of terminal values. The terminology will be simplified by omitting from now on the adjective 'normalized', notwithstanding that terminal figures will be normalized in all the respects mentioned in the preceding two chapters, save that which requires uniformity of capital outlays. For, in general, the technically feasible investment projects, from which the selection must be made, will not all have the same (equivalent) initial outlays.

As for the question of how the purposes, or required services, and the alternative investment options that can be used to provide them, are to be counted, occasions may well arise when the treatment has to be arbitrary. The following rules, however, provide some guidance. (a) The same type of service required in a different locality, or region, is conceived as a different service. (b) If, within a single locality, two or more services can be produced in combination by a single investment project, each different combination of services so producible qualifies as a distinct service. Thus if it is possible to provide flood control alone, possible also to provide electricity alone, and possible also to provide both, though in three different proportions, there will be five different services in that locality. (c) *Per contra,* if two or more investment projects need to combine in order to provide a single service, or a complex of services, each of such combinations of investment projects is to be treated as a single investment option. (d) If there are scale effects in any investment project, each scale of the project is to be distinguished (in the light of the expected demand for the service or services in question) and is to be treated as a separate investment option.

Turning to the question of finance, the more general approach will suppose that the finance for the resulting investment programme is raised in part from the capital budget and in part from the displacing, or at least from the not renewing, of existing public enterprises. There may also be arrangements to encourage private investment to compete with public investment, both sorts of investment being judged solely by the criterion we evolve.

3 Having listed the number of services to be met and the number of alternative investment projects for each service, the first step, after deciding the length of the common period, is to divide the calculated excess terminal benefit (terminal benefit *less* terminal cost) of each of the investment projects by its terminal cost. This gives us a *per dollar* excess terminal benefit (ETB) for each investment option. We can then place in a single row the ETBs of all investment options that are technically able to provide a particular service. There will then be as many such rows as there are services, single and complex, under consideration. The array of such ETBs provides the data we have to work with.

The method of selection will now be illustrated under the assumption that there are but three possible services under consideration: a particular service A, namely a passenger and traffic bridge across the Flo River at a point X, for which there are three investment options, i.e. alternative investment projects; a particular service B, a dam across the river Flo in order to generate electricity for an area marked Y, for which there are five investment options; and a particular service C, another dam which can provide both electricity and irrigation for the same area Y and for which there are four investment options.

The simplest context in which to solve the problem is that in which political constraint I prevails (so that the alternative to investing a dollar in a specific public project is that of placing the dollar in the private investment sector there to amount to $\$(1+\rho)^n$ in the terminal year);[2] also (1) that in which there is no possibility of private enterprise undertaking to meet any of these services, and (2) that in which the initial capital budget available, say $\$5$ million, is raised entirely by additional taxes.[3] The hypothetical ETB data are set out in Table V.8 as the unbracketed figures. Each of the bracketed figures to the right of an ETB figure represents the *terminal* value of the outlays, or capital costs, of each of the investment options in $\$ millions.

The ETB figures in the Table are all positive, as they have to be if the investment option is to qualify for admission, since a positive sum

---

[2] No difference in principle occurs (although a bit more calculation is involved) if political constraint II applies, and the alternative to one dollar in the public projects is, therefore, one dollar in the private sector where $(1-\theta)$ is consumed and where the dollar grows at the rate p_1 or p_2.

[3] This (2) assumption will be removed later on, but the (1) assumption, excluding private enterprise, will be maintained throughout. For a more general treatment in which both assumptions are removed, the reader is referred to the latter part of my 1967 paper.

TABLE V.8

A	0·05 (1·8),	0·20 (1·5),	0·30 (2·0).		
B	0·10 (4·5),	0·20 (4·0),	0·40 (4·0),	0·45 (3·0),	0·50 (3·5).
C	0·22 (5·0),	0·25 (4·0),	0·30 (2·5),	0·35 (3·0).	

indicates that there is an excess of terminal benefit over terminal costs.[4] In other words, all the investment options included in the Table produce a greater terminal value than if, instead, their outlays were placed in the private sector. If it were otherwise, they would not be included in the Table.

As there is only $5 million in the investment budget there is no point in including among the set of investment options any one requiring an *initial* outlay of more than $5 million. However, since we are dealing in terminal values, the initial capital outlays have to be compounded to the common terminal date, t_n, at 20 per cent. We can suppose then that the $5 million budget today becomes $7 million at this terminal date t_n.

4   The problem now reduces itself to the mathematical one of using the data in Table V.8 so as to choose no more than one of the alternative options in each of a number of rows (since no more than one investment option can be adopted for each of the services to be provided), but choosing them so as to obtain the highest total of terminal benefits for the given terminal cost of $7 million.

If, for instance, we pick the investment option in the C row having an ETB of 0·22, and the investment option in the A row having an ETB of 0·30, we shall be picking two investment options which between them have a terminal cost of $7 million, so exhausting the budget. The total excess benefit for this choice will be (0·22 × $5 million) *plus* (0·30 × $2 million) or $1·7 million. If, instead, we pick the 0·50 ETB option in the B row and the 0·35 ETB option in the C row, these two investment options between them use up $6·5 million of terminal capital. Unless we assume that investment options can be increased in any proportion, an unlikely contingency, we shall have left over $0·5 million of capital which, of course, produces no excess terminal benefit. The total excess benefit from this latter choice, however, is (0·50 × $3·5 million) plus (0·35 × $3·0 million), or $2·8 million.

---

[4] The capital costs, under political constraint I, being compounded forward to the terminal date at a ρ of, say, 20 per cent.

Clearly, the latter choice is better than the former. And so we could continue, picking out other combinations of investment projects, the total terminal costs of which do not exceed \$7 million, in order to discover the combination yielding the highest total excess benefit.   Where there are many rows, and many investment options in each row, the selection process can be a lengthy business. A computer programme for selecting the optimal combination of projects from all those allowed by the given budget constraint would require that the problem be formalized, as it is in the footnote below.[5] But if it so happens that along any one row the terminal costs of all the options are equal (though the amount differs from row to row) we can dispense with the computer's service. We should, in that case, choose the highest ETB in each row, and list them in descending order starting from the highest. We work down this list, summing the terminal capital requirements (given in brackets) until the total sum is as close as possible to the available (terminal) capital without exceeding it. This condition that the terminal capital costs (the bracketed figures) in any one row be uniform may seem stringent, but the method will probably

---

[5] The problem is to maximize

$$\sum_{i=1}^{q} \sum_{j=1}^{m} \tau_{ij} W_{ij} K_{ij} \tag{1a}$$

$$\begin{cases} W_{ij} = 0, 1 \\ \tau_{ij} > 0 \end{cases} \tag{2a}$$

$$\sum_{i=1}^{q} \sum_{j=1}^{m} W_{ij} K_{ij} \leqslant K \tag{3a}$$

$$\sum_{j=1}^{m} W_{ij} \leqslant 1 \qquad \text{(for all } i) \tag{4a}$$

There are q possible services, and for each service there are never more than m alternative investment options.

τ_{ij} is the ETB of the jth investment option that caters to the ith service, and K_{ij} is the terminal capital cost corresponding to the ij^{th} investment option.

The first part of the condition (2a), that $W_{ij} = 0, 1$, indicates that the weight W_{ij} is equal to unity if that investment option is selected as part of the programme, and is equal to zero if it is excluded from the programme. The second part of condition (2a) $\tau_{ij} > 0$, indicates that no investment option is to be included in the programme unless it can do better with its capital outlay than can be done with it in the private sector.

Condition (3a) states that the sum of the terminal capital costs of the investment options in the programme should not exceed the terminal value of the capital available (\$7 million in the example above).

Since no more than one option from each row can be chosen we require condition (4a), that the sum of the weight in any row does not exceed unity. This condition means in effect that either one option can be chosen from the ith row, or none.

277

work even where the condition is only approximately met. Indeed, if we tried the method out on the data in Table V.8 where the condition is far from being met, we should form the list:

$$B \quad 0 \cdot 50 \ (3 \cdot 5)$$
$$C \quad 0 \cdot 35 \ (3 \cdot 0)$$
$$A \quad 0 \cdot 30 \ (2 \cdot 0)$$

The highest ETB option for rows B and C will use up $\$6 \cdot 5$ million of terminal capital, and the choice of these two would, on this method, be the solution to the problem. Obviously the highest ETB option in the A row, $0 \cdot 30$, cannot also be included without infringing the budget restraint of $\$7$ million of terminal capital. Thus the total excess benefit from the choice of these two most profitable projects is equal to $(0 \cdot 50 \times 3 \cdot 5 \ \text{million}) + (0 \cdot 35 \times 3 \cdot 0 \ \text{million})$, or $\$2 \cdot 8$ million. This investment programme happens to be also the one yielding the maximum excess terminal value possible under these conditions.

5 We now remove the (2) assumption, and consider the case where the capital sum is to be raised in part by discontinuing existing public enterprises. Let there be three such public enterprises, $x, y,$ and $z,$ that are due to expire this year, but, having recouped their capital through amortization,[6] these enterprises could either be renewed, or their funds used for the new investment programme. If they are renewed their ETBs are calculated respectively as, say, $0 \cdot 05$ (2), $0 \cdot 15$ (1), and $0 \cdot 35$ (3), where, again, the figure in the brackets refers to the terminal worth, in $\$$ million, of the capital required. Let us suppose that the terminal value of the total capital available is $\$7$ million, as before, but that now only $\$4$ million of it is to come from additional taxes, the remainder coming from the amortization funds of the three public enterprises mentioned above. How do we now proceed to select a programme giving the maximum excess terminal benefits for the available funds?

The opportunity cost of obtaining capital *in excess* of the $\$4$ million (in terminal value) being raised by taxation is not simply ρ—as it will be for this $\$4$ million of new investment. On the assumption that the existing enterprises yield at least ρ (for if they yield less than ρ they should not, in any case, be renewed), the opportunity cost of using an additional $\$3$ million by displacing existing public enterprises must be

---

[6] The amortization funds are assumed to be invested in the private sector at ρ, where they are left until particular projects offering more than ρ are available within the existing political constraints.

the expected yields of these enterprises. The procedure, then, is to discontinue first that enterprise having the lowest ETB, provided that the funds so released are used to introduce a new investment option having a higher ETB. The second existing public enterprise to discontinue is, clearly, that having the next lowest ETB, again provided that it is replaced by a new investment having a higher ETB (although one that is as low or lower than the ETB of the new investment(s) replacing the first public enterprise). If this plan is followed, a number of new public investment projects will be financed, up to $3 million, by the funds made available from discontinuing a number of existing public enterprises. Moreover, on this procedure, the ETB of the last public enterprise to be discontinued, though the highest among the discontinued enterprises, will be lower than the ETB of the new investments that replace it (this being the lowest ETB of all the newly introduced investments).[7] It should be manifest that if this latter condition were not met—if the ETB of the last incoming new investment(s) were below that of the last outgoing public enterprise—then we could improve matters by forgoing these new investment(s) in favour of the otherwise to-be-discontinued public enterprise.

Assuming that the new investment options A, B, and C, are as before, we should continue to rank them in order of ETB as B, C, A. The B option will certainly qualify, and the $3 \cdot 5$ million outlay will be financed from the $4 million available from the budget. If no more funds were available, the $\frac{1}{2}$ million left over would be invested in the private sector. However, by discontinuing existing enterprises x and y, having ETBs respectively of $0 \cdot 05$ and $0 \cdot 15$, another $3 million can be made available to finance the new investment C which offers an ETB of $0 \cdot 35$. Since we should require an additional $2 million to introduce A as well, this is as far as we can go within the budget constraints. But the reader will notice that if the budget restraint were, however, extended, say, to $9 million, we could not introduce A by displacing existing enterprise z without violating our rules. For the ETB of enterprise z is $0 \cdot 35$, while that of new investment A is only $0 \cdot 30$.

As in the previous case, that in which the whole of the capital budget is raised by taxes, the solving of the problem appears to be difficult

---

[7] The procedure is analogous with that of increasing output so long as (diminishing) marginal revenue is above (rising) marginal cost. In this case, however, the ETB of the incoming new investments takes the place of marginal revenue, and the ETB of the outgoing public enterprises takes the place of marginal cost.

once we have a large number of services to be met, each attainable by any one of a number of alternative investment projects, and also a large number of public enterprises that can be discontinued and their funds made available for the investment programme. Nevertheless, the problem can be formalized, as in the footnote below,[8] and a systematic

---

[8] Let aK be the terminal value of the capital to be made available from the budget, where a is positive and less than one (in the text, a is 4/7, and aK therefore is $4 million). We have then to maximize

$$\sum_{i=1}^{q} \sum_{j=1}^{m} \tau_{ij} W_{ij} K_{ij} \tag{1a}$$

subject to:

$$\begin{cases} W_{ij} = 0, 1 \\ ij > 0 \end{cases} \tag{2a}$$

subject also to:

$$\sum_{i=1}^{q} \sum_{j=1}^{m} W_{ij} K_{ij} \leqslant K - M \qquad \text{(where } M \geqslant 0) \tag{3a'}$$

$$\sum_{j=1}^{m} W_{ij} \leqslant 1 \qquad \text{(for all } i) \tag{4a}$$

In addition, we are to minimize:

$$\sum_{h=1}^{H} \tau h W h\, K h \tag{5a}$$

subject to:

$$W h = 0, 1 \tag{6a}$$

$$\sum_{h=1}^{H} W h K h \geqslant (1 - a) K - M \tag{7a}$$

$$\tau i^* > \tau h^* \qquad \text{(for all } i) \tag{8a}$$

M is the amount by which the capital to be raised from discontinuing public enterprises will fall short of the maximum allowable (the maximum allowable being $3 million in our example) with M happening to be zero, since the discontinuing of existing enterprises x and y makes the whole of this $3 million available. (If, instead, their discontinuance had made only $2½ million available, M would be $½ million.) To the extent given by the magnitude of M, less capital than K is available for the total of new investments to be introduced, as in equation (3a'), and less capital is to be released from the discontinuation of the existing enterprises, as indicated by equation (7a).

Minimizing the (5a) equation expresses the requirement that we discontinue those among the existing public enterprises that together show the least possible loss of excess benefit.

The last condition (8a) determines the sum M. The symbol τ_i^* represents the ETBs of each of the new investment options that are finally selected, while τ_h^* is the highest ETB of the outgoing public enterprise. The condition (8a) requires that all the adopted investment options have an ETB that is higher than the highest ETB of the outgoing public enterprises.

All the other equations carry the same interpretation as that given for the previous case.

procedure devised to enable the computer to select the optimum investment programme.

6 In conclusion, one must concede the possibility that, owing to past habits of thought, economists might continue to find it easier to think of the problem in terms of the present value of costs and benefits rather than in terms of their terminal values. There is nothing wrong in conceiving and solving the problem in these terms. The method of selecting the investment programme outlined in this chapter can just as well be used if the present value of excess benefits is substituted for their terminal value, and if the present value of outlays is substituted for their terminal values, provided, always, that the normalization technique continues to be employed.

Chapter 40

WHAT CRITERION IS MET WHEN DISCOUNT RATES ARE USED OVER GENERATIONAL TIME?

1 The Pareto criterion on which a cost-benefit analysis is raised has special regard to the economist's basic normative axiom that the value to be attributed to a good or bad at any point in time is that value placed on it by the person(s) at that point of time. Its application requires, *inter alia*, that if a person X values $600 to be received in year 10 as exactly equivalent in welfare to $60 received this year, the economist has to accept this trade-off as part of his 'objective' data.

The single individual raises no problem in this context. Where, however, a number of individuals has to be considered, an arbitrary element may enter whenever the individual time rates of preference do not coincide. So far we have evaded this problem by tacitly supposing that a properly weighted average of the different individual time rates enables us to surmount it. But it is easy to show that this supposition is, in general, erroneous.

If, for example, the introduction of a project affects the welfare of two persons only, X and Y, such that X gains 60 in the first year and Y loses 200 in year 10, we can compare equivalent values in the first year or in the 10th year. If person Y is indifferent as between his loss of 200 in year 10 and a loss of 100 in year one, whereas person X is indifferent as between his gain of 60 in the first year and 600 in year 10, then using the values of year one produces a net loss of 40 from the project in contrast to a net gain of 400 from using the values of year 10. In this example, then, the ratio of X's benefits to Y's losses varies with the reference year chosen in evaluating the project—as is brought out in Figure V.6 in which the time-equivalent values (benefits and losses) of each person are measured vertically as

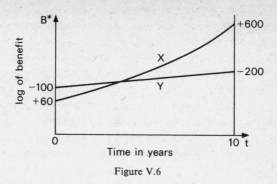

Figure V.6

B^* on a logarithmic scale for each point of time over the period to year 10.

In general, of course, there can be a matrix of rates of time preference, each element of such a matrix denoting the relevant rate for a particular person over a particular period of chronological time. This matrix conception is straightforward. But from our example above we are impelled to conclude that unless the (weighted) time rate of discount is the same both for gainers and for losers from the project, the outcome of a cost-benefit calculation will depend, in general, upon the reference point of time to which all gains and losses are reduced. Since no purely economic consideration favours one point of time over another, the choice of any one point, such as the present, is arbitrary. However, we shall disregard this difficulty in the interests of facing up to the more elusive one.

2 Although not necessary to its demonstration, it will simplify the exposition if, for the time being, we conceive of a public project the finance (and opportunity cost) of which is raised wholly by reducing current consumption, and the benefits from which are entirely consumed as they occur. Moreover, in contrast to the above example, we shall henceforth assume the existence of a money market so accommodating as to produce a rate of discount r that is common to all persons affected by the project over time, this rate r being equal also to the current yield on investment over time.

From these assumptions it follows that *provided that all persons affected expect to remain alive during the investment period* the ratio of benefits to losses (that is, the benefit-cost ratio)—as distinct from the excess benefit over loss magnitude—remains unaltered irrespective of the reference point of time adopted. Inasmuch as a benefit-cost ratio greater than unity entails an excess of benefits over costs, it also meets the Pareto criterion.

The problem addressed in this paper is that which arises when the italicised proviso above is *not* met; when, that is, beneficiaries (and 'maleficiaries') come into being at some point of time later than the initial year and others expire before the terminal date of the investment period.

To illustrate: suppose a benefit of 1000 is to be received by person X in year 100. The common rate of discount r, which also corresponds to X's rate of time preference, is such, we shall suppose, as to discount this 1000 in year 100 to 2 in year zero. But even though this r remains constant over his lifetime, if person X is born in year 80, he cannot be said to be indifferent as between receiving 1000 in year 100 and receiving 2 in year zero, this being 80 years prior to his birth—at least, not without violating the basic axiom.

3 This difficulty has been circumvented up to now by adopting either of two rules. The first is simply that of assuming (implicitly) that the lifetime of each person affected by the project covers the entire investment period, which assumption is incidentally too strict. The second is that of adopting a 'social' rate of discount, one regarded as a political datum which the economist is to accept without question. This latter device has been adopted as a matter of course by a number of writers, and no one will deny that it simplifies matters wonderfully. Yet the implications from introducing politically determined valuations into what are putatively economic calculations are far from acceptable. Certainly, recourse to such a device entails rejection of a purely economic criterion as defined above. And, since it is just possible in any case that the political authority itself may require the economist to produce a purely economic calculation of the project in question, we have some excuse for thinking about it.

4 A three-person community over time is the simplest way of highlighting the problem. In Figure V.7 chronological time is measured along the horizontal axis and the logarithm of the net benefit or loss is measured along the vertical axis. The solid parts of

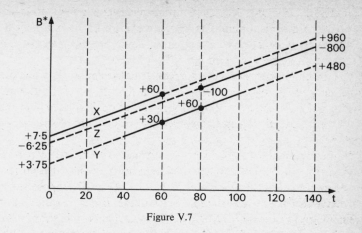

Figure V.7

the lines marked X, Y and Z, are to be interpreted as the 'time-indifference curves' of individuals X, Y and Z, respectively, inasmuch as each individual is indifferent as between any two points along his solid line—since they measure at different times his valuation of the net worth of the project to him.

Given a common rate of time preference r for all persons over time—an r such that $1 compounds to $2 in 20 years' time—the time-indifference curve for each person slopes upward from left to right at the constant angle shown in the Figure. Case (1). Person Z, who lives from year 80 to year 140, is shown to be indifferent as between losing a sum of $100 in year 80 and losing $200 in year 100. Person Y, who lives from year 40 to year 100, is indifferent as between gaining $60 in year 80 and $120 in year 100. Since there is an overlap of twenty years in the lifetimes of these two persons, a comparison between them is made without violating the basic axiom. Whether year 80 or year 100 is chosen, or any year in between, the ratio of benefit to loss of 3/5 remains valid. At year 80, for example, person Z agrees that his loss is equal to $100 and person Y agrees that his benefit is equal to $60. (Discounting these sums to present values or compounding them to terminal values does no more than multiply each sum by the same scalar and leaves the benefit-loss ratio at 3/5).

But in order for a potential Pareto improvement to be realized in this case (1), there has to be some means to enable each person, Y and Z, to move costlessly along his time-indifference curve. Clearly, a money market with a single rate of discount, r, offers such a

285

mechanism. A potential Pareto improvement in such cases is, therefore, conditional upon the existence of such a money market.

The same exercise may be carried out as between persons X and Y, inasmuch as between year 40 and year 60 their lifetimes overlap. The resulting ratio of their respective benefits therefore remains constant at 2:1.

5 Now, consider instead a case (2) for the two persons X and Z whose lifetimes can be seen from Figure V.7 to be separated by a gap of twenty years. To employ r in order to compound person X's benefit of $60 in year 60 to an equivalent benefit of $120 in year 80 violates the basic axiom, since clearly person X is *not* indifferent to receiving $60 in year 60 when he is still alive and receiving $120 in year 80, twenty years after his death. Similar remarks apply to an attempt to discount person Z's loss of $100 in year 80 to an equivalent loss of $50 in year 60, twenty years before his birth.

It should be manifest that we can multiply the number of persons and reduce the time overlap between successive persons indefinitely. But if a time gap between any two persons exist, the use of a discount rate over the whole period is to be ruled out as invalid by reference to the basic axiom.

We conclude that in the absence of some additional institutional mechanism enabling us to transform the project's original net benefit stream into some new pattern through time, it is not possible in general to meet the standard Pareto criterion. The next phase of the analysis should therefore be apparent. First, it will be necessary to show that the use of some institutional mechanism enables society to transform the project's original stream of net benefits into one that meets or fails the Pareto criterion. Secondly, we have to uncover the implications of employing this institutional mechanism so as to interpret the effective criterion. Finally, we have to appraise the ethical appeal of this explicated criterion within the intergeneration context.

6 We have seen that there is no single point of time common to all three persons, X, Y and Z and that, therefore, a mechanism is needed which does more than allow each person to select any point along his time-indifference curve. The institution of a perfect money market, though adequate for case (1) in which the lives of two persons X and Y overlap, is not of itself enough in our three-person case, since person X's lifetime ends in year 60, this being twenty years before person Z's life begins. The link between their lives can, however, be provided by a planning agency entrusted to redistribute individual gains and losses through time in such a manner as to ensure a potential Pareto improvement.

Thus in the example represented by Figure V.7 instead of person X's remaining with a gain of 60 in year 60 and, in the same year, person Y's enjoying a gain of 30 (person Z is not yet born), a government agency could, for example, transfer X's gain of 60 to Y at that point of time, leaving X with zero gain and Y with a gain of 90. This 90 in year 60 could be transformed through the money market to 180 in year 80 (without Y's being any better off as a result of the transformation), in which year it becomes possible to compare the project's benefit of 180 to Y with the loss of 100 to Z. As a consequence, therefore, of the government agency's intervention, the introduction of this project will meet a potential Pareto improvement in year 80: person X is made no worse off by the project, while person Y's benefit of 180 in year 80 exceeds the loss of 100 suffered by person Z. The benefit-cost ratio of the project in year 80 would then be 9/5—which is that ratio also produced by a conventional application of a discount rate to the data, irrespective of whether gains and losses are discounted to time zero or are compounded instead to the terminal year 140.

7 If a government agency could be depended upon automatically to intervene in this way, it might seem to follow that it could go further and, in the example adduced, ensure not merely a *potential* Pareto improvement but an *actual* Pareto improvement simply by transferring Y's gain of 180 in year 80 to person Z. For in that case no person is made worse off by the project and person Z is made better off.

But this final redistribution looks plausible only because no more than three persons are involved. Bearing in mind that the usual run of economic changes that attract political attention involves a welfare distribution covering scores of thousands and even millions of people, it is generally accepted that the task of identifying each person and, even more, that of determining the extent of the loss or gain for each of such persons—to say nothing of the costs of arranging the transfers from gainers to losers—renders an actual Pareto improvement wholly infeasible. Indeed, it is for just this reason that economists have sought to justify fulfilment of a potential Pareto improvement as the relevant criterion.

8 Returning, then, to our example, once we have to treat $X, Y, Z,$ ..., not as persons but as successive generations, we cannot hope to realize more than a potential Pareto improvement. In this connection, it is useful to divide the net gains of generation X into two sums, X_g, the gains of members of the X generation benefitting from the project, and X_l, the losses suffered from the project of other members of the X generation. Hence letting X' stand for the net benefit of generation X, $X' = X_g - X_l = +60$ in year 60. And since we assume a common rate of time preference r, this net gain of 60 for generation X in year 60 is equal to a net gain of 30 in year 40, of 15 in year 20, and of $7\frac{1}{2}$ in year 0.

Similarly, the net benefit of generation Y is denoted by $Y' = Y_g - Y_l = +30$ in year 60, while the net benefit of generation Z is denoted by $Z' = Z_g - Z_l = -100$ in year 80. It follows, therefore, that *prior* to any intervention by a government agency the original project effects a potential Pareto improvement for each of the generations X and Y and a potential Pareto loss for generation Z. However, once the government intervenes in the way described above, each of generations X and Z ends up by realizing a zero potential Pareto improvement (in each of these two generations gains exactly offset losses), whereas generation Y enjoys a potential Pareto improvement (gains to some members of the Y generation exceed the losses suffered by other members of that generation by as much as 80 valued in year 80).

We conclude, therefore, that if the government actually *does* intercede so as to transfer sums from generations X to Y and from generations Y to Z in such a way that, at least, no generations suffer a potential Pareto loss, then a potential Pareto improvement can be secured for at least one generation—in our example, generation Y—whenever the conventional discounting procedure produces a benefit-ratio greater than unity.

9 However, the economist has not, as yet, made the application of his conventional discounting procedure explicitly contingent upon government intervention in the way exemplified above. He has always applied the discount rate directly to the original stream of returns generated by the original investment project irrespective of the time span involved. It follows that if this discounting procedure when applied directly to the stream of returns of the original project shows a benefit-cost ratio greater than unity (or an excess of benefits over costs), an assumption that appropriate transfers as between generations have been made is implicit in the conclusion that a potential Pareto improvement is thereby met. The requirement, then, of hypothetical (costless) transfers as between generations, which are necessary to produce this resulting potential Pareto improvement, entails yet another 'potential' in the criterion.

Put otherwise, a potential Pareto improvement is realized if, within an *existing* community (or generation) a hypothetical (costless) redistribution of the net gains can be so arranged as to make 'everybody' better off. And it now transpires that this sought-for potential Pareto improvement can be realized only if, within an *inter-generation* context, there is in addition a hypothetical (costless) redistribution of each generation's net benefits arranged so as to make each generation enoy a potential Pareto improvement, or—in the limiting case (as in our simple example involving generations X, Y, and Z)—so that no generation suffers a potential Pareto loss and one generation at least enjoys a potential Pareto improvement.

10 It would not be inappropriate to call this dual hypothetical redistribution entailed by the discounting procedure a *potential* potential Pareto improvement, since in order eventually to realize the familiar potential Pareto improvements at particular points in time, hypothetical transfers as between generations have first to be assumed.[1] Irrespective of terminology, however, the dimensions of

---

[1] It is possibly useful to labour the point by analogy—within a static context. Suppose we contemplate introducing a public good and discover that the data show that the algebraic sum of individual valuations is negative. We say it does *not* meet a Pareto criterion; we cannot, that is, reach a position from which, by costless redistribution, 'everyone' can be made better off.

But now some bright lad proves to us that there is some *other* distribution of income, d^*, which differs from the existing distribution d_0 which, could it be costlessly brought about, would show the sum of individual valuations to be positive. Are we to conclude that the public project does, after all, meet a potential Pareto improvement?

No! What has been shown is that a potential Pareto improvement is hypothetically

the hypothetical transfers now involved are manifestly more complex than those involved in the more familiar comparative-statics potential Pareto improvement. And, what is pertinent to the issue, the resulting criterion is less ethically acceptable than the ordinary Pareto criterion; that is to say, it is less likely to command an ethical consensus for the community for which it is intended— namely, the community composed of members of all successive generations covered by the period of investment. Certainly, the economist has never explicitly proposed that such a *potential* potential Pareto improvement be accepted as an economic criterion of social welfare.

To be more explicit, whereas the familiar potential Pareto improvement might commend itself to an existing community at a point of time, since members of the community are aware that there exist distributive mechanisms—the progressive tax structure along with a range of benefits available from the welfare state—which go some way to diffusing the net benefits of public projects among the members of society, no such distributive mechanisms can be counted upon to operate as between generations. An inter-generation project which, using a conventional DPV or CTV method, happens to yield a B/C ratio greater than unity—indicative, therefore, of meeting what we have called a *potential* potential Pareto improvement—might well be one in which the bulk of the benefits accrue to existing or earlier generations, leaving heavy costs to be borne by later generations.[2]

---

[1] (contd) possible. Thus only if the d^* distribution can be brought about costlessly (whether d^* is desirable or not is a separate question) and, if, following that, the resulting positive algebraic sum can be costlessly redistributed, we shall have achieved an actual Pareto improvement. In fact, neither of these operations can be brought about costlessly. Therefore a proposal that the project be adopted because there is a d^* which would generate a positive algebraic sum of individual valuations, is tantamount to adopting a *potential* potential Pareto improvement as a criterion.

[2] What is involved can be brought out more starkly by adopting the somewhat outlandish example used by Freeman (1977) in order to illustrate his assertion that, in project evaluation, it makes economic sense to discount to the present value of damages expected to be suffered by generations who will live many thousands of years from now. Thus a colossal amount of damage, equal in value to $\$D$ and to be experienced in 100,000 years' time, should, he alleges, be discounted to the present to equal, say, \$80 today. If the immediate benefits of such a project are equal to \$100, then the B/C ratio exceeds unity and, on an allocative test, the project should be admitted.

Freeman goes on to argue that justification for this conclusion resides in the fact that if \$80 were invested today and continually reinvested at the discount rate for

11 In general then, by appropriate intervention at points in time over the intergeneration period, an original investment project whose stream of benefits and outlays occurring over the distant future can be discounted to yield a positive net benefit today, is one that may also be converted into any of a number of hypothetical projects, each of which would indeed meet a potential Pareto improvement.

In all such instances, therefore, two sorts of hypothetically costless transfers are involved, not just one. The first has reference to the sums that may be transferred from earlier generations and, possibly, invested for the time necessary to produce zero or positive net benefits for future generations. The second has reference to the distribution among the members of *each* of such generations now having the hypothetical zero or positive net benefits so that no member of it is made worse off. Since the DPV method espoused by Freeman in this intergeneration context is *not* being regarded as

---

[2] (contd) 100,000 years (assuming, always, we could know the relevant rates and that they would continue to be positive, which is questionable), it would compound to this sum D. The beneficiaries from this amount D would then be able exactly to compensate those destined to suffer the D amount of damages, leaving a net gain of $20 for today's generation. According to Freeman, a potential Pareto improvement is thereby met, as required by the economist.

Now, with respect to the *hypothetical* time stream devised by Freeman, a potential Pareto improvement would indeed be met. But clearly this time stream is *not* the original stream which conferred a gain on the present generation of $100 and inflicted damages equal to D on generations living 100,000 years from today. What his argument amounts to, therefore, is the sanctioning of an actual inter-generation project that, by recourse to investment opportunities *could* be changed into a different inter-generation project, which different project could then meet the conventional hypothetical compensation test. Since both a hypothetical project and a hypothetical compensation test are involved in his exercise, he is also, in effect, ascribing allocative virtue to an economic change that meets a *potential* potential Pareto improvement.

The analysis is, of course, symmetric. For if, instead, a colossal benefit equal to B were to be conferred on some group that would be alive in 100,000 years' time by investing today the sum of $80, the project would also be approved on Freeman's logic if the discounted present value of B were equal to, say $100. True, future generations cannot pass benefits backward in time to their predecessors. But it is always possible for current generations to consume $100 of existing capital which, were it not so consumed, would have compounded to B in 100,000 years. Hence, if such action were taken, the generation alive in 100,000 years would, in addition, suffer a loss of potential value equal to B, which loss would exactly offset the benefit B conferred by the project. Future gains and losses would then cancel out, leaving to the present generation a loss of $80 (equal to the outlay on the project) and the gain of $100 from consuming that much of the existing capital which would otherwise have been passed on to the future. This contrived *hypothetical* stream would, therefore, also meet a potential Pareto improvement.

contingent upon actual agreement being reached between governments of all generations involved actually to invest the receipts of earlier generations with the object of presenting later generations with sums calculated to offset the losses they are to suffer, this notional transfer between generations is clearly as hypothetical as the subsequent redistribution of net gains among members of the community at any point of time.

Again, of course, the terminology of the implicit criterion—a *potential* potential Pareto improvement—is itself of no consequence. The reader might indeed prefer simply to envisage instead a more complex form of hypothetical intervention over time, involving both transfers as between generations (via investment opportunities) and as between members of each generation. Yet the same conclusion holds: namely, that whereas a consensus on the acceptability of the familiar potential Pareto improvement as a criterion (involving as it does members of a given generation) may be presumed to exist, in contrast, a consensus as between members of all generations involved in the long-lived investment project may not be presumed—inasmuch as there are no mechanisms which can be presumed to diffuse the net benefits among this inter-generational community.

If, meeting together behind the 'veil of ignorance', the members of all generations involved in the project cannot know when they are to be alive, they will all have a lively apprehension of the disadvantages of being born into one of the later generations to be affected by the project whenever positive rates of discount are used. Projects yielding immense benefits to later generations for very small net costs to the earliest generation can easily be rejected by this earliest generation acting on the conventional criterion. Worse yet, projects inflicting immense damage on later generations in exchange for slight net gains to the earlier generations can easily be accepted by these earlier generations on the conventional criterion.

At all events it is certain that there has been no debate, much less agreement, among economists about the advisability of adopting this implied *potential* potential criterion in an inter-generational context. In the circumstances, the economists are impelled to face directly the intergenerational distributional implications of such projects.[3]

---

[3] It will occur to the reader that even for a project having a relatively short time span, say twenty years, there may not be a common point of overlap; in other words, there

REFERENCES AND BIBLIOGRAPHY FOR PART V

Arrow, K. J. 'Discounting and Public Investment Criteria', in A. V. Kneese and S. C. Smith (eds.), *Water Research*, Baltimore: Johns Hopkins, 1966.

Arrow, K. J. and Lind, R. C. 'Uncertainty and the Evaluation of Public Investment Decisions', *American Economic Review*, 1970.

— 'Uncertainty and the Evaluation of Public Investment Decisions: Reply', *American Economic Review*, 1972.

Baumol, W. J. 'On the Social Rate of Discount', *American Economic Review*, 1968.

Bradford, D. F. 'Constraints on Public Action and Rules for Social Decision', *American Economic Review*, 1970.

— 'Constraints on Government Investment Opportunities and the Choice of Discount Rate', *American Economic Review*, 1975.

Dasgupta, A. K. and Pearce, D. W. *Cost Benefit Analysis: Theory and Practice*, London: Macmillan, 1972.

Dasgupta, P. and Heal, G. 'The Optimal Depletion of Exhaustible Resources', *Review of Economic Studies*, 1974.

Dasgupta, P., Marglin, S. and Sen, A. K. *Guidelines for Project Evaluation*, United Nations, 1972.

Drèze, J. H. 'Discount Rates and Public Investment: A Postscriptum', *Economica*, 1974.

Feldstein, M. 'Net Social Benefit Calculation and the Public Investment Decision', *Oxford Economic Papers*, 1964.

— 'The Inadequacy of Weighted Discount Rates', in R. Layard (ed.), *Cost-Benefit Analysis: Selected Readings*, Harmondsworth: Penguin, 1972.

Fisher, Irving. *The Theory of Interest*, London, Macmillan, 1930.

Freeman, M. 'A Short Argument in Favour of Discounting Intergenerational Effects', *Futures*, 1977.

Harberger, A. C. 'The Opportunity Costs of Public Investment Financed by Borrowing', in R. Layard (ed.), *Cost-Benefit Analysis: Selected Readings*, Harmondsworth:Penguin, 1972.

Haveman, R. H. and Krutilla, J. V. *Unemployment, Idle Capacity and the Evaluation of Public Expenditures*, Baltimore: Johns Hopkins, 1968.

Hertz, D. B. 'Risk Analysis in Capital Investment', *Harvard Business Review*, 1964.

Hirschleifer, J. 'Theory of Optimal Investment Decision', *Journal of Political Economy*, 1958.

— 'Investment Decisions under Uncertainty: Applications of the State-Preference Approach', *Quarterly Journal of Economics*, 1966.

Hirschleifer, J., DeHaven, J. C. and Milliman, J. W., *Water Supply: Economics, Technology, and Policy*, Chicago: University of Chicago Press, 1960.

---

[3] (contd) may be a time gap between the deaths of some members of the community affected by the project and the birth of others affected by the project. In such cases a vindication of the discounting procedure also involves the acceptance of a *potential* potential Pareto improvement as a criterion.

However, within a shorter span of time, one not exceeding a generation of, say, thirty years or so, such a criterion might possibly command a consensus over the period in question based on a belief that institutional mechanisms will continue to operate so that no person affected by these relatively short-term projects is likely to suffer great loss, and that there is a better chance of capturing and diffusing opportunities of increased welfare by adopting this economic criterion than by adopting any other.

Krutilla, J. V. and Eckstein, O. *Multiple Purpose River Development: Studies in Applied Economic Analysis*, Baltimore: Johns Hopkins, 1958.

Lind, R. C. 'The Social Rate of Discount and the Optimal Rate of Investment: Further Comment', *Quarterly Journal of Economics*, 1964.

Marglin, S. 'The Opportunity Costs of Public Investment', *Quarterly Journal of Economics*, 1963(a).

— 'The Social Rate of Discount and the Optimal Rate of Investment', *Quarterly Journal of Economics*, 1963(b).

Massè, P. *Optimal Investment Decisions: Rules for Action and Criteria for Choice*. New Jersey: Prentice-Hall, 1962.

Mishan, E. J. 'A Normalisation Procedure for Public Investment Criteria', *Economic Journal*, 1967.

— 'Flexibility and Consistency in Project Evaluation', *Economica*, 1974.

Musgrave, R. A. 'Cost-Benefit Analysis and the Theory of Public Investment', *Journal of Economic Literature*, 1969.

Nichols, A. 'Normalisation Procedure for Public Investment Criteria: A Further Comment', *Economic Journal*, 1970.

— 'The Opportunity Costs of Public Investment: Comment', *Quarterly Journal of Economics*, 1964.

— 'On the Social Rate of Discount: Comment', *American Economic Review*, 1969.

Page, T. 'Equitable Use of the Resource Base', *Environment and Planning*, 1976.

Ramsey, D. D. 'On the Social Rate of Discount: Comment', *American Economic Review*, 1969.

Ramsey, F. 'A Mathematical Theory of Saving', *Economic Journal*, 1928.

Sandmo, A. and Drèze, J. H. 'Discount Rates for Public Investment in Closed and Open Economies', *Economica*, 1971.

Solomon, E. 'The Arithmetic of Capital-budgeting Decisions', *Journal of Business*, 1956.

Solow, R. H. 'Intergenerational Equity', *Review of Economic Studies*, 1974.

Steiner, P. O. 'Choosing among Alternative Public Investments in the Water Resource Field', *American Economic Review*, 1959.

Strotz, R. H. 'Myopia and Inconsistency in Dynamic Utility Maximisation', *Review of Economic Studies*, 1956.

Weiss, D. *Economic Evaluation of Projects*, Berlin, 1976.

PART VI. PARTICULAR PROBLEMS IN PROJECT EVALUATION

Chapter 41

THE VALUE OF TIME SAVED

1   Transport projects are designed chiefly either to accommodate an increasing number of travellers or to reduce journey time, and sometimes, incidentally, to increase the comfort or convenience of travel.

It is hardly necessary to remark that if a project saves journey-time the compensating variation is equal to the largest sum each person is willing to pay in order to save that amount of time. In the absence of reliable questionnaires, economists have recourse to indirect methods, which may involve interpreting people's behaviour whenever they are faced with clear alternatives,[1] in the attempt to place a social value on the time saved by the introduction of the project in question.

2   A common procedure is to reckon the value of a person's time as equal to the sum he could earn during the time saved. If a man's earnings average $10 an hour, an average saving of time of 25 hours a year might be valued at $250 a year.

The rationale of this procedure derives from the individual's supply schedule of labour. If we simplify the exposition by assuming that the effects of changes in his welfare on his choice of work-time are zero, his marginal valuation curve S in Figure VI.1 cuts the hourly wage line at, say, 42 hours per week. If institutions are such that he is allowed to work the chosen 42 hours per week, then in order to persuade him to part with an hour's leisure—that is, to do another hour's work—he must be paid compensation of at least $10, and more than $10 for each

---

[1] An interesting example is that of Beesley (1965).

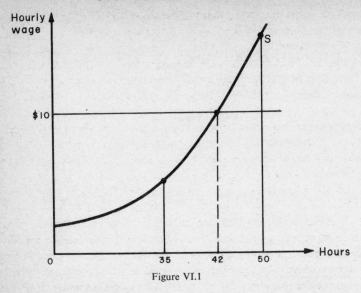

Figure VI.1

additional hour of leisure forgone. For *marginal* deviations from his *choice* of 42 hours, the use of the hourly wage of $10 as the value of his time would seem reasonable.

This familiar construction can be used to explain the chief differences in the average value of time as between different countries or regions. If the value of time, in terms of goods, is very much higher in the United States than it is in India, it is simply because real productivity in the former, and therefore real earnings there, are that much higher. Since we are not primarily interested in inter-country differences in the value of time, but rather in deriving a satisfactory measure for some particular country, we are entitled to be more critical.

Even if we accept the relevance of this approach to the valuation of time, we have to bear in mind that the worker is seldom given the choice of working hours. The hours per day, and days per week, are usually fixed by the employer, possibly in consultation with the labour unions. This implies that the use of the hourly wage rate as a measure of marginal changes in the value of time for any particular worker is less reliable. If, for example, the working week were set at 35 hours, the marginal value of an hour for the worker who would freely choose to work 42 hours would be less than $10. If instead, the working week were set at 50 hours, the marginal value of an hour for this worker would be in excess of $10, as indicated in the Figure.

What is more, the *social* value of the worker's hourly output will be represented by the hourly wage only where price is equal to marginal costs, as in perfect competition. If price exceeds marginal cost in the industry employing the worker then the marginal social valuation of an hour's work—even where the worker chooses the number of hours to work—exceeds the hourly wage he is paid. Again, if there are uncorrected external economies or diseconomies (that have the effect of raising or lowering, respectively, the social value of the product in relation to its market price) the marginal social valuation of an hour's work has, respectively, to be revised upward or downward.

3 Nevertheless, such considerations tend only to qualify the measurement of the value of time. They do not bring into question the idea of valuing time in terms of the social marginal product of labour. And if this social marginal product rises over time, as it does of course with the per capita growth in GNP, then the rise in the real value of labour implies that it becomes increasingly scarce as compared with other goods. As Becker (1965) points out, since time enters also into all consumption activity as well as production activity, economic behaviour implies not only a movement toward the utilization of more labour-saving methods in production, and toward a search for more labour-saving innovations in production, but also a movement toward labour-saving methods in consumption. Thus, the growing scarcity of time induces a switch to consumption goods that economize on time, and this switch of demand provides an incentive to produce labour-saving or time-saving products for the market.

Yet this growing scarcity of time is not to be attributed wholly to the growth over time of labour productivity. It is arguable that the rising standard of consumption will, of itself, reduce the time available per unit of consumption.[2] Thus even if ordinary mortals did not have to work for a living, and goods were liberally bestowed on them by a benevolent technocracy, according as the flow of consumer goods increased so too would the scarcity of time in which to enjoy any quantum of them. Eventually we might become increasingly frantic trying to 'cut corners' and save time in the endeavour to 'enjoy' all our

---

[2] This argument was adumbrated in a footnote by Tipping (1968).

goods; in effect, trying to 'enrich' time by cramming more consumption activities into it. For whereas all other goods can be increased, time cannot.

4   Now if the time saved were in fact invariably to be used for additional output, the marginal social product of labour would indeed be the appropriate concept. Or, again, if in our benevolent technocracy, which freely provides us with an abundance of consumer goods, an extra hour could somehow be tacked on to our twenty-four hour day, the rate of substitution between all other goods and time would be the appropriate concept. But, in general, neither of these considerations is directly in issue wherever the time saved arises from investment in some transport project.

In any specific place or period, that is, the introduction of transport investment that saves time does not require that we evaluate the alternative use of this time saved in producing output or in consuming other goods. Time is not, in such cases, to be regarded as labour time or as leisure time, or as a sort of factor or good that can be distilled from the production or consumption process. Time is not only inseparable from all production and consumption activities, it is complementary to such activities. Time is in fact the unit in which such activities can be measured. When a person is prepared to pay for a good, or to be paid for providing a good, the consumption or provision of the good in question clearly uses up time—a fact which is known to the person who agrees to consuming or to providing the good. Thus, it is not time *per se* for which a person pays, or requires to be paid, but for the specific activity per unit of time, whether that activity involves producing, consuming, creating, playing, idling, or any combination thereof. If a person engages in any less of such activities (all prices and opportunities unchanged), his welfare can increase or decrease; the activity in question, that is, generates a utility or disutility through time.

5   In valuing the saving of time resulting from a transport investment, the tacit assumption is sometimes made that the activity, travelling, is an activity that, for the relevant range, produces a disutility for the individual traveller. Clearly this is not always the case. If a person pays to ride a horse for an hour, an accidental extra quarter of an hour's ride is likely to be welcome. A holiday that is unexpectedly prolonged by a couple of days might be very welcome. The tacit assumption is reasonable only for projects that are designed to reduce travel time that is generally regarded as means only to an end. Nevertheless, the extent of the disagreeability of the journey can vary widely. Thus in evaluating the worth of a reduction in travel time, regard must be had to the particular sort of travel and the relevant alternatives open to the traveller.

There can then be no single correct way of evaluating the saving of time on a journey. For the conditions of travel will vary and the purpose of the journey will vary from case to case. If a person is on his way to a holiday by the sea, some delay at a small railway station with a picturesque view might be enjoyed in a festive spirit. If, on the other hand, a lot depends upon keeping an appointment, a small delay can be excruciating. Thus a young man who is keeping a first date might suffer agony in a traffic jam: he would be willing to pay a large sum to save a few precious minutes. An employee on a business trip may not mind a delay, no matter how long, since it is the firm's time anyway. A business executive having an expense account might positively enjoy travelling as a welcome change from office routine and would as soon have the journey time longer than shorter. He might in fact much prefer to cross the Atlantic by ship rather than by plane. Any saving of journey time would be a loss of benefit so far as he is concerned.

To the corporation who employs him, however, the saving in time might be a gain—but only if the time saved were large enough to enable his presence in the office to add something to profits. Obviously a few hours' saving would be useless in this connection, and it is uncertain whether even a few days would make a difference. Furthermore, even though a saving of the executive's time can be counted on to increase somewhat the corporation's profit, the economist engaged in *social* cost-benefit analysis does not necessarily equate the increased profit with increased social benefit. The increase in profit may well be at the expense of the profits of competitors. Only if the saving in the executive's time resulted in some additional value of output to the economy as a whole (*net* of external effects) would it rate as a social benefit. On the other hand, the owner of a small business, say a retail shop, who can travel only by closing his shop, or by suffering a reduction in sales, would benefit by the saving of a few daylight hours of travelling.

Again, in considering any reduction of an existing delay, the extent of the delay is important. There is obviously some *minimum sensible* below which any delay has no perceptible value for society. An investment that would save about ten seconds' time on a daily journey is not worth having even if many millions of people 'benefit' from it. No one would really care much. Indeed, in a journey that currently takes, say, six hours, a ten-minute saving of time is hardly likely to have a perceptible effect on people's welfare, and there would be a case for ignoring it irrespective of the number of people involved. In general, it is the proportion of time saved that counts as much as the absolute amount of time saved.

There are other fairly obvious factors such as comfort to be considered also. Many people will prefer a journey during which they can sit and read quietly to a shorter journey during which they can do neither, or to a shorter journey during which they have to make one or more changes. They may also prefer a means of transport *A* which arrives punctually to a means of transport *B* which, although it *averages* less on the journey, sometimes takes longer than the *A* transport. Greater frequency of public transport, or a more convenient time-table, may be rated higher than some perceptible saving in existing journey time.[3]

---

[3] For further discussion of such factors the reader is referred to the excellent article by Tipping (1968).

Chapter 42

THE BENEFITS OF A RECREATION AREA (I)

1 In most discussions on the value of facilities for recreation there is some mention of 'non-economic' considerations. Recreational activity may be seen, for instance, as promoting creativity or individual freedom, or as encouraging democratic participation or inculcating a healthy outlook. Whether such values or attitudes can, or should, be brought into the calculus is an open question. There is certainly a repugnance to the idea of attempting to bring humane and perhaps transcendental considerations 'into relation with the measuring rod of money', and though I am in sympathy with it, I am uncertain just where the line should be drawn. For that reason we shall steer away from this controversy, at least until the close of the following chapter, and confine ourselves to the concepts of the direct benefits that the economist should certainly attempt to measure.

2 Let us restrict the analysis to parks, particularly large national parks, as an interesting exercise in the application of cost-benefit principles. Clearly the economic justification for introducing a park of any size whatever is that its total social benefits will exceed its total resource costs. As for the *optimal* size of the park under consideration, it is required in addition that the marginal social benefit be equal to the marginal resource cost.

Once the size and the location of the park have already been determined—when, that is, we are in the 'short period'—visitors are to be admitted into the park until marginal social benefit is equal to marginal variable cost, which cost could, of course, be zero. It is possible, however, for maintenance costs to vary with the number of people admitted. Moreover, the numbers of people entering the park may be such as eventually to cause congestion, or otherwise to impose disamenities on each other, so requiring a subtraction from the schedule of benefits.[1]

To sum up, within the short period, when the size of the park is unalterable, the total conditions require that aggregate social benefits per period (at the optimal inflow of visitors) should exceed total maintenance outlays.

3   Now consider in more detail the long-run determination of the size of a park within some given location. The information we should need from each potential visitor to the park is as follows: for any x acres of park in a given location, what is the incremental value he places on the number of separate trips per annum?[2] To illustrate, for a specific kind of park of one acre, the value the ith person places on successive trips per annum, over and above all costs incidental to reaching this one park,[3] can be plotted in Figure VI.2. Since he is not constrained to take more trips to the park each year than he chooses, we will count trips having only positive values. The Figure reveals that he will choose to make four separate trips each year, the fifth trip having a zero or negative value for him. The total area of these four rectangles represents the maximum sum he is willing to pay per annum for this specific kind of park of one acre.

For a park in the same location of two acres, his marginal valuation of successive trips will be somewhat larger. In consequence he would, as depicted in Figure VI.3, choose to make more trips; in our example, six trips per annum.

We could then introduce parks of three acres, four acres, and so on up to m acres.

4   We now plot marginal valuations for the ith individual for successive *acres* of park, as in Figure VI.4. The first acre has a rectangle

---

[1] Alternatively marginal congestion costs can be added to the marginal resource costs.

[2] We can assume that the duration of the trip is a day, though it could of course be a trip of a number of hours or even minutes.

[3] In the long period, when the decision is taken to introduce a one-acre park in a certain location, the ith person, in evaluating the incremental sums he will pay for additional trips per annum, is assumed to take into account all costs of movement including the expenses, if any, of changing home and job and, also, any psychic losses consequent upon a change of neighbourhood and loss of friends in order to be closer to the park. In short, the positive sums he will pay for successive trips (being compensating variations) are in the nature of surpluses, and are *net* of all expenses incidental to his being able to avail himself of the facilities offered by the park in question.

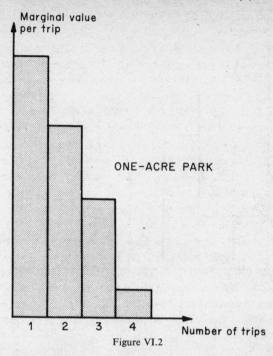

Figure VI.2

equal in area to the total area of successive trips in the one-acre park depicted in Figure VI.2. The size of the second rectangle in Figure VI.4 is equal to the *difference* between the total areas of Figures VI.2 and VI.3, this being the additional amount of money he would be willing to pay for a park having one more acre than the original one-acre park. The size of the third rectangle in Figure VI.4 is the difference between the total area of Figure VI.3 and an area corresponding to the total valuation which the ith person would place on a three-acre park, and so on until m acres—where m is large enough for the mth acre park to have a zero marginal valuation for each of the n persons who will use the park.

Assuming continuity in the construction of the marginal valuation curve per acre, we can derive for each of the n persons a similar curve with respect to the acreage of the given type and location of park. Since the park is a public good inasmuch as (in the absence of congestion) long period costs are not attributable to any one person's activity—the benefits being simultaneously available to all n persons—these indivi-

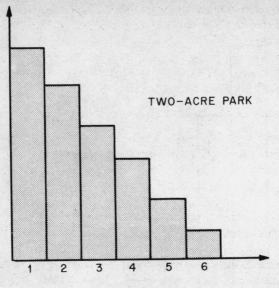

TWO-ACRE PARK

Figure VI.3

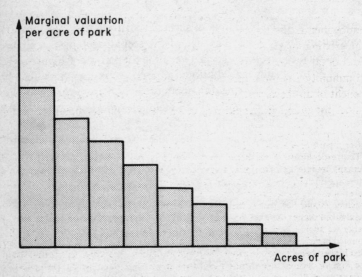

Figure VI.4

304

dual marginal valuation curves are to be vertically aggregated so as to yield the community's joint marginal valuation of successive acres of park per annum.

The intersection of this aggregate marginal valuation curve with the curve of long period marginal cost (of successive acres) will then determine the optimal size of the park. Thus in the long period, the *total* conditions to be met can be summarized as $\sum_{i=1}^{n} V_i > K$, where the Vs are the total valuations placed on this optimal size of park by each of the n persons, and K is the total resource cost of that size of park. As for the necessary (marginal) conditions for the optimal size of park, they are given by $\sum^{n} v_i \gtreqless k$, where v_i is the ith person's marginal valuation per acre of park[4] (never less than zero) and k is the long period marginal cost of adding acreage to the park.[5]

5 Two issues have now to be faced, the implications of the *ceteris paribus* clause relevant to the problem, and the treatment of costs and benefits over time.

The calculation of the benefits by the above method is designed for the introduction of an additional park and for the determination of its size, given the existing spread of population, the existing resource endowments, and the existing product and factor prices, in particular the existing number of parks and recreational facilities provided either free or at some set of prices. Clearly if there are already in the community a number of such parks available, the *apparent* aggregate benefit of all these parks, if obtained simply by aggregating the areas under the marginal benefit curves of the community obtained on the

---

[4] For a park of x acres, $v_i = \delta V_i/\delta x$, and $k = \delta K/\delta x$.

[5] The reader might think that if such information were readily available, he could perhaps use linear programming methods to determine the number, size, location, and other specific features of parks serving the community. But inasmuch as the parks are substitutes, the value people attach to any one of them depends, *inter alia*, on the existing number of parks, their size, location, etc. The objective function to be maximized cannot therefore be calculated. In order to devise some optimal system of parks we should have to use a sequential procedure; finding, say, the highest discounted benefit-cost ratio for the location of some minimal size park, followed by the next highest benefit-cost ratio for some minimal additional park area, either attached to the first or located elsewhere—and so on down to a point where the budget is exhausted, or the benefit-cost ratio of the marginal park acreage is no higher than that of investment projects generally.

above principle, will understate the *true* social benefit—the difference between the apparent and the true benefit being larger the closer can the parks be regarded as substitutes for one another. A correct method of calculating the aggregate social benefit of a number of parks is that outlined in Chapter 8. In principle the method would require that the parks be introduced in hypothetical sequence: to the total benefit of introducing only a single park in the community, there is then added the total benefit of introducing a second park on the assumption that the first park is, indeed, already in existence, and so on. A correct calculation of the total social benefit is, of course, important whenever the economist is concerned with the total contribution to society's welfare of an existing number or a proposed number of parks.

6 In general, the benefits and, to a lesser extent, the outlays, of a project accrue over time. If we choose to adopt the discounted present value method, the question of the appropriate rate of discount arises.

While it is uncertain whether every person would think of each future trip to a national park as having a smaller present value than one to be taken earlier, we might make the conventional assumption that each living person discounts the value of a future benefit. As between generations, however, the conventional discounting of future benefits entails interpersonal comparisons that are not easily acceptable. To my unborn grandson, a trip to the Z national park may be worth no less to him at some future date than it is worth to me today. And economists cannot produce convincing arguments that would justify this future trip being valued today at a smaller figure than that which my grandson will put on it. Valid though the point is, however, it is relevant only if the land in question has no alternative use and requires practically no expense to fashion it into a park, as would be the case in a 'wilderness area'. In such exceptional cases there would then seem to be no more justification for discounting such future benefits to be enjoyed by generations to come than there would be for discounting the existing valuations of different groups alive today.

If, on the other hand, there are indeed alternative uses for the piece of land, or if resources have to be diverted from the production of other goods in order to create a desirable park, the case is otherwise. For the benefits expected to be enjoyed in the future, both by existing and future generations, have now to be compared with those alternative benefits they could enjoy if the resources to be used in creating this park were instead to be used in the production of other assets. It should be borne in mind, however, that the value of man-made assets might well decline over time relative to resources of natural beauty that are preserved by national parks, since the former are becoming increasingly abundant and the latter are becoming increasingly scarce.

One can become involved, at this juncture, in the literature about the choice of an appropriate rate of discount, a choice which depends among other things on the particular methods of finance which are in general subject to political and institutional constraints. Since such a problem is not peculiar to recreational facilities or national parks, we can avoid unnecessary elaboration by assuming (a) that, as a result of income and corporation taxes (to mention only the more familiar factors) the lowest rates of return on private investment exceed the social rate of time preference, (b) that the investible funds are to be raised wholly by reducing private investment, and (c) that all benefits from the project can be translated into cash and reinvested by the public agency at the private rate of return, ρ. With these assumptions we should adopt the private yield ρ as the appropriate discount rate, and unless investment in the park in question can generate a yield at least as great as ρ there is no economic warrant for its introduction. The criterion $PV\rho(B) > K$ has therefore to be met.

There may, of course, be specific alternative uses for the land other than that of a park area, so that the criterion is a necessary but not sufficient condition for introducing the park project. If, for example, prospectors discover valuable minerals under the land, the excess social benefit over cost of using the land for a park and of using it for mineral production have to be directly compared.

Chapter 43

THE BENEFITS OF A
RECREATION AREA (II)

1   Marion Clawson (1959) made an ingenious attempt actually to derive demand curves for recreational activity, in particular for the use of national parks, under a number of simplifying assumptions. Though Clawson touched very lightly on the benefit aspects, if one is interested in policy it is well worth examining the usefulness of the construct he devised from the standpoint of an index of social benefit.

The Clawson concept is that of an already existing park of given acreage and facilities, so the question of determining the optimal size of the park does not arise in his paper. In principle, and considering for the present only direct benefits, one could discover for each person the maximum sum he would be willing to pay (over and above the costs of the journey) for the privilege of one trip a year to this particular park, for two trips a year, and so on, until he would pay nothing for an additional annual trip. The aggregate over all persons of such maximum sums constitutes a measure of the total direct social benefit per annum.

The first relationship estimated by Clawson could be looked at as a sort of gravity model inasmuch as the traffic from any particular area to the park is inversely related to the distance and directly to the population of the area. From areas of varying distance to Yosemite National Park, Clawson estimated the total dollar cost per one day visit, in the year 1953, on the basis of time and mileage, using a number of assumptions of varying degrees of plausibility such as four persons per car travelling 400 miles a day and, more restrictive, that the main purpose of the journey was to visit Yosemite, there being then no entrance charge to the park.

2   The elements of his method can be brought quickly into focus by inventing figures for only three hypothetical areas, *A, B,* and *C,*

situated at varying distances from Yosemite, rather than by introducing his more elaborate estimates. The hypothetical data required is
given in the following Table VI.1.

TABLE VI.1

Area	Population	Distance from Yosemite	Number of visits to Yosemite as a per cent of population[1]	Cost per visit[2]
A	10,000	100 miles	50%	$20
B	20,000	300 miles	15%	$40
C	30,000	800 miles	5%	$100

The corresponding figures of the last two columns enable us to plot
three points, A, B, and C, in Figure VI.5.

If we now make the strong assumption that the population of each of
these areas is a perfect sample with respect to all relevant variables of
the population of all three areas taken together, a curve fitted through
the points A, B, and C, can be interpreted as a relation between the
proportion of the total population visiting Yosemite and the cost per
visit. Thus, if, as stated, 50 per cent of the population of the A area is
willing to make the trip when the cost is $20, we may infer that this
sum is the *least* any person from the A area is willing to pay for the
trip—the marginal trip, that is, is worth just $20 and the intramarginal
trips are worth more. This means that a sort of marginal valuation curve
passes through the point A and—inasmuch as the population samples
of areas B and C are identical with that of A—it passes also through
points B and C.[3]

---

[1] There is, of course, nothing to prevent the number of visits per annum exceeding 100
per cent of that area's population, though in fact this was not the case in the data
unearthed by Clawson.

[2] If it can be assumed that expenditure on food, etc., once in the park, is little different
from what it is at home, we could add together for the visitors coming from any one
area, say the C area, two-day, three-day, and n-day stays in the park along with the one-
day stays there. Since the journey costs are the same for the *marginal n*-day visitor, the
total benefit enjoyed by this marginal n-day visitor can also be taken as just equal to the
total travelling costs.

If these assumptions are implausible, it would be necessary to separate the demand
curves for one-day, two-day, three-day, and n-day visitors.

[3] If it were assumed, instead, that some benefit arises from the journey itself, the curve
passing through points A, B, and C in Figure V.5 would be closer to the horizontal
axis. For the 'true' cost of the journey requires that any incidental benefits are to be
subtracted from the calculated time and resource costs of the journey.

3   If all three areas were of identical size, as in fact they are not, the distances along the horizontal axis of Figure VI.5 could be translated directly from percentages into absolute numbers. By then raising the cost per visit to each area by $1—a result, say, of charging $1 per person entrance fee—we could calculate directly from the curve the reduction in the number of annual visits. These would be different for each of the three areas as each area is associated with a different cost per trip.

Since each area has a different size of population we use the curve to estimate for each area in turn the actual population reduction for a continuous range of entrance charges. Thus an examination of the curve in Figure VI.5 reveals that a rise in costs by $1 results in a reduction of 2% of visits from area A (having a population of 10,000) whereas a rise in cost by $2 results in a reduction of visits equal to 3% of that population—a reduction of 200 visits and 300 visits respectively. Continuing in this way, an exploitable demand curve for area A can be derived as in Figure VI.6, the entrance charge being measured along the vertical axis and the number of visits along the horizontal.

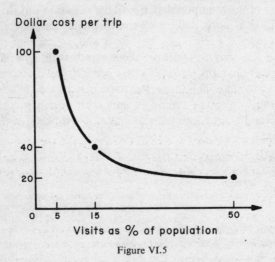

Figure VI.5

This resulting curve can properly be interpreted as a willingness-to-pay curve, or a marginal benefit curve, over and above all costs of the trip. Similar curves can now be derived for the remaining two areas, B

310

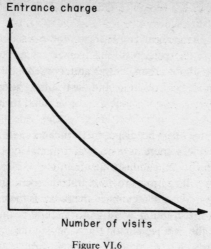

Figure VI.6

and *C*. The horizontal summation of these three curves produces an exploitable demand curve for Yosemite for the entire population of the three areas.

A monopolist contemplating this resultant demand curve could, of course, set a single price, or entrance fee, that would maximize his net benefit. If he were able to discriminate as between the three different areas, the charges would vary inversely with the elasticities of the demand curves for the three areas. A perfectly discriminating monopolist would, by definition, be able to appropriate to himself the whole of the surplus—this being the whole of the benefit otherwise enjoyed by the visitors.

4   In predicting demand over the future, information about population growth, per capita 'real' income growth, and income distribution over time, would be required for all types of investment yielding a stream of future benefits. What is perhaps of particular relevance to the demand for recreation, and is brought out in some of the charts drawn by Clawson and Knetsch (1966), is the relation between the reduction in the working week, and the improvement in roads and travel con-

ditions generally, on the one hand, and, on the other, the demand for recreation facilities.

Other factors that bear emphasis are the external diseconomies, or adverse spillover effects, resulting from a rising population and its agglomeration about urban centres and, consequently, the increase in congestion, noise, air pollution, and the resulting stress and frustration that are likely over time to increase the demand for national parks or wilderness areas. Even if there are as yet no dependable estimates of such trends, one may be disposed to make generous allowance for them. Thus unless there is a radical reversal of current trends in population, traffic, and industrialization, the world inhabited by our grandchildren will be more crowded and built-up than the world today. The average person at some time in the future is then sure to be willing to pay more for recreation facilities, for natural beauty and wilderness areas, than is the average person today having the same 'real' income. In other words, if the trends associated with sustained economic growth persist into the future the terms of trade as between manufactured goods and natural goods will tend to move increasingly in favour of the latter.

If we are unable to estimate the effect of such trends on these terms of trade we should in any critical comparison—say one to decide whether an area should be preserved as a national park or used, instead, for industrial purposes—calculate the hypothetical rate of growth over time of the value of natural goods relative to manufactures that would be necessary to equalize the excess benefits of the two alternative projects. If this hypothetical terms-of-trade growth rate were positive, it could be made a matter of explicit debate whether it fell within the range of plausibility.

5   Two other factors should be entered into the benefits of such reserved areas of natural beauty which, though they appear related, are in fact quite distinct. First, there is the 'option demand' arising from a willingness to pay by all those people who do not anticipate making specific use in the foreseeable future of the particular area, notwithstanding which they are aware of the possibility that their customary sources of recreation might be reduced or withdrawn. They therefore have an interest in supporting the preservation of the area. For instance, they may, at some future date, have to move to another area of the country and, as a form of insurance, they would be willing to

make some contribution to a number of reserved areas that they cannot use today but may want to make use of later.[4]

Secondly there is a 'non-participant' (or 'disinterested') demand arising from the willingness to pay by all those people who are concerned simply that such goods be available to the nation or to humanity at large. They may not be concerned in the least with insuring themselves against future contingencies, and they may well believe that they will never have occasion to enjoy the good in question; but it gives them satisfaction to know it exists. There are, for instance, a large number of people who care that wilderness areas be left on earth, that Venice should not sink beneath the waters, that whales and other species should be preserved, and yet will readily admit that they will never visit a wilderness area, or travel through Venice, or behold a whale. Their welfare would be reduced if they were to know that such things had disappeared from the earth, whereas in recognition of some improvements they would be willing to contribute something.

Such non-participant demand might indeed be thought of as translating into money values, at least, some of those 'non-economic' considerations referred to at the beginning of the preceding chapter. If people's feelings about what is 'right and proper' are sufficiently strong as to induce them to contribute something in order to have their aspirations realized there is no good reason for excluding them in principle from a cost-benefit calculation—always provided that the ends sought are not such as to be precluded by an ethical consensus.

6 Finally, we should remind ourselves that the measure of willingness-to-pay as an index of benefits is appropriate in cost-benefit analysis for the introduction of a good. If the public good, say a park or wilderness area, is already there, and the issue to be decided is whether to transform it into an industrial estate, the benefits that would have to be forgone in destroying the area—which benefits have to be compared with the benefits of the industrial estate—have to be calculated in terms of *minimum compensatory payments* to existing park- or wilderness-area beneficiaries, including those beneficiaries whose welfare

---

[4] The more common example of an optional demand for some facility is that of the willingness of a veteran motorist to pay something toward the upkeep of a bus or rail service that he would not normally make use of, but to which he may have recourse if his car should break down.

313

arises from optional demand and non-participant demand. Granted that welfare effects are normal (or positive), the measure of the benefit forgone from losing the area exceeds the measure of the benefits gained by introducing the area, and this difference in measurement may be crucial in the decision.

Chapter 44

THE OPPORTUNITY COST OF UNEMPLOYED LABOUR

1   In times of low employment there is obviously a stronger case to be made for public projects since they act to absorb otherwise idle resources. The additional employment generated is sometimes regarded as a social good to be evaluated and placed on the benefit side. Alternatively, and as an extension of the above treatment, the advantages of public investment in times of low employment are made manifest by reference to the cost aspect. For where there is substantial unemployment, the opportunity cost of labour, skilled and unskilled, and indeed of specific forms of capital equipment, is much lower than if such factors are already employed. Thus investment projects that would not be economically feasible under conditions of full employment may be economically feasible under conditions of low employment—assuming, of course, that employment is expected to remain low, at least in the absence of these investments.

Now if the public investment in question is to generate additional employment, it has to be financed by 'new money'. In other words, in order to create additional excess aggregate demand in the economy there must be no offsetting reduction of aggregate expenditure elsewhere. The additional money required for these investments can be created directly by the banking system: the central bank, for instance, can create the money needed by the government to finance the (additional) budget deficit that arises from government expenditures exceeding tax revenues. If $1 billion is to be spent on the public projects, then a 'first round' increase of incomes amounting to $1 billion requires that the $1 billion be raised *without* reducing expenditures elsewhere. Raising a part of this sum through taxation, which reduces current expenditures elsewhere by, say, $\frac{1}{4}$ billion, implies that the initial increase of aggregate incomes will only be $\frac{3}{4}$ billion.

Since, in general, an additional aggregate expenditure of $1 billion will generate multiplier effects that will result in the creation of an addition to aggregate income in excess of $1 billion, cost-benefit calculations that take no account of these secondary income and employment effects will underestimate the net benefits of the projects involved. Although allowance for these secondary income effects should obviously be made—at least wherever, under existing political circumstances, no alternative ways of expanding employment are anticipated—we shall restrict ourselves in the remainder of this chapter to the *primary* employment effects; to costing the hitherto idle resources used by the specific public projects in question.

Though not essential to the argument, we can assume that, prior to the introduction of any one or a number of additional public investment projects, prices in the economy are stable. On this assumption, the effectiveness (in terms of generating additional employment) of the amount of the deficit finance associated with the introduction of one or more public investments will depend upon the resulting rise, if any, in factor and product prices. Since this effectiveness in generating employment can be expressed in terms of the probability of drawing the project's factor requirements from the existing unemployment pool, there will, in principle, be a relationship between this probability and the overall rate of unemployment.

This relationship will, of course, depend upon the specific kinds of factors required by the investment project and their location with respect to the project. Primarily, however, this relationship, between the probability of drawing factors from the idle pool and the rate of unemployment, will depend upon the rise in prices (if any) that results from the introduction of this particular project in the given unemployment situation. Much, therefore, depends on the size of the project—or, rather, on its factor requirements relative to factors available in the unemployment pool.

2 To illustrate with extreme examples. Suppose first that overall unemployment is so high that all prices, product and factor, remain constant over the period. Then it may well be that, say, one thousand construction workers required to implement the investment project are initially attracted, not directly from the existing pool of unemployed construction workers, but from existing industries in which they are employed, say industries *A, B, C* ... But since there is no reduction in

316

total expenditure on the goods produced by industries $A, B, C \ldots$, these industries will have to restore the numbers of construction workers in order to maintain their outputs. They can do so only by attracting such workers from other industries or else from unemployed construction workers. Provided that prices remain constant, as assumed, and particularly that the wages of construction workers remain unchanged, the excess demand for one thousand construction workers cannot be satisfied until they are ultimately drawn (or trained) from the unemployment pool.

If the maintenance of constant prices requires, say, 25 per cent unemployment then we should associate 25 per cent unemployment with factor requirements being met wholly from the unemployment pool. More particularly, if it required 25 per cent unemployment among construction workers within some given region, to ensure constancy of their wages, the economist would associate 25 per cent unemployment among them with an eventual 100 per cent withdrawal of construction workers from the unemployment pool—irrespective of the proportion that might initially be withdrawn elsewhere, say from industries $A, B, C \ldots$

Now suppose, instead, the other extreme—overall unemployment being so low that an additional $1 billion of excess aggregate demand is wholly absorbed in price rises. In particular, let us suppose that the $10 million that is earmarked to pay the wage-bill of 1,000 construction workers has the effect only of raising the total wage-bill of the existing population of 10,000 construction workers by the whole of this $10 million—a rise in their wages, let us say, of 10 per cent; that is, from an initial total wage-bill of $100 million to $110 million. If we now discover that unemployment among construction workers is 4 per cent, then a 4 per cent unemployment rate among them is to be associated with an eventual zero per cent probability of construction workers being drawn from the unemployment pool.[1]

3 The more usual case follows in an obvious way and can be illustrated by supposing that, with an 8 per cent unemployment rate among construction workers, of the $10 million of initial excess expenditure on construction workers some $6 million is added to the wage-bill of the *existing* 10,000 construction workers that are already

---

[1] Where prices rise in response to the new projects, the real value of sums proposed— here amounting to $1 billion—has to be deflated accordingly.

employed, leaving only $4 million to be spent on hitherto unemployed construction workers. Thus, in the existing employment situation, the attempt to attract 1,000 construction workers into the new project has resulted in only a small proportion of that number being eventually withdrawn from the unemployment pool. The demand-induced rise of factor prices of, say, 8 per cent absorbs $6 million of the sum of $10 million earmarked for construction workers, the remaining $4 million giving employment to only 377 additional construction workers at the new wage of $10,600. As a result, 8 per cent unemployment among construction workers is to be associated with a probability of about $37\frac{1}{2}$ per cent of the required labour being eventually withdrawn from the unemployment pool.

Such a relationship, indicated in Figure VI.7, between the probability of drawing a worker of any specified skill from the unemployment pool and the rate of unemployment among that group can be discovered and made use of in evaluating public projects. Thus if the opportunity cost of any particular unemployed skilled worker, say the construction worker, is reckoned to be $4,000 per annum and that of an already-employed construction worker—following an induced rise in their earnings to $10,600—is reckoned to be about $12,000 on the average,[2] then the *total* opportunity cost to the project of attracting 1,000 construction workers (when unemployment among them is 8 per cent and, therefore, the probability of drawing an unemployed construction worker is about 0·375) is calculated as a weighted average, namely,

$$\$4,000(0\cdot375 \times 1,000) + \$12,000(0\cdot625 \times 1,000) = \$9 \text{ million.}$$

This opportunity cost of 1,000 construction workers is clearly less than their total wage bill ($12,000 × 1,000) since, in general, it will not be possible to pay the hitherto unemployed construction workers less than those being drawn from existing employment.[3]

---

[2] To the earnings of $10,600 that an already employed construction worker has to forgo in order to take up employment in the public project, some addition must be made for costs of movement, etc.

[3] For an introduction to an ambitious attempt to construct such relationships for all resources, see Haveman and Krutilla (1968).

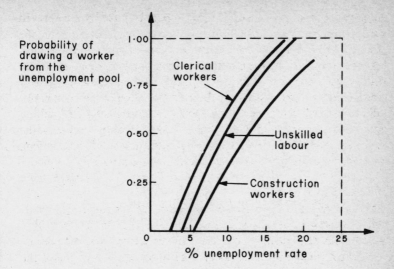

Probability of drawing a worker from the unemployment pool

Clerical workers

Unskilled labour

Construction workers

% unemployment rate

Figure VI.7

319

Chapter 45

LOSS OF LIFE AND LIMB (I)

1 As cost-benefit studies grow in popularity, it is increasingly important to make proper allowance for losses, or gains, arising from changes in the incidence of death, disablement, or disease caused by the operation of new projects or developments.

Since the analysis of saving life is symmetrical with that of losing it, it will simplify the exposition if, initially, we confine ourselves to the analysis of *loss* of life and limb—or, more briefly, to loss of life alone—indicating the necessary extensions later on.

2 (a) Despite repeated expressions of dissatisfaction with the method, the most common way of calculating the economic worth of a person's life and, therefore, the loss to the economy consequent upon his decease, is that of discounting to the present the person's expected future earnings.

A precise expression for the loss to the economy calculated on this method would be L_1, where

$$L_1 = \sum_{t=\tau}^{\infty} Y_t P_\tau^t (1 + r)^{-(t-\tau)}$$

Y_t is the expected gross earnings of (or, alternatively, value added by) the person during the tth year, exclusive of any yields from his ownership of non-human capital.[1] P_τ^t is the probability in the current, or τ^{th}, year of the person being alive during the tth year, and r is the social rate of discount expected to rule during the tth year. This sort of calculation is occasionally supplemented by a suggestion that auxiliary calculations be made in order to take account of the suffering

---

[1] For the returns on his (non-human) assets continue after his death, or during his disablement.

320

of the victim, his loss of utility from ceasing to be alive, and/or of the bereavement of his family.[2] More recently, and as an example perhaps of the economist's finesse, it has been proposed that such calculations be supplemented also by the costs of 'premature burial'[3]—the idea being that the present discounted value of the funeral expenses is higher if they are incurred the sooner owing to an untimely death.

A related calculation, no less plausible than the above, would restrict itself to the individual's loss of expenditure on himself alone. The above formula will serve once Y_t is displaced by C_t, where C_t stands for the personal expenditure of the individual expected during the tth period. Alternatively one could attempt to calculate the individual's loss of consumer's surplus or rent.[4] Neither of these measures has been explicitly proposed however, possibly because a consideration of a man's personal expenditure leads inevitably to a consideration of the utility he also obtains from transferring part of his income to his family and, by extension, to the gains and losses of other members of society.

3 (b) At all events, a second method, which might be thought of as more refined than the first, is that of calculating the present discounted

---

[2] For examples, see Ridker (1967, p. 34). The suggestions, needless to remark, have not been taken up. Presumably they are made in response to an uneasy conscience about the methods actually being employed.

[3] The expression occurs in Ridker's book (1967) on the costs of pollution. For those prone to morbid curiosity, the formula used is on page 39, and takes the form

$$C_a = C_0 \left[1 - \sum_{n=a}^{\infty} \frac{p_a^n}{(1 + r)^{(n-a)}} \right]$$

where C_a is the present value of the net expected gain from delaying burial at age a. C_0 is the cost of burial. P_a^n is the probability that an individual age a will die at age n, and r is the discount rate. It is not impossible that these calculations were made with tongue in cheek, and, if so, it is perhaps an oversight on his part that he omitted a countervailing consideration, viz. that, if the unfortunate person died at a very early age, some useful savings might be effected from the lower cost of a smaller coffin.

[4] Although the concept of rent or economic surplus is conventionally employed within a partial context, it is quite valid in a more general setting (Mishan, 1959, p. 394). However generalized the concept, it still involves comparisons between alternative situations. Any idea of evaluating this surplus by subtracting from a man's total income, or total expenditure, some estimate of a subsistence level of expenditure, can be successful only if this level can be so chosen that the man is indifferent as between surviving at this subsistence level and expiring. But there is no warrant for believing that such a level exists. What casual evidence there is supports the popular impression that, no matter how precarious or hopeless a man's condition, he continues to hang on grimly to his life.

value of the losses over time accruing to *others only* as a result of the death of this person at age τ. A precise expression for the loss to the economy based on this method would be L_2, where

$$L_2 = \sum_{t=\tau}^{\infty} P_\tau^t \cdot (Y_t - C_t)(1 + r)^{-(t-\tau)}$$

where C_t is the personal expenditure of the individual during the tth period that is expected at time τ. This sort of measure, sometimes referred to as being based on the 'net output' approach, in order to distinguish it from the 'gross output' approach associated with the L_1 measure, though occasionally mentioned in the literature,[5] has not been employed apparently because of the assumed policy implications.

(c) A third possible method would repudiate any direct calculation of the loss of potential earnings or spending. Instead, it would approach the problem from a 'social' point of view. Since society, through its political processes, does in fact take decisions on investment expenditures that occasionally increase or reduce the number of deaths, an implicit value of human life can be calculated. This approach receives occasional mention[6] and, indeed, the appeal to the political, or democratic, process is sometimes invoked to provide guidance on broader issues.[7]

(d) The insurance principle is a departure from any of the aforementioned methods. By making use of the premium a man is willing to pay, and the probability of his being killed as a result of engaging in some specific activity, it is thought possible to be able to calculate the value a man sets on his life.[8]

4 Each of these four possible methods of measuring the loss of life is now briefly appraised.

Method (a), turning on the loss of potential future earnings, can be rationalized only if the criterion adopted in any economic reorganization turns on the value of its contribution to GNP, or, more accurately, to net national product. But although financial journalists manage to

[5] For instance, by Devons (1961, p. 107) and Ridker (1967, p. 36).
[6] For instance, by Fromm (1965, p. 193) and by Schelling (1968, p. 147).
[7] Nath (1969, pp. 216–17) proposes that the task of the economist be limited to that of revealing the locus of 'efficient' economic production possibilities available to society, leaving it to democracy to select the collection of goods it wishes.
[8] An example is given by Fromm (1965, p. 194).

convey the contrary impression, maximizing GNP is not an acceptable goal of economic policy. If it were, the simplest way of promoting it would be to adopt a policy of virtually unlimited immigration—accepting immigrants up to the point at which the value of their marginal product is zero. Recourse to this method by the practising economist does not, however, rest on the clear recognition of the desirability of maximizing GNP but rather, obviously on the fact that it lends itself easily to quantification. Notwithstanding its usage, most writers have mental reservations about its validity, and tend to regard it as only part of the total measurement. For instance, Schelling (1968) makes a distinction between the value of livelihood, which is the L_1 measure, and the value of life, which poses a perplexing and possibly unsolvable problem.

The so-called net output method (b) might seem, at first glance, more acceptable than the gross output method: taking a cold-blooded attitude, what matters to the rest of society is simply the resulting loss, or gain, to it following the death of one or more of its members. This *ex post* approach, however, appears to strike some writers as either absurd or dangerous.[9] If accepted, it certainly follows that the death of any person whose L_2 measure is negative confers a net benefit on society. And this category of persons would indeed include all retired people irrespective of their ownership of property. Yet from this undeniable inference, no dread policy implications follow. If the method were satisfactory on economic grounds, the inference would not, of itself, provide any reason for rejecting it. But the method is not satisfactory for the simple reason that it has no regard to the feelings of the potential victims. It restricts itself to the interests only of the surviving members of society: it ignores society *ex ante*, and concentrates wholly on society *ex post*.

As for method (c), which would build on implicit values placed on human life by the political process, the justification appears somewhat circular even when we ignore the political realities of Western democracies: in particular (i) the fact that decisions to invest in certain projects are not determined by popular vote; instead, governments

---

[9] For example, Devons (1961, p. 108) concludes ironically: 'Indeed if we could only kill off enough old people we could show a net gain on accidents as a whole!' As for Ridker (1967, p. 36), the net output method 'suggests that society should not interfere with the death of a person where net value is negative'.

avail themselves of a general mandate, conferred on them by an election, to delegate powers of decision at various levels of the political hierarchy; (ii) the fact that investment decisions are not motivated primarily by the desire to advance the *general* welfare, on any plausible criterion, but are rather the outcome of political conflicts; and (iii) the fact that an implicit value attributable to loss of life by a particular public programme will differ widely from an implicit value derived from another public programme. Ignoring these political realities, and assuming that democratic voting alone determines whether or not a particular investment project, or part of a project, is to be adopted, the idea of deriving quantitative values from the political process is clearly contrary to the idea of deriving them from an independent economic criterion. And where the outcome of the political debate is that of calling upon the economist to provide a quantitative evaluation of the project under consideration, the economist fails to meet his brief in so far as he abandons the attempt to calculate any aspect of the project by reference to an economic criterion and instead attempts to extricate figures from previous political decisions.[10] By recourse to a method that refers a question, or part of a question, received from the political process back again to the political process, the economist appears to be concealing some deficiency in the relevant data or some weakness in the logic of his criteria. Moreover, even it it were agreed that the loss of human life should not be estimated by 'ordinary' economic criteria used in evaluating other gains and losses, the requirements of consistency cannot be met by such implicit—and also arbitrary and erratic—valuations of political outcomes, though they might be met by particular criteria that make the valuation of loss of life explicit and systematic. As we shall see, however, there is no call for evaluating loss of life on a criterion different from that which is basic to the economist's calculation of all the other effects comprehended in a cost-benefit analysis.

Finally, there is method (d) based on the insurance principle. This has about it a superficial plausibility, enough at any rate to attract some

---

[10] Which is not to deny that the economist's criterion or criteria—though independent of the outcome of any particular political process that is sanctioned by the constitution—must themselves be vindicated ultimately by reference to value judgments widely held within the community.

attention.[11] But the insurance policy makes provision, in the event of a man's death, only for compensation to *others*. Thus, the amount of insurance a man takes out may be interpreted as a reflection, *inter alia*, of his concern for his family and dependants, but hardly as an index of the value he sets on his own life.[12] A bachelor with no dependants may have no reason to take out flight insurance, notwithstanding which he could be as reluctant as the next man to depart this fugacious life at short notice.

5 The crucial objection to each of these four methods, however, is that not one of them is consistent with the basic rationale of the economic calculus used in cost-benefit analysis. If we are concerned, as we are in all allocative problems, with increasing society's satisfaction in some sense, and if in addition we eschew interpersonal comparisons of satisfactions, we can always be guided in the ranking of alternative economic arrangements by the notion of a Pareto improvement—an improvement such that at least one person is made better off and

---

[11] An early attempt, for instance, was made by Fromm (1965, pp. 193–6) to attribute a value for loss of life raised on the implied assumption of a straight-line relationship between the probability of a person being killed and the sum that he would pay to cover the risk. If, therefore, the premium y corresponding to the additional risk p is known, the value he places on his life is to be reckoned as y/p. Thus, if a man would pay $100 to reduce his chance of being killed by one per cent—say from an existing chance of $1/10$ to $2/50$—the value he places on his life is to be estimated as $10,000 (or to use Fromm's own calculation, if the probability of being killed in air travel were to be reduced from the existing figure of 0.0000017 per trip of 500 miles to zero, a person who values his life at $400,000 should be willing to pay 68 cents to reduce the existing risk to zero).

The implied assumption of linearity, which has it that a man who accepts $100,000 for an assignment offering him a four to one chance of survival will agree to go to certain death for $500,000, is implausible to say the least. And, indeed, this linearity assumption was later criticized by Fromm himself (1968, p. 174) when it was incidentally posited by Schelling (1968). But even if it were both plausible and proved, the insurance principle does not yield us the required valuation.

[12] An ingenious paper by Eisner and Strotz (1961), after some theorizing on the basis of the Neumann–Morgenstern axioms about the optimal amount of insurance a person should buy, addresses itself to the question of why people continue to buy air-accident insurance when ordinary life insurance is cheaper. They suggest, among other things, that flight insurance could be a gamble (related formally to the increasing marginal-utility segment of the income-utility curve), and they point also to the existence of imperfect knowledge, imperfect markets, and inertia.

However, the paper does not, and is presumably not intended to, throw any light on this question of the valuation of human life. The observation that a man does not insure his life against some specific contingency cannot be taken as evidence that he is indifferent as between being alive and being dead.

nobody is made worse off. A *potential* Pareto improvement,[13] one in which the net gains *can* so be distributed that at least one person is made better off with none being made worse off, provides an alternative criterion, or definition, of social gain—one which, as it happens, provides the rationale of all familiar allocative propositions in economics, and therefore the rationale of all cost-benefit calculations.

When the full range of its economic effects is brought into the calculus, the introduction of a specific investment project will make some of the community of n members better off on balance, some worse off on balance, the remainder being indifferent to it. If the jth person is made better off, a compensating variation (CV) measures the full extent of his improvement, this CV being a maximum sum V_j he will pay rather than go without the project, the sum being prefixed by a positive sign. Per contra, if the jth person is made worse off by the introduction of the project, his CV measures the full decline of his welfare as a minimal sum V_j he will accept to put up with the project, this sum being prefixed by a negative sign.[14] If then, in response to the introduction of this specific project, the aggregate sum

$$\sum_{j}^{n} V_j > 0$$

(where j runs from 1 to n)—if, that is, the algebraic sum of all n individual CVs is positive—there is a potential Pareto improvement, its positive value being interpreted as the excess of benefits over costs arising from the introduction of the project.[15]

---

[13] A 'potential Pareto improvement' is an alternative and simpler nomenclature than a 'hypothetical compensation test'. The problems associated with the concept are important, but need not concern us here if we accept the fact that cost-benefit analyses take place within a partial context, one in which changes in the prices of all the non-project goods can be ignored. If this much is granted, the relevant individuals' compensating variations which is what we are after will be uniquely determined.

[14] These sums may be calculated as annual transfers or as capital sums according to the method being used in the cost-benefit study. Since the flow of costs and benefits are to be valued at a point of time, consistency would require that the CVs also be reckoned as a capital sum at that point of time. If there are no external effects of saving for future generations, the existence of imperfect capital markets will result in different rates of time preference among the persons concerned. In that case, capitalizing their CVs reckoned as annual sums at some single rate of discount will result in corresponding capitalized CVs which would differ from those chosen directly by these same persons, which latter sums should, of course, prevail.

[15] Within the same broad context, and allowing for sufficient divisibility in the

Consistency with the criterion of a potential Pareto improvement and, therefore, consistency with the principle of evaluation in cost-benefit analyses, would require that the loss of a person's life be valued by reference to his CV; by reference, that is, to the minimum sum he is prepared to accept in exchange for its surrender. For unless a project that is held to be responsible for, say, an additional one thousand deaths annually can show an excess of benefits over costs *after* meeting the compensatory sums necessary to restore the welfare of these one thousand victims, it is not possible to make all members of the community better off by a redistribution of the net gains. A potential Pareto improvement cannot then be achieved, and the project in question ought not to be admitted.

If the argument is accepted, however, the requirements of consistency might seem to be highly restrictive. Since an increase in the annual number of deaths can be confidently predicted in connection with a number of particular developments—those, for example, which contribute to an increase in ground and air traffic—such developments would no longer appear as economically feasible. For it would not surprise us to discover that, in ordinary circumstances,[16] no sum of money is large enough to compensate a man for the loss of his life.

6 In conditions of certainty, the logic of the above proposition is unassailable. If in ordinary circumstances we face a person with the choice of continuing his life in the usual way, or of ending it at noon on the morrow, a finite sum large enough to persuade him to choose the latter course of action may not exist. And indeed if the investment project in question unavoidably entailed the death of this specific person or, more generally, a number of specific persons, it is highly unlikely that any conceivable excess benefit over cost, *calculated in the*

---

[15] (contd) construction of such projects, the corresponding rule necessary to determine the optimal output of such projects—or, in short periods, the optimal output of the goods of the existing projects—takes the simple form that $\sum_j^n V_j = 0$, where V_j is the CV of the jth person in response to a marginal increment in the size of the industry, or (in the short period) the size of its output.

[16] If a man and his family were so destitute. and their prospects so hopeless. that one or more members were likely to die of starvation. or at least to suffer from acute deprivation, then the man might well be persuaded to sacrifice himself for the sake of his family. But without dependants. or close and needy friends, the inducement to sacrifice himself for others is not strong.

absence of these fatalities, would warrant its undertaking on the potential Pareto criterion.

It is never the case, however, that a specific person, or a number of specific persons, can be designated in advance as being those who are certain to be killed if a particular project is undertaken.[17] All that can be predicted, though with a high degree of confidence, is that out of a total of n members in the community, an additional x members per annum will be killed (and, say, an additional $10x$ members will be seriously injured). In the absence, therefore, of any breakdown of the circumstances surrounding the additional number of accidents to be expected, the increment of risk of being killed imposed each year on any one member of the community can be taken as x/n (and $10x/n$ for the risk of being seriously injured). And it is this fact of complete ignorance of the identity of each of the potential victims that transforms the calculation. Assuming universal risk aversion,[18] the relevant sums to be subtracted from the benefit side are no longer those which compensate a specific number of persons for their certain death, but are those which compensate each person in the community for the additional risk to which he is to be exposed.[19]

7   Figure VI.8 will enable the reader to form a more precise idea of the concept at issue. Along the vertical axis is measured the person's

---

[17] Cf. Schelling's remarks (1968, pp. 142–6).

[18] Risk-aversion is assumed throughout (unless otherwise stated) solely in the interests of brevity. If some people enjoy the additional risk, their CVs will be positive. In general if the aggregate of the CVs for the additional risk is negative, which is the case for universal risk aversion, there is a subtraction from the benefit side. If, on the other hand, it were positive, there would be an addition to the benefit side.

[19] In a most engaging, and highly perceptive paper, Schelling (1968) divides the problem into three parts: (a) society's interest, (b) an economic interest (in which category a man's contribution to GNP is placed), and (c) a 'consumer's interest'. Discussing this third interest, in connection with a life-saving programme, Schelling correctly poses the relevant question: what will people pay for a government programme that reduces risks? (p. 142). But being uneasy about the actual measurement of such a sum, and absorbed with other fascinating, though in the context irrelevant, considerations, he does not develop the analysis systematically. Indeed, he goes on later to discuss the value of certain loss of life, and comes up with the suggestion that college professors would be prepared to pay an amount equal to something between ten and a hundred times their annual income in order to save the life of one of their family.

If one is interested solely in the conceptual measure, as I am here, one can make use of the notion of external effects to develop the analysis. Fromm's hypercritical comments (1968), on the other hand, make use of external effects, along with the difficulties of measuring, largely to cast doubt upon this valid part of Schelling's paper.

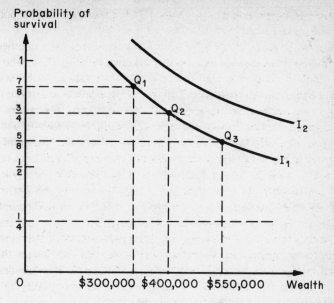

Figure VI.8

expectation of remaining alive over a certain period of time. Along the
horizontal axis is measured the present value of his wealth expected
over that period. The indifference curves are ordered in the usual way,
I_2 having a higher level of utility than I_1. The locus of any difference
curve, say I_1, reveals a continuum of alternative combinations of
wealth and (subjective) survival probabilities as between which this
particular person today is indifferent. The assumption of risk aversion
over the operative range entails the usual downward sloping indifference curves.[20] Thus a person currently at position Q_1 on the I_1
indifference curve has a $\frac{7}{8}$ chance of survival over the period and
anticipates (if he survives) an amount of wealth over that period equal
to a present value of $300,000. The point Q_2 on the same indifference
curve I_1 corresponds to wealth over the period having a present value

---

[20] Risk aversion does not, however, preclude the person's deriving some present utility
from the belief that if he does die within the period in question there will be provision
(which, of course, he can increase by taking out insurance) for his dependants. Indeed,
the more he cares for his dependants and the larger the provision he therefore makes for
them, the less will he fear the loss of his life *in so far* as it reduces their material
prospects. To that extent, but only to that extent, the sum necessary to compensate him
for exposing his life to any given increment of risk will be smaller.

of \$400,000 along with a survival probability of $\frac{3}{4}$. It follows that he would agree to reduce his chance of survival by $\frac{1}{8}$ in return for a minimum sum of \$100,000.

The familiar assumption of convexity implies that the individual will require increasing sums as compensation for exposing himself to equal additional increments of risk. For instance, in order to persuade him to reduce his chances of survival from $\frac{3}{4}$, at Q_2, to $\frac{5}{8}$—that is by another $\frac{1}{8}$—he will require more than \$100,000 in compensation, say \$150,000. Thus the point Q_3 on the I_1 curve represents the combination of \$550,000 and a $\frac{5}{8}$ chance of survival.

Since in ordinary circumstances there is no sum large enough to compensate him for the certainty of death, the indifference curves do not touch the horizontal axis. Indeed, since few persons would be willing to submit voluntarily to fairly high risks of death, the indifference curves may never come closer than some critical distance to the horizontal axis. If, for example, no amount of wealth will induce a person to subject himself to events that would reduce his chance of survival below $\frac{1}{4}$, then all indifference curves eventually become horizontal at a distance of $\frac{1}{4}$ from the horizontal axis.[21]

Finally, the welfare effects on survival can be assumed positive, or 'normal', in that as a person's wealth increases he will require a larger amount of wealth in compensation for the same increment of risk. Or, put otherwise, an increase in his wealth or welfare implies that some part is used to increase his chance of survival, or to reduce mortality risks, for any given rate of exchange between them.

8 In general, of course, every activity will have attached to it some discernible degree of risk (even staying at home in bed bears some risk of mishap—the bed might collapse; the wind might blow the roof in; a marauder might enter). Any change, from one environment to another, from one style of living to another, can be said to alter the balance of risk, sometimes imperceptibly, sometimes substantially. Only the dead opt out of all risk. Yet the actual statistical risk attaching to some activity may be so small that only the hypersensitive would take account of it. In common with all other changes in economic arrangements, there is some *minimum sensible* beyond which an increment, or

---

[21] The shorter the period covered, and the closer therefore to the present is the operation of any change in risk, the higher will be this distance from the horizontal axis and the flatter will be the slope of the indifference curves.

decrement, of risk will go unnoticed. More important, however, what is strictly relevant to the analysis is not the change in the statistical risk *per se*, but the person's response, if any, to such a change. For the change in risk may go unperceived and, if perceived, it may be improperly evaluated. Indeed, people do have difficulty in grasping the objective significance of large numbers and, where chance or risk is at issue, they are prone to underestimate it. One chance in 50,000 of winning a lottery, or of having one's house burned down, seems a better chance, or a greater risk, than it actually is.

The analysis which follows does not, however, depend upon the veracity of such conjectures. All the reader has to accept is the proposition that people's subjective preferences of the worth of a thing is to count. In the market place, the price of a good, or a 'bad' (such as labour-input or other disutility), is fixed by the producer, and the buyer or seller determines the amount by reference to his subjective preferences. Where, however, the amount of a (collective) good, or 'bad', is fixed for each person—as may be the case with a change in risk—a person's subjective preference can only determine the price he will accept or offer for it: in short, his CV. People's imperfect knowledge of economic opportunities, their imprudence and unworldliness, has never prevented economists from accepting as basic data the amounts people freely choose at given prices. Such imperfections cannot therefore consistently be invoked to qualify people's choices when, instead, their preferences are exercised in placing a price on some increment of a good or 'bad'. True, attempts to observe the change of magnitude when people adjust the price to the change in quantity—rather than the more common assumption that they adjust the quantity to the change in price—does pose problems of measurement. But the problems of measurement must not be allowed to obscure the validity of the concept.

Placed within the broadest possible context then, any additional risk of death, associated with the provision of some new facility, takes its place as one of a number of economic consequences (including employment gains and losses, new purchase and sale opportunities, and the withdrawal of existing ones) all of which affect the welfare of each of the *n* members of the community.

Chapter 46

LOSS OF LIFE AND LIMB (II)

1 We shall now consider four types of risk, two of them direct, or physical, risks, the remaining two being indirect, or derivative, risks.

(1) First, there are the direct, or physical, risks that people voluntarily assume whenever they choose to buy a product or avail themselves of a service or facility. Inasmuch as such risks are evaluated by each jth person as a CV, equal say to r^1_{jj}, his benefit from the service or facility is estimated net of such risk; that is, after r^1_{jj} has been subtracted from it. If smoking tobacco causes 20,000 deaths a year, no subtracting from the benefits, on account of this risk, need be entered in a cost-benefit analysis of the tobacco industry inasmuch as smokers are already aware that the tobacco habit is unhealthy. And if, notwithstanding their awareness, they continue to smoke, the economist has no choice but to assume that they consider themselves better off despite the risks. Indeed, the benefits to smokers, net of risk—that is, after subtracting the aggregate $\sum_{j}^{n} r^1_{jj}$—are reflected in the demand schedule for tobacco. Once the area under the demand curve has been estimated, and used as an approximation of the benefit smokers derive from the use of tobacco, any further subtraction for such risks would entail double counting.

Another example will help to clarify the principle and will extend the argument. If, in an initially riskless situation, we observe that the jth person buys a car, we may infer that C_j is positive; that, in his own estimation, he is better off with the car than without it.

The introduction, now, of some personal risk associated with driving the car does not alter this inference.[1] Once he is aware of the

---

[1] The nice distinction made by Schelling (1968, pp. 132–5) between loss of life and

additional element of risk in driving the car, the consequent reduction in the jth person's welfare is valued at the risk compensation r^1_{jj}. If, in spite of the additional risk, the jth person still offers to buy the car, we are compelled to infer that $(C_j. -r^1_{jj}) > 0$, i.e. his original consumer's surplus exceeds the risk compensation or, put otherwise, his consumer's surplus *net of risk* is positive. The evaluation of a new automobile plant will, therefore, disregard this type of risk, since the benefits are roughly equal to the aggregate of consumers' surplus net of risk. Similarly, a cost-benefit study of a highway project which is expected to increase the number of casualties need make no allowance for the expected loss of life, provided, again, that this is the only type of risk. For in this case also, the benefits to be measured are ultimately the maximum sums motorists are willing to pay for the new highway system in full cognizance of the additional risks they choose to assume.

Occasionally, as in the automobile example, the risk assumed by each person will depend also upon the numbers availing themselves of the service or facility. Since the additional degree of risk generated by all the others are imposed on each one, in addition to the risk he would assume in the absence of all others, the analysis must extend itself to include 'external diseconomies internal to the industry'.[2] If we let r^1_{ij} stand for the risk compensation sum required by the jth person for the risk imposed on him by the ith individual, the compensatory sums for the extra risks contributed by all other individuals is given by $\sum_i^n r^1_{ij}$ $(i \neq j)$. Now, although these additional risks are imposed on the jth person, they can always be avoided by his refusal to avail himself of the new service or facility. If, however, he decides to avail himself of it, the economist cannot but assume that he believes he is better off with it than without it. Again, therefore, we must assume that $(C_j - \sum_i^n r^1_{ij}) > 0$, where i now includes j so as to make provision also for the risk that

---

[1] (contd.) loss of livelihood is possibly meaningful, but difficult to capture. Given the 'conjuncture' of circumstances in which a man finds himself, there is, in principle, some amount of money that will just induce him to assume a particular risk of being killed. But it is hardly likely that he will be able to apportion that sum as between 'life' and 'livelihood', and it is not necessary, in this analysis, that he should be able to do so.
[2] The distinction between external effects *internal* to the industry, and those *external* to the industry, was proposed in my 1965 paper.

person j would run if he alone enjoyed the new service or facility.[3] Aggregating over all n members, the net consumers' surplus is $\sum_{j}^{n}$ $(C_j - \sum_{i}^{n} r^1_{ij})$, which can be abbreviated to $C - R^1$.

In so far, then, as additional risks associated with the service or facility are all voluntarily assumed, no subtraction for loss of life need be placed on the benefit side, since the benefits to be measured are already net of risk. However, once we turn from risks that can be voluntarily assumed to those which cannot be avoided (or, rather, cannot be avoided without incurring expenses) we are in the realm of 'external diseconomies that are *external* to the industry', and cost-benefit analyses have to make provision for them.

2   The additional risks that are imposed on the community as a whole, as a by-product of some specific economic activity, and are therefore to be regarded as external diseconomies external to the industry, can be separated into three types. Although all three can be inflicted on the same person, who could propose a single sum in compensation, it is useful to separate them, there being circumstances where only one or two types of risk are of any importance.

---

[3] The external diseconomies of traffic risk are therefore treated exactly as the external diseconomies of traffic congestion. Note, however, that as distinct from the problem of estimating the excess benefit of a *given* project as in a cost benefit study, the determination of an *optimal* traffic flow (which we do not treat in the text) *does* require intervention by the economist in consequence of these mutual diseconomies. For the question raised in determining an *optimal* traffic flow is no longer that of showing that, for a given volume of traffic, total benefits (*net* of risk and congestion) exceed total costs. The question, now, is to *choose* a volume of traffic so as to *maximize* excess benefit over cost, this being realized by equating marginal social benefit to marginal cost. The standard argument is then invoked: although the effects on all others of risk and congestion grow with each additional car, the jth, or marginal vehicle-owner, in deciding whether to use the highway, considers only the term $\sum_{i}^{n} r^1_{ij}$ (ignoring the similar congestion term), as indeed does each of the other members, i.e. he takes account only of the costs to him of each of the n vehicles on the road, including his own. What he does *not* take into account is the effect he himself produces on each of the others by his decision to add his vehicle to theirs; which is to say, he ignores the cost $\sum_{i}^{n} r^1_{ji}$, $(i \neq j)$, the costs imposed on each of the intra-marginal vehicles by introducing his own j^{th} vehicle. This term therefore represents the cost of those external diseconomies generated by the marginal vehicle, diseconomies that are internal to and absorbed by all intra-marginal vehicles, and which are properly attributable to the marginal vehicle in determining the optimal flow of traffic.

(2) The direct *involuntary* risk of death that is inflicted on the jth person by some specific project can be compensated by the sum r^2_{jj}. For example, the establishment of a nuclear power station and the resulting disposal of radioactive waste materials is held to be responsible for an increase in the annual number of deaths. Again, if supersonic flights over inhabited areas are introduced as a regular service, we can anticipate an increase in the annual number of deaths, at least among the frail, the elderly, and among those suffering from heart ailments.

In addition to this primary risk, there is a secondary risk to which the jth person is exposed, which will arise in other instances. For example, in the absence of legal prohibition, a works pours 'sewage' into the air and increases the incidence of death from a number of lung and heart diseases. Apart from those who are the direct victims of this activity, there will be a number of fatalities arising from infection through others. And this possibility of infection obviously increases the risk since, within a given area, every person becomes a source of risk to every other. In addition, therefore to the sum r^2_{jj} to compensate the jth person for the risk imposed on him even if he were the sole inhabitant, he requires also a sum $\sum_{i}^{n} r^2_{ij}(i \neq j)$ to compensate for the risk that each of the other $(n-1)$ persons imposes on him.

There does not seem to be any advantage, however, in upholding this distinction between primary and secondary physical risk. Where the risk of infection through others is acknowledged, it is difficult, if not impossible, to separate primary from secondary risk. In such cases the risk compensation required by each person covers both. We shall therefore employ the general term $\sum_{i}^{n} r^2_{ij}$ for the jth person (which includes the term r^2_{jj} for the risk he runs in the absence of others). Aggregating over the n members of the community, this total risk compensation is to be valued at $\sum_{j}^{n} \sum_{i}^{n} r^2_{ij}$, which can be denoted by R^2.

(3) There is, finally, the indirect, or derivative, risk arising from the general concern of each of the n persons with those physical risks, voluntary and involuntary, to which any of the others is exposed. This additional concern, to which, in general, each member is prone (as a result of the additional physical risks run by others), has, first, a purely financial aspect. If, on balance, the death of the ith person improves the financial position of the jth person, the additional chance of i's death is a

335

benefit to j, and the risk-compensatory sum $r^3{}_{ij}$ is therefore positive. This means that the jth person is willing to pay up to a given sum for the improved chance of his losing some dependent or inheriting some asset—or of inheriting it the sooner.[4] If, on the other hand, the death of the ith person would reduce j's real income, the sum r^3_{ij} is negative; that is, the jth person would have to receive a sum of money to compensate him for the increased risk of suffering a reduction in his real income. Although the jth person's financial condition is likely to be affected by the death of only a few members of the community, his risk compensation, on this account, can be written in general as $\sum\limits_{i.}^{n} r^3_{ij.}(i \neq j)$. Bearing in mind that most of the terms in the sum will be zero, the total expression will be positive or negative according as the increased risk of death run by others makes him, on balance, better off or worse off.

For this financial risk to which the community as a whole is exposed, the total risk compensation is given by aggregating the above expression over the n members to give $\sum\limits_{j.}^{n}\sum\limits_{i}^{n} r^3_{ij.}(i \neq j)$, which can be represented by R^3. This sum can, as suggested, be positive or negative according as the community as a whole expects to be made financially better off, or worse off, by the death of others.[5]

---

[4] It might at first appear that an asset which is transferred from the deceased to his beneficiaries cancels out, as it does in the L_1 or L_2 measure. But although a transfer of wealth is clearly a distribution effect, it may be entered into the calculation of a potential Pareto improvement. And if transfers are generally omitted from such calculations it is simply because they take place between living persons: a transfer of $\$10,000$ from person A to person B implies—ignoring 'interdependent utilities'—that the sum of their CVs is zero. On our criterion there is neither gain nor loss.

When the issue is no longer a voluntary transfer of wealth, but the risk of an involuntary transfer through death, the case is different. If there is an increased risk of person B losing his life, the CV for the risk is negative; that is, there is some minimum amount of money which will restore his welfare. To person A, however, who cares nothing for B's person but who expects to inherit B's vast estate, the increased risk to which B is now exposed is a benefit for which he is willing to pay up to some maximum sum.

[5] Only in an economy in which income was *wholly* from human capital would the R^3 component be comparable with the L_2 measure. A figure for the latter could be got by subtracting the net *losses* to the surviving members, arising from the death of breadwinners, from the net *gains* to the surviving members, arising from the death of dependants. As for R^3, the better the information, and the more constant the relation between income and utility along the relevant range, the closer the figure would be to the aggregate of the actuarial values of the net expected gain or loss to each person. It is the existence of non-human assets, and the possibility of their transfer from deceased to survivors, that adds to the positive value of R^3, and raises it above the L_2 measure.

(4) The other aspect of the concern to which, in general, each member is prone, in consequence of the additional physical risks to which others are exposed, is of a psychic nature. It is convenient, as well as charitable, to suppose that this concern entails a reduction in people's welfare. Thus the compensatory sum $\sum_{i}^{n} r^4_{ij}. \, (i \neq j)$ for the jth person's increased risk of bereavement carries a negative sign, being the sum of money necessary to reconcile him to bearing the additional risk of death to which his friends and members of his family are exposed. The increased risk of bereavement to which the community as a whole is exposed is to be valued at a sum equal to the aggregate $\sum_{j}^{n} \sum_{i}^{n} r_{ij} (i \neq j)$, which sum is abbreviated to R^4.

3 Simplicity of exposition has restricted the analysis to an increase only in the risk of death. The qualifications necessary for the treatment of an increase also in the risk of injury and death are too obvious to justify elaboration. Application of the above analysis to *reduced* risk of death, and to reduced risk of injury and disease, is perhaps slightly less obvious, and it may reassure the reader if its symmetrical nature is briefly illustrated by an example. Just as an increase in the number of accidents and fatalities can be a by-product of some growth in economic activity, so also can a reduction in the number of accidents and fatalities. More familiar, however, is public investment designed primarily to reduce the incidence of disease, suffering and death. And although such activity is to be regarded as a collective good, the relationship between collective goods and external effects (which can be thought of as incidental, 'non-optional', collective goods and 'bads'), is close enough to permit us to make use of our conceptual apparatus without significant modification.

Suppose, then, that the government has a scheme for purifying the air over a vast region, one which is expected to save 20,000 lives annually.[6] The costs of enforcing a clean-air act, and of installing preventive devices wherever needed, has to be set against the above social benefits. In accordance with our scheme, they are to be evaluated as follows.

---

[6] Again, for simplicity of exposition we omit reference, in this example, to the reduction of suffering or enjoyment of better health.

(1) Since, in this example, the reduced risk of death is a collective good, and not an external economy that is internal to some specific economic activity (as there could be, say, in a development that promoted horticulture, regarded as a healthy occupation), there is no R^1 term. There is here no question, that is, of how much a person will pay for some market good after making allowance for the *incidental* reduction of risk. The only good in question here is the collective reduction of risk itself.

(2) If the population of the area is 100 million, and the chance of dying from causes connected with air pollution is independent of age, location, occupation, physical condition, etc., the risk of death to each person in the region is reduced by 2/10,000. More generally, there is for the jth person a reduction of the risk of death from factors connected with air pollution (including infection by others suffering from air-pollution diseases) for which he is prepared to pay up to $\sum_i^n r_{ij}^2$, which on our assumption of universal risk-aversion, is positive. Aggregating over the n members, the total sum of R^2 is, therefore, also positive.[7]

(3) A reduction in the risk of death for everyone implies, for the jth person, a reduction in the chance of his being financially worse off or better off in the future. The risk compensation $\sum_{i.}^n r_{ij}^3. (i \neq j)$ can therefore

---

[7] It is frequently alleged that at low levels, risk can have a positive utility. This would imply that his indifference curve, say I_1 in Fig. VI.8, cuts the vertical (probability) axis before the unity point, and extends itself to the left of that axis. A point on this indifference curve to the left of the axis, having the combination p_i and S_i, indicates a sum he would pay (S_i) in order to enjoy a risk $(1-p_i)$.

But whether this is so, and the extent to which it is so, would seem to depend upon the activity associated with the risk. Driving at 100 miles per hour increases the risk of a fatal accident. And if some people choose gratuitously to drive at this speed, it is not simply in response to the additional risk *per se*. It is partly because a test of skill, physical courage, or manhood, is involved. Even where skill is absent, as in playing Russian roulette, there is a certain bravado in openly flirting with death. On the other hand it is hard to imagine a man deriving positive utility from the information that henceforth he is to be exposed—though anonymously, along with millions of others—to an increased risk of death, one over which he has no semblance of choice or control. The risk of increased infection by some new disease, or by increased radioactive fall-out, would be examples.

Nevertheless, the question of whether risk, at some levels, has a positive utility or a negative utility, in any particular case, is an empirical one, and does not affect the formal analysis.

be positive or negative. The greater the proportion of aggregate income arising from non-human capital, the more likely is the total sum R^3 to be negative for the reduced risk.

(4) Finally, there is the reduced risk of the jth person's suffering bereavement over the future, the corresponding risk compensation $\sum_{i}^{n}$ $r_{ij}^4.$ $(i \neq j)$ being positive. The total sum R^4 will, therefore, also be positive.

Evaluation of the benefits of the government scheme is, then, to be based, ultimately, on the aggregate of maximal sums that all persons in the region affected are willing to pay for the estimated reduction of the risks of death,[8] an aggregate which can usefully be split into three components, R^2, R^3 and R^4.

4 A word on the deficiencies in the information available to each person concerning the degree of risk involved. These deficiencies of information necessarily contribute to the discrepancies experienced by people between anticipated and realized satisfactions. For all that, in determining whether a potential Pareto improvement has been met, economists are generally agreed—either as a canon of faith, as a political tenet, or as an act of expediency—to accept the dictum that each person knows his own interest best. If, therefore, the economist is told that a person A is indifferent as between not assuming a particular risk and assuming it along with a sum of money, V, then, on the Pareto principle, the sum V has to be accepted as the relevant cost of his being exposed to that risk. It may well be the case that, owing either to deficient information, or congenital optimism, person A consistently overestimates his chances of survival. But once the dictum is accepted, as indeed it is in economists' appraisals of allocative efficiency, cost-benefit analysis has to accept V as the only relevant magnitude—this

---

[8] It has been put to me by a colleague that 'the benefits of increased safety from a project can be worth no more than the cost of preserving human life (or of a reduction in accidents) by alternative means'. This statement, however, confuses the measure of the benefits themselves with the measure of the expenditures necessary to produce such benefits. The economist must obviously consider 'alternative means' in order to produce any good at its lowest cost. But he cannot know whether incurring the lowest possible cost is justified until he has independently calculated a figure for the benefits in question, so enabling him to estimate the excess social benefit, or social loss, of preserving human life, etc.

being the sum chosen by A in awareness of his relative ignorance.[9] Certainly all the rest of the economic data used in a cost-benefit analysis, or any other allocative study, whether derived from market prices and quantities, or by other methods of enquiry, is based on this principle of accepting as final only the individual's estimate of what a thing is worth to him at the time the decision is to be made. The thing in question may, of course, also have a direct worth, positive or negative, for persons other than the buyer or seller of it, a possibility which requires a consideration of external effects. Yet, again, on the above dictum, it is the values placed on this thing by these other persons that are to count. Thus, while it is scarcely necessary to urge that more economical ways of refining and disseminating information be explored, the economist engaged in allocative studies traditionally follows the practice of evaluating all social gains and losses solely on the basis of individuals' own evaluations of the relevant effects on their welfare, given the information they have at the time the decision is taken.

5 In sum, any expected loss of life, or saving of life, any expected increase or reduction in suffering, in consequence of economic activity, is to be evaluated for the economy by reference to the Pareto principle; in particular, by reference to what each member of the community is willing to pay, or to receive, for the estimated change of risk. The resulting aggregate of CVs for the community can be usefully regarded as being made up of four components, and, of these, R^1— where it exists—can be ignored on the grounds that the benefit to each individual of the direct activity in question (often estimated as equal to the area under the demand curve) is already net of this risk.

The other components, R^2, R^3, R^4, cannot, in general, be ignored, though one can surmise that with growing material prosperity their magnitude will grow. With the growth in the welfare state, and in particular with an increasingly egalitarian structure of real disposable incomes, the financial risk-compensation, R^3, will tend to decline. The gradual loosening of family ties and the decline of emotional interdependence should cause the magnitude of the bereavement risk-

---

[9] Person A, for example, may find himself disabled for life and rue his decision to take the risk. But this example is only a more painful one of the fact that people come to regret a great many of the choices they make, notwithstanding which they would resent any interference with their future choices.

compensation R^4 to decline also. In a wholly impersonal society, in which, for any jth person, the loss of any member of the community is easily replaceable in j's estimation by many others, R^4 will tend to vanish. R^2, however, is wholly selfish in the sense that it depends on people's preference for staying alive. Until such time as a genetical revolution turns men into pure altruists, or pure automatons, ready, like some species of ants, to sacrifice themselves at a moment's notice for the greater convenience of the whole, it can be expected that R^2 will grow over time.

Before concluding, however, it should be emphasized that the basic concept developed in this chapter is not simply an alternative or an auxiliary to any existing methods[10] that have been proposed for measuring the loss, or saving, of life. It is the only economically justifiable concept. And this assertion does not rest on any novel ethical premise. It follows as a matter of consistency in the application of the Pareto principle in cost-benefit calculations.

In so far as an immediate application of the concepts to the measurement of loss or saving of life is in issue, one's claims must be more muted. In the attempts to measure social benefits and losses, price-quantity statistics lend themselves better to the more familiar examples in which people choose quantities at given market prices than they do to examples in which people have to choose prices for the given quantities. For one can observe the quantities they choose, at least collectively, whereas one cannot generally observe their subjective valuations. In the circumstances, economists seriously concerned to come to grips with the magnitudes may have to consider the possibility that data yielded by surveys based on the questionnaire

---

[10] It is far from impossible that society may choose to refer decisions in matters involving life and death to a representative body or committee, and that a decision may be reached that differs from the one which would arise from the consistent application of cost-benefit techniques. Nevertheless, the economist is free to criticize the decision, to point up inconsistencies, and to discover what features, if any, warrant a departure from the Pareto criterion.

Consistency in this instance requires that the expected change in risk, associated with any contemplated scheme, be evaluated by reference to the same principle as all other relevant economic gains and losses. To evaluate the welfare effect of risk on some other principle, say by voting procedure, entails the adding together of incommensurables: an implicit figure for the effect of risk on welfare attributable to a decision taken by a smaller group (or even by the whole group), by the method of counting heads, is added to a figure for the other economic effects which, using the Pareto principle, aggregates the valuation of each member of the group determined on a CV basis.

method are better than doing nothing, or better than persisting with some of the current measures such as L_1 or L_2.

In view of the existing quantomania one may be forgiven for asserting that there is more to be said for rough estimates of the precise concept than precise estimates of economically irrelevant concepts. The caveat is more to be heeded in this case, bearing in mind that currently used, and currently mooted, measures of saving or loss of life, such as L_1, L_2, L_3 and L_4, have no conceptual affinity with the Pareto basis of cost-benefit analysis.

6 It remains but to comment upon a number of recent proposals for valuing life or for valuing a change in the risk of fatalities which, while they do not reject the basic concept elaborated in these two chapters, yet contrive to produce novel formulae for measuring life or risk based on other concepts.[11]

Although such contributions may make some claim to intrinsic intellectual interest, they are also eloquent testimony to the sceptical belief that, loaded with enough technical hardware, any manuscript today can gatecrash into a respectable professional journal even though it lacks substance, novelty and relevance. The remarks that follow affirm that this is so even where methodological error is evident.

To appreciate this summary judgement, let it be borne in mind that inasmuch as a cost-benefit analysis is an application of normative (or welfare) economics, the economist has perforce to accept the individual's preferences and valuations at the time a social decision has to be made.[12] Thus the validity of any economic calculation can be tested, ultimately, only by reference, *inter alia*, to the relevant individual valuations. As distinct from positive economics, that is, the only admissible test of a net benefit calculation is a direct one involving checks on individual preferences and valuations.

Allowing that the above proposition commands assent, it is

---

[11] See in particular the contributions of Arthur (1981), Conley (1976), Cook and Graham (1977), Jones-Lee (1980), Keeney (1980) and Usher (1971).

[12] Broome (1978) rebels against this basic axiom in any calculation involving changes in a fatality risk. He argues vehemently, though not (in my opinion) persuasively, that an increase in the expectation of the loss of a single life within a community should, in a 'proper' cost-benefit calculation, take on an infinite value. My comments on his views can be found in my 1981 paper.

reasonable to expect that once the concept informing calculations of the value of life and limb has been rescued from error and brought into congruence with the basic axiom of normative economics, it would remain for cost-benefit analysis to be guided by this concept in improving methods for distilling people's risk valuations in a variety of particular cases. But there have also been displays of theoretical virtuosity in constructing models that build on different concepts, in particular on the quaint notion that the worth of a life is related in some fashion to the utility of a person's life or of his lifetime consumption. In view of the observations made in Chapter 45, such efforts would seem to be misdirected if not retrograde— unless, of course, the resulting theories discover proxies that are easier to calculate than direct measures and/or yield implications of importance other than expressions purporting to measure the value of a change in fatality risks or the value of a statistical life.

None of these recent contributions, however, can legitimately claim to meet such desiderata. More important, the authors of the better-known papers, building their models on the utility of expected lifetime economic activities, cannot avoid running into a metho-dological dilemma. Such models all yield some crucial magnitude, call it Q, from which the value of life is to be deduced from some expression containing Q.[13] But in order to test the usefulness of this magnitude Q, it is clearly necessary to calculate the worth of a statistical life (or of a fatality risk) by direct reference to individual valuations. The very implementation of such a test, however— whether or not it vindicates the validity of Q—renders the expression containing Q unnecessary.

7 Nor is it reasonable to expect that a Q magnitude so derived offers a proxy for the direct calculations of individuals' risk valua-tions, which are proposed in this chapter, whenever such calculations are used to estimate the value of a statistical life in the relevant circumstances.[14] If we bear in mind that what is almost invariably

---

[13] This magnitude Q would correspond to H^T in Conley (1976), RL in Jones-Lee (1980) and WE in Arthur (1981).

[14] True, the paper written by Jones-Lee (1980) also introduces an expression for the maximum acceptable risk, but one that he cannot obtain from his RL magnitude alone. He must derive it from direct estimates, or guess at it, or else accept it as a residual from a *direct* estimate of $\delta d/\delta p$, assuming he can place a reliable figure on RL.

wanted, at least in a cost-benefit analysis, is not at all an average value of human life at a given place and time but rather the value of some anticipated *change* in the mortality risk or health risk associated with the introduction of a specific project, we are compelled to conclude that, in the nature of things, there cannot be a unique value of a statistical human life for any age or income group. Given the average income of any age group, the value of a statistical life, as calculated from individuals' own valuations of the relevant risks, will vary greatly according to circumstances. These circumstances include (i) the magnitude of the change in risk, (ii) the type of risk and (iii) the way in which the expected change in risk translates into casualties.

(i) A project that is expected to save each year only one life in 10 million may be depended upon to yield, by direct reference to individuals' valuations, a value of zero for a statistical life. In contrast, the installation of a plant that is expected to increase the death rate by 10 per cent within a given area might yield a value for a statistical life in excess of $1 million.

(ii) The kind of death envisaged also plays a part. Given the same increase in the risk of death, say 1 per cent, the value of a statistical life will turn out to be higher if the death is one that is to be caused by nuclear radiation than if it is to be caused by drowning or influenza.

(iii) Again, as mentioned by Keeney (1980), exactly the same risk of the same kind of death may produce different valuations of a statistical life according (a) as expected death takes form each year as a probability distribution, so that in general it varies from year to year, (b) as the number of expected deaths occur with certainty each year, although they cannot be identified before the event, or (c) as the expected number of deaths—whether as a probability distribution or as a certainty each year—will comprise a whole community within the larger population rather than being diffused throughout the larger population.

In view of the variety of circumstances that arise in different projects, it is less troublesome and certainly more prudent for the economist engaged in a cost-benefit analysis to eschew models that, irrespective of their other defects, seek to produce some average, all-purpose value of life even when normalized for time, place, income and age-group. After all, the project in question is one that offers, among other goods and bads, a particular magnitude of

344

change of fatality or other risk of a specific kind—something he can capture by direct methods without troubling himself to translate the data first into some corresponding value of a statistical life that has relevance only for those particular circumstances.

Chapter 47

MEASURING POLLUTION DAMAGE BY VARIATIONS IN PROPERTY VALUES (I)

1 Apparently some economists believe this is possible. The concept of a rent equal to the capital value of differences in the stream of services that arise from some differential advantage of a piece of land, whether of location or fertility, would seem to be applicable also to a stream of disservices associated with a particular site. Such ideas would predispose economists to seek in rent-differences a comprehensive measure of the social costs of pollution. Those following this line of thought would be apt to regard the problem as being largely a statistical one, that of isolating the effect on equilibrium site prices of different levels of some specific type of pollution. For instance, Ridker (1967 p. 28) writes: 'Despite these problems [the econometric problems and those of adequate information] the potential advantage of using property values is great, for it represents a way to capture in one figure a diverse group of psychic and resource costs associated with real estate that otherwise must be estimated separately.' Though his results were far from encouraging, Ridker continued the quest to uncover this sovereign index. Thus, later in 1967, Ridker and Henning addressed themselves to the difficulties involved in using cross-section data to regress land values on air quality, and although they seemed to be heartened by the results they obtained, their statistical methods were later criticized by Freeman (1971).

The search for significant statistical relationships between pollution and property values continues, though without as yet any close consideration being given to the question of their interpretation. Apparently there is a tacit assumption that an ideally competitive property market which was subject to the influence of only one specific form of pollution would truly reflect social costs and, consequently, an ideal econometric study would be able to produce an exact relation between the degree of pollution and social cost.

Now the application of some simple theory to the problem will reveal that such expectations are doomed from the start: that is to say, it can be shown that variations in property prices of themselves cannot provide a reliable index of the social costs of pollution. The findings which emerge from the following sections are of course applicable to any specific form of pollution, but it will be of topical interest to develop the analysis in terms solely of noise pollution.

2   Although it is possible to reach comparable results using a 'flow' model—one involving current sales and purchases of houses over a set period—we shall confine the analysis to a model based on an existing stock of residential housing situated within a given area. Nothing essential is lost and some convenience is gained by assuming throughout that each family owns one house only. Moreover, in this section we shall ignore all costs associated with moving house, all expectations other than the belief that existing noise levels will continue into the future, and all differences of valuation that arise from a distinction between compensating and equivalent variations with respect to noise disturbance. Finally, since our conclusions are valid for any class of houses that (if we exclude the variable noise) are equally desirable in all other respects, we can restrict the analysis to one particular class of houses.

A partial equilibrium analysis can be expected to disclose only the *differences* in money prices between a quiet house and a noisy house of a given class where all other prices and availabilities remain unchanged. Whether the money price of a quiet house rises or that of the noisy house falls depends, *inter alia,* on the assumptions we make about the flow of newly-built houses that replace old houses and augment the existing stock. If we assume that *quiet* houses of this class can be built for immediate occupation at a cost equal to the market price for houses existing prior to the advent of noise disturbance then the houses which are disturbed by noise will tend to fall in price. If, instead, we assume that *noisy* houses can be built for immediate occupation at a cost equal to the market price that existed before the advent of noise disturbance, then houses unaffected by noise will tend to rise in price. Though whichever assumption we make the *difference* in price will be the same, we shall adopt the latter, and probably more realistic, assumption.

As a first case suppose all the owners of this particular class of houses have identical tastes but different incomes. The *ceteris paribus* valuation of each of these families is ranked in declining order of income, the result being the valuation curve *VC* in Figure VI.9, which is drawn as a straight line.

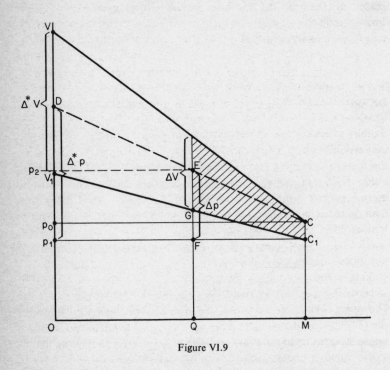

Figure VI.9

Before the introduction of noise, the stock of houses is valued at *OVCM*, and the market clearing price is Op_0, equal to *MC*, which is the value placed on a quiet house by the householder with the lowest income. The vertical distance between the lines *VC* and V_1C_1 (corresponding to the position along *OM* of some particular householder) measures the subjective cost to that householder of some given quantum of noise—assuming always that new noisy houses are available at cost OC_1. If, therefore, *QM* houses are affected by such noise, the amount ΔV in Figure VI.9 is the loss of value to the Qth householder.

Each of the remaining householders, who suffer equally from the noise, puts a smaller value on it according as his income is smaller than that of the Qth person. Their total loss from the noise is therefore equal to the shaded area in the Figure.

Now in equilibrium the market differential between the price of a noisy house and a quiet house, Δp, must be equal to ΔV, the premium placed on quiet by the Qth householder. This implies that a noisy house now sells at p_1, the valuation placed by the Mth householder on a noisy house, and that a quiet house then fetches a market price of $(p_1 + \Delta p)$, or Op_2 as in the Figure.

3   We might remark, in passing, that this resulting equilibrium does not require the assumption that the noise in question initially afflicts those particular householders ranged along QM. For if the houses initially affected by noise were, instead, all to be found in the OQ range they would—under our assumption of costless movement—end up in the hands of the QM householders having the lowest incomes. Any noise-afflicted householder having a higher income than the Qth and, therefore, initially in the OQ range, would be willing to give up more than Δp to exchange his noisy house for a quiet one, whereas any of the householders in the lower income group whose houses are initially unaffected by noise would be willing to accept Δp, or less, in return for putting up with a noisy house.

Thus in the resulting equilibrium, the Qth householder is indifferent as between occupying a noisy house at p_1 or a quiet one at $p_1 + \Delta p$. The QM noisy houses are all held by those having incomes below that of the Qth householder—each of them being satisfied to occupy a noisy house at p_1 since the premium each of them would be willing to pay for a quiet house is less than Δp. As for the quiet houses remaining, each is occupied by a householder with an income greater than that of the Qth at a price equal to $p_1 + \Delta p$ since each is willing to pay more than the market premium of Δp for a quiet house.

It may be noticed also that the construction requires that the straight line curve $V_1 C_1$ be regarded as the demand curve for noisy houses by the community, the demand curve for noisy houses by QM householders being GC_1, and the equilibrium price p_1. With noisy houses available on the market at p_1, the demand for quiet houses is given by DC which passes through point E—the vertical distances between the straight line curve DC and the horizontal line $p_1 C_1$ being at all points equal to those between VC and V_1C_1. Thus if all houses were left quiet, the market price for quiet houses would be p_0. Where there are only OQ quiet houses available, their price will be p_2. And if there were only one quiet house remaining, its market price would be OD (equal to $p_1 + \Delta {}^*p$).

Thus, under our restrictive assumptions, the loss of value as indicated by market prices overstates the social cost of the noise. The former is the price-difference times the number of houses disturbed by noise, or $\Delta p \times QM$, whereas the social cost is the smaller shaded area in the Figure.

4   The construction in Figure VI.9 can be simplified by removing the segment $p_1FC_1\ CED$ which segment is reproduced as Figure VI.10, where the letters OQM replace respectively the letters p_1FC_1 of Figure V.9. The curve DC of Figure V.10 now measures the excess price, or premium, for quiet alone that each householder is willing to pay. Thus when QM households are deprived of quiet, the price-difference, or premium, for quiet Δp (equals Op_2 in the Figure) is equal to the valuation of quiet ΔV by the Qth householder. And the social cost of noise to QM households is, in equilibrium equal to the shaded area $QECM$—equal, by construction, to the shaded area in Figure VI.9.

Exactly the same construction may be used and the same results obtained if, instead, we assume identical incomes but different tastes and, therefore, interpret DC as a ranking of house-evaluation by declining sensitivity to noise.[1] More generally, the value ranking of quiet as indicated by DC arises from a combination of differences both in income and in sensitivity to noise. And since differences in sensitivity are now to affect valuation we may suppose the DC curve continues to N, the Nth household being wholly insensitive to noise. If, moreover, there are a number of households, NN' that are wholly insensitive to noise, we extend the horizontal axis by NN', as shown in Figure VI.10.

In general we conclude that, under existing restrictive assumptions, the market measure of social loss from the introduction of noise always exceeds the true social cost (save for the improbable case in which

---

[1] What households are willing to pay for a good, quiet, is not necessarily positively related to what they are willing to pay for other desirable features of a house. For this reason it simplifies the analysis to isolate the premium they are willing to pay for this desirable feature, quiet, from what they are willing to pay for other desirable features.

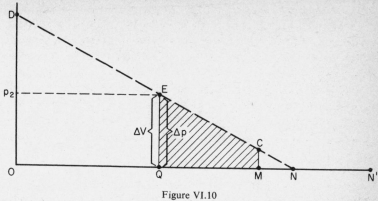

Figure VI.10

every householder has exactly the same valuation of noise, in which case *DC* becomes a horizontal line). Given a straight line valuation curve, the market measures of this loss is equal to, less than, or greater than, twice the true social cost of the noise according as the horizontal axis in Figure VI.10 measures exactly *ON*, or is less than, or greater than, *ON*.

5 It will be convenient henceforth to assume that the least sensitive household alone is wholly insensitive and to construct the Figure as *OQNED,* though bearing in mind the required adjustments if no household is wholly insensitive to noise or if a number of households are wholly insensitive to noise. It goes without saying that the greater the quantum of noise that is introduced the more likely is the former adjustment and the larger, therefore, the true social cost relative to the market measure.

Finally, it should be noticed that in the special case in which all houses in the area become affected by the same degree of noise, there being no quiet house left in the area, a price-difference or premium for quiet cannot emerge in the market. Moreover, if the *ON* or *ON'* case prevailed there would be no difference in house-prices before or after the introduction of noise. If an investigator were to interpret such facts as indicating complete insensitivity to noise by the community he would obviously understate the social cost.

351

Chapter 48

MEASURING POLLUTION DAMAGE BY VARIATIONS IN PROPERTY VALUES (II)

1 The *costs of moving house* is an umbrella term that includes not only the more measurable items such as agents' and solicitors' fees and removal costs, but also search costs (the time, effort, and expenditure involved in searching for a new house), and dislocation costs, which include the 'psychic' costs of adjusting to a new neighbourhood and, for some members of the family, to a new school or place of work, bearing in mind the attendant risks and apprehensions. By assuming that these considerations are additive, we can designate them by the letter C.[1] Thus, if V is the full premium a person is willing to pay for a quiet house in the absence of all movement costs C, the effect of introducing such costs into the model is to drive a wedge between the *net* maximum premium $(V-C)$ he can now afford to pay for a quiet house and the *net* minimal premium $(V+C)$ he will have to receive in order to induce him to part with his quiet house. If we assume that these C costs are the same for each family (an assumption which, when relaxed, will make no qualitative difference to our conclusions), the BB' curve in Figure VI.11, which is the schedule of the effective premia for buying quiet housing, will be uniformly below DN to the same extent that the SS' curve, the schedule of the premia required for selling quiet housing, is above the DN curve.

In general, it should be apparent that if (after introducing a quantum of noise that afflicts a given number of houses) any house-transactions

---

[1] According to the BAA (1970) Survey, (a) removal and search costs varied between 6% and 11% of property prices, and (b) dislocation costs varied enormously but (for finite figures) averaged very much higher than removal and search costs. About 38% of the respondents said no amount of money would induce them to move from their existing neighbourhoods. For calculation purposes, however, a limit of 50% of the value of the property was adopted for dislocation costs.

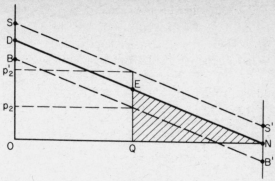

Figure VI.11

take place, the relevant area under *DN* will be less than the full social cost by the costs of movement that are now incurred by buyers and sellers. As a result, the true social cost will exceed a half the market measure of the loss of quiet. On the other hand if, after the introduction of noise, no house-transactions take place, the market premium for the remaining quiet house is determined by reference to the *BB'* curve while the social cost is determined by reference to the *DN* curve. Again, therefore, the true social cost will be greater than a half of the market measure of loss.

Thus in this case (A), if we suppose the *QN* least sensitive householders are afflicted by noise,[2] the equilibrium premium for a quiet house will be p_2, this being the maximum net premium that can be offered by the least insensitive among the *QM* group in the hope of buying a quiet house. No house-transactions take place, however, as the lowest net premium required by a seller of the remaining *OQ* houses is p_2'.

The market measure of the loss from the noise that affects the *QN* least sensitive households is, in such cases, equal to $Op_2 \times QN$ which is less than twice the true social cost indicated in Figure VI.11 by the shaded triangle *QNE*.

For the opposite case (B) in which the households initially affected by the noise are the most sensitive, say the 'S group', three possibilities must be considered: (a) Where the number of houses affected by noise,

---

[2] More generally, the *QN* householders disturbed by noise comprise those having the lowest premia for quiet, whether this is a result of insensitivity or low income or both. For brevity, however, we shall continue to talk only of more sensitive or less sensitive.

OQ_1, is small enough that in equilibrium these noisy houses would come to be held as Q_2N (equals OQ_1), in Figure VI.11a by the least sensitive 'N group'. Thus Q_2N quiet houses would be sold by the N group to the S group at the sellers' premium of p_2'.

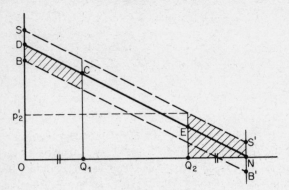

Figure VI.11a

To the resulting minimal subjective loss in equilibrium, the shaded triangle Q_2NE, we have to add the costs of movement to both the selling (N) group and the buying (S) group, these additional costs being indicated respectively by the shaded strip above EN and the shaded strip below DC. The market measure of loss, $p_2' \times Q_2N$ is, here, clearly less than twice the total social cost as measured by the sum of the shaded areas in Figure VI.11a.

(b) The largest number of house-transactions possible is indicated by OQ_1 equal to Q_2N in Figure VI.11b. If exactly OQ_1 houses are affected by noise, the S group will buy exactly this many quiet houses from the N group at a premium of p_2'. In that case the market measure of loss and the true social cost are comparable with those depicted in Figure V.11a.

However, if the number of noise-disturbed houses of the S group is OQ_1', which in Figure VI.11b exceeds OQ_1 but falls short of OQ_2, the equilibrium market premium remains at p_2', at which premium the maximum number of quiet houses, Q_2N, were sold. Since the N group will not sell more quiet houses unless the sellers' premium rises above p_2', and the Q_1Q_1' householders will not buy quiet houses unless the buyers' premium is below p_2', these Q_1Q_1' householders have to remain with noisy houses and suffer a social loss measured by the shaded area

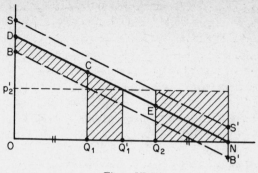

Figure VI.11b

above $Q_1 Q_1$ in Figure VI.11b. Thus the total social cost, in equilibrium, of the noise disturbance is equal to the sum of the shaded areas in Figure VI.11b. Again then the market measure of the loss is $p_2' \times OQ_1'$, equals $p_2' (Q_1 Q_1' + Q_2 N)$, or less than twice this social cost.

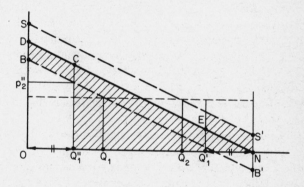

Figure VI.11c

(c) If OQ_1' exceeds OQ_2, as it does in Figure VI.11c, there is only $Q_1' N$ quiet houses left in the area, these (by assumption) being initially in the possession of the N group. Only that number of quiet houses can then be bought by the S group. In equilibrium, therefore, OQ_1'' (equal to $Q_1' N$) quiet houses will be held by the S group. Competition among them for the limited number of quiet houses will produce a market premium of p_2'' for OQ_1'' houses. $Q_1'' Q_1'$ householders will remain with noisy houses, and $Q_1' N$ of the N group will have exchanged quiet for noisy houses. In this equilibrium, the full social cost of the noise

355

disturbance falling initially on OQ'_1 households is measured as the shaded areas in Figure VI.11c. They can be decomposed into (i) the area under the DN curve for all those remaining, in equilibrium, with noisy houses (equal to the Q''_1N households in Figure VI.11c) plus (ii) the two shaded strips, to represent costs of movements of buyers and sellers respectively, that below DC and that above EN.

Thus for all these possibilities in the (B) case also, in which noise initially affects the houses of the S group, the market measure of the loss from noise is less than twice the social cost—which, of course, does not preclude the market measure of loss being significantly less than the social cost. It may reasonably be inferred that for cases intermediate between (A) and (B)—those in which the houses affected by noise are held initially partly by the S group and partly by the N group—the same relationship holds as that for (A) and (B).

It may be observed, finally, that the larger the costs of movement C the greater is the vertical distance between BB'' and SS'' and the greater, therefore, is the true social cost relative to the market measure of loss. In the limiting case the costs of movement will be large enough to prevent any premium for quiet houses being established in the market no matter which houses are initially affected by noise.

2 *The Model when Compensating and Equivalent Variations are Distinguished*

Removing the assumption of no difference between a person's equivalent variation and compensating variation for the introduction of a 'bad', noise, broadens the difference between the schedules of buying and selling prices of quiet houses. Instead of the premia for quiet over noisy houses being measured uniquely by DN, we now have a curve of equivalent variation, D_1N in Figure VI.12, which at any point measures the maximum sum the corresponding household will pay for a quiet house over a noisy one, and a curve of compensating variation, D_2N in Figure VI.12, which at any point measures the minimum sum the corresponding household will accept in order to give up a quiet house in exchange for a noisy one. Assuming 'normal' welfare effects D_2N will be above D_1N at all points other than N (since the Nth person attaches no value to quiet).

It is not implausible to believe that the minimum amount of money

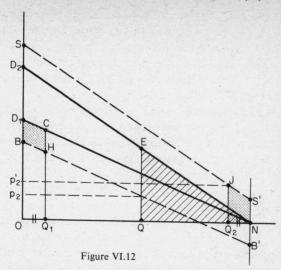

Figure VI.12

some persons are willing to accept in order to go without may be several times larger than the maximum sum they are ready to pay for some good which they regard as crucial to their wellbeing, if only because the latter sum is limited by their current and expected wealth while the former sum is not limited.[3] And one may generalize to the extent of asserting that the greater the volume of noise in question the greater is the divergence between these two curves and, consequently, between SS' and BB'. For in buying a house the relevant schedule of maximal premia is D_1N. Therefore the *effective* schedule of premia offered for buying a quiet house, BB', is got by subtracting from D_1N the costs of movement C. On the other hand, in selling a quiet house the relevant schedule of lowest acceptable premia is D_2N, and the effective schedule of premia demanded for selling a quiet house, SS', is got by adding to D_2N the cost of movement C.

Two modifications of our results follow from this analytic refinement. The consequent widening of the vertical distances between BB' and SS' reduces the maximum possible house-transactions. Secondly, the true cost of noise is to be measured by reference to the higher D_2N curve which, at any point, indicates the minimum sum the corresponding householder will accept to bear with it. Thus in the case in which

---

[3] For example, 54% of the respondents in the BAA survey said that nothing would induce them to live close to a major airport.

QN of the N group is initially afflicted with noise, the resultant market premium for quiet, p_2 in Figure VI.12, is yet further below the marginal social cost of quiet QE. The market measure of loss is $p_2 \times QN$, and the social cost is the shaded triangle QNE. In the opposite case in which OQ_1 houses of the S group are affected by noise, the market premium at which they are able to buy Q_2N (equals OQ_1) quiet houses from the N group is p_2'. The measure of market loss is then $p_2' \times Q_2N$ while the social cost is equal to the sum of the two dotted areas in Figure VI.12 D_1CHB and $Q_2NS'J$. Clearly, there is nothing in this construction to prevent the social cost being much larger than the market measure.

3 The Model Revised for Expectations

In determining the market measure of noise the tacit assumption has been made that the households unaffected by the introduction of some quantum of noise will continue to remain so. If this is not the case, or if it is believed that it will not be the case, our results require further revision.

If the introduction of noise is associated with expectations that it will extend over the future to houses currently free from noise, such houses will anticipate a declining time-profile of quiet. In consequence, the capital premium a household is willing to pay for a currently quiet house is below that which would hold in the absence of such expectations. The *operative* equivalent variation schedule $D_1'N$ in Figure VI.13 will then be below D_1N, the equivalent variation schedule for expectations that currently quiet houses will continue to remain quiet over the foreseeable future. Similarly the *operative* compensating variation schedule $D_2'N$ in Figure VI.13 will be below D_2N the compensating variation schedule for unchanged expectations.

The effect of such expectations in reducing the market measure of the loss from the introduction of noise into the area is quite manifest without elaborating Figure VI.13 to include the cost of movement. If QN of the N group were initially afflicted by noise their attempts to buy a quiet house—given the prevalence of expectations that issue in the operative schedules $D_2'N$ and $D_1'N$—produce an equilibrium for a quiet house of p_2. The social cost to QN householders of their being deprived of quiet is, however, measured by reference to the D_2N curve (which indicates the minimum sums needed to compensate them for putting up with noise indefinitely in exchange for quiet indefinitely). It

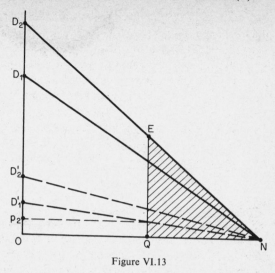

Figure VI.13

is therefore equal to the area of the shaded triangle QNE. Clearly, when such expectations are introduced, the social cost can exceed the market measure of loss $(p_2 \times QN)$ many times over—a conclusion which continues to hold if, instead, the S group of households were initially affected by the noise.

Whether expectations about future noise patterns are not realized, or are more than realized, will make no difference to the equilibrium relationship between the true social cost of the current loss of quiet and its market measure. Even if currently quiet houses were destined never to be disturbed by noise, the belief that they would be disturbed in the near future—which is not an implausible expectation in the light of postwar experience—might drastically reduce their current market premium p_2. In the limiting case in which prevailing expectations are that the quiet houses remaining will very soon become as noisy as the others the operative schedules $D_2'N$ and $D_1'N$ will become horizontal and there will be no differential in market prices between quiet and noisy houses. In these circumstances, an econometric study that succeeded in isolating the difference in house prices attributable solely to noise in that area would seem to show that householders cared little or nothing about the degree of noise.

4 Generalizing from this case of noise pollution to other kinds of pollution, one is tempted to conclude that a little more patience with the theory could save a lot of econometric effort. For it would now seem that even if differences in property values were successfully identified as arising solely from differences in the incidence of a specific type of pollution, they could not be counted on to bear any reliable relation to the true social costs of that pollution.

Under a number of highly restrictive assumptions—including no costs of movement, no differences between equivalent and compensating variations, and no expectations about currently quiet houses becoming noisy in the future—true social costs can be taken as roughly a half the market measure of the noise damage. But this tidy result disintegrates as the restrictive assumptions are discarded and we draw closer to the real world. From our brief examination of the problem, we may generalize as follows: the greater the degree of noise involved, the greater the costs of movement, the greater the difference between equivalent and compensating variations, and the less sanguine are expectations of continuing quiet, the larger becomes the true social cost of the noise damage relative to its market measure. As we elaborate the model to reflect the main features of the real world, even the utmost restraint in the way of casual estimates of any of these magnitudes does not weaken the broad conclusion that the market measure of the incidence of noise can be a large or small or negligible fraction of the true social cost. Indeed the market measure of loss can be zero in circumstances that generate a substantial social cost.

The moral of the story is that the endeavour to extract a dependable relationship between specific pollution damage and social cost by reference to variations in property values is doomed to failure. Much more is to be hoped for in this regard from attempts to evolve more sophisticated interviewing techniques.[4]

REFERENCES AND BIBLIOGRAPHY FOR PART VI

Anderson, R. J. and Crocker, T. D. 'Air Pollution and Property Values', *Urban Studies*, 1971.

Arthur, W. B. 'The Economics of Risks to Life', *American Economic Review*, 1981.

British Airports Authority. Evidence submitted to Roskill Commission on Siting of Third London Airport (1970).

---

[4] Among economists who, though critical of current work in the subject, are hopeful of the possibilities of measuring the social cost of noise by more elaborate questionnaires and other direct methods. are Paul (1971). Pearce (1972). and Plowden (1970).

REFERENCES

Becker, G. 'A Theory of the Allocation of Time', *Economic Journal*, 1965.

Beesley, M. 'The Value of Time Spent in Travelling: Some New Evidence', *Economica*, 1965.

Broome, J. 'Trying to Value a Life', *Journal of Public Economy*, 1978.

Clawson, M. 'Method of Measuring the Demand for and Value of Outdoor Recreation', *Resources for the Future*, Washington, DC: Brookings Institution, 1959.

Clawson, M. and Knetsch, J. *The Economics of Outdoor Recreation*, Baltimore: Johns Hopkins, 1966.

Commission on the Third London Airport, Report, London: HMSO, 1971 (sometimes known as the Roskill Report).

Commission on the Third London Airport, Papers and Proceedings, Vol. VII, Stage III, London: HMSO, 1970 (the Roskill Commission's Research Team Study).

Conley, B. C. 'The Value of Human Life in the Demand for Safety', *American Economic Review*, 1976.

Cook, P. J. and Graham, D. A. 'The Demand for Insurance and Protection: The Case of Irreplaceable Commodities', *Quarterly Journal of Economics*, 1977.

Devons, E. *Essays in Economics*, London: Allen & Unwin, 1961.

Eisner, R. and Strotz, R. H. 'Flight Insurance and the Theory of Choice', *Journal of Political Economy*, 1961.

Flowerdew, A. D. J. 'The Cost of Airport Noise', *The Statistician*, 1971.

Freeman, A. M. 'Air Pollution and Property Values: A Comment', *Review of Economics and Statistics*, 1971.

Fromm, G. 'Civil Aviation Expenditure', in R. Dorfman (ed.) *Measuring Benefits of Government Investment*, Washington, DC: Brookings Institution, 1965.

— Comment on T. C. Schelling's paper, 'The Life You Save may be Your Own', in S. B. Chase Jr (ed.) *Problems in Public Expenditure*, Washington DC: Brookings Institution, 1968.

Haveman, R. H. and Krutilla, J. V. *Unemployment, Idle Capacity and the Evaluation of Public Expenditure*, Washington, DC: Resources for the Future, Inc., 1968.

Jones-Lee, N. W. 'Maximum Acceptable Physical Risk and a New Measure of Financial Risk Aversion', *Economic Journal*, 1980.

Keeney, R. L. 'Equity and Public Risk', *Operations Research*, 1980.

Krutilla, J. V. 'Conservation Reconsidered', *American Economic Review*, 1967.

Linnerooth, J. 'The Value of Human Life: A Review of the Models', *Economic Inquiry*, 1979.

Mishan, E. J. 'Rent as a Measure of Welfare Change', *American Economic Review*, 1959.

— 'The Recent Debate on Welfare Criteria', *Oxford Economic Papers*, 1965.

— 'What is Wrong with Roskill?', *Journal of Transport Economics and Policy*, 1970.

— 'Pangloss on Pollution', *Swedish Economic Journal*, 1971.

— 'The Value of Trying to Value Life', *Journal of Public Economy*, 1981.

Nath, S. K. *A Reappraisal of Welfare Economics*, London: Routledge and Kegan Paul, 1969.

Needleman, L. 'Valuing Other People's Lives', *Manchester School*, 1976.

Paul, M. E. 'Can Airport Noise be Measured in Money?', *Oxford Economic Papers*, 1971.

Pearce, D. 'The Economic Evaluation of Noise', *Problems of Environmental Economics*, Paris: OECD, 1972.

Plowden, S. 'The Cost of Noise', *Metra* monograph, 1970.

Ridker, R. G. *The Economics of Air Pollution*, New York: Praeger, 1967.

Ridker, R. G. and Henning, J. A. 'The Determination of Residential Property Values with Special Reference to Air Pollution', *Review of Economics and Statistics*, 1967.

Schelling, T. C. 'The Life You Save may be Your Own', in S. B. Chase Jr (ed.) *Problems in Public Expenditure*, Washington DC: Brookings Institution, 1968.

Thaler, R. and Rosen, S. 'The Value of Saving a Life: Evidence from the Labor Market', Paper 74–2, New York: University of Rochester, 1974.

Tipping, D. G. 'Time Savings in Transport Studies', *Economic Journal*, 1968.

Turvey, R. 'The Price of Time in a Technological Age' (unpublished ms.), 1972.

Usher, D. 'An Imputation to the Measure of Economic Growth for Changes in Life Expectancy', New York: National Bureau of Economic Research, 1971.

Walters, A. A. 'Mrs Paul on Aircraft Noise—a Comment', *Oxford Economic Papers*, 1971.

— *Noise and Prices*, Oxford: Clarendon Press, 1975.

Wilkinson, R. K. 'House Prices and the Measurement of Externalities', *Economic Journal*, 1973.

Zeckhauser, R. 'Procedures for Valuing Lives', *Public Policy*, 1975.

PART VII. UNCERTAINTY

Chapter 49

CERTAINTY EQUIVALENCE

1   The treatment in this section of the methods for dealing with uncertainty in project evaluation is, inevitably perhaps, the least satisfactory feature of this introductory volume. In the evaluation of any project there is sure to be some guesswork about the magnitudes of future costs and benefits, arising in the main from technological innovations and shifts in demand which may affect the prices of the inputs and outputs. In consequence, economists making use of the methods discussed in this section cannot be sure of arriving at a common figure or set of figures for a specific project. The problem of how to make decisions in any situation where the past affords little if any guidance is not one that can be satisfactorily resolved either by logic or empiricism, and what rules have been formulated are either of limited application or of no practical value. We shall, however, consider briefly and in a simple-minded way the various methods that have been proposed to deal with this problem of uncertainty, beginning with the device of reducing an uncertain prospect to an equivalent certainty.

2   Suppose that I am uncertain of the price my house will fetch on the market when I come to sell it in five years' time. Though uncertain of the exact price, I will surely entertain some ideas of what the price is likely to be. With luck, I think it could be $60,000, possibly even more. Allowing for this, that and the other, it is, however, more likely to be $50,000. Yet it could well be as low as $40,000, and one cannot altogether exclude the possibility of its fetching a sum lower even than this.

I should be glad to be free of the anxiety caused by this uncertainty about the sales price of my house for a guaranteed price of $50,000 five years hence. Indeed, I could be induced to agree to a smaller sum than $50,000. The question naturally arises: what is the lowest guaranteed sum I would be prepared to accept in five years' time to be rid of uncertainty? If it were $45,000, then $45,000 is said to represent the certainty equivalent that corresponds to the range of my uncertain prospects.

If, on the other hand, I contemplated buying a particular house in five years' time for a sum which could be as low as $72,000 but might be as high as $100,000, I might be induced to agree to pay, in five years' time, as much as (but no more than) $86,000. If so, $86,000 becomes the certainty equivalent corresponding to the uncertain purchase price.[1]

In general, it is asserted that to any *uncertain* future sum of money—to be paid or to be received—there corresponds a *guaranteed* sum as between which and the uncertain sum in question the individual is indifferent.

On the more common assumption of risk-aversion for transactions of some importance, a person is prepared to pay some premium for safety. If, therefore, the expected figure for the sale of his house appears to be $50,000, by accepting a guaranteed price of $45,000 he can be said to be paying a risk premium of $5,000. If, on the other hand, he is concerned with the problem of buying a particular house in five years' time, and the most likely price is $80,000, by accepting a guaranteed future price of $86,000, he can be said to be paying a risk premium of $6,000. It goes without saying that the higher the degree of uncertainty about the future price,[2] the greater the risk premium a person will be willing to pay.

---

[1] If there were only two possible outcomes, $100,000, expected with a probability of $\frac{1}{4}$, and $72,000 expected with a probability of $\frac{3}{4}$, the certainty equivalent might be thought equal to $(\frac{1}{4} \times \$100,000) + (\frac{3}{4} \times \$72,000)$, or $79,000. In 'normal' cases, it would be less than $79,000, as explained in Chapter 52. In the present chapter we do not, however, assume that probabilities can be attached to each of a range of possible outcomes.

[2] The higher degree of uncertainty might be measured by a higher degree of variance if it were possible to talk of likelihood in a probabilistic sense, one arising from repeated experiment in an unchanged universe—which is not, however, the case for uncertainty.

3 This notion of uncertainty equivalence is, perhaps, a useful ploy in working through abstract economic constructs where the troublesome fact of uncertainty can be formally accommodated, without any amendment to the theory, simply by attributing a certainty equivalent to every uncertain magnitude. But it provides little guidance to the economist engaged in evaluating a project. If he cannot be sure of a figure at any time in the future he will have to guess at it, and if he is at all sensible he will choose to err on the conservative side. There is no way of insuring himself. The knowledge that some rational being, when faced with the problem of placing a value on some future magnitude, might well choose a value very different from that chosen by another equally rational individual, may be of some consolation to him in his perplexity. But it cannot provide him with a clear decision rule.

4 Further theoretical elaboration is of interest but of small practical value. For example, by measuring expected value (or arithmetic mean) along the horizontal axis and variance on the vertical axis, a 'gambler's indifference map' can be constructed. The indifference curves will slope upward from left to right indicating that increasing uncertainty (as measured by variance) has to be compensated by an increase in expected value. If we now have a number of alternative future benefits to choose from, all incurring the same cost, and each identified by a particular expected value and variance, that touching the highest indifference curve is chosen.

Such a construction enables us formally to rank a number of alternative uncertain benefits without first reducing each to a certainty equivalent. But though, formally speaking, the method is more direct, exception can be taken to the idea of being able to measure mean and variance in situations of genuine uncertainty. For uncertainty, strictly interpreted, implies ignorance of the probability distribution. Moreover, in the absence of a *community* indifference map, and in the absence of agreement on the characteristics of the data, the method provides no more guidance in the face of uncertainty than does the method of uncertainty equivalents; which is to say it provides practically no guidance at all.

Chapter 50

GAME THEORY (I)

1 Since game theory can be used as a technique for dealing with cases of complete ignorance of the initial probabilities of possible outcomes, the reader might be inclined to pitch his hopes for useful guidance a little higher. Again, I think he will be disappointed. But before pronouncing judgment we shall illustrate with one or two simple examples the relevant techniques know as the 'two-person zero-sum game', so-called for the rather obvious reason (1) that the game is played between two persons or groups, one of which may be 'nature', and (2) that there are no mutual gains to be made; the gains to one party being exactly equal to the losses suffered by the other party.

2 Consider first a reservoir which is full at the beginning of the season and can be used both for irrigation and for flood-control. Without any prior knowledge of whether or not a flood will occur, a decision is required on the amount of water to be released. If a little water is released now it will be good for the harvest, but it will be ineffectual as a contribution to preventing future flood damage. If, instead, a lot of water is released now it will make flood damage virtually impossible, but it will damage the harvest to some extent.

Now the amount of water that can be released from the reservoir can range, in general, from nothing at all to the whole lot. As for the flood, if it occurs it can be either negligible or highly destructive. In order to illustrate the principle, however, we can restrict ourselves to two possible outcomes, (b_1) full flood and (b_2) no flood. The options open to the decision-maker are also to be restricted for simplicity of exposition: they will be (a_1) release one-third of the water in the reservoir, (a_2) release two-thirds of the water in the reservoir, and (a_3) release all the water in the reservoir.[1] In addition

---

[1] This example is taken from R. Dorfman (1962), p. 130 ff.

to the possible states of nature, (b_1) and (b_2), and the options open to the decision maker, (a_1), (a_2), and (a_3), we are also assumed to have a clear idea of the quantitative result corresponding to the particular outcome and the option adopted. If, for example, a decision is taken to release two-thirds of the reservoir, which is option (a_2), and a full flood, (b_1), happens to occur, the net benefit—that is the value of the harvest *less* the value of the damage done by the flood—is assumed to be known. In this example we shall assume it is equal to $140,000. Again, if instead we choose the (a_3) option, that of releasing all the water, the net benefit that arises if the full flood (b_1) occurs is assumed equal to $80,000. Since there are three options, or strategies, and two possible occurrences, or states of nature, there will be altogether six possible outcomes each identified by a net benefit figure. The scheme is depicted in Table VII.1 below.

TABLE VII.1

	b_1 Flood	b_2 No Flood
a_1	$130,000	$400,000
a_2	140,000	260,000
a_3	80,000	90,000

A glance at the Table will convince the reader that, provided the six figures above are all accepted as correct estimates of net benefits, option a_3—requiring the release of all the water in the reservoir—will never be adopted. Whether b_1 or b_2 occurs the net benefits of adopting the a_3 option will be lower than those of either a_1 or a_2. In the jargon, option a_3 is *dominated* by the other options, a fact that is revealed by the figures in the a_1 row (130,000 and 400,000) and those in the a_2 row (140,000 and 260,000), both sets of figures being larger than the a_3 row figures (80,000 and 90,000). We could then save some unnecessary calculation by eliminating the dominated option a_3, since there are no circumstances in which it would pay to adopt it. Nevertheless we shall retain it in this simplified example as the additional exercise will be useful while the additional calculation will be slight.

Given no information other than in Table VII.1 we could employ either of two standard methods to produce a decision: a *maximin* procedure and a *minimax* procedure. We shall illustrate the former in the remainder of the present chapter, and the latter in the following chapter.

3 *The maximin procedure.* If he looks along the first row of Table VII.1 showing the net revenues, $130,000 and $400,000, corresponding to each of the two possible alternative states of nature, b_1 and b_2, when the decision-maker chooses option a_1, it will be realized that the worst that can happen is the occurrence of b_1, yielding a revenue of only $130,000. Assuming that the decision-maker is a conservative person, he will want to compare this worst result, or minimal net revenue, that he can obtain from choosing a_1 with those minima he might obtain if instead he adopts the a_2 or a_3 option. Now the choice of a_2 can realize a net yield of either 140,000 or 260,000 according as b_1 or b_2 occurs respectively. He can then be sure of at least 140,000. Similarly if he chooses option a_3 he can be sure of obtaining at least 80,000. These three row minima, 130,000 for a_1, 140,000 for a_2, and 80,000 for a_3 are all shown in the third column of Table VII.2— which is the same as Table VII.1 except for the addition of two columns.

TABLE VII.2

	b_1	b_2	Row minima	Maximin (maximum of row minima)
	$	$	$	$
a_1	130,000	400,000	130,000	
a_2	140,000	260,000	140,000	140,000
a_3	80,000	90,000	80,000	

Down this third column he reads off the worst possible outcome corresponding to each option. If he chooses a_1, he can be sure of not getting less than 130,000. If he chooses a_2, he can be sure of not getting less than 140,000. If he chooses a_3, he can be sure of not getting less than 80,000. It will then occur to him that if he chooses any option *other than* a_2 he might get less than 140,000; for example, if having chosen a_1, b_1 occurs, he will receive only 130,000, whereas if he chooses a_3 he will receive only 80,000 or 90,000 according as event b_1 or event b_2 occurs. The largest net revenue he can be *sure* of obtaining is, then, $140,000. The maximin principle therefore requires that he choose option a_2 (releasing two-thirds of the reservoir), and assure himself of no less than 140,000.

The guiding idea has been to pick out the maximum figure from column three, which column contains the minimum possible net revenues corresponding to each option. Hence the figure chosen—140,000 in column four of Table VII.2—is spoken of as the *Maximin*.

4 One feature of the above example is that capital costs are taken to be constant for each of the alternative options. This enables us to compare directly the net revenues—annual revenues *less* annual loss— in each of the first two columns. If we assume instead that revenues are fixed and that costs alone vary according to the decision made and the event which takes place, we can go through the same sort of exercise.

An example would be the installation of a boiler in a works.[2] Again we can suppose three options: a_1, installing a coal-fired boiler, a_2, installing an oil-fired boiler, or a_3, installing a dual boiler, one that could be switched from using coal to using oil, and vice versa, at negligible cost. Three possible occurrences are to be considered: b_1, coal prices rise relative to oil prices over the next twenty years by an average of 25 per cent; b_2, the reverse of this; and b_3, the relative prices of the two fuels remain on the average unchanged.

The outcomes of the relevant calculations are summarized in Table VII.3, the figures being the present discounted values (in thousands of dollars) of the streams of future costs associated with each option for each of the three possible outcomes.

By convention costs are to be regarded as *negative* revenues, so the figures in Table VII.3 are all negative. Looking along the a_1 row the worst outcome is $-13 \cdot 0$. If a_1 is chosen and b_1 should occur, the cost

TABLE VII.3

	b_1	b_2	b_3	Row Minimum	Maximin
a_1	$-13 \cdot 0$	$-12 \cdot 0$	$-12 \cdot 0$	$-13 \cdot 0$	
a_2	$-11 \cdot 3$	$-12 \cdot 5$	$-11 \cdot 3$	$-12 \cdot 5$	$-12 \cdot 5$
a_3	$-12 \cdot 8$	$-12 \cdot 8$	$-12 \cdot 8$	$-12 \cdot 8$	

[2] This example has been adapted from that given in Moore (1968).

would be 13. (13 is the highest absolute figure in the row but, seen as a negative revenue and considered algebraically, -13 is less than -12. Thus -13 is the lowest figure in the row.) The largest costs, or the smallest gains, corresponding to options a_2 and a_3 are, respectively, -12.5 and -12.8, which figures are entered in the fourth column. Of these row minima, the maximum (or least cost) is -12.5 corresponding to option a_2 which, on the maximum principle, would be the one to be chosen. Having chosen a_2, we can be sure that the cost to which the firm can be subjected cannot exceed 12.5. this cost would be incurred if event b_2 took place. If, however, event b_1 or b_3 occurred the cost would be only 11.3.

Chapter 51

GAME THEORY (II)

1 There is one implication of this maximin principle that is obviously unsatisfactory. It seeks security above all, and is therefore highly conservative. In Table VII.1, for instance, we are led by it to choose a_2 rather than a_1 simply because in choosing a_2 we can be sure of obtaining at least \$140,000 whereas if we choose a_1 we can be sure of obtaining at least \$130,000. If we feel pretty certain of getting the least in all cases, we should indeed be wise to choose that least which is largest. And the least for a_2 is \$10,000 larger than that for a_1. But if it so happens that the event b_2 does take place, our choice of a_2 yields us only \$260,000, whereas had we instead chosen option a_1 event b_2 would yield as much as \$400,000. In other words, if b_2 takes place after all, we shall forgo an extra gain of \$140,000 (\$400,000 *minus* \$260,000). The cost of playing safe— if ensuring \$10,000 more if the worst should happen—is that of losing the opportunity of gaining \$140,000 more if the best should happen.

2 We can 'cook up' another set of figures for this example, those in Table VII.4 below, in order to bring out this defect even more sharply.

TABLE VII.4

	b_1	b_2	Row Minimum	Maximin
a_1	13	5,000	13	
a_2	14	15	14	14

The row minima for options a_1 and a_2 are shown, in the third column, to be 13 and 14 respectively. On the maximin principle, the a_2 option is to be chosen as that which guarantees a net receipt of no less than 14—but it is clear that the most that can be gained from choosing option a_2 is only 15. By comparing this choice with the

371

rejected option a_1, we cannot but realize that we are sacrificing the chance of gaining 5,000 in order to increase our guaranteed minimum receipts from 13 to 14. With outcomes such as those in the columns of Table VII.4 it is hard to think of anyone employing the maximin method and choosing a_2. For he will be aware that if event b_2 turns up, he will receive 15 only, whereas if he had instead chosen a_1 he would receive 5,000: he becomes aware then that by choosing a_2 (so as to ensure that if the worst happens he will receive one more than if, instead, he chooses a_1) he lays himself open to a potential loss of 4,985 (5,000 *minus* 15) should the best, b_2, occur.

A less conservative person would not want to guide his choice by the maximin principle even if the figures were less enticing than those in Table VII.4. Indeed, if he were at all enterprising, and had an eye open for the larger gains that are possible, he would adopt something like the reverse of the maximin principle. What he would want to avoid is the possibility of an outcome which will make him regret his choice. Since his regret will increase with the size of the loss of possible gain —4,985, in the above example, if he chooses a_2—he will adopt the principle of minimizing his regret. Hence, the alternative *minimax-regret* procedure suggested by economists.

3 *The minimax procedure.* We can illustrate this procedure by constructing Table VII.5 below using the primary data given in Table VII.1. Suppose a flood occurs, which is to say that the b_1 event takes place, the initial choice of option a_2 would have secured for the b_1 event the largest net revenue of 140,000. If, on the other hand, a_1 had been chosen, the net revenue would have been 130,000; or 10,000 less than could have been got had we chosen a_2. We therefore put a 10,000 in the cell opposite a_1 and below b_1 in Table VII.5. This 10,000 entry is to be interpreted as follows: if b_1 occurs, the prior choice of option a_2 yields the largest receipt, 140,000. By choosing some other option, say a_1, we receive only 130,000, a *potential loss* of 10,000. Below b_1 and opposite a_3, however, we place the figure 60,000 since, if b_1 occurs, our prior choice of a_3 would yield 80,000—a potential loss of 60,000 (140,000 *minus* 80,000) compared with the largest yield of 140,000 that would come from having chosen a_2. Opposite a_2 itself we obviously put a zero, as there is no potential loss from having chosen a_2 if event b_1 occurs.

We now fill the cells down the second column. The highest net

372

revenue if event b_2 occurs is 400,000 corresponding to the choice of option a_1: hence a zero opposite a_1 and below b_2. If a_2 instead is chosen only 260,000 can be collected—a potential loss of 140,000 (400,000 *minus* 260,000) is involved. Below b_2 and opposite a_2, therefore, we place the figure 140,000. If, finally, a_3 is chosen, only 90,000 can be collected, involving a potential loss of 310,000 (400,000 *minus* 90,000). Below b_2 and opposite a_3 we therefore place the figure 310,000.

TABLE VII.5

	b_1	b_2	Row Maxima (of potential losses)	Minimax (minimum of row maxima)
a_1	10,000	0	10,000	10,000
a_2	0	140,000	140,000	
a_3	60,000	310,000	310,000	

Since the derived figures in the first two columns are now to be regarded as potential losses, row a_3 is again dominated by the other rows. Its potential losses for either event, b_1 or b_2, are larger than those of any other row. The standard computational procedure would be to eliminate a_3 before calculating the figures for the Row Maxima column. But, again, in so simple an example, it adds to the interest while causing no difficulty.

As it is regret-at-potential-losses we now seek to minimize, we glance along the rows and pick out the largest potential loss that could arise from each option in turn. The largest figure along the a_1 row is 10,000. It is therefore placed opposite a_1 under the third column containing the row maxima. For the a_2 row the largest potential loss figure is 140,000, and it is entered accordingly opposite a_2 and in the third column. For the a_3 row the largest potential loss figure is 310,000 and this is shown opposite a_3 in the third column.

Of these largest potential losses from choosing a_1, a_2 or a_3, the decision-maker chooses the smallest, which is 10,000 corresponding to option a_1. Accordingly the figure of 10,000 is entered in the fourth column of Table VII.5. By choosing option a_1 he can be sure of one thing; that whichever event occurs, his potential loss—that is, the additional gain he might, in that event, have obtained had he instead selected one of the other options—can be no greater than 10,000. For clearly, if he chooses instead a_2, the potential loss he may suffer is 140,000. While if he chooses a_3 the potential loss he may suffer is 310,000.[1]

As a further illustration of the minimax-regret method, Table VII.6 below is constructed from the primary data given in Table VII.3. For the first column, below b_1 the best choice is a_2, since it would entail the least cost 11·3. If option a_1 were chosen instead, the cost would be 13, and therefore the loss of potential saving would be 1·7 (13 *minus* 11·3). Similarly, if a_3 were chosen the cost would be 12·8, and the loss of potential saving 1·5 (12·8 *minus* 11·3). The figures in the next two columns are obtained in the same way. In the fourth column we put the row maxima. From these the smallest potential loss, 0·5 corresponding to option a_2, is chosen and entered in the fifth column.

TABLE VII.6

	b_1	b_2	b_3	Row Maxima	Minimax
a_1	1·7	0	0·7	1·7	
a_2	0	0·5	0	0·5	0·5
a_3	1·5	0·8	1·5	1·5	

4 Not surprisingly perhaps, the more obvious defect of this minimax method is the opposite of that found in the maximin. The conservatism of the maximin, it will be recalled, is such that cases can arise in which large potential gains are sacrificed for very little extra security. In order to skirt this contingency, the so-called minimax-regret method courts

---

[1] This 'minimax-regret', or 'minimax-risk' (of loss), principle, as it is sometimes called, is really a misnomer. The figures for losses in Table VII.5 are given without sign. But if we follow the convention of treating losses as negative signs we should write all the figures in Table VII.5 with a minus sign. For instance, if a_3 is chosen and b_1 occurs, the potential *gain* is 80,000 *minus* 140,000 or −60,000.

The largest potential loss in each row of Table VII.5 should then really be expressed as a *negative* figure: −10,000 for a_1, −140,000 for a_2, −310,000 for a_3. These negative figures can then be regarded as the lowest or minimal row gains. Of these (algebraic) row minima we choose the (algebraic) maximum; namely −10,000 corresponding to option a_1.

The formal procedure is in fact no different from that used in connection with Table VII.3, where the negative items happen to refer to costs.

In effect then the same *maximin* procedure as before is employed, with the important difference that the row minima figures we are now maximizing refer to (negative) *potential* gains (as compared with other options) instead of *actual* gains.

However, we shall here follow the convention of using positive figures to refer to potential losses, and of describing the procedure as 'minimaxing-regret'.

the opposite danger. For cases can arise in which the application of this more enterprising minimax method will effectively jettison the chance of a good gain for the hope of getting a bit more.

The net revenue figures in Table VII.7 below are chosen to bring out this defect of the minimax regret procedure.

TABLE VII.7

	b_1	b_2	b_3	b_4
a_1	300	300	300	300
a_2	120	500	120	120

Application of the maximum principle would select option a_1 so assuring a receipt of 300. Table VII.8 below, however, uses the data in Table VII.7 to derive corresponding figures in each cell for potential losses.

TABLE VI.8

	b_1	b_2	b_3	b_4	Row Maxima	Minimax
a_1	0	200	0	0	200	
a_2	180	0	180	180	180	180

In the concern (should event b_2 occur) *not* to regret the loss of 200, the person employing the minimax-regret principle incurs instead the risk of the somewhat smaller potential loss of 180 should any of the other three events, b_1, b_3, b_4, occur. Put more directly, his choice of a_2 ensures that if event b_2 occurs he will obtain 500 rather than the 300 he would obtain by choosing a_1. If, however, either b_1, b_2 or b_4 occurs, he will collect only 120 rather than the 300 he would obtain by choosing a_1.

5   A minor characteristic—sometimes regarded as a defect—arising from the use of the minimax method is that if one of the rejected options is withdrawn, then that option which had been chosen before its withdrawal might not be the option chosen by this method in the new circumstances. This possibility is illustrated by using the figures in Table VII.9 below, which happen to be the same as those used in Table VII.1 except for the last line.

TABLE VII.9

	b_1	b_2
a_1	130,000	400,000
a_2	140,000	260,000
a_3	300,000	200,000

On the maximin method a_3 would be chosen. Using the minimax procedure, however, we first derive from Table VII.9 the potential loss figures which appear in Table VII.10 below, and from the row maxima column, we choose the lowest figure, namely 160,000 corresponding to option a_2.

TABLE VII.10

	b_1	b_2	Row Maxima	Minimax
a_1	170,000	0	170,000	
a_2	160,000	140,000	160,000	160,000
a_3	0	200,000	200,000	

Now if, in Table VII.9, option a_1 were withdrawn, the resulting potential loss figures for the remaining options, a_2 and a_3, are given in Table VII.11. The row maxima are now 160,000 and 60,000 for a_2 and a_3 respectively. Therefore on the minimax procedure, a_3 becomes the chosen option.

TABLE VII.11

	b_1	b_2	Row Maxima	Minimax
a_2	160,000	0	160,000	
a_3	0	60,000	60,000	60,000

If, on the other hand, option a_3 were to be withdrawn from Table VII.9, the potential loss figures for the remaining options, a_1 and a_2, are those given in Table VII.12. The row maxima corresponding to a_1 and a_2 are now 10,000 and 140,000, so that on this principle the a_1 is chosen.

TABLE VII.12

	b_1	b_2	Row Maxima	Minimax
a_1	10,000	0	10,000	10,000
a_2	0	140,000	140,000	

There is, however, nothing paradoxical about such results. From the standpoint of the minimax-regret principle, the initially rejected options that are removed are indeed relevant to the decision. Thus, in withdrawing option a_1, the yield of 400,000 if event b_2 occurs is no longer available to us. Thus when a_1 is no longer available the potential loss from choosing a_3 falls from 200,000 (when a_1 was available) to only 60,000, as shown in Table VII.11.

Similarly if option a_3 alone is withdrawn, leaving us with a_1 and a_2, the 300,000 outcome if b_1 occurs is no longer available to us. The potential loss from choosing option a_1 if b_1 occurs falls therefore from 170,000 (when a_3 was available) to only 10,000 (when a_3 is no longer available), as a result of which the a_1 option is then chosen, as indicated in Table VII.12.

We need not therefore regard this feature of the minimax procedure as a defect of the method. Rather we should confine our criticism to that already indicated in the preceding section as illustrated by Tables VII.7 and VII.8, in which the chance of some minimum gain is put at risk in the hope of securing a bit more.

6 In sum, it would appear that the choice of maximin or minimax-regret would not be adopted in advance of, and independently of, the primary data by any person unless he were cautious to a fault (in which case he would always apply the maximin principle) or recklessly opportunistic or, more precisely, fearful of losing potential gains (in which case he would always apply the minimax-regret principle).

One must conclude that even where conditions are such that these methods can be applied, the fact alone that the choice of whether to use maximin or minimax-regret will depend upon the person and upon the data makes the application of game theory techniques somewhat unsatisfactory. Since subjective judgement enters into the choice of whether to use maximin or minimax-regret, competent economists inspecting the same data can come up with different decisions.

Chapter 52

SIMPLE PROBABILITY IN DECISION MAKING

1 The techniques illustrated in the preceding two chapters are based on the assumption that there is no knowledge at all available that could throw any light on the likelihood of each of the alternative events, b_1, b_2, b_3, occurring over the period in question. In the complete absence of such knowledge we can no more suppose that b_1 is as likely to occur as b_2 than we can suppose that b_1 is more (or less) likely to occur. We can say no more of the events in question than that each is *possible*. Once a suspicion about the greater likelihood of one, or more, of the possible events occurring begins to form, the simple game-theory method may require modification. In general, the more information about likelihoods we can obtain the more agreement about the best decision we can hope to secure. If, from years of keeping records about floods, we could attach probabilities to each of the possible outcomes in our first example, our procedure would be to include those probabilities as weights in working out a solution.

2 Suppose that event b_1 (flood) can be expected with a probability of p_1, say $\frac{3}{5}$, and event b_2 (no flood) therefore with a probability p_2 of $(1-p_1)$, or $\frac{2}{5}$, we make our calculations in a way to be illustrated by reference to Table VII.13 below.

TABLE VII.13

	$b_1\ (p_1=\frac{3}{5})$	$b_2(p_2=\frac{2}{5})$	Weighted average	Largest weighted average
a_1	$130{,}000 \times \frac{3}{5}$	$400{,}000 \times \frac{2}{5}$	238,000	238,000
a_2	$140{,}000 \times \frac{3}{5}$	$260{,}000 \times \frac{2}{5}$	188,000	
a_3	$80{,}000 \times \frac{3}{5}$	$90{,}000 \times \frac{2}{5}$	84,000	

If option a_1 is chosen, each of the outcomes—130,000 and 400,000—corresponding to the possible events, b_1 and b_2 respectively, is multiplied by the probability of the occurrence of the event, $\frac{3}{5}$ and $\frac{2}{5}$. The weighted average, or mathematical expectation, of the gains from choosing a_1 is entered in the third column, as also is the weighted average of gains from choosing a_2 and a_3. The largest weighted average is obviously 238,000 arising from the choice of option a_1, which can be regarded in the circumstances as the proper decision.

Now if this figure of 238,000 could be regarded as the anticipated value of net revenue from choosing a_1, in the sense that there is a stronger likelihood of a net revenue 238,000 occurring when a_1 is chosen than of any other single value, we might have less hesitation in opting for a₁ rather than a_2 or a_3. But this figure of 238,000 for a_1 can be regarded as the expected value only in the conventional statistical sense; that is to say, if it were possible to repeat this experiment year after year for, say, the next hundred years or so then—provided that the relevant climatic conditions remain unaltered—the *average* net revenue from choosing a_1, taken over the hundred years, would be close to 238,000. For roughly $\frac{3}{5}$ of the century, or for roughly sixty out of the hundred years, event b_1 would occur, and for the remaining years event b_2 would occur.

It is clear, then, that if we are thinking in terms of many years ahead, we can (if relevant conditions are not expected to change very much) expect to come close to the (undiscounted) average of 238,000 by repeatedly opting for a_1. If, on the other hand, we are interested in the outcome next year alone we obviously cannot expect a net revenue of 238,000 from choosing a_1. For in one year only one event will occur. If b_1 occurs the net revenue will be 130,000. If, instead, b_2 occurs the net revenue will be 400,000. All we can say is that, on the basis of past evidence, there is more chance of b_1 occurring than b_2. And the higher the probability of b_1's occurring the more we are disposed to expect it and to have our decision governed by the thought of its occurrence.

If, to take more extreme probabilities, we discovered from the records that floods occur, on the average, in nine years out of ten, we should be justified in expecting a flood next year, and in being surprised if it did not occur. The net revenue we can most reasonably expect if we choose a_1 is therefore 130,000. By the same logic, the net revenue we should be inclined to expect by choosing option a_2 is 140,000. This being so, we might conclude that the rational thing is to choose a_2. But once we have probabilities attached to the various events it would *not* be very sensible to focus our expectations on the event with the highest probability and ignore the possibility of the other events occurring. Thus whether the probability of event b_1 occurring is $\frac{3}{5}$ or $\frac{9}{10}$, the decision-maker is not completely indifferent to the outcome arising from event b_2—unless that outcome is the same, say 200,000 whatever option is chosen. The greater the gain in choosing a_1 (given that b_2 occurs) compared with that in choosing a_2, the more weight he will give to the a_1 option. To illustrate with extreme figures; if choice of a_1 would entail an outcome of 1,000,000 if event b_2 occurred whereas the choice of a_2 entailed an outcome of zero for the same event, the nine chances out of ten that b_1 would occur— conferring an additional 10,000 if a_2 were chosen rather than a_1— would hardly be likely to prevail against the thought that if, despite its slim chance, b_2 did occur a net gain of 1,000,000 would be collected.

3   We may conclude tentatively that dependable probabilities will be taken into account by the decision-maker in such cases; moreover, that the use of these probabilities as weights in the method indicated above, by reference to Table VII.13, would be acceptable to many as a rough general rule. By choosing an option on the basis of a weighted average of events, rather than on the basis of a single most likely event, we are in effect refusing to neglect the possible impact of the less likely event(s) on our decision, and doing so in a systematic and conventional manner.

Chapter 53

CONDITIONAL PROBABILITY IN DECISION MAKING

1 Records covering many years can provide information *additional to* the probability of each of a number of alternative events occurring such as b_1 and b_2. For instance, in addition to discovering that over, say, a hundred years event b_1 (flood) occurred in sixty out of a hundred years, that is with a frequency of $\frac{3}{5}$, and event b_2 (no flood) therefore with a frequency of $\frac{2}{5}$, the records may reveal the following information: (1) prior to event b_1, a period of several weeks of cloudy weather—a condition we refer to as z_1—was observed in half the number of b_1 events; (2) prior to event b_1, a period of several weeks of mixed weather—referred to as z_2—was observed in one-third of the number of b_1 events; (3) prior to event b_1, a period of several weeks of clear weather—say z_3—was observed in one-sixth of the number of b_1 events.

The same sort of information will be available for event b_2 which, it is assumed, is completely independent of b_1. Let us suppose, therefore, that z_1 (several weeks of cloudy weather) was observed prior to one-sixth of the number of b_2 (no flood) events; that z_2 (several weeks of mixed weather) was observed prior to one-third of the number of b_2 events; and that z_3 (several weeks of clear weather) was observed prior to one-half of the number of b_2 events. If we can assume that basic climatic and other relevant conditions will remain much the same, we can treat these frequencies as probabilities. And if so, we can get better results than those reached by adopting what are called 'pure' strategies; that is, by adopting *either* option a_1 or a_2 or a_3. These better results are attained by recourse to 'mixed' strategies, which are no more than a *combination* of pure options—adopting a_1 a fraction of the time, a_2 another fraction of the time, and a_3 the remainder of the time.

2 Thus, instead of the choice between the three simple options, a_1, a_2

and a_3, let the reader think of a larger number of quite arbitrary mixed strategies; call them $s_1, s_2, s_3, \ldots, s_n$. For example, strategy s_1 might require that if z_1 is observed then a_1 is to be chosen; if z_2 occurs a_2 is to be chosen; if z_3 occurs a_3 is to be chosen. Strategy s_2 might be as follows: if z_1 occurs choose a_1; if z_2 occurs choose a_2, while if z_3 occurs choose a_2 again. Strategy s_3 might be, if either z_1 or z_2 or z_3 occurs choose a_2, and so on.

Now suppose event b_1 were to take place, we should, as indicated above, expect to observe weather condition z_1 with a probability of $\frac{1}{2}$, z_2 with a probability of $\frac{1}{3}$, and z_3 with a probability of $\frac{1}{6}$. The expected or average outcome over a period of time from adopting, say, strategy s_1 (in the event that b_1 occurs) is got by weighting each of the net revenues attaching to the options designated by strategy s_1 by the probabilities of the z's. Thus, strategy s_1 prescribes that we select option a_1 (with outcome 130 in case of event b_1) should z_1 occur, which it does with a probability of $\frac{1}{2}$. The first component of strategy s_1, in that event, is $\frac{1}{2} \times 130$. The second component of strategy s_1 requires we select a_2 (with outcome 140 for event b_1) should z_2 occur, which it does with a probability of $\frac{1}{3}$. Consequently the second component of strategy s_1 is equal to $\frac{1}{3} \times 140$. Similarly, the third component of strategy s_1 prescribes option a_3 (with outcome of 80 for b_1) should z_3 occur, which it does with a probability of $\frac{1}{6}$. Hence it is equal to $\frac{1}{6} \times 80$.

Given event b_1 then, the expected value of revenue from employing strategy s_1 is equal to

$$(\tfrac{1}{2} \times 130) + (\tfrac{1}{3} \times 140) + (\tfrac{1}{6} \times 80) = 125.$$

Given the same b_1 event, we could work out the expected value of the revenue from employing strategy s_2. The same steps in the calculation give it as

$$(\tfrac{1}{2} \times 130) + (\tfrac{1}{3} \times 140) + (\tfrac{1}{6} \times 140) = 136.$$

Given the same b_1 event again, the employment of strategy s_3 will realize an expected value equal to

$$(\tfrac{1}{2} \times 140) + (\tfrac{1}{3} \times 140) + (\tfrac{1}{6} \times 140) = 140.$$

And so we could go on calculating expected revenues, in the event b_1 takes place, for all the other strategies.

If, instead, event b_2 occurred then the relevant probabilities of z_1, z_2 and z_3, would be $\frac{1}{6}, \frac{1}{3}$ and $\frac{1}{2}$ respectively. And employing the original

s_1 strategy would, therefore, yield an expected value of revenue equal to

$$(\tfrac{1}{6} \times 400) + (\tfrac{1}{3} \times 200) + (\tfrac{1}{2} \times 90) = 199.$$

Employing strategy s_2, however, would yield an expected value of net revenue equal to

$$(\tfrac{1}{6} \times 400) + (\tfrac{1}{3} \times 260) + (\tfrac{1}{2} \times 260) = 284.$$

While recourse to strategy s_3 would yield an expected value of revenue equal to

$$(\tfrac{1}{6} \times 260) + (\tfrac{1}{3} \times 260) + (\tfrac{1}{2} \times 260) = 260.$$

TABLE VII.14

(in thousand dollars per annum)

	b_1	b_2
s_1	125	199
s_2	136	284
s_3	140	260
.	.	.
.	.	.
s_n	140	260

These results can be displayed in Table VII.14 for all n possible strategies, though in fact only the first three strategies and the last strategy are represented there. Some strategies are likely to be dominated by others and would not stay in the Table. After eliminating all the dominated strategies, we are left with a choice of mixed strategies which we could renumber $S_1, S_3, \ldots, S_m$.

3   What is the advantage of all this? On the surface of things it would appear to offer a larger range of choices.[1] Granted that the use of these strategies offers us more choice, how do we go about selecting the best strategy?

In fact we are 'back to square one'—*except* that there are apparently

---

[1] We can, of course, include the pure strategies (the choice of option a_1 alone, a_2 alone, or a_3 alone) among these mixed strategies. The choice of a_1 alone might be numbered strategy S_8, with a_1 being chosen irrespective of the occurrence of z_1, z_2 and z_3, so yielding 130 for b_1, and 400 for b_2 as in Table VII.13. The choice of a_2 alone would enter, say, as strategy s_9 with a_2 being chosen regardless of the occurrence of z_1, z_2 and z_3, so yielding 140 for b_1 and 260 for b_2 as in Table VII.13.

many more choices of strategy than the initial three options. With the data given by Table VII.14, that is, we could employ the maximin method, or the minimax-regret method, or some other method in order to select one of these new strategies. Indeed, where we can attach probabilities also to events b_1 and b_2, we can employ the method outlined in the preceding chapter: we can, that is, calculate the weighted average net revenue for each of the listed strategies, and choose that yielding the highest revenue.

Again, however, if we are concerned with the outcome over the next one or two years only, the method outlined is of much less use than if, instead, we can adopt the strategy for a largish number of years. Consider, for instance, the calculated net revenue of 125 that arises from employing strategy s_1 in the event that b_1 takes place. True, if b_1 is to occur, we shall observe z_1 with a probability of $\frac{1}{2}$, z_2 with a probability of $\frac{1}{3}$, and z_3 with a probability of $\frac{1}{6}$. But in responding to the z's according to the adopted strategy, here s_1, we cannot hope to realize in this same year a revenue of 125. For in the one year *either z_1, or z_2, or z_3*, is observed and, therefore, according to the strategy chosen, *either a_1, or a_2, or a_3*, is adopted. The net revenue in that event is *either* 130, *or* 140, *or* 80—*not* 125 however, which is but an average figure to which the revenues will converge only if, whenever b_1 occurs (which is about $\frac{3}{5}$ of the total number of years), we *continue to* use strategy s_1. Similar remarks apply to the figure of 199. It follows that if, say, over the next hundred years event b_1 could be expected to occur $\frac{3}{5}$ of the time and event b_2 the remaining $\frac{2}{5}$ of the time, the repeated use of strategy s_1 could be expected to give a series of (undiscounted) revenues that would average about $(\frac{3}{5} \times 125) + (\frac{3}{5} \times 199)$, or 155. If, over the same period s_2 instead were repeatedly employed, the average (undiscounted) revenue to expect would be $(\frac{3}{5} \times 136) + (\frac{2}{5} \times 284)$, or 196. We could work out the (undiscounted) average revenues for all the mixed strategies listed, and expect in general that at least one such strategy would produce a weighted average about the highest (238) for the pure strategy which makes no use of the z's.[2]

4 We may conclude that the information about such indicators as the

---

[2] Given an appropriate rate of discount, we could, of course, calculate the present discounted value of any future net revenue, and produce a strategy that would yield a highest weighted average *discounted* net revenue.

z's can be of use in improving the decision process through mixed strategies only when events over a large number of years or over a large number of similar projects are anticipated. If, for example, a reservoir is to be used under the same environmental conditions for many years to come, or if a large number of similar reservoirs are to be constructed, there can be advantages in using information provided by the z's in order to produce a variety of mixed strategies. Having chosen the maximum-yielding strategy, it has to be employed repeatedly over the future in the first case, or applied to each of the many reservoirs in the second case. If, however, what matters is the revenue for only one or two years and/or for only one or two reservoirs; or if, alternatively, environmental conditions cannot be expected to remain unchanged (so that one cannot reasonably attach probabilities to the events b_1, b_2, or to the indicators z_1, z_2, z_3), the method of contingent probabilities outlined above is of little practical use.

Chapter 54

HOW PRACTICAL ARE GAME THEORY DECISION TECHNIQUES?

1 The final stage of a typical cost-benefit study requires that we evaluate a stream of net benefits,

$$(B_1 - K_1), (B_2 - K_2), ..., (B_n - K_n)$$

in which the B's, or benefits, and the K's, or costs, are uncertain, and, indeed, increase in uncertainty the further they are from the present.

The difficulties we encounter in the attempt to apply game theory principles may be illustrated by recourse to a simple example in which the net benefits of a project are spread over four years as follows: −100, 30, 80, 50. The −100 figure indicates a net capital outlay of 100 in the first year, and the remaining figures are net benefits in successive years. The penumbra of uncertainty surrounding each of these figures might suggest, for example, that for the −100 figure we substitute a *range* −95 to −105; for the figure of 30, a range 25 to 35, and so on. For practical purposes, however, we would not use a continuous range, only discrete figures. The range −95 to −105 could, for instance, be split into three possible outcomes, −95, −100, and −105. The range 25 to 35 could also be split into three outcomes, or perhaps five, say, 25, 38, 30, 32 and 35. Similarly for the other two figures. If we take these arbitrarily chosen figures from the range of net benefits in any period to be independent of the arbitrarily chosen figures from the range of any other period's net benefits, then a combination that included one of the possible net-benefit outcomes from each of the four periods—say −95 from the first period, 32 from the second, 75 from the third, and 50 from the fourth—would add up to the outcome of a single event. There are obviously as many events as

386

there are combinations of such possible outcomes for the four-year period.[1]

2   The uncertainty about the net-benefit figures in each period can, however, be attributed instead to the uncertainty about future *price-*movements of both the inputs and outputs associated with the project. It is true that the price-movements themselves depend upon a number of future possible events, such as technical innovations, changes in domestic and foreign policies, and alterations in the conditions of demand and supply. But for each combination of such possible events there will correspond a range of possible prices for both the inputs and outputs in question. We may therefore express the uncertainty about all future events in each period by reference to some price-range of each of the inputs and outputs.

Suppose that in the A_1 investment project, giving rise to a four-year stream of net benefits (including the initial year's capital outlay), there are the prices of only four items to be anticipated; that of homogeneous labour, that of homogeneous material, that of homogeneous machinery, and that of homogeneous output. Since prices do become more uncertain as we move into the future, the range of possible prices becomes wider and, as it becomes wider, it may be split into a larger number of possible prices. In token of this consideration we shall divide the price-range of each item into three alternative prices for the first period, but into five alternative prices for the second, third, and fourth periods. In each of the four periods there will be a larger number of possible net benefits, each possible net benefit corresponding to a different combination of the prices of each of the above-mentioned four items. Thus, for the first period, the three alternative prices for each of these four items will generate 3^4, or 81, possible outcomes, each of such outcomes being an alternative net benefit in the first period. For the second period, the five different prices for each of the four items will generate 5^4, or 625, possible outcomes, each being an alternative net benefit. Similarly, there will be 625 possible net benefits for each of the two remaining periods.

Matching any one of the 81 alternative net benefits in the first period with any one of the 625 possible benefits from each of the other three

---

[1] It is hardly necessary to say that in adding these four figures, those for the second, third, and fourth periods have to be discounted at the relevant rate.

periods so as to produce a particular permutation of four successive benefits, provides us with (in the terminology of game theory) a single event, b_1. Since there are 81 different net-benefit outcomes in the first period, and 625 different net-benefit outcomes in each of the three remaining periods, the total number of different events which are possible is given by 81×625^3, or close to 20 billion different events.

3 If we now introduce another investment option A_2, which also yields a stream of possible net benefits over four years and uses the same inputs and outputs, we have to calculate figures for roughly another 20 billion events. If, on the other hand, the A_2 stream covers more periods than the A_1 stream, or if there are additional inputs or outputs to contend with, we shall have to increase the number of events. Each of these additional events will carry a net-benefit figure for A_2, positive, zero or negative. Corresponding to these additional events for A_2 there will be zeros for A_1. There may, however, be inputs or outputs in the A_2 investment option that replace those in the A_1 option; for example, steel may be the only material used in the A_1 investment option, and aluminium the only material used in the A_2 option. In that case there will be a number of b's that are strictly relevant only to A_1 and a number that are strictly relevant only to A_2. Corresponding to those events that are strictly relevant to A_1 there will be net revenues (positive, zero, or negative) for the A_1 option, and zeros for the A_2 option, and vice versa.

One has but to reflect (a) that the price-range of any important item can be split into more than three or five possible prices, (b) that the number of important items to be bought or sold over the lifetime of a project can easily exceed four, (c) that the number of periods of any of the investment streams under comparison can exceed four and, indeed, is often likely to exceed ten, (d) that there are frequently more than two investment options to compare, to realize that the number of possible events, or outcomes, can run into billions of billions. Attempts to deal with the uncertainty aspects of cost-benefit studies in this game-theory fashion is, therefore, hardly a practical proposition even with the most advanced computers.

When it is further recalled that, as distinct from simple game-theory techniques, not only is the number of distinct events *not* given to us exogenously (as indicated above, it is generated from alternative prices chosen arbitrarily from guesses about the likely range), but also that not all events are equally likely, inasmuch as not all the alternative prices are equally likely, it is not surprising that in any practical evaluation of investment projects no recourse is had to the formal apparata of game theory.

Chapter 55

THE UTILITY APPROACH

1 Up to the present, net revenues or costs have been expressed in money terms, though they could just as well have been expressed in 'real' terms by using a price-index as deflator. Whether in money or in 'real' terms, however, the absolute or proportional differences between the figures may not be a good index of the sense of gain or loss to the decision-maker.

2 A coin is tossed and if it comes down heads $10 is paid to me, while if it comes down tails I have to pay $10. This sort of gamble would be called an actuarially fair gamble if it were believed that an unbiased coin would have an equal chance of coming down heads as of coming down tails. In fact if the coin were tossed many hundreds of times, heads would appear about half the number of times, and at the end of the game I would be no better or worse off—or nearly so.

It might be thought then that, if I am indifferent to the joys of gambling, I could have no objection to taking part in an actuarially fair gamble. But if the coin is to be tossed only a few times—in the limiting case, say, once only—I may demur. To be more accurate, my willingness to gamble in this way may be observed to diminish the larger is the bet. If it is no more than $10, I may have no objection. If the bet is $10,000 I will almost certainly not agree to a fair gamble.

Maintaining the fiction that I derive no pleasure from the act of gambling, the reluctance to participate in a fair gamble for large stakes is not irrational. For I would not feel the gain of $10,000 as keenly as I would feel the loss of $10,000. Put more formally, the utility added by $10,000 is for me smaller than the amount of utility lost when I lose $10,000. This inference would follow from the assumption that my income is subject to diminishing marginal utility.

Indeed, for any consistent person an ideal experiment can be planned. The truthful answers to the questions asked would enable us to draw a curve relating total number of utils to 'real' income. If we are interested, as we are here, only in *differences* in utility corresponding to differences in income, it is only the shape of this utility curve that matters, not the particular scale or origin we adopt.

3 To illustrate, let us suppose the experiment just mentioned has been performed and we have emerged with the utility curve, *UU*, shown in Figure VII.1. On the vertical axis the utility index marked (a):1 util, 2 utils, 3 utils, and so on, could be changed to (b):10 utils, 20 utils, 30 utils, respectively, or for that matter to (c): 200 utils, 400 utils, 600 utils respectively, without in any way altering the shape of the utility curve, *UU*. Again, if the origin were changed from zero, as shown in Figure VII.1, to some other number, say 50, then instead of (a) above we should read off 51 utils, 52 utils, 53 utils; instead of (b), we should read off 60 utils, 70 utils, 80 utils; or instead of (c), we should read off 250 utils, 450 utils, 650 utils. Thus, neither of these alterations—neither those of scale nor those of origin—will change the shape of the *UU* curve in Figure VII.1. In the jargon, the utility function is determined up to a linear transformation.

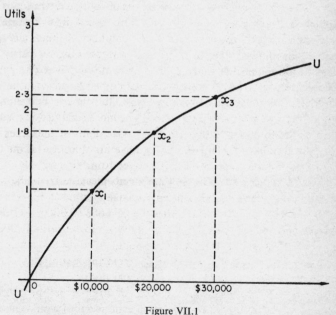

Figure VII.1

391

More specifically, suppose we moved from point x_2 on the UU curve, which point corresponds to an income of $20,000, to the point x_1 which corresponds to an income of $10,000, then using the (a)-scale (and irrespective of the value of the origin) the experienced loss of real income is measured as 0.8 utils. Using the (b)-scale, the loss would be measured as 8 utils. Using the (c)-scale it would be measured as 160 utils. Now let us move from x_2 on the UU curve to x_3, an increase in utility corresponding to an increase in income from $20,000 to $30,000. Again, irrespective of origin, the gain in utility is measured on the (a)-scale as 0.5 utils, on the (b)-scale as 5 utils, and on the (c)-scale as 100 utils.

It follows that, beginning with an income of $20,000, the *ratio* of utility lost by the *subtraction* of $10,000 to the utility gained by the *addition* of $10,000—that is, $U(-\$10,000)/U(+\$10,000)$—is for the (a)-scale $-0.8/0.5$, for the (b)-scale $-8/5$, and for the (c)-scale $-160/200$. Clearly the *ratio* of these differences (in cardinal utilities) remains the same at $-8/5$ regardless of the scale and origin.[1] And this ratio is, indeed, all we require to explain why our perfectly consistent individual will not accept an actuarially fair gamble. On the assumption that his behaviour is determined only by reference to the shape of his utility curve, it can be shown that he would accept such a fair gamble only if the marginal utility of his 'real' income were constant (or increasing). For in that case the total utility curve UU would be a straight line sloping upwards to the right (or one that is concave from above). The utility lost would then be equal to (or less than) the utility to be gained. If, however, diminishing marginal utility prevails, the utility curve will be shaped as in the figure. In that case the utility of the loss of $10,000 ($0.8$ utils on the a-scale) exceeds the utility of the gain of $30,000 (0.5 on the (a)-scale) by 0.3, the actuarial value of the gamble in terms of the (a)-scale being $-0.3/2$, or -0.15, which is negative.[2] From the utility point of view it is obviously not a fair gamble, but one having a negative value.

4   Now in order to be able to plot such a utility curve from the

---

[1] Though we have recourse here only to the ratio of the first differences, it is easy to show that this constancy attaches to the ratio of the second, the third, fourth, ... and nth differences also.

[2] The actuarial value of the gamble as a *proportion* of the difference in utility as between an income of $10,000 and $30,000 remains constant at $-15/130$ for any scale and origin.

consistent and perceptive answers given by such a person, it should be clear that we could begin by attributing to some initial income, say $10,000, some arbitrary number of utils, say 100 utils, and also to some smaller income, say $1,000, a smaller but still quite arbitrary number of utils, say 95 utils—or it could be 10 utils, or zero utils, or even −55 utils. For as we have said, the origin is arbitrary: it can be zero or positive or negative. However, once we have chosen 100 utils for $10,000 and, say, 95 utils for $1,000, we can show how the answers given by our individual enable us to plot enough points to draw a total utility curve over the range $1,000 to $10.000, and indeed beyond that range.

The key assumption we have to make throughout, in order to be able to plot the points of his utility curve, is one that equates, say, (1) the utility of a $\frac{2}{3}$ chance of winning $100, with (2) $\frac{2}{3}$ of the utility of $100. Put generally, the assumption is that (1) the utility of the *probability* of winning a sum x, is equal to (2) that probability *times* the utility of the sum x: $U.pr(x) = pr.U(x)$. This assumption may or may not be plausible, but for the purpose in hand we have to accept it. As indicated above, we start the construct by choosing two levels of income and arbitrarily attribute a higher utility to the larger. Since within this limitation the choices are arbitrary, we may as well choose the figures with an eye to maximum convenience. We shall, therefore, choose zero income and $10,000 and attribute zero utils to zero income and 100 utils to the income of $10,000.

5   Now in order to discover the appropriate utility of some intermediate income, say $5,000, we have only to put the following question to our rational individual: which option would you choose: (1) $5,000 with certainty, or (2) a gamble in which the result is either zero or $10,000? The reply will always be that it depends upon the sort of gamble.[3] If there were 9/10 of a chance of winning $10,000 and therefore only 1/10 of winning nothing, he would be very likely to choose (2) the gambling option. If the odds were the other way round, he would almost surely choose the certain option (1). We may legitimately surmise, however, that there will be some gambling odds which would make our individual indifferent as between the two options.

[3] We may suppose the individual begins with zero income, or else that the above sums are *additional* to his existing income.

Suppose the gambling odds which make him indifferent as between options (1) and (2) are 7 chances of winning $10,000 to 3 chances of winning nothing. In other words, when the probability of winning $10,000 is set at 7/10 and that of winning nothing at $(1 - 7/10)$, or 3/10, the utility to our individual of each of these two options is exactly equal. We therefore have the equation:

(1) Utility of $5,000 = (2) Utility of probability (7/10) of $10,000
+ Utility of probability (3/10) of zero

More briefly, $U(5,000) = U$ of a 7/10 probability of 10,000 + U of a 3/10 probability of 0.

It is our key assumption however that now enables us to rewrite the right-hand side of the equation as $[(0 \cdot 7 \times U(10,000)) + (0 \cdot 3 \times U(0))]$.

Since we have already chosen 100 utils for $10,000 and zero utils for zero income, by substituting these utils for the corresponding sums on the right-hand side of the equation we have:

$$U(5,000) = (0 \cdot 7 \times 100 \text{ utils}) + (0 \cdot 3 \times 0 \text{ utils}) = 70 \text{ utils}$$

In Figure VII.2, we already have two points, zero utils corresponding to zero income, and a point where 100 utils corresponds to an income of $10,000. Since we have just discovered that $5,000 is valued at 70 utils, we mark off a third point 70 utils on the vertical scale above $5,000. We know the utility curve for this person must pass through this point.

To find another point, we could take some other certain sum, say $7,500, and once more put the question before our imaginary person who, we shall suppose, is now indifferent between the options only if there are 9 chances out of 10 of winning $10,000. Once again therefore we have an equation:

$U(7,500) = U$ of a 9/10 probability of 10,000 + U
of a 1/10 probability of 0

which, using our key assumption, we can rewrite as:
$U(7,500) = (0 \cdot 9 \times 100 \text{ utils}) + (0 \cdot 1 \times 0 \text{ utils}) = 90 \text{ utils}$

We mark off a fourth point 90 utils, on the vertical scale, above $7,500. Any number of additional points can be plotted by this means and we may continue generating such points until we can draw the utility curve with confidence between zero and $10,000.

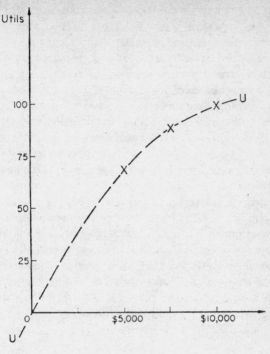

Figure VII.2

Indeed, we can extend the utility curve beyond $10,000. Consider the utils corresponding to $20,000. We let option (1) be the certainty of $10,000 and option (2) a gamble between receiving $20,000 or nothing. If the individual is indifferent between options where there is a 0·6 probability of winning $20,000 we can write:

$$U(10,000) = [0·6 \times U(20,000)] + [0·4 \times U(0)]$$

Therefore, 100 utils = 0·6 × U(20,000), and U(20,000) must equal 166·2/3 utils.

6 Having mapped out the utilities corresponding to the dollar values we can replace the net revenues in each of the Tables of the preceding chapters by their util equivalents. The same decision rules discussed there may now be applied to these new figures, the result being that, in some cases, a different option or decision strategy will emerge.

This method of deriving a utility curve from such experiments was originally put forward as a hypothesis to explain—by reference to both diminishing and increasing marginal-utility segments of the curve—why the same person both insures and gambles.[4] An extension of this precedure, whereby money, or 'real' revenues are translated into utilities, to the problems of practical decision-taking does not appear to have been a resounding success. For a one-man enterprise, or even a partnership, the experiment could conceivably be carried out—assuming that anticipated risks could be expressed in terms of probabilities—and, if successful, the resulting utility curve might be used to replace money sums by utilities in the hope of approaching closer to an optimal decision. But, on the face of things, it would seem quite impracticable to derive such a curve uniquely for a large number of people; and for society in general quite impossible.[5] Even if the method were practicable it runs into the objection that its employment would be unnecessary and, indeed, would go beyond the Pareto basis of cost-benefit analysis. For the Pareto criterion requires only that the sum of the money gains in any project exceed the money sum of the losses: no weighting of these gains and losses by reference to a utility scale, nor their arbitrary addition, is called for.

---

[4] The interested reader might wish to consult Friedman & Savage (1948).

[5] The single figure for revenue that is used as a possible outcome in a cost-benefit analysis is not a possible gain to a single person. In a cost-benefit analysis such a figure is the resultant of the possible gains and losses of a large number of different people. If we wanted to replace such a gain by a figure for total utility, the utilities of all the persons affected have to be added together by some arbitrary weighting system.

Chapter 56

POPULAR DEVICES FOR
COPING WITH UNCERTAINTY

1 Of the variety of methods proposed for dealing with uncertainty only four are in common use for making allowance over the future for unforeseeable changes in the magnitudes and prices of benefits and outlays. These are (a) the cut-off period, (b) discount rate adjustments, (c) subjective probability, and (d) use of the market to yield a discount rate.

2 (a) The crudest way of dealing with uncertainty is that of adopting some arbitrary cut-off period. In the case of very risky projects the period chosen can be as short as two or three years. This means that unless capital outlays are expected wholly to be recouped within two or three years the investment project would not be undertaken. Projects as risky as this are not, however, usually undertaken by the public sector. A large part of the investment by the public sector is in utilities, such as gas, electricity, water, buildings, transport, bridges, highways, docks—today referred to as 'infrastructure'—the future demand for which is believed to be more dependable. If cut-off periods are used at all for these sorts of public investment, they will range up to 30 years or more. It is hardly worth going much further beyond 30 years, however, for even if the benefits are expected with near certainty over the distant future, a benefit of $x expected in, say, 30 years' time has a present social value of only a fraction of $x. If, for example, the social rate of time preference is 10 per cent, each dollar of net benefit that is expected in 30 years' time has a social value today of about 6 cents. Indeed, under these conditions, a formal cut-off period of 30 years is hardly necessary since, of each dollar of net benefit appearing in yet later years, 95 per cent or more of its worth is in any case lost in its translation to present social value.

3 (b) Another device that is hardly less crude is that of adding a percentage to the riskless rate of discount that would otherwise be adopted. Apart from the difficulty of discovering such a riskless rate, this device reduces the hypothetical expected value of net benefits at a compound and quite arbitrary rate. If, for example, 2 per cent is added to a riskless discount rate of 10 per cent so to allow for uncertainty, then we use a 12 per cent discount rate on the assumption that we can somehow obtain a single figure for each expected future net benefit or outlay.

Alternatively, it is possible to express the uncertainty of a particular net revenue by widening the upper and lower limits of the later period as compared with those for the net revenue of an earlier period. If in the first and second period the upper and lower figures are set respectively at 90 per cent and 110 per cent of the most likely figure, the corresponding percentages for, say, the fifth and sixth periods might be set at 80 per cent and 120 per cent of the most likely figure. A certain arbitrariness clearly enters the calculation by either method, but the latter is more direct and more flexible than that of raising the discount rate and, moreover, allows for an optimistic as well as a pessimistic expectation. At all events, this alternative has a close affinity with the next method (c), the difference being in the extent of the formalization.

4 (c) If we allow that rationality in the actuarial sense is applicable to public investments, we can make use of subjective estimates of likelihood to generate something less crude than a simple triple-valued outcome consisting of a most likely figure for the value of some future benefit plus an upper (most optimist) figure and a lower (most pessimistic) figure. We can, as it happens, generate a probability distribution covering the full range of net-benefit possibilities simply by making use of subjective probabilities attaching to several possible values of each variable in each period.

To appreciate the advantages of this procedure, let us first illustrate the deficiency of the simple triple-value method. This can be readily appreciated by an extremely simplified example of a project in which there are no more than four future prices about which there is some uncertainty; say they are the input prices of a specific grade of iron ore in years 1 and 2, and the output prices of a specific type of steel tubing in years 1 and 2. To simplify further, suppose that the most likely price in each of the four cases is reckoned to have a 60 per cent chance of occurring. The most likely estimate, or expected estimate, of the net benefit of the project (whatever it happens to work out at) is that, of course, which corresponds to the occurrence of the four most likely prices, and it will have only a $(0.6)^4$ or, roughly, a 13 per cent chance of occurring. As for the most *optimistic* and also the most *pessimistic* estimates, each will have a much smaller than a 13 per cent chance of occurring. For example, if there is a 20 per cent chance of each of the four most optimistic prices occurring, there will be a $(0.2)^4$, or a 1.6 per cent chance, of the most optimistic net benefit estimate being realized. Similarly for the most pessimistic estimate. Ordinary prudence then would suggest that we attempt to discover more about the chances of the other possible outcomes before reaching a decision on whether or not to undertake the investment. Indeed, we should prefer to have as complete a distribution as possible of the range of alternative cost-benefit outcomes.

This subjective probabilistic approach can be illustrated by reference to the four uncertain prices mentioned above; call them p_1, p_2, p_3, and p_4. The first step is to obtain from the experts estimates of the most likely magnitudes of each price over the future. In the case of the p_1 price, for instance, we should want from them not only their estimates of the chance of some most-likely value of p_1 occurring in that year, but also their estimates of the chances of some lower and higher values occurring. For example, after some discussion with the experts, we might decide that there is a 60 per cent chance of p_1 being $\$1.20$, a 30 per cent chance of its being $\$1.00$ and a 10 per cent chance of its being $\$1.40$. Having obtained three such estimates for each of the four prices, the next step—given that the movements of p_1, p_2, p_3, and p_4 are independent of one another[1]—is to calculate an excess benefit figure with each possible combination of the four prices. Since each price has three alternative values, there will be $(3.0)^4$, or 81, possible net-benefit outcomes, each with its own probability. For example, one of these 81 combinations of the four prices might consist of $\$1.40$ for p_1 with a 10 per cent probability, $\$3.50$ for p_2 with a 60 per cent probability, $\$2.0$ for p_3 with a 20 per cent probability, and $\$1.80$ for p_4 with a 30 per cent probability. This one possible combination of the four prices would have a net-benefit figure of, say, $\$125,000$, and the probability of its occurring would be equal to the product of these four probabilities, or

---

[1] If the values of different variables are *not* independent, then clearly they cannot enter

0·36 per cent (equal to $0·1 \times 0·6 \times 0·2 \times 0·3) \times 100$ per cent. All together, the 81 possible outcomes, along with their corresponding probabilities, provide a fairly detailed probability distribution, one which, in general, will have the normal shape.

Such a distribution cannot, of course, be any more accurate than the initial estimates made by the experts. The information contained by such a distribution is the result only of bringing out the full implications of these initial estimates. But by accepting the basis of such information we can now say a good deal more than before. Having got the mean and standard deviation of the distribution we can say, for example, that there is a 90 per cent chance of the excess-benefit outcome falling between, say, $110,000 and $175,000; that there is only a 3 per cent chance of the excess benefit being zero or negative; and so on. When there are a number of investment projects to be ranked, this method of dealing with uncertainty implies that their corresponding net-benefit *distributions* are to be compared. And unless some of these distributions are dominant, they can be ranked only by comparing larger gains on one project's distribution with smaller ones having a higher probability on the distribution of another project. Subjective judgement in project selection enters again at this final stage, for there is no economic expertise that can say just how much additional risk an additional one per cent gain is worth.

In the above simple example, involving four variables with a three-level estimate for each, the eighty-one possible outcomes could be worked out with pencil and paper. In general, however, there will be far

---

[2](*contd*) the calculation as independent variables. The relationship between them has to be spelled out and attention given to the distribution of the 'independent' variable. For example, the amount of an output sold and the price of that output may both be uncertain, but if the quantity to be sold will depend upon the price, we need only an estimate of the distribution of the price. Suppose the relationship adopted was $S = 100 + 25p + e$, where S is the amount sold, p the price, and e an error term. If the most likely estimate for p is, say, 10, then the most likely estimate for S is 350. If the likelihood of a price of 10 occurring is 60 per cent then the likelihood of S being 350 is 60 per cent also (with a total sales value of 3,500) *provided* the error term e is zero. If, however, the error term is not zero, but instead is such that when p is equal to 10 the chance of S being 350 is 80 per cent, with a 10 per cent chance of its being either 400 or 300, a distribution of three possible sales values is generated. For the 60 per cent probability of p being 10, that is, we shall now have a $(0·6 \times 0·8)$ or 48 per cent chance of a sales revenue of 3,500 *plus a* $(0·6 \times 0·1)$ or 6 per cent chance of a sales revenue of 4,000 *plus* a $(0·6 \times 0·1)$ or 6 per cent chance of a sales revenue of 3,000. Once we take into account the two other possible prices, having between them a probability of 40 per cent, we generate nine independent values for the sales revenue.

more than four uncertain variables and sometimes—especially where
there is information arising from variations in price or quantity over
the past—more than three probability estimates for each variable. All
possible cost-benefit outcomes of a single project might then run into
millions or thousands of millions. Nevertheless, a sample distribution
can be simulated with the aid of a computer that is set to select at
random from the distributions of each of the uncertain variables
(according to the probability of its occurring) one particular value, and
from this chosen combination of values to compute the corresponding
net-benefit figure. After a run of, say, 200 or 300 'observations' the
resulting sample will usually be a reliable enough distribution to work
with.[2]

---

[2] If there is any doubt about the adequacy of the sample, the computer can be run for
another 200 or 300 'observations'. If there is then no discernible difference in the
resulting distributions, the sample is deemed to be large enough.

Chapter 57

RECOURSE TO THE YIELD ON RISKY PRIVATE INVESTMENT

1 (d) In a Western economy having a large private investment sector and well organized capital markets there is less need to calculate this sort of subjective probability distribution for any particular public project provided, as is generally the case, public investment forms a large proportion of total investment. Assuming that the risks run by each type of private investment can be arranged as a probability distribution, the expected or actuarial rates of return on the different types of private investments may be regarded as alternative opportunity yields on the investible funds at the disposal of public agencies.

2 It has been remarked, however,[1] that the yield on private investment can properly be regarded as the appropriate opportunity yield for public investment purposes only if the (subjective) cost of risk-bearing is the same for the taxpayer as it is for the individual private investor. The argument is that if the benefits and costs are to be measured, as they should be, in terms of compensation variations—willingness to pay a maximum sum for benefits received, willingness to accept a minimal sum for losses incurred—the (subjective) costs of risk-bearing have to be subtracted from the net benefit of the investment project in order to obtain a correct measure of its value to the recipient. According to this analysis, where the number of taxpayers is large, the risk borne by each one in respect of any particular public investment project becomes negligible. In contrast, the risk-bearing costs of a similar project to a limited number of private investors can be appreciable. Hence, it is concluded, it is not so much the government's

---

[1] By Arrow and Lind (1970).

402

pooling of investment risks from its undertaking of a large number of investment projects that justifies the ignoring of the risks—or not only such investment-pooling—but rather the fact of spreading the risk of any single investment over a very large number of taxpayers.[2] As a corollary, it follows that a public investment having an expected rate of return below that of a private investment may yet be economically superior. For what is relevant in the comparison is not the expected rates of return *per se* but the expected rates of return *net* of the (subjective) costs of risk bearing.[3]

Allowing that increased investment in the public sector entails reduced expenditure in the private sector, the above argument is valid wherever funds are raised by tax revenues (not by selling government securities), and wherever the public agency is restricted in the use of its investible funds to specified projects. It does not apply if the public agency is permitted to use these funds either (i) to invest directly in the private sector, which option enables it to avail itself of any expected rate of return on private investment, or (ii) to buy out private investment projects already undertaken—buying them out at (not less than) the capitalized value of their expected net benefits, *net* of the private costs of risk bearing. For under either of these options the opportunity yield open to the public funds will again be the full actuarial rate of return on private investment. Indeed, inasmuch as permitting public agencies these options of investing in, or buying assets from, the private investment sector promotes a more economic use of investible funds, the economist should in fact recommend their universal adoption in the absence of specific objections.

3   Obviously the riskier the type of private investment the higher is

---

[2] It may be contended, of course, that if the risk for each taxpayer becomes negligible as their numbers increase indefinitely so also does the benefit per taxpayer. However, on the principle of increasing cost of risk bearing, the rate of diminution of risk-bearing costs per person as numbers increase is assumed to be faster than the rate of diminution of the benefits.

If the assumptions of rationality and full information are relaxed, we could justify neglecting the risk-costs of public investment in so far as the taxpayer experiences no anxiety about possible losses simply because he overlooks any connection between a loss incurred by a public investment and a possible increase in his tax payments.

[3] A amendment to the Arrow–Lind thesis has been made by Fisher (1973). He points out that in so far as the risks involved are external diseconomies, or 'public bads', the damage experienced by each person does not diminish with the increase in the number of people who, also, will be the beneficiaries of the public investment.

the expected rate of return—a consequence both of risk-aversion and the tax disadvantages of investing in projects that yield highly variable returns.[4] But whatever the reasons for the higher gross rates of return expected on riskier private investments, the conclusion remains unaffected. If the placing of public funds in the riskier type of private investment can in fact realize higher gross returns over time, then no public investment ought to be undertaken that is expected to yield gross returns that are any lower.

To illustrate, if the A-type of private investment has an expected yield of 10 per cent before tax and the B-type of investment, which is riskier, has an expected yield of 14 per cent before tax, then for society as a whole continued investment in the A-type investment produces a return of 10 per cent whereas continued investment in the B-type investment produces a return of 14 per cent.[5] If a succession of specific public projects is expected to yield, say, 12 per cent then, in undertaking them, the agency is forgoing the opportunity of earning an additional 2 per cent by investing instead in the B-type investment.

Of course, one might do better yet if more information could be secured at low cost. If it were possible to know in advance the actual return to be realized on each particular B-type investment that the government could undertake as an alternative to a given public project, then such actual private yields—which would vary over time from one B-type of investment to another—could properly be used as the appropriate opportunity yield rather than the over-all actuarial rate of return on the risky B-type investment. Such information, alas, is just not available at low cost: if it were there would be no problem of uncertainty. The information we can more reasonably hope for is an average rate of return for the B-type investment when a fair number of such investments have been undertaken. And, under given conditions, we might reasonably anticipate that this average rate, say 14 per cent, will continue over the near future. Only if this 14 per cent can reasonably be expected to continue up to the terminal year of the public project in question, however, can it be regarded as the appropriate opportunity

---

[4] The individual investor in risky projects may, however, be able to overcome the tax disadvantages to some extent by spreading his investment over a number of such projects.

[5] Ignoring the tendency for the return to decline as more B-type investment is undertaken. This consideration, however, affects only the magnitude of public investment, not the principle.

yield in any public investment criterion. If the return on this B-type investment is expected to rise or fall over that period, modifications have to be made accordingly.

4 Care must be taken in the use of this highest actuarial rate of return, say ρ, that is to be adopted as the basis of the social opportunity yield in public investment criteria. Only where the political constraint is such that the public agency has the option of wholly reinvesting at ρ all the returns of any project, is ρ to be used as the appropriate discount rate, or—if, instead, the method of compounding outlays and benefits forward to the terminal date is adopted—as the appropriate reinvestment rate (in the absence of superior public reinvestment opportunities). The reader will recall from our treatment of investment criteria in Part V that in other cases the public agency is constrained to distribute the benefits in cash or kind direct to the public, i.e. it is not permitted wholly to reinvest these returns in the private investment sector. Since in these other cases the common behaviour assumption that is adopted has it that the public saves only a fraction of any additional returns, the benefits of any project are to be compounded forward at a rate below ρ, say p, in which case such benefits can also be discounted to the present at p.

In the presence of uncertainty, in sum, it is appropriate to regard the highest actuarial rate of return ρ on the riskier private investments as the basis of the opportunity yield ρ for public investment. This ρ has then to be used as indicated in our discussion of public investment criteria in Part V.

5 We began this chapter by referring to the fact that Western economies have large private investment sectors and also use a sizeable proportion of their public funds for investment purposes. The larger the private investment sector the more appropriate is the use of the highest actuarial rate of return ρ as the basis of the opportunity yield of the public investment sector—provided, always, that the latter is large enough to avail itself, if necessary, of an average return of ρ over time. Where private investment is limited, or where public investments are few, reference to the private sector for a social opportunity yield is less appropriate, and we should seek more information. For if private investment is limited we can place little confidence on an average yield ρ being maintained on risky private investment. If, on the other hand, the private investment sector were large enough to enable us to treat ρ with some confidence, public investment projects may be too few to enable us to place any confidence in their expected returns being realized.

For instance, suppose that the country is contemplating only three investment projects over the next five years, each requiring an outlay of about a billion dollars. The alternative use of the funds in the private investment sector may involve spreading these sums over a large number of much smaller high-risk enterprises where they could virtually be certain of earning something very close to ρ—which yield, we shall assume for simplicity, is wholly reinvested. But the expected rate of return on these three large public projects is much less certain: in terms of probability, the variance is high. In that case it would be imprudent to make the decision whether or not to undertake these large public projects turn on a direct comparison of their expected rates of return with the opportunity yield ρ—or to use single figures for their expected benefits over time.

Each of these three large public projects has a range of outcomes other than the most probable outcome, and in the circumstances these other outcomes should receive more attention. We should therefore attempt to supplement information about the most likely return to each public investment with the sort of data required for a (subjective) probability distribution of outcomes as discussed in method (c) in the preceding chapter. The narrower the range of outcomes, and the smaller the variance, the greater the confidence we can repose in comparing, say, the normalized internal rate of return (based on the expected net benefits) with the social opportunity yield, ρ. According as the range of outcomes is wider, and the variance greater, we pay more attention to outcomes other than the most likely one. We should want to form a judgement on the eligibility of each project by reference to this (subjective) probability distribution of all outcomes—say the probability distribution of the normalized terminal values of the net benefits.

If the costs of constructing such (subjective) probability distributions are not high they may be usefully employed even where public projects are numerous. Such a distribution adds an extra dimension to the adopted investment criterion and, according to the skill and consistency with which it is used, it should serve to raise somewhat the average return on public investment.

In the more general case we might, indeed, wish to compare directly the probability distribution of the outcomes of a particular public investment with the probability distributions of the outcomes of the particular private investments that will be displaced if the public project is adopted.

REFERENCES AND BIBLIOGRAPHY FOR PART VII

Arrow, K. J. and Lind, R. C. 'Uncertainty and the Evaluation of Public Investment Decisions'. *American Economic Review*, 1970.

Baumol, W. J. 'On the Social Rate of Discount', *American Economic Review*, 1968.

Carter, C. F. and others (eds.). *Uncertainty and Business Decisions*, Liverpool: University Press, 1957.

Churchman, C. W. *Introduction to Operations Research*, New York: Wiley, 1957.

Dorfman, R. 'Basic Economic and Technological Concepts', in Maass and others. *Design of Water Resources Systems*. London: Macmillan, 1962.

Fisher, A. 'Environmental Externalities and the Arrow-Lind Public Investment Theorem', *American Economic Review*, 1973.

Friedman, M. and Savage, L. J. 'The Utility Analysis of Choices Involving Risk', *Journal of Political Economy*, 1948.

Hertz, D. B. 'Risk Analysis in Capital Investment', *Harvard Business Review*, Jan./Feb. 1964.

Hillier, F. S. 'The Derivation of Probabilistic Information for the Evaluation of Risky Investments', *Managerial Science*, April 1963.

King, W. R. *Probability for Management Decisions*, New York: Wiley, 1968.

Luce, R. D. and Raiffa, H. *Games and Decisions: Introduction to Critical Survey*, New York: Wiley, 1967.

Moore, P. G. *Basic Operation Research*, London: Pitman & Son, 1968.

Reutlinger, S. *Techniques for Project Appraisal Under Uncertainty* (World Bank Staff Paper No. 10). Baltimore: Johns Hopkins, 1970.

Schlaiffer, R. *Probability and Statistics for Business Decisions*, New York: McGraw-Hill, 1969.

— *Introduction to Statistics for Business Decisions*, New York: McGraw-Hill, 1961.

PART VIII. FURTHER NOTES RELATING TO COST-BENEFIT ANALYSIS

NOTE A: MORE ACCURATE MEASURES OF ECONOMIC SURPLUS

Chapter 58

THE CONCEPT AND MEASURE OF CONSUMER'S SURPLUS

1 Notwithstanding some ill-considered utterances about consumer's surplus by well-known economists,[1] it is a concept so crucial to allocative economics generally, and in particular to cost-benefit analysis, that there is everything to be said for clarifying both the concept itself, and the relationship between the concept and its measurable proxy, the demand curve.

Marshall's (1924) definition of the individual's consumer's surplus, the amount of money a man is willing to pay rather than go without

---

[1] For instance, Little (1957) stated that it was no more than a 'theoretical toy' (p. 180). According to Samuelson (1963), 'The subject is of historical and doctrinal interest with a limited amount of appeal as a purely mathematical puzzle' (p. 195). This latter remark could be said with some truth of a large number of topics in contemporary economics, but it cannot be accepted as a judgement about consumer's surplus. Without this concept how does the economist justify the free use of roads, bridges, parks, etc., or the operation of industries at outputs for which prices are below marginal costs, or two-part tariffs? Without attempts to measure increments of consumers' surpluses, and rents, cost-benefit analyses would be primitive indeed.

the thing over that which he actually pays, though it has strong intuitive appeal, is not altogether satisfactory: for it implies a constraint on the quantity to be bought. The sum of money the consumer is willing to pay, say, for a licence to buy the good at some given price rather than go without it, depends on how much he is expected to buy. And if, as Marshall implicitly assumed, the amount of the good he is to buy—on paying for this licence—is the same amount as that which he buys at the price *in the absence of* any need for a licence, then he will *not*, generally, pay as much for the licence as he would if, instead, he is allowed to buy as much of the good as he wants. His having to pay for a licence makes him worse off, and if his income effect is positive he would then—at the same price—choose a smaller amount than if he could buy freely without a licence. Consequently, if he is constrained to buy the initial (larger) amount, he will pay less for the licence.[2]

2   Such considerations prompted Hicks' definition (1939) of a *compensating variation* measure of the consumer's surplus. For the privilege of being able to buy the good at the existing price, *in whatever amount he chooses,* the consumer is willing to pay some maximum sum—his compensating variation. In 1943 Henderson pointed out that the exact measure proposed by Hicks would differ according to whether the consumer had to pay for the opportunity of buying the good at the given price or whether, instead, he was to be paid for abandoning this opportunity. This distinction is illustrated by reference to the indifference curve for a single individual in Figure VIII.1.

Along the horizontal axis is measured the good x, to be introduced into the economy at a fixed price given by the budget line Y_0X_0. OY_0

---

[2] Marshall's dissatisfaction, and eventual disillusion, with the concept of consumer's surplus, arose from his utility analysis. Aware that the fall in the price of a good which made the consumer better off had some effect on the amount he would buy, Marshall tried to circumvent the problem by holding the individual's marginal utility of income constant. But this was plausible only for minute changes in the individual's welfare. Moreover, in extending the concept to the market, Marshall's choice of working in terms of cardinal, and interpersonal, utility proved cumbersome and unconvincing.

Once Hicks introduced the more operational distinction between income and substitution effects, it became evident that it was real income, and not the marginal utility of money, that was to be held constant. And despite popular belief to the contrary, these are not alternative methods of expressing the same condition. A constant marginal utility of money does *not* imply constant real income, and vice versa.

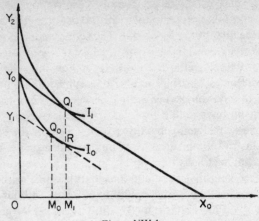

Figure VIII.1

measures his money income over a period during which the prices of all goods other than x remain constant. Prior to the introduction of good x, the individual's money income Y_0 corresponds to a real income indicated by the indifference curve I_0. Once x is introduced at the price given by the budget line Y_0X_0, the individual chooses the point Q_1 on the higher indifference curve I_1, and therefore consumes OM_1 of x.

The difference made to the person's real income, $I_1 - I_0$, is unambiguous. Ambiguity arises simply because we are to measure the real gain in terms of money income, as defined, along the vertical axis. Hicks' compensating variation, CV, is equal to Y_0Y_1. For if the consumer is made to pay this sum in order to be permitted to buy x at the price (given by the slope of Y_0X_0), he could just reach Q_0 on his original indifference curve I_0. That is, if he is to be exactly as well off as he was originally before x was introduced, Y_0Y_1 is the maximum sum he can afford to pay for the privilege of buying x at the given price. And if called upon to pay this maximum, the amount of x that he would in fact buy is given here by OM_0.

Turning to Henderson's distinction, we now ask a different question: what is the minimum sum the consumer will accept to give up entirely the opportunity of buying the new good x at the market price, given by the slope of Y_0X_0? The answer is a sum equal to Y_0Y_2. For adding this sum to his initial income, OY_0, his total income becomes OY_2, and this income, without any x, is on his indifference curve I_1. He is then just as well off as he would have been if, at his

410

original income OY_0, he was able to buy x at the given price. This measure of consumer's surplus was called by Hicks (1944) the *Equivalent Variation*, EV, inasmuch as, in the absence of x, such a sum provides the consumer with an equivalent improvement in his welfare.

Provided the income effect is positive ('normal'), Q_1 will be to the right of Q_0 on the parallel budget lines. OM_1 will therefore be larger than OM_0, and Y_0Y_2 will be larger than Y_0Y_1. If, instead, the income effect were negative, the ranking would be reversed: Q_1 would be to the left of Q_0, ON_0 would be smaller than OM_0, and Y_0Y_2 would be smaller than Y_0Y_1.[3]

3   More generally, the definition of CV is the sum of money—to be paid by the consumer when the price falls: to be received by him when the price rises—which, following a change in the price, leaves him at his initial level of welfare. The EV, on the other hand, is that sum of money—to be received by the consumer when the price falls; to be paid by him when it rises—which, if he were exempted from the change in price, would yet provide him with the same welfare change. These two measures have been illustrated in Figure VIII.1 for the special case of the introduction of a new good x at a given price, rather than for a change in the existing price of x. They are illustrated in Figure VIII.2 for the case of a fall in the existing price of x.

Initial money income is again represented by OY_0, initial real income being given by the indifference curve I_1 which is reached by the tangency of the price-line p_1 at Q_1. If the price of x falls to p_2, the tangency of the p_2 price-line at Q_2 raises the consumer's real income from I_1 to I_2. His CV is then equal to Y_0Y_1, this being the maximum sum he could afford to pay for the lower price p_2 without being any worse off. For if he pays this sum, so reducing his money income to OY_1, the now lower price p_2 enables him to reach B on his original I_1 curve. His EV, on the other hand, is equal to Y_0Y_2, this being the minimal sum he will accept to forgo the opportunity to buy what he wants at the lower price p_2. For with this sum his total income would be equal to OY_2, and with this income and the old price p_1 he could just reach the higher indifference curve I_2 at C. This increase in his welfare

---

[3] The reader will note that these relationships hold irrespective of whether marginal utility of real income is diminishing, constant, or increasing—these three possibilities being consistent with any given indifference map of the individual.

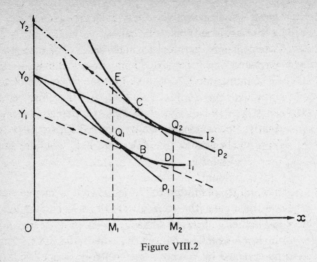

Figure VIII.2

is exactly equal to that which he could attain with this new price p_2 and with his original money income OY_0. Once more, Y_0Y_2 will exceed Y_0Y_2 for a 'normal' good x, as drawn; the reverse being true if x, instead, were an 'inferior' good.

We can now go through the same exercise for a rise in the price of x. With income OY_0, we begin with the consumer being faced with p_2 and, therefore, choosing point Q_2 on indifference curve I_2. A rise in the price of x to p_1 now induces him to take up the position Q_1 on the I_1 indifference curve. Our definitions would therefore measure the CV of such a price-rise by Y_2Y_0, this being the minimum sum that would restore the individual's welfare to its original level I_2 when the price rises to p_1. The EV is now to be measured as equal to Y_0Y_1, this being the maximum sum the consumer is prepared to give up if he is exempted from the higher price p_1. For giving up this sum, and retaining the old price p_2, would enable him to reach I_1 (at B), which is the level of welfare he reaches if he is not exempted from the rise in price to p_1.

4   These two measures, the CV and the EV, are all that are needed in ordinary circumstances. Solely as a matter of curiosity, however, we might wish to go back to Figure VIII.1 for a precise measure of the definition put forward by Marshall. This turns out to be a sum equal to the vertical distance Q_1R, this being the maximum sum the consumer

412

will pay for the privilege of being able to buy x at the given price *provided* he is constrained to buy OM_1 of x—this amount of x being that which the consumer actually buys when he is permitted (without having to pay anything for the privilege) to buy freely at the given price. For if he moves along the price line from Y_0 to Q_1, and is then obliged to stay with the quantity OM_1 of x, he must give up Q_1R in order to be at R on his original indifference curve I_0. This measure Q_1R is smaller than Y_0Y_1, as indeed it should be, since the consumer would pay less for the privilege of being able to buy x if he were compelled to buy a particular amount of it (here OM_1) than if, instead, he could choose whatever amount of x he wished.[4]

Thus the Marshallian measure differs from the CV measure only in its having a quantity constraint attached to it. Extending the Marshallian-type measure to a change in the price, we return to Figure VII.3. For a fall in price from p_1 to p_2, the relevant quantity-constraint is OM_2, and the quantity-constrained CV is therefore measured as Q_2D. A quantity-constrained EV, requiring the consumer to purchase only OM_1 of X—this being the amount he buys at the original price p_1 without receiving any compensation—is measured as Q_1E.[5]

Again, for a rise in price from p_2 to p_1 these measures are reversed. Q_1E becomes the quantity-constrained CV, and Q_2D becomes the quantity-constrained EV. Q_2D is smaller than Y_0Y_1, and Q_1E is larger than Y_0Y_2.

---

[4] This is true (that is the Marshallian measure is smaller than the CV) irrespective of whether x is a 'normal' or an 'inferior' good.

[5] It is clear from Figure VIII.2 that the quantity-constrained CV measure, Q_2D, is smaller than the unconstrained CV measure, Y_0Y, which is as it should be since he would always pay less for a constrained privilege than for an unconstrained one. For the analogous reason that he would want to receive a larger compensation if he were to be constrained with respect to quantity than if he were not to be so constrained, the quantity-constrained EV measure, EQ_1, is larger than the ordinary EV measure, Y_0Y_2.

Chapter 59

MARGINAL CURVE MEASURES OF CONSUMER'S SURPLUS

1 The two more popular measures of consumer's surplus, CV and EV, can be represented on the marginal diagram, Figure VIII.3. I_0' is the marginal indifference curve corresponding to indifference curve I_0 in Figure VIII.1 of the preceding chapter. In fact, I_0' is the curve of the first derivative of I_0 with respect to x. Similarly, the marginal indifference curve I_1' is the first derivative of the I_1 curve of Figure VIII.1. For convenience both marginal indifference curves are represented as straight lines in Figure VIII.3. And, since in Figure VIII.1 I_1 is indicative of a higher level of welfare than I_0, the assumption of a 'normal' good x requires that marginal indifference curve I_1' be drawn above (or to the right of) I_0'.[1]

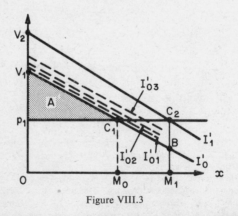

Figure VIII.3

---

[1] If, instead, the income effect on x were negative, the reverse would be true; the I_1' marginal indifference curve would be below the I_0' marginal indifference curve.

414

If we regard individual welfare as continuously variable the indifference curves are infinitely dense, and so also, therefore, are the marginal indifference curves. For illustrative purposes, however, we could select an arbitrary number of marginal indifference curves, I'_{01}, I'_{02}, and so on, as indicated by the broken lines in Figure VIII.3.

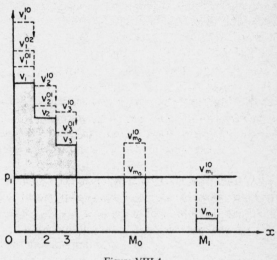

Figure VIII.4

We shall return to this diagram presently, after taking a closer view of the origin and of the point M_1 by means of an incremental diagram, Figure VIII.4. The story opens with no x being available and our consumer having I_0 welfare. The maximum sum he will pay for a single unit of x is shown as the first unit column having height v_1. Let us suppose that he pays this maximum sum, in which case his welfare remains unchanged at level I_0. He is then offered a second unit of x. The maximum he can now afford to pay for this second unit is given by the height of the second column, v_2. Again we suppose that he is required to pay this maximum, so retaining his original welfare at I_0, and a third unit of x is offered to him, for which he can pay as much as v_3, the height of the third column. If we continue in this way, he will eventually, after purchasing M_0 units of x, have offered as much as v_{m0} for the M_0^{th} unit of x.

If he buys M_0 units of x on these terms, he will be no better off after

415

buying them than he was before he bought any x. His level of welfare, that is, remains at I_0. Now, let the price p_1 be set at height v_{m0}. The sum of the portions of the solid columns that stick up above the price line (their dotted segments) has now to be interpreted. Since his payment of this sum, in addition to price p_1 per unit for OM_0 units of x, is such that he is no better off than he was originally without x, this sum is to be regarded as the CV for introducing x at a price p_1. It is the maximum sum he will be able to pay for the privilege of buying x at p_1 without his being any worse off than he was originally. On the Figure VIII.3 diagram, having continuous curves, this CV is represented as the area of the dotted triangle A.

2 Let us now return to our consumer in a more charitable humour, and allow him to buy all the x he wants at the introductory price p_1. His welfare, or real income, increases from I_0 to I_1, and—because his real income effect is assumed positive—he buys more of x; in fact OM_1 of x in Figure VIII.3.

Looking at things in the light of the incremental diagram, Figure VIII.4, we notice that, because of this increase in real income, the value of the final M_1^{th} unit is now valued at v_{m1}^{10}, equal to price p_1, and not at the smaller value v_{m1}—the maximum he would have paid for the M_1^{th} unit on the first procedure, which retained his welfare at the level I_0. Indeed, because of the increase in the level of his welfare from I_0 to I_1 when he is allowed to buy x freely at p_1 (and ends up buying OM_1 units) the valuation of all preceding units of x are raised; the M_0^{th} unit being valued at v_{m0}^{10}, the third unit being valued at v_3^{10}, and the first unit being valued at v_1^{10}, and so on. The stepped line joining the top of these revised columns in Figure VIII.4, from the first to the M_1^{th} unit, can be represented, however, by the segment $V_2 C_2$ of the continuous marginal indifference curve I_1' in Figure VIII.3. Once the consumer has been allowed to buy all he wants of x at the price p_1, and his welfare rises from I_0 to I_1, the area $OV_2 C_2 M_1$ is the exact measure of what the OM_1 units of x are worth to him.

If the privilege of buying x at p_1 were now withdrawn, he would have to be returned his expenditure on OM_1 units of x, or $Op_1 C_2 M_1$. But unless he were also paid a sum equal to the area of the triangle $p_1 V_2 C_2$, he would be worse off than he was with the privilege of buying all he wanted at price p_1; his welfare, that is, would be below I_1. The triangle $p_1 V_2 C_2$ is, then, the measure of his EV. It is the minimum sum that is needed to make him as well off when the privilege of buying x at p_1 is withdrawn as he was when he enjoyed that privilege.[2]

3 We now return, once more, to Figure VIII.4 in order to throw more light on two issues that are somewhat obscure. As mentioned, beginning with welfare at level I_0, the maximum the consumer will pay for the first unit of x is given by the height v_1 of the first solid column. But if, instead of paying this maximal sum, he pays no more than the price p_1, he makes a surplus on this first unit equal to the column segment $p_1 v_1$. As a result his welfare rises, say, to I_{01} (greater than I_0), and the maximum he is now prepared to pay for the second, third, and subsequent units of x is—on the assumption of a positive income effect—raised somewhat to v_2^{01} for the second unit, to v_3^{01} for the third unit of x, and so on. Let him now be offered a second unit of x at the same price p_1, and he makes as a surplus on this second unit an amount equal to $p_1 v_2^{01}$. His welfare has risen by another increment to, say, I_{02}, and the maximum sum he will pay for successive units also rises. For the third unit he will now pay as much as v_3^{02}, (above v_3^{01}, but not shown in the Figure) and so on. Proceeding in this way, determining the resulting maximum sum the consumer will pay for each successive unit prior to allowing him to buy it at price p_1, we can trace a locus that has been called (Hicks, 1944), the 'marginal valuation', MV, curve. Its relation to the marginal indifference curves of Figure VIII.3 could be shown there, but in order not to clutter up the picture we have reproduced the main features of Figure VIII.3 in Figure VIII.5, and shown this MV curve as the *broken* line joining V_1 to C_2.

This MV curve is not, however, to be identified with the demand curve. For in order to generate a demand curve for x we trace the path of consumer purchases by gradually *lowering the price* from V_1 to p_1. Although both the MV and the demand curves pass through C_2 when

---

[2] The reader might care to note that the quantity-constrained CV—corresponding to the Marshallian definition of consumer's surplus—is smaller than the Hicksian CV. In Figure VIII.3, it can be represented as the dotted triangle A *less* the triangle $C_1 C_2 B$. For the quantity constraint requires of the consumer that, in paying a maximum for the privilege of buying x at p_1, he continue to buy OM_1 units (and not the OM_0 units he would have chosen to buy). Since the marginal indifference curve I_0' shows the maximum he is prepared to pay for these additional $M_0 M_1$ units of x, and shows that this maximum for each such unit is below the price p_1, his welfare can be maintained—after paying a sum equal to the triangle A—only by refunding him the losses he must sustain on the additional $M_0 M_1$ units, a total loss given by the triangle $C_1 C_2 B$.

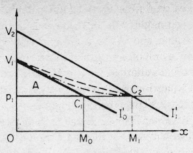

Figure VIII.5

the price is p_1, for all previous quantities of x the MV curve (for a 'normal' good) is above the demand curve, shown as the *dotted* curve joining V_1 to C_2. The reason is simply that, in tracing the locus of the MV curve, the consumer is deemed to buy each successive unit of x, from the first onward, at the actual price p_1. In contrast, the demand curve is generated by having the consumer pay a price that is first equal to OV_1 and, though gradually lowered, remains above p_1 until the final $M_1{}^{\text{th}}$ unit is bought. As a result, the surplus of welfare gained in the purchase of the first, second, third, and subsequent units of x (save for the final $M_1{}^{\text{th}}$ unit) is greater for the MV curve procedure than for the demand curve procedure. At each unit of x, save the final $M_1{}^{\text{th}}$ unit, the consumer's valuation is, therefore, higher for the MV curve than for the demand curve.

4 In order to broach the second issue, we return to Figure VIII.4, and recall that the maximum sum the consumer will pay for the first unit is given by the height v_1 of the first column. If he is permitted to buy this one unit at p_1, his CV for that one unit is equal, as indicated, to the dotted segment of the column above the p_1 line. Suppose we now ask the question: what is the minimum sum he will accept in order to give up the privilege of buying this one unit of x at p_1? Now if this question is asked prior to his having bought any unit of x at a price (such as p_1) below his maximum valuation of a first unit, his welfare will still be at the I_0 level. The minimum sum he would accept to forgo having the one unit of x might then be thought equal to the maximum sum he would pay for it. But whether in fact he has bought this x unit at p_1, and his welfare has risen to the level I_{01} (greater than initial level I_0), or whether he has *not* yet bought this unit of x, and his existing welfare is

418

still at I_0, makes no difference. The minimum sum he will require to forgo the unit he bought at p_1, or the opportunity to buy it at p_1, is in either case the same, and larger, than the maximum sum he would pay to be able to buy a unit of x at p_1. For assume that he has not yet bought any x at p_1, and his welfare is still therefore at I_0, the individual has to ask himself the question: what is the level of welfare I *could* reach if I were permitted to avail myself of the opportunity of buying this unit of x at p_1? And the answer, as indicated above, is the level I_{01}, greater than I_0. The sum of money which, therefore, exactly compensates him for *not* being able to attain this I_{01} level of welfare (through the purchase of a unit of x at p_1) is equal to the column segment $p_1 v_1^{01}$.

This description of the sum of money, however, corresponds exactly with the definition of the EV—the sum which, if he is exempted from the economic change in question, provides him with the equivalent change in his welfare.[3] More generally, if no constraint is placed on the amount of x the consumer would wish to buy, the EV necessary to induce him to forgo the opportunity of buying x at p_1 is equal to the area of triangle $p_1 V_2 C_2$ in Figure VIII.5.

5 Let us summarize these interpretations. The CV for introducing x at price p_1 is given by the dotted triangle A in Figure VIII.5. Once x is introduced at that price, the consumer, in the absence of constraint, will buy OM_1 units and achieve a welfare level corresponding to indifference curve I_1. In order to persuade him to forgo this opportunity to buy x at p_1, which takes him to I_1 welfare, he must receive a minimum sum equal to the area of the large triangle, $p_1 V_2 C_2$. By definition this is his EV.

If, on the other hand, he has already been given the price p_1, and the economic change consists of withdrawing it entirely, this same minimum sum, equal to triangle $p_1 C_2 V_2$, now represents the consumer's CV, being the sum that must be paid him in order to maintain his existing welfare at I_1. His EV in this circumstance is the smaller triangle A, this being the maximum sum he would pay to be exempt from losing the opportunity to buy at p_1, which payment would

---

[3] If, however, the economic change being contemplated is the exact opposite of this; viz. the *withdrawal* of the opportunity of buying a unit of x at p_1 and, as a result, a reduction of the consumer's welfare level from I_{01}, the payment of this sum is the appropriate CV for such an economic change. For it is the sum the consumer must receive in order to maintain his existing level of welfare, I_{01}, following such a change.

in fact reduce his level of welfare to I_0,[4] the level prior to the introduction of good x.

Confining ourselves to the CV and EV of introducing a normal good x at price p_1, it is clear that the area between the price and the individual's demand curve, D, is greater than the CV area and less than the EV area; i.e. for 'normal' goods, $CV < D < EV$. It is obvious that the smaller is the income effect the smaller will be the difference between these areas regarded as measures of consumer's surplus. In the limiting case of zero effect, the three areas coincide.[5]

6 Finally, we can translate the CV and EV measures of Figure VIII.2, featuring a fall in the price from p_1 to p_2 onto the marginal diagram of Figure VIII.6. At p_1 the consumer is buying OM_1 units. At p_2 he is buying OM_2 units. The marginal indifference curves I_0', I_1', and I_2', are indicated as solid lines, and the demand curve passing through VDH as the dotted line.

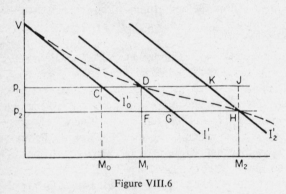

Figure VIII.6

The CV of the fall in the price from p_1 to p_2 is equal to the cost difference for OM_1 units of x, or rectangle p_1p_2FD, *plus* the triangle DFG. The EV for that fall in price is equal to the cost-difference for

[4] It should be self-evident that the maximum sum a consumer will pay to acquire a benefit (his CV) is the same maximum sum he will pay to hold on to it (his EV); that is, to be exempt from its removal once he already has it.

[5] If x had a negative income effect we should have $EV < D < CV$. Figure VIII.5 would have to be revised by exchanging points M_0 and M_1, C_1 and C_2, V_1 and V_2. The demand curve joining the new V_1 to the new C_2 would then be steeper than either of the two marginal indifference curves. In the extreme case, the demand curve over a range slopes upwards from left to right.

OM_2 units, or rectangle p_1p_2HJ *less* the triangle HJK. These measures of CV and EV are, of course, reversed for a price rise from p_1 to p_2.

The horizontal slice of consumer's surplus under the demand curve, the area p_1p_2HD is an approximation to either of the exact measures, being clearly greater than the CV measure, and smaller than the EV measure, for a price-fall. Again, the smaller the income effect, the closer is the coincidence of the three measures. For a zero income effect the measures coincide. Goods having zero income effect are hard to come by, but for a great many purposes the income-effect involved is small enough for economists to make use of the area under the demand curve as a close approximation of the relevant benefit or loss.

Chapter 60

THE CONCEPT AND
MEASURE OF RENT

1 Although the concept of rent, in the specific sense of a surplus to factor-owners, is not so popular in cost-benefit analyses as the concept of consumers' surplus, it is possible that, with growing awareness of allocation theory and growing refinements in techniques of measurement, it will become increasingly employed. The concept deserves more detailed treatment for another reason: the use of the area above the supply price of a factor is a less reliable proxy for the measurement of rent than is the area below the consumer's demand curve à proxy for his surplus. The reader will appreciate this remark more readily after the concept of rent has been defined.

Textbook definitions that are still in current use can be divided into two types. One conceives of rent as a payment in excess of that necessary to maintain a factor in its current occupation. The other would describe it as the difference between the factor's current earnings and its 'transfer earnings'—the latter term denoting its earnings in the next most highly paid use. As we shall see, the first type of definition is ambiguous because of the quantity constraint. The second type of definition is even more restricted, however, as its validity would require that, in the choice of occupation, men are motivated solely by pecuniary considerations. Indeed, it will transpire that, like consumer's surplus, rent is a measure of change in a person's welfare and, again, like consumer's surplus, can have both a CV and an EV measure.

2 As with the treatment of consumer's surplus, our first recourse will be to the indifference map. Figure VIII.7 indicates four quadrants of a diagram in which money income, Y, is again measured vertically, and the good L (which can be thought of as labour services) is measured horizontally. Any horizontal distance to the right of the origin, O, would measure the amount of L acquired by the individual; any horizontal distance to the left of the origin, the amount of L given up. Similarly, any distance above the origin measures the amount of income acquired, and any distance below it the amount of income given up. As distinct from the consumer goods' situation which is depicted in the north-east quadrant, the factor supplies' situation is here depicted in the north-west quadrant.[1]

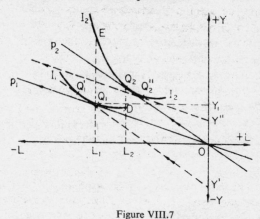

Figure VIII.7

If we construct a price-line p_1 passing through the origin and tangent at Q_1 to the indifference curve I_1, the individual is represented as in his chosen equilibrium position, giving up OL_1 of this particular sort of

---

[1] This construction has three advantages over the more common leisure-income diagram which is placed in the usual north-east quadrant.

(1) First, the choice among available combinations of two goods, leisure (regarded as a homogeneous good) and money, fails to convey the more general notion of the individual as a demander and a *supplier* of any number of goods and factors, electing to provide a particular combination of them according to market prices. In general, each of the variety of factors the individual can offer requires a different skill and entails a different degree of hardship.

(2) One avoids the artifice of a limit to the amount of the 'good' leisure, say twenty-four hours of the day, which artifice has the awkward result that an improvement in welfare is represented along one axis as equivalent to more than twenty-four hours of leisure a day. In the construction of Figure VIII.7, the limit to the supply of any factor is governed directly by the shape of the person's indifference curves, and the measure of any welfare change is in terms of the one good, money income.

(3) The indifference map of Figure VIII.7, whose curves can be extended to cross the vertical axis, is the correct prior construction to that useful textbook diagram in which a downward-sloping curve from left to right crosses a price-axis, to the right of which the line is interpreted as a demand curve for the good, and to the left of which the line is interpreted as a supply curve of it.

423

labour and, in exchange, acquiring OY_1 units of money income. Let the market supply price for this sort of labour rise from p_1 to p_2, and the individual's new equilibrium is given by the combination Q_2 on the I_2 indifference curve. The resulting change from Q_1 to Q_2 may be divided, in the usual Hicksian way, into a pure substitution effect—a movement from Q_1 to Q_1'—and a pure welfare effect—a movement from Q_1' to Q_2. Although the welfare effect can, of course, go either way, it should be noticed that a positive welfare effect—implying a welfare-induced increase in the *demand* for a good or factor—constitutes a reduction in the *supply* of a good or factor. Thus a positive, or 'normal' welfare effect, following a rise in the price of a factor, acts to reduce the amount put on the market. As we shall see the 'backward-bending' supply curve of the factor owner is the outcome of a strong positive welfare effect overcoming the unambiguous substitution effect.

The increase in the individual's welfare that follows the rise in the price of his labour from p_1 to p_2 can be measured, first as a CV—here, the exact amount of money that has to be taken from him to restore his welfare to its original I_1 level. The measurement of the CV on the vertical axis is, therefore, OY'. It is the maximum sum of money he could give up for the opportunity of selling his labour at the higher price p_2. If he gives up this sum OY', he will have the negative income indicated by Y' and, with price p_2, he can just reach I_1 at Q_1'.

This increase in his welfare can also be measured as an EV—here, the exact amount of money which has to be given to him to ensure that, if the opportunity to sell his labour at p_2 is not extended to him, he is still able to reach the new welfare level as indicated by indifference curve I_2. The EV is, therefore, measured as OY'', along the vertical axis. If he is paid this sum, he will be able to reach I_2 at Q_2'' with the original price p_1. It will be observed that, in the 'normal' case (positive welfare effect), the CV measure of an increase in welfare that follows a rise in the supply price exceeds the EV measure.

Since rent is frequently regarded as a surplus which may be partly or wholly appropriated without having any effect on the supply of factors, it is important to notice that—provided the welfare effects are not zero—wherever the individual has to pay an amount less than, or equal to, his rent (as measured, say, by his CV), the amount of factors he will offer will differ from the original amount. To illustrate, if, after the price has risen to p_2 and he supplies Q_2 of the factor, the CV measure of his rent is equal to OY', as stated. Let him be taxed the full amount of this rent and, with the new price p_2, he will reach Q_1', and supply a larger amount of factors than before.

3 As with consumer's surplus we could also trace out a quantity-constrained CV and EV. This constrained CV, sometimes associated with the Marshallian concept of rent, would be the sum of money the individual would surrender in order to retain p_2 when, at the same time, he were restrained from providing no more than OL_2 of the factor (this being the amount he chose to supply at p_2). This restriction on his choice of quantity, not surprisingly, reduces the sum he is willing to pay for the opportunity of having the higher price p_2 from OY' to Q_2D. Similarly, the constrained EV, the minimum sum he will accept to forgo p_2 when he is compelled to supply the original amount OL_1, is EQ_1 which is larger than the unconstrained EV of OY'. There is obviously nothing 'wrong' in using the quantity-constrained CV and EV. But on grounds of plausibility and convenience they are to be rejected in favour of the CV and EV proper.

4 It is instructive to turn briefly to the case of the supply of a factor in two alternative occupations A and B. Although the individual might choose to work part time in each occupation, owing to institutional arrangements this is not always feasible. We shall therefore confine the analysis to the case of placing his factor L entirely in the A occupation, or entirely in the B.

Figure VIII.8 represents a section of a three-dimensional indifference map, with the same vertical axis Y and two horizontal axes, L_a and L_b, crossing at right angles. If we imagine our three-dimensional figure were cut vertically into four equal parts, the figure is the space left after the removal of the vertical quarter in which L_a and L_b are both negative. Our attention is largely restricted to the upper, the positive part, of the diagram.

The rate of pay in A is given by p_a which is higher than p_b. If he chose to work in A at p_a, his earnings, OY_a, would be higher than his earnings, OY_b, in B. Nevertheless, the individual chooses to place his factors entirely in the B occupation, his equilibrium being Q_b on the indifference surface I_2 which is above the indifference surface I_1 on which is found his alternative choice, Q_a. As compared with the equilibrium he could reach in the A occupation, the individual enjoys a positive economic rent which, as an EV, can be measured as OY'—this

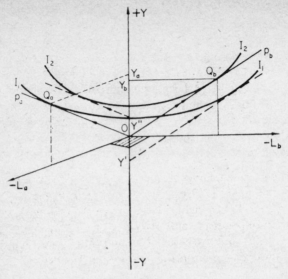

Figure VIII.8

being the maximum sum he is prepared to pay to remain in B. For after paying as much as OY' he can just reach the I_1 indifference surface—the new, lower, level of welfare which he would reach if he had to move into the A occupation. Conceived as a CV the rent is measured as a sum equal to OY'', this being the minimum sum the individual must be paid in order to induce him to transfer to occupation A. For, after receiving the sum OY''', he will be able, moving along p_a, to reach the I_2 indifference surface—representing his original level of welfare.

It should be manifest that, because of his occupational preference for B, the positive rent from working in B rather than A is accompanied by a smaller money return. Indeed, the textbook definition of rent, turning on the difference between the factor's current earnings and their transfer earnings, would in this instance be negative for the worker who chooses the B occupation, whereas it is clearly a positive rent on the CV or EV definition.[2]

---

[2] By a *positive* rent in this connection we mean an *increment* in his welfare from being in B rather than in A; an increment of welfare that can be measured either as the EV or as the CV of the move from A to B.

Chapter 61

MARGINAL CURVE
MEASURES OF RENT

1 The marginal curves I_1' and I_2' in Figure VIII.9 correspond to I_1 and I_2 in Figure VIII.7, except that, for conventional reasons, they are drawn from left to right. The I_0' marginal indifference curve in the figure corresponds to some original I_0 curve (not depicted in Figure VIII.7) before any price was offered for the factor L. It is convenient, again, to draw these three curves as straight lines.

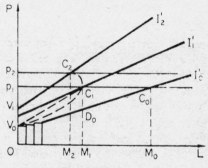

Figure VIII.9

To fix our ideas we shall suppose L to be labour of a given skill, measured along the horizontal axis in hours per week in a specific industry A, the prices of all other factors and goods being taken as constant.[1]

---

[1] We could have used a larger diagram to disclose the nature of the marginal indifference curve I_0' by taking hourly increments of this labour and—parallel with our treatment of consumer's surplus—constructing successive columns, the heights of which would indicate the individual's valuation of each successive hour offered. Having gone through this process in connection with consumer's surplus in some detail already, we shall not repeat it—though we have drawn in the first three columns under the I_0' to remind us of the process.

When the individual first contemplates employment in A, the I_0' curve is the locus of minimal payments required to induce him to offer there his successive increments of labour. If he receives these minimal payments, and no more, as he moves from left to right along the I_0', he is no better off at any point along it than he is at the beginning, prior to his employment there. The introduction now of an hourly wage, p_1, enables us to represent triangular areas corresponding to his CV and EV.

2   The individual's CV is a sum of money equal to the area of the larger triangle $V_0C_0p_1$, determined as follows. The area beneath the I_0' curve up to the M_0^{th} unit, equal to $OV_0C_0M_0$, is the minimum sum of money needed to induce him to work the OM_0 hours, whereas the rectangular area, $Op_1C_0M_0$, is what he would be paid for working the OM_0 hours. The *excess* of this rectangular area over that minimum sum, equal to the triangle $V_0C_0p_1$, is therefore the maximum sum he can afford to pay for having the opportunity to sell his labour in A at p_1. For if he pays this maximum sum in exchange for this opportunity of selling his labour at p_1, he is just able—by choosing to work OM_0 hours—to maintain his welfare at the original I_0 level; being then no better off than he was before the p_1 opportunity was presented to him.

His EV, on the other hand, is a sum that is equal to the area of the smaller triangle $V_1p_1C_1$, explained as follows. Having availed himself of the p_1 price to offer OM_1 units of labour and reached the I_1 level of welfare, we put the question: what is the maximum sum he is willing to pay in order not to have to do any work in A?[2] This is equal to the area $OV_1C_1M_1$ under the I_1' curve. However, if he gives up the opportunity to sell his labour at p_1, the total income he forgoes is equal to the rectangular area $Op_1C_1M_1$. And this loss of income exceeds the most that he is willing to pay by the area of the triangle $V_1p_1C_1$. In order, then, to retain this I_1 level of welfare (which he was able to reach with

---

[2] Along any marginal indifference curve, a movement *rising upward* (to the right, as drawn in the figure) implies a *giving up* of units, the vertical height therefore measures the *minimum* sums required for successive units offered. A movement *sloping downward* (to the left, as drawn in the figure) implies the *acquiring* of additional units—or the withdrawal of units once supplied. The vertical height therefore measures the *maximum* sums he will pay for additional units.

The same interpretation holds for the consumer's marginal indifference curves, although downward-sloping is, in contradistinction to the above Figure, to the right, and upward-sloping is to the left.

p_1) when p_1 is no longer available to him, he must receive a sum equal to the area of this triangle.[3]

By starting with a supply price equal to V_0 in Figure VIII.9, a price at which the individual supplies nothing, and gradually raising the price to p_1 at which he supplies OM_1 units, we generate the dotted-line supply curve of labour joining V_0 to C_1. For a 'normal' good or factor being offered (one for which *less* is offered as welfare increases), the supply curve will be steeper than the relevant marginal indifference curves. For an 'inferior' good or factor, on the other hand, the supply curve will be flatter than the marginal indifference curves. In the 'normal' case, Hicks' Marginal Valuation curve will also be steeper than the marginal indifference curves. And since, for each successive unit offered, the welfare effect (until the M_1^{th} unit is reached) is greater than that produced in generating the supply curve, the MV curve, indicated by the broken-line curve $V_0 C_1$, will be above the supply curve.

3 We must now face the critical question: how well does the area between the price and the individual's supply price approximate the CV and EV measures of rent? Although the construction of diagrams of this sort can be somewhat arbitrary, it is well known that the supply curve can be much steeper than the marginal indifference curves and, indeed, can be backward-bending—implying a welfare effect that is positive and large relative to the substitution effect. What makes the welfare effect so important in the factor market are the existing economic institutions under which men tend to place all their labour in single occupations. The welfare of each worker, therefore, depends exclusively, or largely, on the level of a single factor price. It is quite possible, in fact as well as in theory, that a further rise in price from p_1 to p_2 would (if he were allowed to choose) result in the worker's choosing to supply OM_2 units, a smaller amount of labour than the OM_1 units he supplies at p_1. The resulting supply curve, passing through $V_0 C_1 C_2$, though it lies between the CV and EV measures of

---

[3] The quantity-constrained CV, associated with the Marshallian measure, can also be represented in Figure VIII.9. Once price p_1 is introduced the amount the individual chooses to supply is OM_1. The most he is willing to pay to obtain this price p_1, while at the same time being constrained to purchase OM_1 units, is a sum equal to the area $V_0 D_0 C_1 p_1$, which is clearly smaller than the unconstrained CV, $V_0 C_0 p_1$, as indeed it has to be.

rent, could be very different from either. This would be bad enough if either measure were acceptable as satisfactory for the purpose in hand. But in a cost-benefit analysis, guided by the criterion of a potential Pareto improvement, it is the CV measure that is usually employed.

Granted 'normal' welfare effects, a project that *raises* the supply price of the factor produces a CV measure of rent that could be significantly *larger* than the area above the supply price. The consequent underestimation of the rent accruing to the factor-owner might, erroneously, preclude an economically feasible project. On the other hand, for a project that *lowers* the supply price of a factor, the area defined by the CV could be significantly *smaller* than the area above the supply curve. The consequent overestimation of the loss of rent resulting from using the area above the supply price as a proxy for the CV measure might then, again, erroneously preclude projects that are economically feasible.[4] How important is this consideration likely to be?

4   As indicated earlier, in modern industry it is the general practice to offer workers a 'package deal'; in its simplest form, a wage rate plus a constraint on the number of hours per day, and also on the number of days per week. Such constraints vary from industry to industry, and in occupations within the industry, but this fact makes no difference to the analysis of rent in such circumstances.

Suppose the hours per week in the A industry are set at forty, except in the particular case in which the worker, when offered p_1 per hour, would have in any case chosen to work forty hours, the constraint will be operative. If so, his CV under the forty-hour constraint will be smaller than it would be without it. Provided it is positive, however, he will accept the all-or-nothing offer and make some rent from it. The worker's CV under this constraint—the maximum sum he will pay in

---

[4] Under the same conditions, the conclusion for changes in the demand price is the opposite of that for the supply price. A project that *raises* the demand price of a good will, in the 'normal' case, have a CV (the minimum sum the consumer will accept as compensation) that is *larger* than the area under the demand curve. If the welfare involved is substantial, the consequent underestimation of the loss could result in a cost-benefit analysis admitting projects that do not meet the criterion.

One the other hand, for a project that results in a *reduction* of the price of a good to the consumer, the CV is smaller than the area under the demand curve. The consequent overestimate of the gain from using the area under the demand curve as a proxy for the CV might again admit projects that are not economically feasible.

order to have the opportunity to work the forty-hour week in A at p_1—is the excess of the weekly wage over the minimum payment he will require. And this minimum weekly payment he would accept can be represented in Figure VIII.10, as the area of a unit L column with height equal to such minimum sum. Since the figure ranks the columns in ascending order of height, column L_1 corresponds to the minimal sum of the first worker; he would accept a sum lower than all the others and, in consequence, makes the largest (constrained) CV rent. Letting the total pay for the forty-hour week be measured as OW_1 on the vertical axis, the CV measure of rent for the first worker is represented by R_1; the shaded extension of column L_1 to height W_1. Similarly, the areas of R_2, R_3, R_4, . . . indicate the rents of workers 2, 3, 4, and so on.

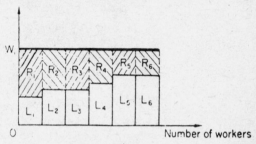

Figure VIII.10

Clearly the stepped line got by tracing the tops of the L columns indicates the beginning of the supply curve of labour for that industry. If we continued adding workers in ascending order of height we should eventually engage a worker, say the nth worker whose L column was just below, or equal to, the height of the W_1 line. All workers in the industry, save possibly the nth, will be making a rent.

Where large numbers of workers are involved we may draw a continuous supply curve to the point of intersection with the weekly-wage line, the total rent to the workers in this industry being the area enclosed between the wage line and the supply curve. A lengthening of the working week, or any other restriction, would be represented as an upward shifting of this supply curve. The equilibrium number of workers would fall, and the rents of each of the remaining number would be reduced.

We may conclude, tentatively, that notwithstanding the difficulties discussed in connection with the *individual* supply curve, the

431

constraints imposed by industry are such that the area above the supply curve of a particular type of labour to an industry offers a good measure of the rent enjoyed by the number employed. The gain or loss of rent resulting from a rise or fall in the weekly wage can now also be measured in the conventional way.

Chapter 62

THE CHOICE OF L LAW OR $\overline{\text{L}}$ LAW

1 The effects of the law of liability both on the valuation of the spillovers and on the magnitude of costs of implementing potential improvements have been considered separately in Part III. Each is important in itself, but when added together, as they are in this chapter, they strengthen the argument that the law of liability is a potent factor in determining the economic feasibility of investment projects and the level of optimal outputs. To pursue the argument further, we shall continue to restrict our attention to a mutual-agreement solution in which, provisionally, the only way of dealing with spillovers is taken to be through output-reduction. The conclusions are, however, readily extended to the other ways of dealing with spillovers by mutual agreement.

2 Figure VIII.11 is similar to Figure III.1 (p. 145) except that two marginal spillover curves have been drawn, $E_L E_L'$ corresponding to the L law, and $E_{\overline{L}} E_{\overline{L}}'$ corresponding to the $\overline{\text{L}}$ law. BB_1 represents, as before, the excess commercial benefit curve which is here assumed to be invariant to the state of the law.

If the L law prevails, competitive equilibrium is initially at B_1. This L-determined output of x, OB_1, plus its accompanying spillover, determines the welfare level of the victims. Their CV of the spillover produced by the last unit of x—the maximum sum they would collectively offer for its elimination—is, by reference to the $E_L E_L'$ curve, calculated as equal to the vertical distance $E_L' B_1$. The most the

433

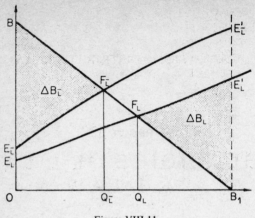

Figure VIII.11

victims will offer to the manufacturer to forgo the production of successive units of x, *less* the associated reduction of excess commercial benefit, continues to be positive until an optimal output Q_L is reached. The resulting dotted triangular area, ΔB_L, measures the ESB_L (the potential Pareto improvement) of reducing output under the L law to its optimal. If this area exceeds G_L, the G costs under the L law, then RSB_L, the residual social benefit under the L law, is positive, and the optimal output Q_1 will be established. On the other hand, if G_L exceeds ESB_L, the RSB_L is negative, and output remains at OB_1. In that case the overall net benefit to society of producing this output OB_1 is equal to the triangle BE_LF_L *less* ΔB_L. This may be positive, zero, or negative. If negative, it would mean that as a result of G_L being larger than ESB_L, and too large, therefore, to justify a reduction of output to Q_L, the production of x will be carried on at a level that, on balance, entails an overall loss to society. Any subsequent inference by the economist that a *reduction* of the competitive equilibrium output OB_1 should not be undertaken, on the grounds that RSB of the movement to the Q_L optimum is negative, is clearly unwarranted. Once we take a step toward realism, and introduce the costs of implementation, G, into the calculation, we have therefore to look again at the overall social gain of producing the good at all—at the *total* conditions, in effect.

If, now, the $\overline{L}$ law prevailed, the spillover being prohibited (in the absence of mutual agreement), the initial output of x, and its spillovers, would be zero. Under the $\overline{L}$ law, therefore, the welfare level of the potential spillover victims will initially be higher than it is under L law. The sum of the minimal payments they are ready to accept for bearing with successive units of spillover, so maintaining their initial welfare, is given by spillover evaluation curve $E_{\overline{\text{L}}}E'_{\overline{\text{L}}}$ and—assuming they receive no more than the sums indicated by this curve—the optimal output under the $\overline{\text{L}}$ law is $OQ_{\overline{\text{L}}}$ and the corresponding $ESB_{\overline{\text{L}}}$ is the dotted triangular area $B_{\overline{\text{L}}}$. If this $ESB_{\overline{\text{L}}}$ exceeds the corresponding $G_{\overline{\text{L}}}$ necessary for its implementation, the $RSB_{\overline{\text{L}}}$ is positive, and the output $Q_{\overline{\text{L}}}$ will be reached. If, however, the magnitude of G_{L} exceeds $ESB_{\overline{\text{L}}}$, the output x will not be produced at all. In producing a zero output there is, of course, neither loss nor gain.

3   Let us consider all the possibilities: first, if the RSB is positive under either law, the optimal output-adjustment always takes place. Under the L law this will be output OQ_{L}, which is smaller than the output $OQ_{\overline{\text{L}}}$ under the $\overline{\text{L}}$ law. Second, if the RSB differs according to the law of liability, we have two interesting cases; (a) RSB_{L} is positive while $RSB_{\overline{\text{L}}}$ is negative, in which cases the optimal output OQ_{L} is reached under the L law, whereas if the $\overline{\text{L}}$ law prevails, the output produced is zero, and (b), the reverse of this, RSB_{L} is negative while $RSB_{\overline{\text{L}}}$ is positive, in which cases the full output, OB_1, tends to be produced under the L law, whereas, if the $\overline{\text{L}}$ law prevails, the optimal output $OQ_{\overline{\text{L}}}$ is realized.

The (a) case means simply that if $\overline{\text{L}}$ law prevails there can be no output of x which is socially desirable. In other words, only in the absence of any production of x can the economy be at an optimal position; any output of x (including the 'optimal' output $Q_{\overline{\text{L}}}$) entails a potential Pareto loss. If, however, the L law prevails, and the unchecked commercial output tends to OB_1, the optimal output OQ_{L} tends to be realized.[1] Case (b) shows that if L law prevails, the competitive output OB_1 appears socially desirable, whereas if $\overline{\text{L}}$ law prevails the socially desirable solution, and the one which tends to occur, requires that output $OQ_{\overline{\text{L}}}$ be produced.

The third possibility is that the RSB is negative under either law. No output at all is produced under the $\overline{\text{L}}$ law whereas (unless the

---

[1] Moreover, if the law is changed from $\overline{\text{L}}$ to L, then output of x is changed from zero to Q_{L}, whereas if it is changed from being L to $\overline{\text{L}}$, the change in output is merely from Q_{L} to $Q_{\overline{\text{L}}}$.

economist intervenes with an argument about the total conditions) under the L law the competitive output OB_1 is produced.

These three possibilities, (1) each RSB positive under either law, (2) RSB_L positive under L, negative under $\overline{L}$ law (and the reverse for $RSB_{\overline{L}}$) and (3) each RSB negative under either law, have one result in common: that under L law the output of x is always larger than under $\overline{L}$ law, the difference being least for (1) and most for (3). Thus, for (1) the difference is only that between Q_L and $Q_{\overline{L}}$; for (2) it is either (a) that between Q_L and zero, or (b) that between B_1 output and $Q_{\overline{L}}$,[2] while for (3) the difference is between B_1 output and zero output.

This third possibility is the more interesting one. If, owing to G costs being too large, we have a choice of law under which we produce 'all or nothing', we shall be getting 'too much' spillover under the L law and 'too little' under the $\overline{L}$ law. There is no way of knowing in advance, in such an event, which law offers more (or less) social gain. Under the $\overline{L}$, with zero output being the overall optimal outcome, nothing is to be added to social welfare. Under an L law, with OB_1 output being the overall optimal outcome, the potential Pareto improvement of producing OB_1, as compared with producing nothing, is given by area of triangle BE_LF_L less that of triangle ΔB_L, and this, as indicated, can be positive, zero, or negative.[3]

4 Thinking of this all-or-nothing case, we conclude that there are some spillover-generating activities which under an L law will be completely unhampered, and under an $\overline{L}$ law completely suppressed. But if on allocative grounds alone we have to choose as between L and $\overline{L}$ law, we cannot determine where the balance of advantage lies without empirical knowledge—provided that mutual agreement about dealing with spillovers is confined to the output changes of method I.

---

[2] The analysis requires a slight modification because of the likelihood that where compensation is received from, or paid to, the potential spillover victims, they are likely to receive more than the absolute minimum they will accept, or pay less than the absolute maximum they can afford. If so, their post-agreement welfare will be greater than it is in the pre-agreement stage under either law and as a consequence the spillover-valuation curves will be above those in the figure. The optimal outputs resulting will, therefore, be somewhat to the left of Q_L and $Q_{\overline{L}}$ in the Figure.

[3] Where (a) $RSB_{\overline{L}}$ is negative and RSB_L is positive, the $\overline{L}$ law yields no social gain, while the L law entails a potential Pareto improvement (after taking account of G_L). Where (b) $RSB_{\overline{L}}$ is positive and RSB_L is negative, the $\overline{L}$ entails a potential Pareto improvement (after taking account of $G_{\overline{L}}$) while under the L law the potential Pareto improvement can be positive, zero, or negative.

If, however, we now consider method II (the use of preventive devices), there appears to be a case on allocative grounds for preferring $\overline{\text{L}}$ law. And we should, indeed, consider the II method for the good reason that preventive devices are generally believed to be a less costly way of dealing with spillovers than that of reducing output.

Although the three possibilities with respect to L and $\overline{\text{L}}$ law discussed in connection with method I have their counterparts in connection with method II concerning preventive devices—except, of course, that with method II the amount of spillover alone is affected, and not output of x also—there is now a significant and 'dynamic' factor to be reckoned with. Once the burden of spillover-compensation enters into the costs of production (or the costs of using a good), as it does under $\overline{\text{L}}$ law, private industry—searching for the lowest cost method of conforming with the legal requirements—has an interest in discovering preventive devices to avoid comparatively heavy compensatory payments. Wherever industry succeeds, a real economic saving is effected. Under the L law in contrast, there is no similar incentive for industry to investigate and develop as cheap a preventive device as possible. Putting the matter more formally, under L law the entrepreneur, allocating his research funds among alternatives according to equi-marginal principles, will tend to ignore all opportunities for social gains (of replacing welfare-compensatory costs by the lower costs of preventive devices) which might be made by directing research funds into developing improved preventive devices. So long as he is not held accountable for the spillover effects, he concludes, correctly, that directing resources into research to diminish the magnitude of these social afflictions, which necessarily reduce social welfare, serves only to reduce his profit. Under the $\overline{\text{L}}$ law, on the other hand, organized research into ways of reducing spillover costs counts as much, as indeed it should, as research into other ways of reducing costs.

5   Although, as has been stated repeatedly, the rationale of cost-benefit analysis derives solely from the Pareto principle, it is not true that the liberal economist is impervious to a consideration of all other social issues. In particular, taking his values from the community for which he is evaluating the projects in question, he is concerned with the distribution of real income and with the broader issue of equity. The question of such social considerations entering separately into the final decision and, possibly, qualifying, or conflicting with, the cost-benefit

calculation is not being raised here. The question at issue is that of facing a choice he has so far unwittingly evaded in this connection, the choice of basing his cost-benefit evaluations on L law or $\overline{L}$ law. Where the spillovers of a project are large, it can, as suggested, make a crucial difference. The case made out above for habitual recourse to $\overline{L}$ law can be strengthened by some reflection on its implications for welfare distribution and equity.

With respect to welfare distribution, the arguments are tentative but far from negligible. It may be possible to show that the goods which generate significant spillovers earn incomes for, and/or are bought by, groups having higher incomes than average. It may also be possible to show that spillovers such as pollutants and traffic noise tend to fall more heavily on poorer neighbourhoods.[4] Inasmuch as environmental quality enters heavily into welfare (though not into GNP) the distribution of welfare may be more regressive than that of 'real' disposable income.

6   Equity is better served by $\overline{L}$ law. In the absence of comprehensive sanctions against trespass on the citizen's amenity, existing institutions lend themselves inadvertently to a process of blackmail in so far as they place the burden of reaching agreement on the person or group whose interests have been damaged. Although the disamenities inflicted on innocent parties may be judged with less severity when they are generated as a by-product of the pursuit of profit or pleasure than when, instead, they are generated for the sole purpose of exacting payment from the victim, in either case a Pareto improvement is met by agreement between the parties.

The alleged neutrality of the Pareto principle, in respect of the question of who should compensate whom, is to be interpreted only as a matter of complete indifference as between the two alternative ways of giving effect to it. Indeed, the principle, as it were, deliberately opts out of the question. So far as it can be invoked, person N compensating

---

[4] 'Rich' and 'poor' neighbourhoods must be identified before the spillovers appear. If, in fact, spillovers are randomly spread among 'rich' and 'poor' neighbourhoods to start with, and that, as a result the poor began to move into spillover-affected areas (in consequence of the decline in property values) and the rich began to move into the unaffected areas, the resulting association between spillover areas and income-groups could not be adduced as evidence for the thesis that spillovers reduce the welfare of the poor more than the rich. In the real world, the existing situation is likely to be the result both of initial discrimination against poorer neighbourhoods and of the subsequent reaction of rich and poor to the spread of spillovers.

person S to desist is as valid an application of the principle as that of person S compensating person N in order to indulge himself.

But the two situations may be Pareto symmetric without their being ethically symmetric. The fact that the conflict of interest is mutual does not of itself imply that the sort of settlement effected is a matter of *indifference* to society. Indeed, the neutrality of the Pareto principle is to be conceived simply as a *disregard* of the ethics involved. It is true that if the non-smoker's enjoyment is reduced by the smoker's freedom to smoke, so also is the smoker's enjoyment reduced by having to refrain from smoking to satisfy the non-smoker. Yet smoker and non-smoker are not thereby on an equal footing. In accordance with the liberal maxim, the freedom of any man, say, to smoke what he wants and where he wants is conceded—but along with the critical proviso that his smoking take place in circumstances which do not reduce the welfare of others. In so far as this critical proviso is not met, the freedom of the smoker to smoke is not symmetric with the freedom desired by the non-smoker. For the non-smoker's desired freedom does not go beyond the breathing of smokeless air. And, unlike the freedom sought by the smoker, it does not reduce the amenity of the other party. The logic of this example is to be extended to the satisfaction a person enjoys as a result of his operating a noisy vehicle, lawn-mower, or transistor, a satisfaction that has the incidental effect of destroying the amenity of others. The person who is content to live quietly does not, thereby, damage the welfare of others. In short, the fact that there is a conflict of interest—and also an opportunity for mutual benefit—does not imply equal culpability. Unless, therefore, the law is altered so as to provide effective and comprehensive safeguards for the citizen—which is implied by $\overline{L}$ law—no agreement concluded under the existing L law can be vindicated on ethical grounds.[5]

---

[5] Unless there are constant costs over the likely range of output variation—a not unlikely circumstance—an exogenous change in, say, the demand of a group will, as indicated earlier, affect the welfare of others through changes in goods and factor prices. The attempt to trace welfare changes back to those whose market actions caused them would be too costly a venture to be feasible. The market is justly regarded as an impersonal mechanism. But it is not feasibility alone that differentiates the market-induced welfare changes from those resulting from external effects. Whether an increase, say, in the demand for good x causes its price, and those of related goods, to rise or fall, the resulting distribution of real income may be progressive or regressive. If a judgement were to be made of the market-induced welfare effects, it could be made on grounds of distribution only. It could not be made—as it can in the case of external diseconomies—on grounds of equity alone.

7 Once the inequity of the L law, in an economy producing adverse spillovers, is acknowledged, reflection suggests that it is more serious than might appear from the consideration alone of a single spillover event. For any Pareto improvement under the L law is one which must begin from the distribution of welfare as determined by reference to the existing amounts of spillover in the economy. Since under L law the initial loss of welfare from those subjected to the spillovers of some new project is estimated as the maximum they would offer to be rid of it—and *not* the larger sum; the minimum they would accept for bearing with it—$\Sigma Vi > 0$ is not necessarily met, and there is therefore no assurance that ESB or RSB could be met. Yet the project may qualify under the L law. Since potential victims, under such a law, have no means of limiting in advance the level to which their welfares may be reduced in consequence of the spillovers yet to be produced along with market goods, their welfare may decline so far as to make life well-nigh intolerable.

Even if negotiation costs fall over time, or if the government appoints an agency to provide the initiative necessary to reach voluntary agreements where possible, the mere fact of the spillovers having grown over time will make any worthwhile Pareto improvement less likely. For the effect of maintaining L law for some time is to permit the growth of spillover-creating industries, and perhaps also to allow some industries to flourish which would not have come into being at all under an $\overline{L}$ law. Eventually, the numbers using the products of such industries, the numbers employed in them, the wealth of the owners, and the power and influence of the managers, combine to create a formidable interest that is as difficult to oppose on economic principle as it is difficult to dislodge by political means. For as the magnitude of the spillovers, and of the numbers and wealth of those interested in maintaining them, have grown, the reduction of spillovers back to any initial tolerable level becomes increasingly costly—whether in terms of compensatory payments, preventive devices, or any other method. It becomes, therefore, increasingly unlikely that such a reduction of spillovers will qualify as a Pareto improvement (ESB). Let the L law remain in force long enough, and such a Pareto improvement may become a virtual impossibility. And if, therefore, from such time on all decisions on the spillover problem are referred by the economist to the Pareto principle, there will be nothing to prevent these spillovers increasing without limit, and nothing to prevent the environment sinking ever lower in the scale of amenity. In such circumstances, the case in equity for seeking guidance via the Pareto principle alone is very weak, and the case for establishing $\overline{\text{L}}$ law to redress the existing inequity is very strong.

REFERENCES AND BIBLIOGRAPHY FOR PART VIII

Hicks, J. R. *Value and Capital*, Oxford: Clarendon Press, 1939.

— 'The Four Consumers' Surpluses', *Review of Economic Studies*, 1944.

Little, I. M. D. *A Critique of Welfare Economics* (2nd edn.), Oxford: Oxford University Press, 1957.

Marshall, A. *Principles of Economics* (8th edn.), London: Macmillan, 1924.

Mishan, E. J. 'Rent as a Measure of Welfare Change', *American Economic Review*, 1958.

— *Introduction to Normative Economics*, New York: Oxford University Press, 1980.

Samuelson, P. A. *Foundations of Economic Analysis* (2nd edn.), Cambridge, Mass.: Harvard University Press, 1963.

Index